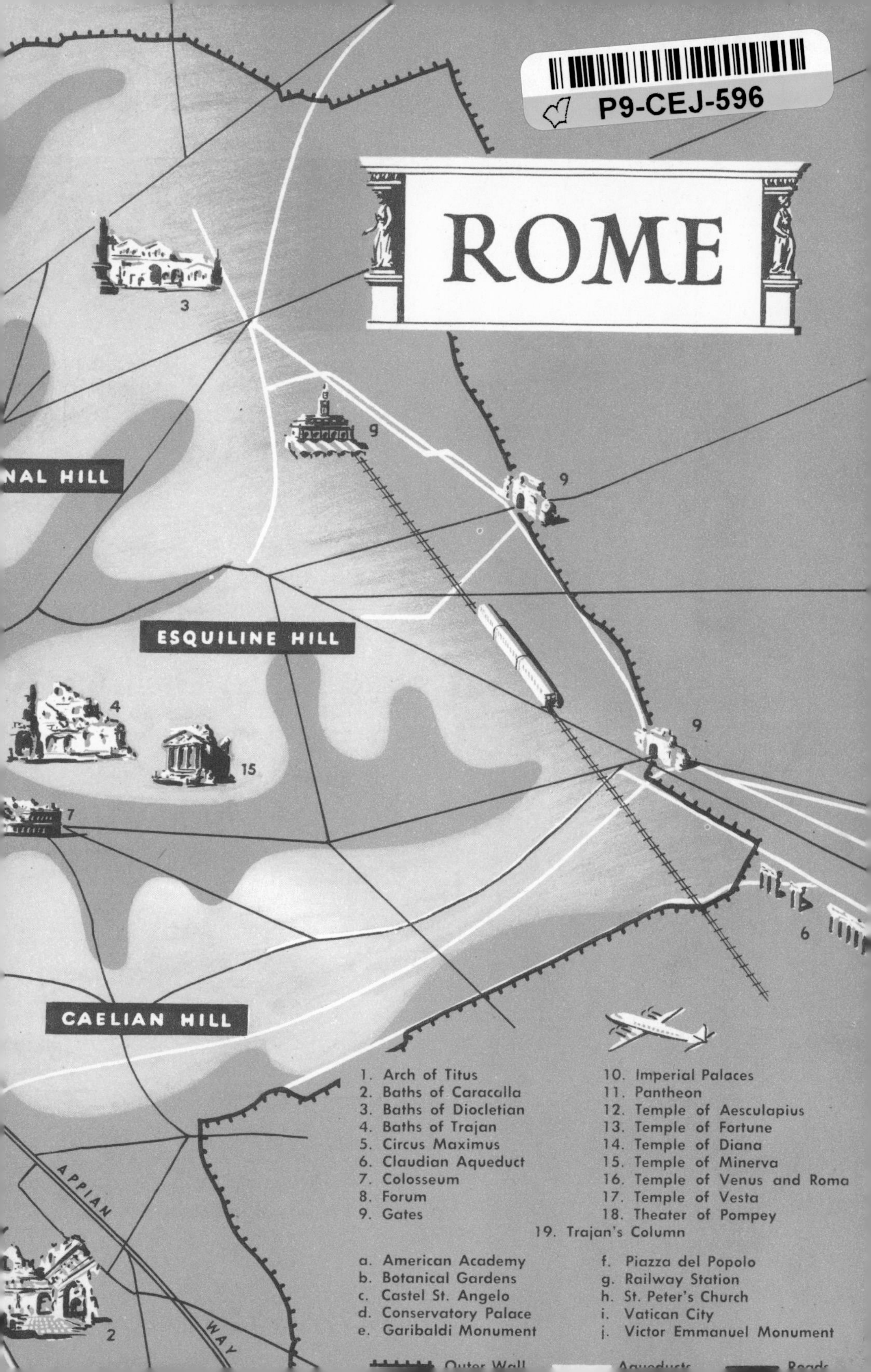

P9-CEJ-596
ROME
3
9
9
NAL HILL
ESQUILINE HILL
4
15
7
9
6
CAELIAN HILL
APPIAN
WAY
2
1. Arch of Titus
2. Baths of Caracalla
3. Baths of Diocletian
4. Baths of Trajan
5. Circus Maximus
6. Claudian Aqueduct
7. Colosseum
8. Forum
9. Gates
10. Imperial Palaces
11. Pantheon
12. Temple of Aesculapius
13. Temple of Fortune
14. Temple of Diana
15. Temple of Minerva
16. Temple of Venus and Roma
17. Temple of Vesta
18. Theater of Pompey
19. Trajan's Column
a. American Academy
b. Botanical Gardens
c. Castel St. Angelo
d. Conservatory Palace
e. Garibaldi Monument
f. Piazza del Popolo
g. Railway Station
h. St. Peter's Church
i. Vatican City
j. Victor Emmanuel Monument

LANGUAGE, LITERATURE, AND LIFE

USING LATIN

BOOK ONE

BY

JOHN FLAGG GUMMERE
WILLIAM PENN CHARTER SCHOOL

ANNABEL HORN
WESLEYAN COLLEGE

SCOTT, FORESMAN AND COMPANY

CHICAGO ATLANTA DALLAS PALO ALTO NEW YORK

PRINTED IN THE UNITED STATES OF AMERICA

CONTENTS

UNIT I AMERICA AND OTHER LANDS

I PATRIA NOSTRA: Nouns · Sentences · The Subject · Verbs · Adjectives 9
II AMERICA ET EURŌPA: *The, A, An* · Position of the Adjective · The Predicate · Predicate Noun · Predicate Adjective · Translation 12
III CASA PULCHRA: Direct Object · Adjective Endings · Position of the Verb · Use of *do* in Negative Sentences and in Questions 15
IV TERRAE PULCHRAE: The Plural · Adjectives with Plural Nouns · Two Adjectives Modifying One Noun · Phrases 18
V BONAE EPISTULAE: Omission of the Subject · Case 23
REVIEW OF UNIT I 26

UNIT II ON LAND AND SEA

VI VĪTA PERĪCULŌSA: English Nouns and Latin Nouns · Nouns Denoting Possession · Two Forms of Translation for the Genitive · Adjectives Modifying Nouns in the Genitive 28
VII POĒTA ET NAUTA: Person and Number of Verbs · The Forms of *sum* · *You,* Singular and Plural 31
VIII FĪLIA NAUTAE: The Infinitive · Conjugation of *portō* · The First Conjugation 34
IX GALBA ET PĪRĀTAE: Transitive and Intransitive Verbs 37
REVIEW OF UNIT II. 39

UNIT III PEOPLE OF THE PAST

X GALBA ET FĪLIA: Indirect Object · Dative Case · Adjectives Modifying Nouns in the Dative 43
XI PUELLA BENIGNA: English Nouns and Latin Nouns · Adjectives with a Dependent Dative · Position of Genitive and Dative 46
XII ĪNSULA NOSTRA: Use of Prepositions · The Preposition *ē, ex* · Ablative Case · Adjectives Modifying Nouns in the Ablative · The Expletive *there* 50
XIII LĀTŌNA ET RĀNAE: Declension · First Declension · Apposition 52
REVIEW OF UNIT III 56

UNIT IV GOOD STORIES

XIV SICILIA: Clauses · Conjunctions · Ablative with *ā* or *ab* 57
XV LŪNA ET STELLAE: Moods of Verbs · Indicative Mood · Imperative Mood · Imperative of the First Conjugation · Imperative of *dō* · Vocative Case 64
XVI URSA: Tense of Verbs · Present Tense · Future Tense · Future of *portō* · Stem of the Future 67
XVII NAUTA ET EPISTULA: Future of *sum* · Future of *dō* · The Conjunction *cum* 70
REVIEW OF UNIT IV 73

UNIT V STORIES OF EARTH AND SKY

XVIII AGRICOLA LABŌRAT: The Pronoun · Forms of Questions · Answers to Questions 75

XIX CORNĒLIA ET URSA: Perfect Tense · Stem of the Perfect · Person Endings · Perfect of the First Conjugation · Perfect of *sum* 78

XX RĒGĪNA SUPERBA: English Nouns from Latin Nouns of the First Declension 80

XXI ARCA PĪRĀTĀRUM: Imperfect Tense · Tense Sign of the Imperfect · Person Endings · Imperfect of *portō* · Present System · Imperfect of *sum* 84

REVIEW OF UNIT V 91

UNIT VI STORIES OF GODS AND MEN

XXII DEAE NŌTAE: Declension of *templum* · Endings · Second Declension · Forms of Questions 92

XXIII TEMPLUM ANTĪQUUM: Gender · Agreement of Adjectives in Gender 95

XXIV HERCULĒS ET LEŌ: Declension of *amīcus* · Adjectives in *-us* 98

XXV CĒNA BONA: English Nouns and Latin Nouns · Second-Declension Nouns in *-er* 101

XXVI AMĪCUS FĪDUS: Imperfect of *dō* · Summary of Second-Declension Nouns · Endings of the Second Declension · Vocative Case of the Second Declension 104

REVIEW OF UNIT VI 110

UNIT VII STORIES FROM HISTORY AND LEGEND

XXVII DOLUS BELLĪ: Declension of *bonus* in All Genders · Adjectives with Masculine in *-er* · Adjectives with Masculine Nouns of the First Declension · Declension of *vir* 112

XXVIII MĪDĀS ET AURUM: Adjectives Used as Nouns 115

XXIX LIBRĪ PRETIŌSĪ: The Adverb · Distinction Between *nunc* and *jam* . . . 118

XXX RĀMUS AUREUS: Case Use with Prepositions · Phrases with *to* · *In* with the Accusative 124

XXXI DAPHNĒ ET APOLLŌ: English Nouns and Latin Nouns · Ablative of Means 128

REVIEW OF UNIT VII 131

UNIT VIII MYTHS AND OTHER TALES

XXXII DEUCALIŌN ET PYRRHA: Second Conjugation · Present System of the Second Conjugation · Present Imperative of *moneō* 132

XXXIII PERSEUS ET MEDŪSA: Perfect Tense of the Second Conjugation . . . 138

XXXIV CENTUM PĪRĀTAE!: Use of Passive Voice · Present Passive of *portō* and *moneō* · Passive Endings · *ā* or *ab* Meaning *by* 140

XXXV ARACHNĒ ET MINERVA: Declension of *hic* 144

XXXVI AEACUS ET FORMĪCAE: English Nouns and Latin Nouns 146

XXXVII VICTŌRIA PYRRHĪ 148

REVIEW OF UNIT VIII 150

UNIT IX STORIES OF FACT AND FICTION

XXXVIII FORMĪCA ET CICĀDA: The Preposition *sub* · The Demonstrative *ille* 155
XXXIX FĀMA APPIĪ CLAUDIĪ: English Adjectives and Latin Adjectives · The Verbs *adsum* and *absum* 158
XL VIR TIMIDUS: Interrogative Pronoun · Case of the Interrogative . . . 161
XLI VESUVIUS ET POMPEIĪ: Interrogative Adjective 164
XLII THĒSEUS ET MĪNŌTAURUS: Imperfect Passive 169
XLIII PRĪMUS AVIĀTOR: The Demonstrative *is* · Pronoun Use of *is* · *hic* and *ille* as Pronouns 173
REVIEW OF UNIT IX 176

UNIT X TALES FROM ROMAN HISTORY

XLIV DOLUS ANNAE: English Verbs and Latin Verbs 178
XLV RŌMĀNĪ VEIŌS OCCUPANT: Future Passive of *portō* and *moneō* 181
XLVI CLOELIA 183
XLVII MĀNLIUS CAPITŌLIUM SERVAT: Reflexive Pronoun 185
XLVIII ASCANIUS ET CERVUS ALBUS: Use of *suus* · Declension of *suus* · *ejus* and *eōrum* 188
REVIEW OF UNIT X 191

UNIT XI STORIES OF ADVENTURE

XLIX SERTŌRIUS ET CERVA DIĀNAE: Third Declension · Masculine and Feminine Nouns of the First Class · Endings 196
L FRĀTER PERFIDUS: Masculine and Feminine Nouns of the Third Declension 200
LI DANIĒL ET LEŌNĒS: Latin Nouns and English Nouns 204
LII EPISTULA RŌMĀNA: Neuter Nouns of the First Class 206
LIII POĒTA CAECUS: Masculine and Feminine Nouns of the Second Class 208
LIV ERROR CŌNSIDIĪ: Neuter Nouns of the Second Class · Gender in the Third Declension 210
REVIEW OF UNIT XI 212

UNIT XII FAMOUS STORIES RETOLD

LV CĪVĒS RŌMAM ITERUM AEDIFICANT: Latin Nouns and English Nouns 214
LVI ANDROCLĒS ET LEŌ: Use of Participles · Forms of the Perfect Participle · Declension of the Participle 217
LVII PĪCUS—RĒX ET AVIS: Principal Parts of the Verb · Principal Parts of First-Conjugation Verbs · Stems of the Verb 220
LVIII PRŌ AMĪCŌ: Principal Parts of Second-Conjugation Verbs · Different Endings of the Perfect Stem 223
LIX ŌMINA MALA: Perfect Passive of *portō* and *moneō* · Predicate Noun with Passive Forms 225
REVIEW OF UNIT XII 230

UNIT XIII STORIES FROM VERGIL: I. A KINGDOM SOUGHT

LX MĀTER ANTĪQUA: Ablative with *cum* · Kinds of Ablatives 231
LXI NŪLLUM DOMICILIUM IDŌNEUM: The Independent Participial Construction · The Ablative Absolute · Free Translation of the Ablative Absolute 233
LXII AENĒĀS ET DĪDŌ: Third Conjugation · Present Tense of *-ō* Verbs of the Third Conjugation · Imperative of *-ō* Verbs of the Third Conjugation 236
LXIII CONJŪNX AENĒAE PRŌMITTITUR: Present Tense of Third-Conjugation *-iō* Verbs · Imperatives of *-iō* Verbs 240
LXIV AENĒĀS AUXILIUM PETIT: Latin and English Nouns 243
REVIEW OF UNIT XIII 245

UNIT XIV STORIES FROM VERGIL: II. A KINGDOM WON

LXV AUDĀCIA TURNĪ: Fourth Conjugation · Imperative of Fourth-Conjugation Verbs 247
LXVI FOEDUS FRĀCTUM: Perfect Active of the Third and Fourth Conjugations · Perfect Passive of the Third and Fourth Conjugations · Principal Parts of Third-Conjugation Verbs · Principal Parts of Fourth-Conjugation Verbs 250
LXVII ĪRA AENĒAE: Related Latin Words · Imperfect of the Third and Fourth Conjugations 254
LXVIII TURNUS RELICTUS Ā DEĪS: Future of the Third and Fourth Conjugations · Tense Sign of the Future 257
LXIX FĪNIS CERTĀMINIS: Present Infinitives of the Four Conjugations . . . 260
REVIEW OF UNIT XIV 263

UNIT XV MYTHS

LXX VELLUS AUREUM: Third-Declension Adjectives · Adjectives of Two Endings · Adjectives of Three Endings 268
LXXI UXOR ĪNFĒLĪX: Latin Prefixes · Third-Declension Adjectives of One Ending 272
LXXII UXOR ĀMISSA: Latin and English Prefixes · Present Active Participle · Declension of the Present Participle 275
LXXIII FĒMINA CŪRIŌSA: Latin Adjectives and English Adjectives · Cardinal Numbers 278
REVIEW OF UNIT XV 280

UNIT XVI STORIES OF THE TROJAN WAR

LXXIV JŪDICIUM PARIDIS: Meaning and Use of the Relative Pronoun · Forms of the Latin Relative Pronoun · Agreement of the Relative Pronoun · Relative Pronoun with *cum* 282
LXXV PARIS ET HELENA: Direct Quotations · Indirect Quotations · Indirect Discourse · Predicate Noun or Adjective in Indirect Discourse · Present Infinitive in Indirect Discourse 285
LXXVI DOLĪ ULĪXIS 288
LXXVII HELENA ET MENDICUS: Conjugation of *eō* · Compounds of *eō* 292
LXXVIII EQUUS LIGNEUS: Fourth Declension of Nouns · Endings 296
REVIEW OF UNIT XVI 299

UNIT XVII THE STORY OF IPHIGENIA

LXXIX EPISTULA FALSA: Use of Personal Pronouns · Declension of *ego* and *tū* · Reflexive Pronouns of the First and Second Persons · Pronouns with *cum* 301

LXXX MĀTER ET FĪLIA PERVENIUNT: Meaning of the Past Perfect · Formation of the Past Perfect Active · Past Perfect Passive 305

LXXXI ACHILLĒS DOLUM INVENIT: Latin Participles and English Adjectives · Perfect Active Infinitives · Passive Infinitives · Tense of Infinitives in Indirect Discourse 308

LXXXII SACRIFICIUM ĪPHIGENĪAE: Fifth Declension · Endings · Accusative of Duration of Time · Ablative of Time at Which 311

LXXXIII ĪPHIGENĪA INVENTA EST: Latin Nouns and English Nouns 314

REVIEW OF UNIT XVII 316

UNIT XVIII THE RETURN OF ULYSSES

LXXXIV ULĪXĒS AD PATRIAM REDIT: Future Active Participle · Future Active Infinitive 317

LXXXV TĒLEMACHUS PATREM VIDET: Conjugation of *possum* · Imperative of *eō* and *sum* · Negative Commands 320

LXXXVI ULĪXĒS RECOGNŌSCITUR: Declension and Use of *ipse* · Meaning of the Future Perfect · Formation of the Future Perfect Active · Future Perfect Passive · Perfect System 322

LXXXVII PĒNELOPĒ LĪBERĀTA EST: Latin Adverbs and Adjectives · Declension and Use of *īdem* · *mīlle* and *mīlia* · Accusative of Extent of Space 326

REVIEW OF UNIT XVIII 329

UNIT XIX STORIES FROM CAESAR

LXXXVIII UTER FORTIOR ERAT?: Latin Verbs and Related Nouns and Adjectives · Comparison of Adjectives · Formation of the Comparative and Superlative · Declension of Comparatives and Superlatives · Translation of Comparatives and Superlatives 330

LXXXIX TERROR EXERCITUM RŌMĀNUM OCCUPAT: Latin Words Made with Suffixes · Comparison of Adjectives in *-er* · Special Adjectives in *-lis* 334

XC DUX ĪRĀTISSIMUS: Latin Word Families · Adjectives Compared Irregularly 337

XCI CAESAR TAMESIM TRĀNSIT: Adverbs Compared Regularly · Irregular Adverbs 340

REVIEW OF UNIT XIX 342

UNIT XX ANCIENT AND MODERN PROFESSIONS

XCII ARCHITECTĪ ET FABRĪ · Mīrābile Dictū! 344

XCIII CORPUS JŪRIS CĪVĪLIS · Mīrābile Dictū! · Using Legal Terms and Phrases from Latin 346

XCIV MEDICAE ARTĒS · Then and Now · Mīrābile Dictū! · The Romans Had a Word for It 348

XCV AGRICULTŪRA RŌMĀNA · Mīrābile Dictū! 350

Roman life and times

THE ETERNAL CITY . . . 21
DIGGING UP THE PAST . . . 40
THE ROMAN EMPIRE . . . 61
THE ROMAN HOUSE . . . 88
FROM EGG TO APPLES . . . 108
ROMAN COINS . . . 117
ROMAN DRESS . . . 121
THE ROMAN THEATER . . . 136
FURNISHINGS OF A ROMAN HOUSE . . . 152
ROMAN SPORTS . . . 167
ROMAN INDUSTRIES . . . 193
ROMAN BATHS . . . 228
THE GODS OF THE ROMANS . . . 265
SCHOOLS AND BOOKS . . . 290
COMING OF AGE . . . 295

Latin for pleasure

DĒ TRIBUS ANIMĀLIBUS (*Fun with prepositions*) . . . 352
ROME AND AMERICA . . . 354
LATIN MOTTOES . . . 358
HORĀTIUS (*A play*) . . . 359
CIRCĒ (*A play*) . . . 365
PUER AEGER (*A play*) . . . 372
FAMILIAR SONGS IN LATIN . . . 376

Word mastery

ENGLISH NOUNS FROM LATIN NOUNS OF THE FIRST DECLENSION . . 28, 47, 82
ENGLISH NOUNS FROM LATIN NOUNS OF THE SECOND DECLENSION 102, 128, 147
ENGLISH ADJECTIVES AND LATIN ADJECTIVES IN *-us* . . . 159
ENGLISH VERBS AND LATIN VERBS . . . 179
ENGLISH NOUNS FROM LATIN NOUNS OF THE THIRD DECLENSION . . 205, 215
LATIN AND ENGLISH NOUNS . . . 244
RELATED LATIN WORDS . . . 254
LATIN AND ENGLISH PREFIXES . . . 273, 276
LATIN ADJECTIVES AND ENGLISH ADJECTIVES . . . 279
LATIN PARTICIPLES AND ENGLISH ADJECTIVES . . . 309
ENGLISH NOUNS FROM LATIN NOUNS OF THE FOURTH DECLENSION . . 315
LATIN ADVERBS AND ADJECTIVES . . . 327
LATIN VERBS AND RELATED NOUNS AND ADJECTIVES . . . 331
LATIN WORDS MADE WITH SUFFIXES . . . 335
LATIN WORD FAMILIES . . . 338
REVIEW OF WORD MASTERY . . . 343

Helps for the student

REVIEW OF GRAMMAR . . . 380
LATIN-ENGLISH VOCABULARY . . . 399
ENGLISH-LATIN VOCABULARY . . . 419
SUMMARY OF PRONUNCIATION . . . 428
LIST OF PROPER NAMES . . . 429
LATIN FOR CLASSROOM USE . . . 436
LIST OF ILLUSTRATIONS . . . 437
INDEX OF GRAMMAR . . . 442

Our national Capitol at Washington, D. C., is similar in design to public buildings that stood in Rome two thousand years ago.

UNIT
I

I. PATRIA NOSTRA

America est patria mea. America est patria tua. America est patria nostra.

Patria tua est terra pulchra. Patria mea est terra pulchra. Patria nostra est terra pulchra. America est pulchra.

Patria nostra est terra lībera. America est terra lībera. America est patria nostra.

Ame′rica,[1] America
est, is
lī′bera, free
me′a, my
nos′tra, our
pa′tria, native country, native land
pul′chra, beautiful
ter′ra, land, country
tu′a, your

Most of the letters in these Latin words represent approximately the same sounds as in English. Short **a** (that is, **a** without a long mark) has the sound of the first *a* in *aha′*. Short **e** is always pronounced like *e* in *met*, never like *e* in *her*. Short **o** is like *o* in *obey*. Short **u** is like *u* in *full*.

Notice that **i** in **lībera** has a long mark; long **i** (ī) is pronounced like *i* in *machine*. Latin **ch** is about like English *k*.

[1]While *America* was not a word known to the Romans, it has a Latin form.

The Roman aqueduct on the left was built eighteen hundred years before the American bridge which so closely resembles it.

NOUNS

The names of persons, places, or things are *nouns*. Thus the words *boy, city, Italy, house* are nouns. The names of qualities or ideas are also nouns; for example, *bravery, mercy, freedom, truth.*

You have had the following Latin nouns: **America, patria, terra.**

SENTENCES

A sentence is a group of words which expresses a thought.

America est patria tua, *America is your native country.*
Patria nostra est terra lībera, *Our country is a free land.*

Usually a sentence states something or asks a question.

THE SUBJECT

The noun about which we state or ask something is called the *subject* of the sentence.

America est pulchra, *America is beautiful.*

In this sentence we state something about **America.** Therefore, **America** is the subject of the sentence.

VERBS

A *verb* is a word used to tell what the subject does or what is done to the subject.

The boy walks.
The boy is called.

In the first sentence *walks* tells what the boy does. In the second sentence *is called* tells what is done to the boy.

Some verbs do not show any action, but merely show existence, continuance in a place, or connection. In the following sentences *is* and *shall stay* are verbs of this kind.

He is in the city.
We shall stay here.
He is good.

The Latin verb **est** is of this kind.

America est patria mea, *America is my native country.*

ADJECTIVES

In Latin, as in English, we often use some other word with a noun to describe the person or thing.

America est terra pulchra, *America is a beautiful land.*

In this sentence **pulchra** describes **terra.** Such a word is called an *adjective,* and is said to modify the noun.

Give the English equivalent of: **est, lībera, nostra, patria.**

Give the Latin equivalent of: *my, beautiful, land, your.*

Pronounce after your teacher, giving each vowel and consonant its proper sound in Latin: **Ame′rica, lī′bera, pa′tria, pul′chra.**

LATIN LIVES TODAY

Latin is a key to English. As you learn the meaning of Latin words, you will add many new English words to your vocabulary and find new meanings for words you already know.

Because Columbus discovered America, our country is sometimes poetically called *Columbia.* The word *America* comes from the first name of another explorer, who was called in Latin **Americus.**

Since many of the discoverers of parts of North and South America spoke Italian, Spanish, or French—languages derived from Latin—we have numerous place names which are either Latinized forms of persons' names or really of Latin origin.[1] Such are: Argentina (**argentum,** *silver*), Carolina (**Carolus,** *Charles*), Florida (**flores,** *flowers*), Montana (**montes,** *mountains*). Find five names of towns in your state ending in *-a* which you think come from Latin.

[1]Not all place names ending in *-a* are of Latin origin. *Iowa, Minnesota,* and *Oklahoma,* for example, are from Indian words.

II. AMERICA ET EUROPA

America nōn est īnsula. Eurōpa nōn est īnsula. Britannia est īnsula, et Sardinia est īnsula.

Britannia est magna īnsula. Britannia nōn est patria nostra, sed Britannia est terra pulchra.

5 Sardinia est īnsula, sed Sardinia nōn est parva īnsula. Sardinia est magna īnsula. Sardinia est terra pulchra.

Ītalia est terra pulchra, sed Ītalia nōn est īnsula. Ītalia nōn est parva. Hispānia nōn est īnsula, sed Hispānia est terra pulchra. Hispānia nōn est patria tua.

10 Eurōpa nōn est patria nostra. Britannia nōn est patria mea. Sardinia nōn est patria mea, et Ītalia nōn est patria tua. America est patria nostra.

Britan′nia, Britain
et, and
Eurō′pa, Europe
Hispā′nia, Spain
īn′sula, island
Īta′lia, Italy
mag′na, large, great
nōn, not
par′va, small
sed, but

Latin long **a** (ā) is pronounced like English *a*, as in *father*. Long **o** (ō) has a sound like English long *o*, as in *hole*. Latin **g** is always pronounced like *g* in *get*. Latin **s** is always pronounced like *s* in English *say*. Latin **v** is pronounced like English *w*.

When the English name of a person or place is spelled the same as the Latin, the word will not be included in the vocabulary following the story; e.g., *Sardinia*. All such words may, however, be found in the List of Proper Names (p. 429).

THE, A, AN

In English a noun is usually preceded by *the, a,* or *an.* Latin has no such words. In translating Latin into English, we supply *the, a,* or *an* as needed.

POSITION OF THE ADJECTIVE

The Latin adjective often follows its noun: **terra pulchra.** But **magna** and other adjectives denoting size or number commonly stand before their nouns, as in English: **magna terra.**

THE PREDICATE

What we say or ask about the subject is called the *predicate.*

Sardinia nōn est parva īnsula, *Sardinia is not a small island.*

In the sentence just given, **nōn est parva īnsula** is what is said about the subject. It is the predicate of the Latin sentence. Similarly, *is not a small island* is the predicate of the English sentence.

PREDICATE NOUN

A noun in the predicate which is linked to the subject by a form of the verb *to be* (*is, are, was, were, will be, has been, had been,* etc.) is called a *predicate noun.*

A predicate noun denotes the same person or thing as the subject.

Sardinia est īnsula, *Sardinia is an island.*

In this sentence **īnsula** is linked to the subject by **est.** It denotes the same thing as the subject. The word **īnsula** is a predicate noun.

Any form of the Latin verb meaning *to be* (**est,** etc.) may be used to link the predicate noun to the subject.

This mosaic picture, which adorned a wall in Pompeii, is made of many tiny pieces of colored glass.

PREDICATE ADJECTIVE

An adjective linked to the subject by any form of the verb meaning *to be* is a *predicate adjective.*

Īnsula est pulchra, *The island is beautiful.*

A predicate adjective modifies the subject of the sentence.

TRANSLATION

Translation is changing the expression of thought from one language to another. Thus we speak of translating from Latin into English and from English into Latin.

In every lesson of this book there is a Latin story which you will want to read, understand, and translate into English. Help in understanding and translating the story is given in the vocabulary (list of new words) and in the grammatical explanations. There are also Latin sentences to be translated into English, English sentences to be put into Latin, and varied exercises to give practice in understanding.

When you are translating Latin, try to express the exact thought in good English. You will find translating English into Latin a help with both languages.

Translate: 1. My native country is small. 2. Italy is not an island. 3. Your native country is a free land. 4. The island is large and beautiful. 5. Our native country is not an island.

Point out: 1. The subjects in the sentences you have just translated. 2. The predicate nouns. 3. The predicate adjectives.

HELP YOURSELF If you were translating into Latin the sentence, *The man is a sailor*, for which English words would there be no separate Latin words?

LLT Many of the words that you hear and use daily come from Latin. So familiar will many Latin words look that you will immediately connect them with English words. For example, we have some common words connected with **insula** and **magna.**

Why are the Hawaiians an *insular* people? What is an *insulated* wire? What is the covering of an *insulated* wire called?

Why is the Capitol at Washington, D. C., considered a *magnificent* building? Can Australia be said to be an island of great *magnitude?* What is the meaning of *magnified* in the following sentence? "In this drawing the insect is so *magnified* that it looks ferocious."

III. CASA PULCHRA

Jūlius. Agricola casam pulchram habet, sed casa nōn est magna. Casa est alba. Agricola parvam casam amat.

Mārcus. Agricola parvam fīliam habet. Parva fīlia agricolam amat, et agricola parvam fīliam amat. Fīlia parvam casam amat.

Jūlius. Casa nostra est magna et alba. Casam nostram amō. Cūr 5 fīlia casam amat?

Mārcus. Fīlia casam amat quod casa est alba.

Jūlius. Parvam casam amō; magnam casam nōn amō.

Mārcus. Cūr parvam casam amās?

Jūlius. Parvam casam amō quod casa est pulchra. 10

Mārcus. Casa mea est magna. Casam meam amō quod casa mea est magna et pulchra.

Jūlius. Casa tua est pulchra. Casam tuam amō.

Mārcus. Casam nostram amō quod casa nostra est pulchra.

agri′cola, farmer
al′ba, white
a′mās, you love, do love; like, do like
a′mat, loves, does love; likes, does like
a′mō, I love, do love; like, do like
ca′sa, cottage, house
cūr, why
fī′lia, daughter
ha′bet, has, does have
quod, because

Long **u** (ū) is pronounced like *u* in *rude*. Latin **c** is like English *k*. In Latin, **j** has the sound of *y* in *yes*. Latin **qu** is like *qu* in *queer*.

Prosperous people once lived in this section of an ancient town on the seacoast of Italy.

The Museum of Science and Industry in Chicago looks like a group of buildings in ancient Rome.

DIRECT OBJECT

In the following sentence **Americam** denotes the thing which the subject, **agricola**, loves.

Agricola <u>Americam</u> amat, *The farmer loves America.*

A word denoting the person or thing directly affected by an act is called the *direct object.* In this lesson the direct objects end in **-am.**

ADJECTIVE ENDINGS

In Latin an adjective has different endings, depending on its use in the sentence. Notice that adjectives modifying direct objects end in **-am** in this lesson, while those modifying subjects or predicate nouns end in **-a.** Since a predicate adjective modifies the subject, predicate adjectives in this lesson end in **-a.**

The Latin words **mea, nostra,** and **tua** are adjectives, and their endings, like those of other adjectives, are determined by the words with which they are used.

POSITION OF THE VERB

The Latin verb commonly stands at the end of the sentence. But forms of the verb meaning *to be* (*is, are, was, were, will be,* etc.) frequently come before the predicate noun or adjective.

America est terra pulchra, *America is a beautiful land.*

USE OF *do* IN NEGATIVE SENTENCES AND IN QUESTIONS

The English sentence *I do not like the cottage* is translated **Casam nōn amō.** Similarly, *Why does the farmer love the island?* is in Latin **Cūr agricola īnsulam amat?** In such sentences there is no separate Latin word for *do* or *does.*

Give the proper ending (**-a** or **-am**) for each incomplete word and explain your choice.

1. Casa nostr__ est alb__.
2. Patria me__ est terra līber__.
3. Fīlia tu__ īnsul__ nōn amat.
4. Magn__ īnsul__ amās.
5. Britannia est magn__ et pulchr__ īnsul__.
6. Fīlia tu__ cas__ nostr__ amat.
7. Cūr magn__ īnsul__ amās?

HELP YOURSELF

In Latin the endings of most words show their different uses in the sentence. In "Casa Pulchra," what ending do all the subjects have? The direct objects? In the sentences above, how can you tell the predicate nouns from the direct objects?

LLT

With the help of the Latin words you have learned, choose the word in parentheses that completes each sentence correctly.

1. A free country has (liberty, slavery).
2. Sylvia shows filial devotion to her (brother, father).
3. An agriculturist is a (sailor, farmer).

The state capitol of Arkansas, like many other state capitols, looks like a Roman building.

This Roman wall still stretches across many miles of northern England.

IV. TERRAE PULCHRAE

Britannia et Sardinia sunt īnsulae pulchrae. Saepe Britanniam et Sardiniam laudāmus quod īnsulae sunt pulchrae. Americam et Ītaliam quoque laudāmus, sed America et Ītalia nōn sunt īnsulae.

Americam amāmus quod America est patria nostra. Eurōpam 5 quoque amāmus, sed Eurōpa nōn est patria nostra. Eurōpa multās et magnās silvās habet. America quoque multās et magnās silvās habet; silvae sunt pulchrae. Sardinia parvās silvās habet.

Sardiniam amāmus quod Sardinia est īnsula pulchra. Agricolae Sardiniam amant, sed Hispāniam quoque amant. Agricolae His- 10 pāniam amant quod Hispānia magnās silvās nōn habet.

Agricolae silvās nōn amant sed agricolae terrās pulchrās amant.

amā'mus, we love, do love; like, do like
a'mant, (they) love, do love; like, do like
laudā'mus, we praise, do praise
mul'tae, many
quo'que, also
sae'pe, often
sil'va, forest
sunt, (they) are

Latin **ae** is pronounced like *i* in *like*. Such a blending of two vowel sounds is called a *diphthong*. Latin **au** is pronounced like *ou* in the word *round*.

THE PLURAL

In English we use different forms of nouns to show whether we mean one person or thing or more than one. Thus *book* refers to one thing, and *books* refers to more than one. The form *book* is in the *singular number*, and *books* is in the *plural number*.

In Latin, too, there are different forms for the singular and plural. In the following sentence the subject is plural and ends in **-ae**.

> **Agricolae casam amant,** *The farmers like the cottage.*

In the following sentence the predicate noun is in the plural and ends in **-ae**.

> **Britannia et Sardinia sunt īnsulae,** *Britain and Sardinia are islands.*

In the following sentence the direct object is plural and ends in **-ās**.

> **Agricolae casās amant,** *The farmers like the cottages.*

The plural nouns used as subjects or predicate nouns in this lesson end in **-ae**. The direct objects in the plural end in **-ās**.

ADJECTIVES WITH PLURAL NOUNS

In English an adjective does not change its form when used with a plural noun; in Latin it does. In this lesson the adjectives which modify plural subjects or plural predicate nouns end in **-ae**; those which modify plural direct objects end in **-ās**.

TWO ADJECTIVES MODIFYING ONE NOUN

In English we often have two adjectives modifying the same noun, without any connective.

> *He was driving a shabby old car.*

In Latin two adjectives modifying the same noun are sometimes connected by **et**. Often the **et** need not be translated.

> **America multās et magnās silvās habet,** *America has many large forests.*

PHRASES

Any group of connected words not containing a subject and verb is called a *phrase*.

> **Britannia et Sardinia,** *Britain and Sardinia*
> **patria nostra,** *our country*
> **multās et magnās īnsulās,** *many large islands*

1. Saepe fīliam tuam laudāmus; saepe fīliās tuās laudāmus. 2. Casae pulchrae sunt magnae. 3. Agricolae patriam amant; agricola patriam amat. 4. Silvam pulchram amō; silvās pulchrās amāmus. 5. Multās terrās laudāmus; patriam tuam quoque laudāmus. 6. Agricola casam habet; casa est parva. 7. Britannia est magna et pulchra īnsula. 8. Britannia et Sardinia sunt magnae īnsulae.

Translate the italicized words: 1. Your daughters like the *small white cottage.* 2. We often praise the *beautiful islands.* 3. My *daughter* loves *your daughters.* 4. The farmer also loves a *free country.* 5. We like *many lands.* 6. The *forests* are *beautiful.*

HW Translate into Latin the six English sentences above.

LLT

Some interesting English words are related to Latin words in the vocabulary of this lesson.

silva { Pennsylvania, silvan (sylvan), Sylvia }

multae { multimillionaire, multiply, multitude }

Give the meaning of each word connected with **multae.** What other words connected with **multae** can you think of?

With what Latin word is *laud* connected? What does *laudable* mean?

Compare the modern building in which the Supreme Court of the United States meets and one of the Roman temples on page 93.

In the famous Colosseum the Romans watched games and sports.

THE ETERNAL CITY

The "Eternal City" is Rome on its seven hills by the Tiber River. We think of Rome as eternal, not only because the city is very old but also because it was the center of the ancient Roman civilization which has had such great influence on the western world.

In the days of its great glory, Rome had a population of about a million—Roman citizens, their families and slaves, as well as foreigners from many countries. There were also transients, for people often came to Rome on business, to see the sights, or to visit friends.

As in a modern city with a great population, there were in ancient Rome rich homes and poor tenements, shops and taverns, crowded streets and busy markets, public buildings and fine parks.

An artist's idea of the Roman Forum as it once was. Here the government of the empire was carried on, and here the Roman came to fulfill his duties as a citizen.

Rome was a busy city. Boats bearing freight crowded the Tiber, and the warehouses on the docks were jammed with goods from all over the world. Along the highways which led to Rome rumbled a steady procession of wagons and carts bringing in supplies.

Rome had many amusement places: theaters, luxurious public baths, racing tracks, and a vast athletic field. Greatest of all was the Colosseum, the amphitheater shown on page 21.

Above all, Rome was a city of magnificent temples and government buildings. Nowhere in the city were there more splendid structures than in the Forum, which consisted of an open square and numerous buildings where the Senate met and the people voted, where magistrates held court and officials had their headquarters.

Just as the Forum was the heart of Roman legislative, judicial, and executive life, so Rome itself was the heart of the ancient world, important in the lives of men everywhere.

Excavations have revealed the site of the Roman Forum. From these ruins and accounts by ancient writers an artist was able to make the picture at the top of this page.

V. BONAE EPISTULAE

Cornēlius est nauta et Americam amat quod America est patria. America quoque est patria nostra. America est magna et pulchra terra. Cornēlius saepe Hispāniam, Britanniam, Ītaliam videt. Cornēlius epistulās bonās scrībit quod multās terrās videt. Saepe epistulās vidēmus. Epistulae nōn sunt longae, sed sunt bonae. 5

Anna multās epistulās habet. Anna est parva puella, sed epistulās bonās amat. Jūlia quoque epistulās bonās amat. Puellae nautam laudant quod nauta epistulās bonās scrībit.

Anna quoque multās epistulās scrībit. Epistulae sunt longae, sed nōn sunt bonae. Jūlia longās epistulās nōn scrībit, sed bonās epistulās 10 scrībit. Epistulae Americam laudant quod Jūlia Americam amat.

Jūlia Eurōpam nōn laudat quod Eurōpam nōn videt. Jūlia nōn est nauta; multās terrās nōn videt. Cornēlius multās terrās videt quod est nauta. Cornēlius Americam amat, sed saepe Eurōpam quoque laudat. 15

bo′na, good, excellent
epis′tula, letter
lau′dant, (they) praise, do praise, approve of
lau′dat, (he) praises, does praise, approves of
lon′ga, long
nau′ta, sailor
puel′la, girl
scrī′bit, (he) writes, does write
vidē′mus, we see, do see
vi′det, (he) sees, does see

In Latin long **e** (ē) is pronounced like *e* in *they;* short **i** is like *i* in *this.*

OMISSION OF THE SUBJECT

We have seen that **amō** is used to mean *I love,* without a separate word for *I.* In the same manner **amat,** which is translated *loves* when it has a noun subject, is translated *he loves* or *she loves* when there is no noun subject.

Fīlia mea fīliās tuās amat; casam tuam quoque amat, *My daughter loves your daughters; she likes your house, too.*

In the same way, we may translate **scrībit** *he writes* or *she writes,* **videt,** *he sees* or *she sees,* and **est,** *he is* or *she is* or *it is.*

Jūlia Eurōpam nōn laudat quod Eurōpam nōn videt, *Julia does not praise Europe because she does not see Europe.*

The Jefferson Memorial, one of the newer public buildings in Washington, D. C., is Roman in design, like many of the others.

CASE

In English some words have different forms to show how they are used in sentences.

He walks. Marcus sees him.

Here *he* is the subject form, and *him* is the direct-object form of the same word.

A noun in English has the same form for the subject and for the direct object, but it has a different form to refer to a person as possessing something.

The boy walks. I see the boy. I have the boy's book.

These different forms and uses of words in sentences are called *cases* or *case uses.* The subject is in the *nominative case*, the direct object is in the *objective* (or *accusative*) *case*, and the word referring to the possessor is in the *possessive case.*

In Latin also, the subject is said to be in the *nominative case*, and the direct object is said to be in the *accusative case.*

The Latin endings for the nominative and accusative of all the nouns we have had thus far are as follows:

	SINGULAR	PLURAL
Nominative:	**-a**	**-ae**
Accusative:	**-am**	**-ās**

1. Epistulam tuam vidēmus. 2. Nauta bonās epistulās scrībit. 3. Nauta epistulam longam habet; epistulās longās amat. 4. Casam vidēmus; est magna casa. 5. Casās vidēmus; sunt magnae casae. 6. Nautae casam tuam laudant; casās nostrās quoque laudant. 7. Puella silvās pulchrās videt; silvae sunt magnae. 8. Fīliam meam amō; casam tuam amāmus. 9. Fīliam tuam amō; fīliās tuās amāmus.

Select the correct word to complete each sentence below, and tell why you chose it.

1. Casa est (magnam, magna).
2. Epistulae sunt (longae, longa).
3. Silvās (pulchrās, pulchrae) amāmus.
4. Agricola (fīlia, fīliam) habet.
5. (Patria, Patriam) amās.
6. Patria nostra est (līberam, lībera).
7. Silvae sunt (magnae, magnās).
8. (Epistulae, Epistulās) laudat.

From the list at the left below, select the word or phrase that translates the word or words in each parenthesis.

bonae	**multās terrās**
epistula longa	**nauta**
epistulam longam	**nautās**
epistulās	**parva īnsula**
multae epistulae	**parvam īnsulam**
multās epistulās	**puellae**

1. (*the long letter*) laudāmus.
2. (*a sailor*) (*many lands*) videt.
3. (*a small island*) vidēmus.
4. (*the girls*) sunt (*good*).
5. Puella (*many letters*) nōn scrībit, sed (*letters*) amat.

HELP YOURSELF Point out the subjects in the fourth paragraph of "Bonae Epistulae." In the third paragraph of the story which subjects are singular? Which are plural? In the third and fourth paragraphs find some predicate nouns and adjectives.

LLT

Why is a *bonus* so called?

An *epistle* is a letter. Paul's Epistles in the New Testament are actually letters which he wrote to Christians of his time.

What is the meaning of *nautical?* Is there anyone in the class who can tell how long a *nautical* mile is? Why is it so called?

You know what **scribit** means. What is the meaning of the English words *scribble, scribe, inscribe?* What is a radio *script?*

REVIEW OF UNIT I LESSONS I-V

Nouns	*Verbs*		*Adjectives*		*Other Words*
agricola	**amō**	**laudat**	**alba**	**multae**	**cūr**
casa	**amās**	**laudāmus**	**bona**	**nostra**	**et**
epistula	**amat**	**laudant**	**lībera**	**parva**	**nōn**
fīlia	**amāmus**	**scrībit**	**longa**	**pulchra**	**quod**
īnsula	**amant**	**sunt**	**magna**	**tua**	**quoque**
nauta	**est**	**videt**	**mea**		**saepe**
patria	**habet**	**vidēmus**			**sed**
puella					
silva					
terra					

I. From the list of words below, choose one to fill each blank in the sentences that follow.

albam	**casam**	**fīlia**	**patriam**
bonae	**epistula**	**īnsulae**	**puellae**
bonam	**epistulae**	**līberam**	**pulchra**
casa	**epistulam**	**longa**	**pulchram**
casae	**epistulās**	**patria**	**silvae**

1. __ sunt pulchrae. 2. __ est alba. 3. __ sunt longae. 4. Nauta __ saepe scrībit. 5. Terram __ amāmus. 6. Īnsula __ est quoque magna. 7. Sunt bonae __. 8. __ tua est bona. 9. __ nostrae sunt albae. 10. __ mea est America.

II. For each blank give the correct form of a word in the review vocabulary above. Use a different word each time, and explain the form.

1. Agricola casam __ habet.
2. Cūr īnsulam __ amās?
3. Patria __ est terra __.
4. __ amō, quod īnsula est __.
5. Fīlia __ īnsulam __ amat.
6. Nauta __ scrībit.

III. In the following sentences change each singular noun to plural and make other necessary changes.

1. Bona puella casam albam amat.
2. Silvam pulchram amō.
3. Īnsula est parva.

IV. Tell which word does not belong in each list and give the reason.

Sample: **fīlia, nauta, habet, terra, patria**
Answer: **Habet,** because it is a verb and all the others are nouns.

1. **agricola, casa, epistula, est, īnsula**
2. **amat, habet, laudāmus, nōn, sunt**
3. **alba, bona, fīlia, lībera, mea**
4. **longa, magna, nostra, nauta, pulchra**
5. **nauta, patria, quod, silva, terra**

V. Supply the correct Latin form of the English word.

1. Īnsula est ___. (*long*)
2. Nauta ___ longās scrībit. (*letters*)
3. Agricola ___ nōn videt. (*house*)
4. Mārcus est ___. (*farmer*)
5. Agricolae nōn sunt ___. (*sailors*)

LATIN LIVES TODAY

Complete each of the following sentences by using one of the words given.

1. Some rich men are famous for { liberty. / liberality. / liberation. }

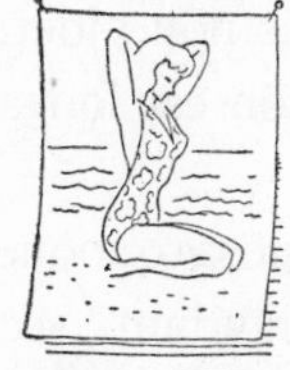

2. Girls in Hollywood are noted for { magnitude. / longitude. / pulchritude. }

3. In the evening we sat on the { terrace. / territory. / terrier. }

4. In addition to his salary the man received a { bonbon. / bonus. / bone. }

5. When you take a magazine regularly, you are a { scribbler. / describer. / subscriber. }

Roman ships like this model carried passengers and freight on the Mediterranean

UNIT

II

VI. VITA PERICULOSA

Vīta nautae est perīculōsa, sed vīta agricolae nōn est perīculōsa. Nautae vītam perīculōsam amant; agricolae vītam quiētam parvae īnsulae amant.

Corsica et Sardinia et Melita[1] sunt īnsulae pulchrae. Corsica et 5 Sardinia sunt magnae īnsulae; Melita est parva īnsula. Incolae īnsulārum pulchrārum sunt agricolae et nautae. Casae nautārum sunt parvae, sed agricolae magnās casās habent.

Vīta agricolae saepe est longa, sed agricola multās terrās nōn videt. Nautae multās terrās vident, sed interdum vīta nautae nōn est longa 10 quod vīta nautae est perīculōsa.

Saepe vīta quiēta est vīta bona; interdum vīta perīculōsa quoque est bona. Poētae saepe perīculōsam nautārum vītam laudant, sed quiētam agricolārum vītam amō.

ha′bent, (they) have
in′cola, inhabitant
inter′dum, sometimes
perīculō′sa, dangerous

poē′ta, poet
quiē′ta, quiet
vi′dent, (they) see
vī′ta, life

Such words as **poēta** and **quiēta** each have three syllables: **po ē′ta, qui ē′ta.**

ENGLISH NOUNS AND LATIN NOUNS

In the list above, you see the word **poeta.** How does it differ in spelling from the English noun with the same meaning?

Some other Latin nouns give us English nouns with this same change in spelling: **caverna,** *cavern.*

[1]Now called Malta.

If **matrona** is a word of this kind, what English noun comes from it? What word comes from **palma?**

When you meet a Latin word like **poeta,** you will know its meaning at once. Such words will not appear in the lesson vocabulary, and will be starred in the review list for the unit. All such words will be found in the reference vocabulary at the back of the book.

NOUNS DENOTING POSSESSION

As you know, most English nouns show possession by adding an apostrophe and *s* (*'s*) in the singular or simply an apostrophe in the plural: *the girl's desk; the boys' books.*

We say that such nouns are in the *possessive* case. This case in Latin is called the *genitive.*

In "Vīta Perīculōsa" you met some Latin nouns in the genitive case. Notice that these nouns have the ending **-ae** in the singular.

Vīta nautae est perīculōsa, *The sailor's life is dangerous.*

Latin nouns which end in **-a** in the nominative and **-am** in the accusative end in **-ae** in the genitive singular. The genitive plural ends in **-ārum.**

Casae nautārum sunt parvae, *The sailors' cottages are small.*

TWO FORMS OF TRANSLATION FOR THE GENITIVE

The genitive may be translated either by the possessive case or by *of* and the noun.

casa nautae, *the sailor's cottage* or *the cottage of the sailor*

In the nouns you have had thus far, the genitive singular has the same ending as the nominative plural.

Genitive Singular: **Casa nautae est parva,** *The sailor's cottage is small.*

Nominative Plural: **Nautae sunt incolae īnsulae,** *The sailors are inhabitants of the island.*

You can decide from the general meaning of the sentences whether a form ending in **-ae** is nominative plural or genitive singular. The position of the words will also help you, as a genitive usually follows the noun upon which it depends.

ADJECTIVES MODIFYING NOUNS IN THE GENITIVE

An adjective modifying a noun in the genitive is also in the genitive and is in the same number as the noun. In this lesson the adjectives which modify singular nouns in the genitive end in **-ae**; those which modify plural nouns end in **-ārum.**

1. Interdum vītam agricolārum laudāmus. 2. Nautae interdum vītam agricolārum laudant. 3. Agricolae interdum vītam nautārum laudant. 4. Vīta tua nōn est perīculōsa. 5. Vīta poētae nōn saepe est perīculōsa. 6. Incolae īnsulae pulchrae terram vident. 7. Agricolae parvās casās habent. 8. Epistula nautae quiētam vītam laudat.

Select the correct word to complete each sentence and tell why you chose it.

1. Britannia est patria __. { nauta / nautae / nautam }

2. Interdum casās __ vidēmus. { agricolam / agricola / agricolārum }

3. Incolae __ patriam meam laudant. { īnsula / īnsulās / īnsulārum }

4. Jūlia fīliās __ amat. { poētae / poētam / poētās }

5. Fīliae __ casās amant. { poētās / poētārum / poēta }

HY Find in the first paragraph of "Vīta Perīculōsa" a noun used both in the genitive singular and the nominative plural. How do you know which is genitive and which is nominative?

LLT The English words *poet* and *quiet* are almost like the Latin words. What other English words connected with **poeta** and **quieta** can you think of?

From **vita** come *vital, vitality, vitamins.* Complete each sentence with one of these words.

1. The heart is a __ organ.
2. An athlete needs great __.
3. Lack of __ may cause disease.
4. Many kinds of __ are sold in drug stores.
5. The __ of the invalid was surprising.
6. Air is a __ necessity.

VII. POETA ET NAUTA

Anna. Sum fīlia poētae.

Fulvia et Secunda. Sumus fīliae nautae.

Anna. Sardinia est patria mea. Sardinia est magna īnsula et multās silvās habet. Silvae nōn sunt magnae, sed sunt pulchrae. Incolae Sardiniae silvās pulchrās amant. 5

Fulvia. Es incola Sardiniae, sed sumus incolae Hispāniae. Hispānia nōn est īnsula, sed est terra pulchra. Hispānia quoque parvās silvās habet. Incolae Hispāniae parvās silvās amant.

Anna. Nautae multās terrās vident, sed vīta nautārum est perīculōsa. Vīta poētārum nōn est perīculōsa. Sum laeta quod sum fīlia 10 poētae.

Secunda. Sum laeta quod sum fīlia nautae. Poēta fābulās bonās scrībit et fābulās bene legit, sed multam pecūniam nōn habet. Vīta nautae est perīculōsa, sed nauta saepe multam pecūniam habet.

Fulvia. Sum quoque laeta quod sum fīlia nautae. Nauta fābulās 15 nōn scrībit, sed fābulās bene nārrat.

Anna. Vīta nautārum est laeta quod nautae vītam perīculōsam amant. Poētae vītam quiētam amant, sed vīta poētārum est quoque laeta.

be′ne, well
fā′bula, story
lae′ta, happy, glad
le′git, (he) reads
mul′ta, much
nār′rat, (he) tells
pecū′nia, money
sum, I am

A theater in Spain where Romans once applauded their favorite shows

PERSON AND NUMBER OF VERBS

A verb may be in the *first person,* the *second person,* or the *third person.*

First Person: I walk
Second Person: you walk
Third Person: he walks

The first person of a verb shows that the speaker is performing the action. The second person shows that the person spoken to is performing the action. The third person shows that a person or thing spoken of is performing the action.

Observe that the third person is different in form from the first and second persons. The third person plural also is different from the third person singular.

Singular: he walks
Plural: they walk

A verb always agrees with its subject; that is, the person and number of the verb are always the same as the person and number of the subject.

The man walks fast.

In the sentence above, the subject, *man,* is third person singular. Since it agrees with the subject, the verb, *walks,* is also third person singular.

In Latin the verb has different forms to show person and number. You have already had such forms as **amō,** first person singular, and **amat,** third person singular.

THE FORMS OF *sum*

You are familiar with the forms **est,** *he, she, it is,* and **sunt,** *they are.* These are two forms of the verb **sum,** meaning *I am.*

Now you will learn how this verb changes to show person and number.

	SINGULAR	PLURAL
First Person:	**sum,** I am	**su′mus,** we are
Second Person:	**es,** you are	**es′tis,** you are
Third Person:	**est,** he, she, it is	**sunt,** they are

The forms of a verb when arranged in regular order make a *conjugation.* When we recite these forms, we *conjugate* the verb.

This picture of a villa was painted on the wall of a Roman house. (*See p. 74.*)

You, SINGULAR AND PLURAL

In English the word *you* may be either singular or plural.

Singular: *You are a farmer.*

Plural: *You are farmers.*

Latin, however, has different forms for the singular and plural of the word meaning *you*, although the Latin word for *you* is not often used as the subject of a verb.

The Latin verb forms for the second person are also different in the singular and plural.

Singular: **Es agricola.**

Plural: **Estis agricolae.**

1. Sum incola Britanniae; fīlia mea incola Hispāniae est. 2. Patria nostra est America, et patriam nostram amāmus. 3. Estis incolae Ītaliae; Ītalia est terra pulchra. 4. Ītaliam saepe laudāmus, sed Americam quoque amāmus. 5. Poēta bene scrībit; puella fābulās poētae nārrat. 6. Es puella laeta; fābulās longās amās. 7. Poēta fābulās longās scrībit. 8. Sumus agricolae; casae nostrae nōn sunt magnae. 9. Puellae sunt laetae, sed multam pecūniam nōn habent.

1. I am an inhabitant of America. 2. The poet's daughter praises my cottage. 3. My cottage is white. 4. We are inhabitants of a beautiful island. 5. You are sailors. 6. You are a farmer; you love your country.

Change the verbs to the singular and make other necessary changes: 1. Estis fīliae nautārum. 2. Sumus incolae Hispāniae. 3. Sunt agricolae.

Change the subjects to the singular and make other necessary changes: 1. Casae sunt albae. 2. Puellae sunt laetae. 3. Fābulae sunt bonae.

VIII. FILIA NAUTAE

Anna. Cūr casam spectātis? Cūr nōn ambulātis?

Lūcia. Nōn ambulāmus quod puellam expectāmus.

Cornēlia. Casam spectāmus quod est casa nautae. Puella est fīlia nautae. Cūr casam spectās?

5 *Anna.* Casam spectō quod casa est pulchra. Casās pulchrās spectāre amō. Cūr fīliam nautae nunc expectātis?

Lūcia. Puellam nunc expectāmus quod fābulās saepe nārrat. Puella fābulās bene nārrat. Fābulās bonās amāmus. Interdum puella quoque pecūniam portat.

10 *Cornēlia.* Nōn multam pecūniam portat, sed nauta multam pecūniam habet. Nauta multās terrās videt et fābulās bonās nārrat. Interdum fābulae nautae sunt longae.

Anna. Fābulās bonās quoque amō. Sum fīlia poētae. Saepe poētae fābulās bonās nārrant.

15 *Lūcia.* Fābulās poētārum quoque amāmus quod sunt bonae, sed poētae multās terrās nōn vident.

Cornēlia. Fīliam nautae amāmus quod fābulās pulchrās nārrāre amat. Fīlia nautae est laeta quod fābulās amāmus.

This house in Herculaneum had the plain exterior common to Roman houses. All the beautiful color and design were inside.

am'bulō, -āre, walk
expec'tō, -āre, wait for, expect
nunc, now
por'tō, -āre, carry, bring
spec'tō, -āre, look at, watch

In this lesson you meet a Latin word spelled with the letter x: **expectō**. Latin **x** is always pronounced like English *ks*.

Hereafter, in the vocabularies, the infinitive of each first-conjugation verb will be indicated. Thus, **ambulō, -āre** indicates that the infinitive of **ambulō** is **ambulāre** and that **ambulō** belongs to the first conjugation.

THE INFINITIVE

You are familiar with such English verb forms as *to go, to ride, to carry.*

I want to carry the package.

Such a verb form is called an *infinitive.*

The Latin infinitive meaning *to carry* is **portāre.**

CONJUGATION OF *portō*

You have learned how to conjugate **sum,** and now you will learn how to conjugate **portō.**

SINGULAR	PLURAL
por′tō, I carry, I am carrying	**portā′mus,** we carry, we are carrying
por′tās, you carry, you are carrying	**portā′tis,** you carry, you are carrying
por′tat, he, she, it carries; he, she, it is carrying	**por′tant,** they carry, they are carrying

The *stem* of a verb is found by dropping the **-re** of the infinitive. The stem of **portō** is **portā-.**

Infinitive: **portāre** *Stem:* **portā-**

To this stem the person endings are added.

You will observe that the characteristic vowel of the stem, **-ā-,** disappears before the ending **-ō** and becomes short before **-t** and **-nt.**

As you have seen, the person endings are:

	SINGULAR	PLURAL
First Person:	**-ō** or **-m**[1] (I)	**-mus** (we)
Second Person:	**-s** (you)	**-tis** (you)
Third Person:	**-t** (he, she, it)	**-nt** (they)

THE FIRST CONJUGATION

Many verbs have the infinitive ending in **-āre** and are conjugated like **portō.** We say that such verbs are of the *first conjugation.* The verbs **ambulō, amō, expectō, laudō, nārrō,** and **spectō,** forms of which appear in this or preceding lessons, are of the first conjugation.

[1]The person ending **-m** appears in **sum** and will be seen in certain forms to be learned later.

1. Puellās nunc expectāmus. 2. Bonās fābulās nārrātis, sed fābulās nārrāre nōn amāmus. 3. Agricolae fābulās laudant, sed agricolās nōn laudāmus. 4. Nauta incolās īnsulae spectat. 5. Nunc sum nauta; vīta mea est perīculōsa. 6. Agricolās laudās; agricolae nautās laudant. 7. Es agricola; vīta tua nōn est perīculōsa. 8. Estis agricolae; agricolae vītam quiētam amant. 9. Sumus poētae; vīta nostra quoque est quiēta.

Select the Latin word which correctly translates the English, and tell why you chose it.

1. To walk (ambulāre, ambulant, ambulat)
2. We see (spectō, spectātis, spectāmus)
3. They tell (nārrās, nārrat, nārrant)
4. He is carrying (portō, portāre, portat)
5. You are telling (nārrō, nārrāmus, nārrās)

For each blank supply a form of **laudō.**

1. Fābulās poētārum __. (*I*)	4. Casās agricolārum __. (*we*)
2. Agricolās __. (*you, sing.*)	5. Vītam perīculōsam __. (*you, pl.*)
3. Nautās __. (*he*)	6. Casās albās __. (*they*)

From the following list of words select one to complete each sentence below. Use each verb only once. Explain your choices.

amat **ambulant** **expectō** **laudās** **nārrāmus** **spectātis**

1. Fīliās meās __.	3. Poēta pecūniam __.	5. Casam albam __.
2. Casam magnam __.	4. Fābulās bonās __.	6. Fīliae meae __.

HW In the Latin sentences at the top of the page change the plural verbs to singular and make any other necessary changes.

HELP YOURSELF Find in "Fīlia Nautae" two verbs which end in **-mus.** What is the subject of each? Find a verb ending in **-t** or **-nt** which must have a subject supplied in translation.

LLT

What does a *porter* do? What is a *portfolio?* How does a *portable* radio differ from a cabinet radio?

Each of the sentences below contains a word which has the same meaning as an English word connected with **specto.** Substitute the derivative in each sentence.

The flower show was a gorgeous sight. All day long, crowds of onlookers exclaimed over the exquisite blooms. The chrysanthemums were the most showy.

IX. GALBA ET PIRATAE

Sum incola Siciliae. Incolae Siciliae sunt agricolae et nautae. Sum nauta; Galba est fīlius (*my son*).

Vīta incolārum Siciliae est perīculōsa quod pīrātae incolās īnsulae saepe superant et abdūcunt (*carry off*). Interdum agricolās et nautās necant. Pīrātae pecūniam et gemmās incolārum amant; casās agricolārum et nautārum saepe occupant. 5

Pīrātae casās nostrās spectant, sed pīrātās nōn vidēmus. Pīrātae Galbam vident, sed Galba pīrātās nōn videt. Pīrātae Galbam abdūcunt, sed Galbam nōn necant. Galba clāmat; fēminās et puellās vocat. Nunc fēminae et puellae clāmant; Galbam et pīrātās mōnstrant. 10

Nautās et agricolās vocō. Pīrātās superāmus. Īnsulam pīrātārum occupāmus; pīrātās necāmus. Galbam nōn vidēmus, sed parva pīrātae fīlia Galbam mōnstrat. Galbam et parvam puellam servāmus. Parva puella est laeta quod pīrātae Galbam nōn necant.

Nunc pīrātae agricolās et nautās nōn abdūcunt; nunc pecūniam et gemmās incolārum nōn occupant. Fēminae et puellae sunt laetae quod gemmās pulchrās habent. 15

clā′mō, -āre, shout, scream
fē′mina, woman
gem′ma, jewel, gem
mōn′strō, -āre, point out, show
ne′cō, -āre, kill, slay
oc′cupō, -āre, seize, occupy
pīrā′ta, pirate
ser′vō, -āre, save, preserve
su′perō, -āre, overcome, conquer
vo′cō, -āre, call, summon

All proper names with their pronunciation are included in the list beginning on page 429. Unless you are sure you know how to pronounce a name, look it up there.

When there are more than two consonants between two vowels, all but the first go with the following vowel: **mōn′strō, pul′chra.**

These Roman dishes of gold and silver, with the jewelry and bags of money, would have been rich booty for the pirates.

TRANSITIVE AND INTRANSITIVE VERBS

A verb which has a direct object is *transitive.*

Nauta fābulam nārrat, *The sailor tells a story.*

If a verb does not have an object, it is *intransitive.*

Ambulant, *They walk.*

In this example the action is complete in itself; the verb has no object and is intransitive.

Some verbs are transitive or intransitive according to the way they are used. But such verbs as *be, appear, seem* cannot take an object and are therefore always intransitive.

Thus the forms of **sum** are intransitive. In the following sentence the verb **est** merely links the predicate noun, **īnsula,** to the subject, **Sicilia.**

Sicilia est īnsula pulchra, *Sicily is a beautiful island.*

1. Pīrātae gemmās fēminae nōn habent; pīrātae īnsulam nōn occupant; pīrātās necāmus. 2. Nunc fēminae et puellae pīrātās vident; nautae fēminās et puellās servant. 3. Agricolam vocātis; agricola Galbam servat. 4. Gemmae sunt pulchrae; fēminae pecūniam et gemmās amant. 5. Ītalia est patria tua; patriam tuam servās; patriam nostram servāmus. 6. Agricola casam meam mōnstrat; casam meam laudat. 7. Pīrāta nautam superat; pīrātam superās.

Translate the English words into Latin.

1. (*I am*) agricola. 3. (*He is*) nauta. 5. (*You are*) pīrātae.
2. (*You are*) poēta. 4. (*We are*) puellae. 6. (*They are*) fābulae.

Translate the verbs: 1. The pirates are watching our little island. 2. You (*pl.*) seize the pirates' island; you save the jewels and money. 3. The pirate calls the woman; now the woman screams; we overcome the pirate; we save the woman.

LLT

Find in the vocabulary of this lesson a Latin word connected with each italicized word in the following paragraph.

The burglar entered the room *occupied* by the *vocalist* and seized her *gems.* She made a great *clamor; feminine* screams *demonstrated* her alarm. "Give back my jewels, you *pirate!*" she cried.

REVIEW OF UNIT II LESSONS VI-IX

Nouns	*Verbs*		*Adjectives*	*Other Words*
fābula	**ambulō, -āre**	**occupō, -āre**	**laeta**	**bene**
fēmina	**clāmō, -āre**	**portō, -āre**	**multa**	**interdum**
gemma	**expectō, -āre**	**servō, -āre**	**perīculōsa**	**nunc**
incola	**habent**	**spectō, -āre**	**quiēta**	
pecūnia	**legit**	**sum**		
pīrāta	**mōnstrō, -āre**	**superō, -āre**		
poēta	**nārrō, -āre**	**vident**		
vīta	**necō, -āre**	**vocō, -āre**		

I. In the first two columns below, are the Latin person endings you have had. Find in the last two columns the English pronoun corresponding to each one.

1. -ō or -m	4. **-mus**	(*a*) you (*pl.*)	(*d*) you (*sing.*)
2. **-s**	5. **-tis**	(*b*) he	(*e*) they
3. **-t**	6. **-nt**	(*c*) we	(*f*) I

II. Give the stem of **ambulō, expectō, mōnstrō, necō, servō,** and tell how you found it.

III. Name the case or cases shown by each of these endings: **-ās, -a, -am, -ārum, -ae.**

IV. Change to plural: **ambulās; laudās; nārrat; spectō.** Change to singular: **ambulant; expectātis; laudant; spectāmus.**

V. Choose the correct word to complete each sentence.

1. Casae (agricolam, agricolārum, agricolās) sunt pulchrae.
2. Puella (casārum, casae, casam) mōnstrat.
3. (Fēmina, Fēminam, Fēminae) interdum ambulat.
4. Pīrātae (incola, incolās, incolae) spectant.
5. (Gemmās, Gemma, Gemmae) est pulchra.
6. Fēminae et (puellam, puellās, puellae) sunt laetae.

LLT

Which Latin noun in the review vocabulary above has no common English derivative? Give one or more English words connected with each of the other Latin nouns in the list. Select at least six verbs from the list with each of which you connect an English word. With which adjectives in the list do you connect English words?

Through an arch in Pompeii, Mount Vesuvius is seen today, looking very peaceful, but still capable of pouring out destruction.

DIGGING UP THE PAST

On a fine summer morning in the year we call A.D. 79, the people in the cities of Pompeii and Herculaneum, at the foot of Mount Vesuvius, were going about their business as usual. Suddenly a column of smoke shot up from the mountain and spread over the sky, until day was turned into night. Showers of hot cinders, small stones, and ashes fell over the two cities and the countryside. Lightning flashed, and one earthquake after another shook the ground. Those who fled at once saved their lives, but those who hesitated perished in their homes, on the streets, or outside the city gates.

All that now remains of a street corner in Pompeii which many people must have passed each day

After the volcano was once more quiet, survivors came back to find both Herculaneum and Pompeii buried deep. At Pompeii people dug through the ashes in search of valuables, but no attempt was made to uncover the cities. For centuries they were forgotten.

Eventually the work of uncovering these two towns began, and now large sections have been laid open. Today one can walk into the buildings of Pompeii and Herculaneum and imagine how they used to look and how the inhabitants worked and played. Because they fled in haste, the people left houses and shops just as they were.

When large sections of a building remain standing, as in the case of the house with the balcony shown in the upper picture, it is not hard to imagine that it once looked like the picture below. However, sometimes it is possible for experts to determine how other buildings looked from a study of their foundations, walls, and the rubbish of the materials from which they were constructed.

The same street corner with its raised sidewalk, cobbled street, and stepping stones, as it must have looked when people still lived in the houses and walked in the streets

An open excavation in Herculaneum. All the dirt in the baskets and cars will be sifted; every scrap of metal and crockery will be saved and examined.

The men who make a special study of things of the past are really detectives searching for clues —not to crime but to the customs and habits of early peoples. Among the various clues these men find are tools, pottery, jewelry, inscriptions, weapons. These things tell much about the people who made them or used them.

This picture shows how such clues are being recovered today. It has been much more difficult to uncover Herculaneum than Pompeii, because a rain followed the eruption and turned the ashes into mud that became almost as hard as rock. Moreover, a modern city extends over much of the site of the ancient one. Some of the excavating, therefore, has been done through underground passages.

For the people of Pompeii and Herculaneum the burial of their cities by Vesuvius was a frightful disaster, but for us it was a piece of good fortune, because the eruption made it possible for two Roman towns of the past to be studied in modern times.

X. GALBA ET FILIA

Fīlia mea Fulviam saepe videt. Fulvia est fīlia Galbae. Galba multās terrās videt; nauta est et bene labōrat. Galba et Fulvia magnam casam habent. Casa pictūrās pulchrās habet.

Fulvia gemmās dēsīderat. Galba multam pecūniam habet, itaque Fulviae multās et pulchrās gemmās dat. Fulviae multam pecūniam quoque dat. 5

Fīlia mea gemmās amat et dēsīderat, sed multās gemmās nōn habet. Pecūniam quoque amat et dēsīderat, sed nōn multam pecūniam habet.

Interdum Fulvia fīliae meae gemmās mōnstrat. Mihi quoque gemmās mōnstrat; gemmae sunt pulchrae. 10

Fulvia fīliae meae multās et pulchrās pictūrās mōnstrat; fīlia mea pictūrās amat. Nunc Fulvia fīliae meae pictūram pīrātārum mōnstrat. Fīlia mea pictūram nōn amat; pīrātās timet. Fulvia pictūrās nōn timet; pīrātās nōn timet.

Galba puellīs fābulās nārrat. Bonās fābulās nārrat quod nauta 15 est et multās terrās videt. Galbam amō, quod puellīs fābulās bene nārrat.

dēsī′derō, -āre, want, desire
dō, da′re, give
i′taque, and so, therefore
labō′rō, -āre, work, labor
mi′hi, me, to me (*as ind. obj.*)
pictū′ra, painting on the wall, picture
ti′met, fears, is afraid of

In the division of words into syllables, a syllable must always have a vowel or diphthong. In the word **timet** the first syllable is **ti,** and the second is **met.** There are definite rules for the division of Latin words into syllables. One of these rules is: A consonant between two vowels is taken with the vowel which follows it: **ti met.** In the vocabularies of this lesson and preceding lessons the accented syllable is indicated; e.g., in **labō′rō** the accent falls on the syllable **bō.**

This picture was painted on the wall of a Pompeian house. The costume indicates that the woman was of high rank.

As we use framed pictures, flowered carpets, and patterned linoleum, the Romans used such mosaics for decoration.

INDIRECT OBJECT

A word denoting the person to whom something is given, said, or shown is the *indirect object.*

I gave Mary the letter.

In the following Latin sentence **nautae** is the indirect object, because it denotes the person to whom something is given.

Pīrāta nautae epistulam dat, *The pirate gives the sailor a letter.*

In English we sometimes use a phrase instead of an indirect object.

I gave the letter to Mary. The pirate gives a letter to the sailor.

In Latin a phrase is never used for this purpose; there is only one way to express the indirect object.

DATIVE CASE

A Latin noun used as an indirect object is in the *dative case.* All the nouns used thus far end in **-ae** in the dative singular. Notice that this ending is the same as that of the genitive singular and the nominative plural.

All dative plural forms in this lesson and the lessons immediately following end in **-īs.**

Galba incolīs epistulam mōnstrat, *Galba shows the inhabitants the letter.*

ADJECTIVES MODIFYING NOUNS IN THE DATIVE

An adjective modifying a noun in the dative case is also in the dative, and is in the same number as its noun. In this lesson the adjectives which modify singular nouns in the dative end in **-ae**; those which modify plural nouns in the dative end in **-īs.**

1. Fēminae pulchrae gemmās dō; fēminīs pulchrīs gemmās damus. 2. Poēta pecūniam dēsīderat, itaque agricolae poētae pecūniam dant. 3. Incolae īnsulae nautae epistulās dant; nautae incolīs īnsulae pecūniam dant. 4. Fābulam fīliae meae nārrō; fīlia tua fābulam legit. 5. Nautae epistulam dās, et nauta epistulam mihi mōnstrat. 6. Agricolae bene labōrant. 7. Fīlia agricolam amat, itaque puella bene labōrat.

Complete each sentence by adding one of the words or phrases below. Use each word or phrase only once.

1. Parva puella pecūniam __ dat.
2. Parvae puellae multam pecūniam __ dant.
3. Agricola gemmās __ dat.
4. Agricolae gemmās pulchrās __ dant.
5. Poēta __ pictūram pulchram mōnstrat.

agricolae **agricolīs** **nautīs** **parvae puellae** **parvīs puellīs**

Write the following words, dividing them into syllables:

bona **laudant** **nauta** **saepe** **vīta**

In the Latin sentences above, what forms of **dō** do you find? Write the conjugation of **dō.** (Notice that **dō,** unlike **portō,** has short **a** in the infinitive and in the first and second person plural.)

HW Make five Latin sentences, each of which contains a noun in the dative modified by an adjective.

HY In "Galba et Fīlia" find five indirect objects and point out the verb with which each is used. Find two nouns ending in **-ae** which are not indirect objects, and tell the case of each.

Complete each sentence with a word connected with **laboro.**

1. __ is work.
2. A __ task is a hard task.
3. __ Day comes in September.
4. Our school has a science __.
5. A __ is a person who works.

XI. PUELLA BENIGNA

Galba. Vīlla alba est vīlla poētae et fīliae. Poētam videō, sed fīliam nōn videō.

Cornēlia. Fenestrae vīllae sunt apertae; jānua quoque est aperta. Nunc poētam videō; epistulam scrībit.

5 *Galba.* Poēta epistulam nōn scrībit; fābulam scrībit. Fābulae poētārum mihi grātae sunt. Nunc Annam videō. Anna est fīlia poētae.

Cornēlia. Fēminam quoque videō. Fēmina et parva puella pictūram spectant.

10 *Galba.* Fēminam nōn spectās, sed Fulviam spectās. Fulvia nōn fēmina est; puella est. Annae pictūram mōnstrat et fābulam nārrat. Fulvia est puella benigna.

Cornēlia. Cūr Fulvia parvīs puellīs benigna est?

Galba. Fulvia parvās puellās amat et fābulās nārrāre amat. Fulvia
15 parvīs puellīs cāra est quod est benigna. Fulvia quoque mihi benigna est.

Cornēlia. Cūr Fulvia tibi benigna est?

Galba. Fulvia est fīlia mea. Fulviam amō quod est fīlia mea; sed Fulvia mihi quoque grāta est quod est puella benigna.

aper′ta, open
benig′na, kind
cā′ra, dear
fenes′tra, window
grā′ta, pleasing
jā′nua, door
ti′bi, to you, you (*as ind. obj.*)
vi′deō, I see

These figures were part of a mosaic floor in a bath at Ostia, near Rome.

When a word is divided into syllables, two consonants between two vowels are separated, one going with the vowel which precedes and one with the vowel which follows: **sil′va, be nig′na.** However, there is an exception to this rule. When **b, p, d, t, g, c,** or **f** is followed by **l** or **r,** both letters are taken with the following vowel, as in **a gri′co la.** Also the combination **ch** is treated as a single letter and, when it is followed by **l** or **r,** the three letters are taken together, as in **pul′chra.**

The pieces of a Roman mosaic, exposed by the bombing of an English city in World War II, are being put together in the original design.

ENGLISH NOUNS AND LATIN NOUNS

On pages 28-29 you met some Latin nouns that are much like English nouns: **caverna**, *cavern;* **poeta**, *poet.*

You have also met one Latin noun ending in **-a** which gives us an English noun in *-e:* **Europa**, *Europe.* Another such word is **rosa**, *rose.*

If **causa** is a word of this kind, what is the English word which comes from it? What is the English for **pluma?**

Some words are exactly alike in Latin and English: **alumna, arena.**

For each of the Latin nouns below, there is an English noun whose form is like *poet, Europe,* or *alumna.* Give the English nouns.

agricultura	**columna**	**forma**	**nympha**	**ruina**
area	**fama**	**fortuna**	**pictura**	**villa**

ADJECTIVES WITH A DEPENDENT DATIVE

In the following sentence, **puellae** is in the dative case because it depends on the adjective **benigna.**

Fulvia puellae benigna est, *Fulvia is kind to the girl.*

With adjectives meaning *kind, friendly, dear, pleasing, hostile, near,* and some others the dative is often used as the equivalent of an English phrase with *to.* This use is called the *dependent dative.*

POSITION OF GENITIVE AND DATIVE

The English noun in the possessive case stands before the word on which it depends, but in Latin the genitive commonly follows.

the poet's house, **casa poētae**

In Latin the dependent dative commonly precedes the word on which it depends.

kind to the girl, **puellae benigna**

The indirect object may either precede or follow the direct object.

Fīlia puellae gemmam dat.

Fīlia gemmam puellae dat.

1. Epistula mea tibi grāta est; epistulae meae tibi grātae sunt. 2. Casa tua magnam fenestram habet; casa mea multās fenestrās habet; fenestrae sunt apertae. 3. Pictūram jānuae apertae videō; pictūrās jānuārum apertārum videō. 4. Puella est bona et benigna; fīliae meae benigna est. 5. Jānuae casārum albārum sunt apertae. 6. Bene labōrās; itaque pecūniam tibi damus. 7. Īnsulam longam spectās. 8. Fābulās parvīs puellīs nārrātis. 9. Magnās silvās nautae mōnstrāmus; nauta silvās timet. 10. Agricolae labōrant; poēta agricolās laudat.

This picture shows a modern artist's idea of a Roman villa in Britain. Such villas were the homes of Romans who lived in the provinces.

Give the Latin for the italicized words: 1. Italy is *dear to poets.* 2. Anna is *kind to your daughter.* 3. The pictures are *pleasing to the little girl.* 4. You give *the little girl* a letter. 5. Your letters are not *pleasing to me.*

Using what you have learned about syllabication, explain the division of each of the following words:

a gri′co la	**fe nes′tra**	**lau′dat**	**pe rī cu lō′sa**
Bri tan′ni a	**His pā′ni a**	**nau tā′rum**	**pul′chra**
e pis′tu la	**jā′nu a**	**pa′tri a**	**sae′pe**

HW Translate completely the five English sentences above.

HY In "Puella Benigna" find some datives depending on adjectives.

LATIN LIVES TODAY For each italicized word substitute another one that is connected with a Latin word in the vocabulary of this lesson.

1. Praise is *pleasing* to everyone.
2. The old man had a *kind* expression.
3. John is the *caretaker* of our building.
4. The cat could scarcely squeeze through the small *opening.*

XII. INSULA NOSTRA

Galba casam in magnā īnsulā habet; īnsula est Sardinia. Casa mea quoque in Sardiniā est, et saepe Galbam videō.

In īnsulā sunt multae viae. Viae nōn sunt bonae, sed agricolae saepe ibi ambulant. Interdum cum agricolīs in viīs ambulō.

5 Casa mea est in viā longā. Ē jānuā casae meae vīllam videō; vīlla fenestrās apertās habet. Vīlla est magna, et fāma vīllae est magna.

In īnsulā nostrā sunt silvae. Ē jānuā apertā casae meae parvam silvam videō. Interdum cum incolīs ibi ambulō, sed Jūlia in silvā nōn ambulat. Jūlia est fīlia mea. Jūlia silvās nōn amat.

10 Cornēlia et Fulvia quoque in īnsulā nostrā habitant. Cornēlia et Fulvia sunt fīliae Galbae, et cum Galbā in casā magnā habitant. Cornēlia et Fulvia sunt Jūliae cārae; Jūlia est Cornēliae et Fulviae cāra. Jūlia cum Cornēliā et Fulviā in viīs ambulat; in magnīs silvīs nōn ambulant.

15 Fāma Sardiniae magna est. Īnsula est patria nostra. Mihi īnsula grāta est, sed puellīs nōn grāta est.

cum, with
ē, ex, from
ha'bitō, -āre, live, dwell
i'bi, there, in that place
in, in, on
vi'a, street, road, way

USE OF PREPOSITIONS

Words like *from, with, in, by* are called *prepositions.* A preposition is frequently followed by a noun: *with the farmer.*

The noun *farmer* is the object of the preposition *with.* The preposition and its object together form a *prepositional phrase.*

A preposition shows the relation between its object and some other word, such as a verb or a noun. In the first sentence below, *from* shows the relation between its object, *Italy,* and the verb *comes.* In the second, *with* shows the relation between its object, *eyes,* and the noun *boy.*

He comes from Italy.
The boy with the blue eyes is Arthur.

Latin also has numerous prepositions, which you will frequently meet in your study of the language. In this lesson you become acquainted with three Latin prepositions: **cum, ex,** and **in.**

THE PREPOSITION *ē, ex*

The preposition meaning *from* given in this vocabulary has two forms, **ē** and **ex.** Before a vowel or *h*, **ex** is always used. Before some consonants (but not all) **ē** is used.

ABLATIVE CASE

Latin prepositions meaning *with, from,* or *in* are followed by the *ablative case.* Notice that the prepositions **cum, ex,** and **in** are followed by the ablative in the story of this lesson.

In the nouns used thus far, the ablative ends in **-ā** in the singular and in **-īs** in the plural.

Cum Jūliā et nautīs ambulō, *I walk with Julia and the sailors.*

ADJECTIVES MODIFYING NOUNS IN THE ABLATIVE

An adjective modifying a noun in the ablative case is also in the ablative. Remember also that an adjective is always in the same number as its noun.

Silva est in īnsulā pulchrā, *The forest is on a beautiful island.*

Agricolae ē magnīs vīllīs ambulant, *The farmers walk out of the large farmhouses.*

In this lesson adjectives modifying singular nouns in the ablative end in **-ā**; those modifying plural nouns in the ablative end in **-īs.**

THE EXPLETIVE *there*

As you learn from the vocabulary of this lesson, *there,* meaning *in that place,* is in Latin **ibi.** But in such a sentence as *There is no danger, there* does not mean *in that place;* it is used merely to introduce the sentence. When thus used, *there* is called an *expletive.*

Latin does not use any word for the expletive *there,* and the sentence *There is a house on the island* is expressed by **Est casa in īnsulā.** In such sentences the Latin verb usually stands before the subject.

1. In viā; in viīs; ex casā; ex casīs; cum puellā; cum puellīs. 2. In silvā habitāmus; ex silvā ambulās; cum agricolā ambulātis. 3. Ē jānuā nautam vidēmus; in viā nautam vidēmus; cum Cornēliā nautam vidēmus. 4. Est vīlla in parvā īnsulā; sunt vīllae in parvīs īnsulīs. 5. Fīlia agricolae nunc in Ītaliā est, itaque ex Ītaliā

epistulam scrībit. 6. Fīlia agricolae cum fīliā tuā est. 7. Poētae īnsulam amant et ibi ambulant. 8. Agricolae in īnsulā habitant. 9. Fāma īnsulārum est magna. 10. Patria tua tibi cāra est.

Translate the prepositional phrases: 1. The girls walk in the forest; the girls walk from the farmhouses; the girls walk with the farmer. 2. I walk on the island; I do not walk in the street now. 3. There is a forest on the island. 4. The daughters of the poet sometimes walk there. 5. There are sailors on the streets; the farmer gives money to the sailors. 6. My daughter is walking with the daughter of the sailor.

Fill each blank with a form of **puella** and give the reason for your choice.

1. ___ fābulam nārrat. 4. ___ vidēmus. 7. Casae ___ sunt magnae.
2. Casa ___ est parva. 5. Cum ___ ambulō. 8. Multās ___ videō.
3. Pictūra est ___ grāta. 6. ___ mihi cārae sunt. 9. Cum ___ ambulant.

Some Latin expressions have been taken into English without change of spelling or meaning. A good example is **cum laude,** *with praise.* If you graduate from college with high honors, you will be described as graduating **cum laude,** or even **magna cum laude,** *with great* (or *high*) *praise.*

Via is now used as an English word. What does *via* mean in the sentence, "The shipment was made from New York to San Francisco *via* Chicago"?

XIII. LATONA ET RANAE

In scholā nostrā linguam Latīnam discimus. Nunc in fābulā Latīnā dē rānīs discimus.

Incolae Graeciae saepe deās vident, quod deae saepe in silvīs Graeciae ambulant. Interdum Lātōna in silvīs ambulat. Fēminae Graeciae Lātōnam, deam pulchram, amant, quod Lātōna est fēminīs benigna.

Nunc Lātōna in silvā ambulat. Cum Lātōnā sunt īnfantēs (*infants*) Diāna et Apollō.

Agricolae Lātōnam et īnfantēs spectant; deam timent. Dea agricolās videt; itaque agricolās vocat. Aquam ōrat. Lātōna aquam nōn dēsīderat, sed īnfantēs aquam dēsīderant.

Est aqua in lacūnā (*pond*), sed agricolae Lātōnae aquam dare nōn dēsīderant. Itaque in lacūnā ambulant; nunc aqua nōn est bona. Lātōna est īrāta quod agricolae sunt in aquā.

Dea īrāta clāmat.

Nunc agricolae sunt rānae. Nunc agricolae in casīs nōn habitant; in lacūnā habitant, quod sunt rānae.

a'qua, -ae, water
dē, *prep. with abl.*, about, concerning
de'a,[1] **-ae,** goddess
dis'cimus, we learn
īrā'ta, angry
lin'gua, -ae, language, speech
ō'rō, -āre, ask for, beg for, pray to
rā'na, -ae, frog
scho'la, -ae, school
ti'ment, (they) fear

Remember that the combination **ch** is always pronounced like English *k;* **schola** is pronounced *sko'la.*

Hereafter, in the vocabularies, the genitive singular of each noun will be indicated after the nominative. Thus **lingua, -ae** indicates that the genitive singular of **lingua** is **linguae** and that **lingua** belongs to the first declension.

[1]The dative and ablative plural of **dea** and **fīlia** end in **-ābus.**

Nunc aqua non est bona.

DECLENSION

You have now learned five cases of Latin nouns. A list of the cases and numbers of a noun, adjective, or pronoun given in order, with or without the meanings, is called a *declension*. When you give all the forms of a word, you *decline* it.

FIRST DECLENSION

Nouns with the nominative ending in **-a** and the genitive in **-ae** belong to the *first declension*. All first-declension nouns form their cases with the same endings as **silva**.

	SINGULAR
Nominative:	**sil′va,** a forest (*as subject or predicate noun*)
Genitive:	**sil′vae,** of a forest, a forest's (*possessive*)
Dative:	**sil′vae,** to a forest, a forest (*as indirect object*)
Accusative:	**sil′vam,** a forest (*as direct object*)
Ablative:	**sil′vā,** (from, with, in, *etc.*) a forest
	PLURAL
Nominative:	**sil′vae,** forests (*as subject or predicate noun*)
Genitive:	**silvā′rum,** of forests, forests' (*possessive*)
Dative:	**sil′vīs,** to forests, forests (*as indirect object*)
Accusative:	**sil′vās,** forests (*as direct object*)
Ablative:	**sil′vīs,** (from, with, in, *etc.*) forests

The part of a noun to which the endings are added is called the *base*. The base may be found by dropping the ending of the genitive singular. Thus, the base of **silva** (found from the genitive **silvae**) is **silv-**. The following sentences illustrate the use of the Latin cases.

The forest (**silva**) is beautiful.
The trees of the forest (**silvae**) are green.
The sunshine gives color to the forest (**silvae**).
The girl saw the forest (**silvam**).
Bears are in the forest (**in silvā**).

The forests (**silvae**) are beautiful.
The trees of the forests (**silvārum**) are green.
The sunshine gives color to the forests (**silvīs**).
The girl saw the forests (**silvās**).
Bears are in the forests (**in silvīs**).

APPOSITION

A noun is sometimes set beside another noun to explain its meaning by indicating more definitely who or what is meant.

Fīlia mea <u>Fulvia</u> puellās expectat, *My daughter Fulvia is waiting for the girls.*

A noun thus used is in *apposition* with the noun it explains. In this sentence **Fulvia** is in apposition with **fīlia.**

A noun in apposition is in the same case as the noun it explains. Thus, in the sentence on page 54, **Fulvia** is in the nominative to agree with **fīlia.** A noun in apposition is called an *appositive.*

In English we often use *of* in translating an appositive that is a place name.

In īnsulā Siciliā habitō, *I live on the island of Sicily.*

1. Americam, patriam nostram, amāmus; Ītaliam, patriam tuam, amās. 2. Puella ex silvā ambulat; nautae ē viīs casās spectant. 3. Cornēliae, fīliae tuae, pecūniam damus. 4. Nunc dea īrāta aquam ōrat. 5. Fāma linguae Ītaliae, patriae tuae, est magna. 6. Jānua casae aperta est; jānuae casārum apertae sunt. 7. Ē jānuā aquam videō; ē jānuīs silvam vidēmus. 8. In scholā nostrā dē Lātōnā et rānīs discimus. 9. In Americā linguam Latīnam in scholā discimus. 10. Puellae gemmās ōrant.

Select the phrase in parenthesis that completes each sentence correctly and give the reason for your choice.

1. In ___ habitāmus (īnsulam Siciliam; īnsulae Siciliae; īnsulā Siciliā).
2. Jānuam apertam ___ videō (casae tuae; casam tuam; casā tuā).
3. Lingua īnsulārum magnārum nōn est ___ (lingua Latīna; linguam Latīnam; linguās Latīnās).
4. Fīlia tua in viā ___ expectat (parvam puellam; parvae puellae; parvīs puellīs).
5. Agricolae aquam Lātōnae ___ nōn dant (deam pulchram; deae pulchrae; deā pulchrā).

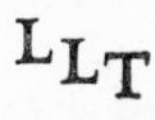

The pictures illustrate three English nouns that can be described by the word *aquatic,* which is derived from the Latin word **aqua.** What are the nouns?

An aquatic ___. An aquatic ___. An aquatic ___.

With what Latin word is *aquarium* connected? What is an *aquarium?*

When the police reported that the owner of the store which had been robbed was *irate,* were they describing the man's personal appearance, his state of mind, or his nationality?

An *orator* is a skillful speaker. What is an *oratorical* contest?

What do you think a *ranologist* is?

REVIEW OF UNIT III LESSONS X–XIII

Nouns	*Verbs*	*Adjectives*	*Other Words*
aqua, -ae	dēsīderō, -āre	aperta	ibi
dea, -ae	discimus	benigna	itaque
*fāma, -ae	dō, dare	cāra	mihi
fenestra, -ae	habitō, -āre	grāta	tibi
jānua, -ae	labōrō, -āre	īrāta	
lingua, -ae	ōrō, -āre	*Prepositions*	
pictūra, -ae	timet	cum	
rāna, -ae	timent	dē	
schola, -ae	videō	ē, ex	
via, -ae		in	
*vīlla, -ae			

I. In each list of words below, find one word that does not belong there and tell why it does not belong.

aqua, deārum, fenestrīs, ōrātis, schola, viīs
aperta, benigna, cāra, fāma, grāta, īrāta
damus, dēsīderās, habitāmus, labōrās, ōrās, pictūrās
ē, cum, dē, dō, ex, in

II. Supply the Latin word that completes each of the following sentences and explain its form.

1. Poēta pictūram __ dat. (*to the girl*)
2. Fenestrae __ sunt. (*open*)
3. Fābula est __ grāta. (*to the women*)
4. Aquam __ damus. (*to the goddess*)
5. Puella __ benigna est. (*to me*)
6. Fīliae sunt __ cārae. (*to the farmers*)

LLT

Janua

In the following sentences find English words connected with Latin words you know and tell from what Latin word each comes. The number after each sentence indicates how many such words it contains.

1. I am working for a scholarship. (1)
2. Orators are not timid speakers. (2)
3. Baseball writers use a strange lingo. (1)
4. The famous poet had a villa in Italy. (4)
5. Sylvia drew a picture of her aquarium. (3)
6. The benign old lady liberated the frog. (2)
7. The janitor of the building labors early and late. (2)
8. The inhabitants of the village are proud of their school. (3)

Although this recent photograph shows Mount Etna in a peaceful setting, there has been an eruption since this picture was taken.

UNIT
IV

XIV. SICILIA

Sicilia est magna īnsula Eurōpae. In Siciliā sunt multae casae et villae. Sunt multae silvae quoque, sed silvae Siciliae nōn sunt magnae.

Incolae ōrae maritimae sunt nautae, sed casae agricolārum ōrae maritimae propinquae nōn sunt. 5

Aetna est in īnsulā Siciliā. Incolae Siciliae Aetnam timent. Cūr incolae īnsulae Aetnam timent? Incolae Aetnam timent quod flammās Aetnae saepe vident.

Sicilia Ītaliae propinqua est. Ex Siciliā Ītaliam vidēmus. Incolae Ītaliae quoque Siciliam vident. Flammās Aetnae vident. Aqua 10 Siciliam ab Ītaliā sēparat, sed aqua est angusta.

Messāna est in ōrā maritimā Siciliae, et incolae Messānae ōram maritimam Ītaliae vident. Casās et vīllās Ītaliae vident. Incolae Ītaliae īnsulam Siciliam quoque vident.

Sicilia est īnsula amoena. Incolae Aetnam timent, sed Siciliam 15 amant, quod est īnsula amoena.

ā, ab, *prep. with abl.*, from

amoe′na, pleasant

angus′ta, narrow

flam′ma, -ae, fire, flame

ō′ra, -ae, shore; **ō′ra mari′tima,** seacoast, seashore

propin′qua, near, nearby

sē′parō, -āre, separate

In Latin, the diphthong **oe,** as in **amoena,** is pronounced like *oi* in English *boil.*

The adjective **propinqua** takes a dependent dative.

CLAUSES

A part of a sentence containing a subject and predicate is called a *clause.*

incolae īnsulae sunt nautae, *the inhabitants of the island are sailors*

quod est īnsula amoena, *because it is a pleasant island*

Clauses are said to be of two kinds: *independent* and *dependent.* An *independent* clause expresses a complete thought.

Aqua Siciliam ab Ītaliā sēparat, *Water separates Sicily from Italy.*

Incolae Siciliae Aetnam timent, *The inhabitants of Sicily fear Etna.*

A *dependent* clause modifies a word in the independent clause.

Incolae Siciliae Aetnam timent quod flammās saepe vident, *The inhabitants of Sicily fear Etna because they often see the flames.*

The dependent clause, in the example above, is **quod flammās saepe vident;** it modifies **timent.**

CONJUNCTIONS

As you have seen, the words **et,** *and,* and **sed,** *but,* are used to join words.

Sicilia et Sardinia sunt īnsulae, *Sicily and Sardinia are islands.*

Sunt parvae sed pulchrae silvae in īnsulā, *There are small but beautiful forests on the island.*

In the first sentence **et** joins the nouns **Sicilia** and **Sardinia;** in the second, **sed** joins the adjectives **parvae** and **pulchrae.**

Words used in this way are called *conjunctions.*

Conjunctions also join phrases and clauses.

Rānae in aquā et in terrā habitant, *Frogs live in water and on land.*

Here **et** connects the phrases **in aquā** and **in terrā.**

Incolae Aetnam timent, sed Siciliam amant quod est terra amoena, *The inhabitants are afraid of Etna, but they love Sicily because it is a pleasant land.*

The conjunctions **sed** and **quod** join the three clauses of the sentence above.

ABLATIVE WITH *ā* OR *ab*

You have previously had one preposition meaning *from:* **ē** or **ex**. In "Sicilia" you find **ā** or **ab** used with the ablative to mean *from.*

Nautae ab ōrā maritimā properant, *The sailors hurry away from the seashore.*

While both prepositions may be translated by the English word *from,* **ā** or **ab** means *away from,* while **ē** or **ex** means *from* in the sense of *out of.*

Nauta ā casā ambulat, *The sailor walks away from the house.*

Agricola rānam ex casā portat, *The farmer carries the frog from (out of) the house.*

The preposition **ā** or **ab** has two forms. Before a word beginning with a vowel or *h,* **ab** is used; before most consonants, **ā** is used.

Nauta ā Siciliā properat; poēta ab Ītaliā properat, *The sailor hurries away from Sicily; the poet hurries away from Italy.*

1. In terrā amoenā; ab īnsulā angustā; ab īnsulīs angustīs. 2. Ex fenestrīs casae flammās vidēmus. 3. Fīliae tuae ē vīllā ambulant. 4. Via angusta vīllam ā casā sēparat. 5. Messāna multās et angustās viās habet. 6. Incola Messānae tibi ōram maritimam Ītaliae mōnstrat. 7. Flammae Aetnae sunt magnae. 8. Ōra maritima Siciliae est Ītaliae propinqua. 9. Viae angustae sunt perīculōsae. 10. In Ītaliā nōn habitāmus, sed linguam Latīnam discimus.

1. Your farmhouse is near the forest. 2. From the seashore we see the fires of Etna. 3. The island is long and narrow. 4. The seacoast is pleasant, and I often walk there. 5. There are small islands near Sicily. 6. Water separates the islands from Italy. 7. The girl walks away from the seashore. 8. The woman carries the money out of the house.

A present-day Sicilian and his donkey jog along over an ancient Roman bridge, which seems as strong as ever.

THE ROMAN EMPIRE
BRITANNIA
Vallum Hadriani
Aquae Solis (Bath)
Tamesis
GERMANIA
SARMATIA (RUSSIA)
EUROPA
Rhenus
GALLIA
Vesontio
Rhodanus
Arelate (Arles)
HISPANIA
ITALIA
ETRURIA
Tiberis
Arretium
CORSICA
Veii
Roma
Lacus Albanus
Ostia
LATIUM
Cumae
Capua
SARDINIA
Misenum
Via Appia
Tarentum
Vesuvius
Herculaneum
Pompeii
Paestum
Aetna
SICILIA
Messana
MARE MEDITERRANEUM
Carthago
MELITA
ITHACA
ARCADIA
GRAECIA
Aulis
Athenae
DELOS
Sparta
CRETA
Troja
Ida
Danuvius
PONTUS EUXINUS (BLACK SEA)
Colchis
ASIA
Babylonia
PHOENICIA
AFRICA

The Mediterranean coast looked much the same in Roman days as now.

THE ROMAN EMPIRE

For more than five hundred years, Rome was called the ruler of the world, because most of the world known at that time was included in the Roman Empire.

Long before there was an empire, the city of Rome existed. History and legend tell of the flight to Italy of the Trojan Aeneas, whose marriage with the Latin princess Lavinia united the Latins and the Trojans. Their descendant Romulus is said to have founded Rome in 753 B.C. and to have been the first king. Romulus was followed by other kings, Roman and Etruscan. Rome was a kingdom for nearly two hundred fifty years, but finally the last of the kings was deposed, and the city-state became a republic. The republic lasted for five hundred years; then came the Empire, with Augustus as the first emperor (27 B.C.).

To secure peace, Rome, while still a republic, conquered hostile lands outside the borders of Italy and made them provinces. Under the Empire, more provinces were added, until Rome ruled all the lands bordering the Mediterranean, which became *mare nostrum*, "our sea." Britain, too, came under Roman domination, as well as other northern parts of Europe. At their greatest extent, the boundaries of the Empire were measured in thousands of miles.

On a plain beside the Danube River, which once formed part of the northern boundary of the Empire, this arch marks the site of a Roman camp and town.

The pictures on these pages indicate the size of the far-flung Empire. (See also pp. 18, 59, 70, 143, 178, and 206.) The remains of walls and bridges, temples and amphitheaters continue to remind us of Roman occupation in Austria, France, Russia, Africa, England, Spain, Portugal, and Sicily.

Included in the Roman Empire were peoples of many different races, some highly civilized, others barbaric. Conquered nations began at once to feel both the power of Roman government and the influence of Roman life and thought.

Into each new province came a Roman governor, with judges, treasurers, and other officials. Teachers came also to establish Roman schools, and architects to build houses and public buildings in Roman style. The social and religious life of the province was Romanized. Amphitheaters were built, so that sports and public entertainments could be introduced. Temples rose to Roman gods. Everywhere Latin was spoken.

In an inland town of Portugal stand the pillars of this temple to Diana, built when Rome held the Spanish peninsula.

In the far north-eastern part of the Empire on the Black Sea there was once a Roman colony. The Romans built this pit for storing fish.

The extent of the Empire gave Rome a wide variety of crops, lumber, and minerals. These, together with a few manufactured articles, were the basis for a brisk trade. The fine Roman roads built in Italy and in the provinces for the armies were also useful in peace. All roads led to Rome, it was said, and all were heavy with traffic. Moreover, merchant ships sailed the Mediterranean, carrying valuable cargoes.

Gradually the Romans permitted corrupt practices in government, business, society, and religion, until the Empire crumbled and was no more. Many of the institutions, however, that made Rome great have survived. Her laws and government, her art and culture, her language and literature still influence the lives of civilized peoples all over the world.

Arches recently unearthed in the north African desert, once a fertile Roman province.

XV. LUNA ET STELLAE

Anna. Noctū lūna et stellae sunt pulchrae, sed nōn semper lūnam et stellās vidēmus. Nunc sunt multae stellae in caelō. Nunc lūna et stellae sunt clārae.

Tullia. Lūnam clāram et stellās clārās amō.

5 *Anna.* Lūnam et stellās quoque amō.

Tullia. Nārrā mihi, Anna, dē lūnā.

Anna. Lūna est pulchra. Dea lūnae est Diāna. Diāna sagittās habet; radiī (*rays*) lūnae sunt sagittae Diānae. Sagittae Diānae sunt clārae.

10 *Tullia.* Cūr lūnam interdiū nōn vidēmus?

Anna. Noctū Diāna in caelō habitat, sed interdiū in terrā habitat. Diāna est dea lūnae, sed est quoque dea silvārum. Itaque magnās silvās amat.

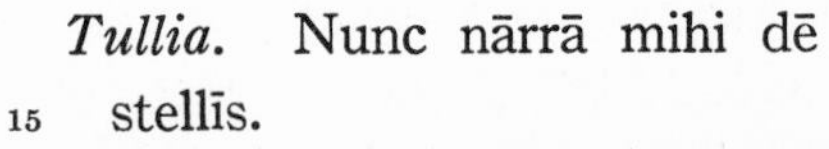

Tullia. Nunc nārrā mihi dē
15 stellīs.

Anna. Multae stellae sunt in caelō. Stellae semper in caelō sunt, sed interdiū stellās nōn vidēmus. Stellae sagittās
20 nōn habent.

Tullia. Diāna sagittās habet. Cūr stellae sagittās nōn habent?

Anna. Stellae deae nōn sunt;
25 sunt gemmae deae.

Anna et Tullia. Tuae gemmae sunt clārae, dea lūnae. Spectāte nōs, stellae clārae! Spectā nōs, Diāna pulchra!

Diana, goddess of the moon, as the Italian artist Correggio painted her. Here she is driving across the sky.

cae′lō, *abl.*, sky
clā′ra, bright, clear; famous
inter′diū, by day, during the day
lū′na, -ae, moon
noc′tū, at night
nōs, *nom. and acc. pl.*, we, us
sagit′ta, -ae, arrow
sem′per, always
stel′la, -ae, star

MOODS OF VERBS

In Latin, as in English, the way in which a verb is used determines its *mood*. In this book you will learn two moods, the *indicative* and the *imperative*. The verbs you have had thus far have been in the *indicative*.

INDICATIVE MOOD

A verb that is used to state a fact is in the *indicative mood*. A verb used in a question which requires a statement of fact for an answer is also in the *indicative*.

Aquam portō, *I am carrying water.*

Cūr aquam portās? *Why are you carrying water?*

IMPERATIVE MOOD

In "Lūna et Stellae" you meet the imperative mood. A verb that is used to express a command is in the *imperative mood*. In the following Latin sentences, **nārrā** and **spectāte** express commands, just as *tell* and *look* do in the English translations.

Nārrā mihi dē lūnā, *Tell me about the moon.*

Spectāte nōs! *Look at us!*

IMPERATIVE OF THE FIRST CONJUGATION

The imperative of **portō** is:

Singular: **portā,** carry (*said to one person*)
Plural: **portāte,** carry (*said to more than one*)

As you see, the singular imperative is like the present stem of the verb.

nārrā, laudā, vocā

The plural imperative is made up of the present stem and **-te.**

nārrāte, laudāte, vocāte

IMPERATIVE OF *dō*

The imperative forms of **dō** are **dā, date.** Are your eyes sharp enough to detect the slight difference between them and the imperative forms of other verbs?

VOCATIVE CASE

In addition to the cases which have been given so far, there is another case, called the *vocative*, which is used in addressing a person. In most Latin nouns the vocative has the same form as the nominative.

> **Noctū, Anna, stellās vidēmus,** *At night, Anna, we see the stars.*
> **Vocāte agricolās, puellae,** *Girls, call the farmers.*

In a Latin sentence the vocative is usually preceded by one or more words.

1. Nunc, Galba, in Americā sumus; dā mihi epistulam. 2. Nunc, puellae, estis in Siciliā; nārrāte agricolīs dē pīrātīs. 3. Interdiū in casā estis; noctū stellās in caelō spectātis. 4. Interdum estis quiētae, puellae; cūr quiētae estis? 5. Dea lūnae sagittās clārās semper habet. 6. Cūr nōs in viā expectātis? 7. Diānam in pictūrīs saepe spectāmus. Cūr sagittās portat?

1. Girls, look at the stars! The stars are bright at night. 2. Look at the moon, Fulvia! The moon is bright, too. 3. You (*sing.*) are kind to Cornelia, and Cornelia is kind to you. 4. During the day I watch the little girl from my window. 5. Give me the arrows, girls, and call the women.

Answer each of the following questions by a Latin sentence. 1. Who is the goddess of the moon? 2. Does Diana ever live on the earth? 3. When does she live in the sky? 4. Why does Diana love forests? 5. What are the rays of the moon?

In the first four Latin sentences above, change each plural verb to the corresponding singular form, and make other necessary changes.

What is a *constellation?* Have you ever seen the *constellation* called the Big Dipper?

The twelve signs of the zodiac have the same names as twelve of the *constellations.* All of them have Latin names. *Sagittarius* is related to a word in today's vocabulary. Can you find another name that is related to a Latin word you know?

If you can locate the Big Dipper on a starry night, you can easily recognize Ursa Major, the great bear.

XVI. URSA

Jūnō est pulchra; in caelō habitat, sed saepe in terrā ambulat. Jūnō est dea invidiōsa et fēminās pulchrās nōn amat.

Callistō, fēmina pulchra, in terrā amoenā Arcadiā habitat. Interdum in silvīs Arcadiae ambulat.

Hodiē Callistō in silvīs ambulat et dīcit, "Incolae Arcadiae mē laudābunt quod pulchra sum. Jūnō quoque est pulchra, sed incolae deam nōn laudābunt, quod Jūnō invidiōsa est." 5

Jūnō ex caelō fēminam spectat et dīcit, "Nunc es pulchra, sed nōn semper eris pulchra. Mox eris ursa. Interdiū et noctū in silvīs habitābis. Vīta tua erit perīculōsa, quod agricolae tē necāre temptābunt." 10

Nunc Callistō est ursa; nunc in silvīs ambulat. Saepe agricolae ursam vident et interdum ursam necāre temptant.

Juppiter deam invidiōsam nōn laudat. Juppiter dīcit, "Fēminam pulchram servābō. Callistō in caelō habitābit."

Nunc incolae terrae stellās clārās in caelō vident. Ursam in stellīs vident. Ursa est Callistō. 15

dī'cit, speaks, says
e'ris, you will be
e'rit, (he, she, it) will be
ho'diē, today
invidiō'sa, jealous
mē, *acc. sing.*, me
mox, soon
tē, *acc. sing.*, you
temp'tō, -āre, try, attempt
ur'sa, -ae, bear

TENSE OF VERBS

When someone says, *The boy stands in the street,* we know that the act is going on while we are being told about it; that is, in the present time. If the sentence is *The boy stood in the street,* we know that the act took place at some past time. Similarly, the sentence *The boy will stand in the street* shows that the act is going to take place in the future.

In these sentences the form of the verb shows the time of the act. The forms of a verb which show time are called *tenses.* There are six tenses in English. Their names are *present, past, future, present perfect, past perfect,* and *future perfect.* The following forms of the verb *walk* with the subject *I* show how these tenses are used.

Present:	I walk	*Present Perfect:*	I have walked
Past:	I walked	*Past Perfect:*	I had walked
Future:	I shall walk	*Future Perfect:*	I shall have walked

PRESENT TENSE

All the Latin verbs you have had up to this time are in the *present tense;* that is, each one shows that an act is taking place in the present time.

Epistulam portās, *You are carrying the letter.*

The stem **portā-,** which is used to form the present tense of **portō,** is called the *present stem.*

FUTURE TENSE

In the following sentence *shall go* indicates an act to be done in the future.

I shall go tomorrow.

So we say that *shall go* is in the *future tense.* In English *shall* and *will* are the signs of the future tense.

I shall, or will, praise. *You will praise.*

In Latin verbs of the first conjugation the tense sign of the future appears as **-b-** in the first person singular, **-bu-** in the third person plural, and **-bi-** in the other forms.

FUTURE OF *portō*

The verb **portō** is conjugated as follows in the future tense:

SINGULAR	PLURAL
portā'bō, I shall carry	**portā'bimus,** we shall carry
portā'bis, you will carry	**portā'bitis,** you will carry
portā'bit, he, she, it will carry	**portā'bunt,** they will carry

STEM OF THE FUTURE

The *future tense,* like the present, is formed on the present stem of the verb, which is, as you know, found by dropping the **-re** of the infinitive.

Present = present stem + person endings
Future = present stem + **-bi-** (**-b-**, **-bu-**) + person endings

The tenses of the verb which are formed on the present stem are said to belong to the *present system.*

1. In viā angustā ambulās; in viīs angustīs ambulābis. 2. Pecūniam habent; in vīllā habitant; in casīs tuīs habitābunt. 3. Ursae in silvīs ambulābunt; ursās necāre temptābis. 4. Fīliās nautārum hodiē expectāmus; nautās nōn expectābimus. 5. Epistulās meās laudātis, sed fābulam meam nōn laudābitis. 6. Pīrāta casam nautae mox occupābit, sed nautam nōn necābit. 7. Ē vīllā fēminae invidiōsae ambulābō; in vīllā nōn habitābō. 8. Dea īrāta dīcit, "Fēmina erit ursa; in silvā ambulābit." 9. Agricolae ursās necāre mox temptābunt.

Change the verbs to future tense: 1. Fēmina invidiōsa fīliam meam nōn laudat. 2. Agricolae magnās ursās in silvīs necant. 3. Rānās spectāmus. 4. Nauta ursam pulchram mihi mōnstrat. 5. Noctū et interdiū ursae in silvā ambulant.

Complete each sentence (1) with a form of the present indicative of **temptō,** (2) with a form of the future indicative of **temptō.**

1. Fābulam nārrāre __ (*I*).
2. Pictūram mōnstrāre __ (*you, sing.*).
3. Agricola ursam necāre __.
4. Bene labōrāre __ (*we*).
5. Sagittās portāre __ (*you, pl.*).
6. Nautae fēminās servāre __.

HY In the first paragraph of "Ursa" find present forms of three different verbs. In the fourth paragraph find future forms of three different verbs. How can you tell they are future?

XVII. NAUTA ET EPISTULA

Cornēlia. Cūr hīc in jānuā casae amitae meae stās?

Fulvia. In jānuā casae stō, quod ē jānuā ōram maritimam videō. Mox nautae epistulās ex prōvinciīs iterum portābunt.

Cornēlia. In prōvinciā quoque habitō, sed nautae mihi epistulās
5 nōn dabunt.

Fulvia. Ubi habitās?

Cornēlia. In īnsulā Siciliā habitō, et casa mea est in ōrā maritimā. Cum in Siciliā sum, ex fenestrīs casae nostrae aquam videō. Saepe in ōrā maritimā vesperī ambulō. Interdum noctū ibi ambulō et
10 lūnam clāram spectō. Ubi est casa tua?

Fulvia. Casa mea est in Hispāniā. Mox erō in Hispāniā. Hispānia nōn est īnsula. Casa nostra nōn est ōrae maritimae propinqua; est silvīs propinqua. Ē jānuā casae magnās silvās vidēmus, sed aquam nōn vidēmus. Hīc esse amō, sed quoque in Hispāniā esse amō.

15 *Cornēlia.* Amita mea Hispāniam quoque amat; mox erimus ibi in casā nostrā.

Fulvia. Spectā, spectā! Nautam videō; celeriter ambulat. Mox mihi epistulam dabit.

Puellae clāmant. Nōn puellīs, sed amitae nauta epistulam dat.

For twenty centuries this Roman aqueduct carried water to Segovia, Spain.

Roman books were rolled and kept in a case. The other articles are writing materials.

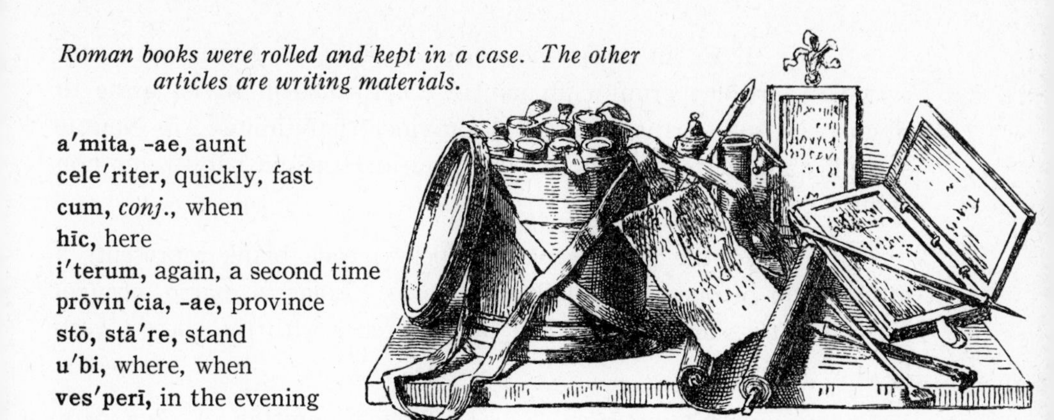

a'mita, -ae, aunt
cele'riter, quickly, fast
cum, *conj.*, when
hīc, here
i'terum, again, a second time
prōvin'cia, -ae, province
stō, stā're, stand
u'bi, where, when
ves'perī, in the evening

FUTURE OF *sum*

The English verb *to be* has such different forms as *be, am, is;* and so we call it an *irregular verb.* In the same way the Latin verb **sum** is irregular. In the present tense, as you know, it has such different forms as **sum, es,** and **sunt.**

Sum is irregular in the future, too. It does not have the tense signs you have seen in the future of regular verbs. The future of **sum** is:

SINGULAR	PLURAL
e'rō, I shall (will) be	**e'rimus,** we shall (will) be
e'ris, you will be	**e'ritis,** you will be
e'rit, he, she, it will be	**e'runt,** they will be

The infinitive of **sum** is **esse,** *to be.*

FUTURE OF *dō*

As you know, the stem vowel, **-a-**, is short in the present of **dō** (except the second person singular, **dās**). In all forms of the future, the stem vowel is also short.

THE CONJUNCTION *cum*

You have already met the conjunctions **et** and **sed.** In "Nauta et Epistula" you meet the Latin conjunction **cum,** meaning *when.* Do not confuse this word with the preposition **cum,** which you have already learned.

Preposition: **Cum puellīs ambulābō,** *I shall walk with the girls.*
Conjunction: **Saepe ambulant cum lūna est clāra.** *They often walk when the moon is bright.*

1. Es in casā; mox eris in vīllā. 2. Nauta erit cum agricolā; agricolae erunt cum nautīs. 3. Erimus in silvīs; ursae in silvīs erunt. 4. Eritis nautae; in prōvinciā habitābitis. 5. Nautae epistulās amitae meae dabunt. 6. Cum in Hispāniā habitō, hīc nōn habitō.

In the seven sentences below, each blank represents a future form of one of the following verbs: **mōnstrō, nārrō, occupō, portō, spectō, sum, vocō.** Read each sentence with the correct verb form.

1. Puellae pulchrās pictūrās __ .
2. Agricola __ in casā.
3. Nauta bonās fābulās __.
4. Magnās īnsulās __ (*1st pers. pl.*).
5. Longās sagittās __ (*2nd pers. sing.*).
6. Puellās bonās __ (*1st pers. sing.*).
7. Nautae lūnam et stellās __.

Supply the Latin verb in each sentence below.

1. In jānuā cum Cornēliā __. (*we will be*)
2. In viā vesperī __. (*you [pl.] will be*)
3. Ursae in silvā noctū __. (*will be*)
4. In ōrā maritimā iterum __. (*we shall stand*)
5. Multae vīllae in ōrā maritimā __. (*will be*)
6. In viā angustā celeriter __ temptābit. (*to walk*)
7. In casā nostrā __ dēsīderat. (*to be*)

Divide the following words into syllables.

fenestra nostra pulchra

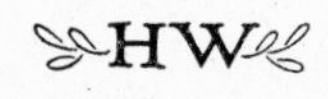

Translate: 1. The large pictures will be beautiful. 2. Poets tell good stories. 3. The girl is standing in the door.

The name of a part of an automobile, the *accelerator*, is connected with a word in "Nauta et Epistula." Why is this part so called?

A number of English words are related to **sto**. A *stable* government is one that stands, or lasts. His *stature* is six feet (he stands that high). What is a *stabilizer?* What is a railway *station?*

When are *vesper* services held? When does the *vesper* sparrow sing? The evening star is sometimes called *Vesper*.

REVIEW OF UNIT IV LESSONS XIV–XVII

Nouns	*Verbs*	*Adjectives*	*Other Words*	
amita, -ae	dīcit	amoena	celeriter	noctū
caelō	eris	angusta	hīc	nōs
flamma, -ae	erit	clāra	hodiē	semper
lūna, -ae	sēparō, -āre	invidiōsa	interdiū	tē
ōra, -ae	stō, stāre	maritima	iterum	ubi
prōvincia, -ae	temptō, -āre	propinqua	mē	vesperī
sagitta, -ae			mox	
stella, -ae	*Conjunction*	*Preposition*		
ursa, -ae	cum	ā, ab		

I. Find, in the list of verbs below, the one which completes each sentence.

dat	habitat	sēparātis	stās
dēsīderō	labōrat	stant	temptāmus

1. Sagittās sēparāre ___. (*we are trying*)
2. In ōrā maritimā ___. (*they stand*)
3. Nōs ___. (*you are separating*)
4. Prōvinciam propinquam ___. (*I do desire*)
5. In īnsulā amoenā ___. (*he lives*)
6. Interdiū agricola bene ___. (*does work*)
7. Pecūniam amitae ___. (*she gives*)
8. In casā ___. (*you are standing*)

II. In each sentence below, supply a form of **sum.**

1. (*We shall be*) deae.
2. Mox (*you will be*) ursa.
3. Noctū (*there are*) stellae in caelō.
4. Cornēlius hodiē (*is*) in scholā.
5. (*You will be*) poētae.
6. Semper (*I shall be*) incola līberae īnsulae.
7. Jūlia (*will be*) invidiōsa.
8. Vesperī flammae (*will be*) clārae.

III. Fill each blank with the imperative of the verb given.

1. ___ hīc in jānuā, Anna. (stō)
2. ___ ursam, agricolae. (necō)
3. ___ (*pl.*) celeriter sagittās. (portō)
4. ___ pīrātam, nauta. (necō)
5. ___ lūnam clāram, amita. (spectō)

IV. Give the tense, person, and number of (1) **sēparant,** (2) **spectās,** (3) **stābunt,** (4) **temptābitis.**

This wall of a Pompeian house was decorated with beautiful colored pictures. On page 33 there is a colored picture of the villa in the left panel.

v. Find in the group at the right the Latin word for each verb form in the group at the left.

1. he will try
2. they will tell
3. we shall praise
4. I shall be
5. you (*sing.*) will praise
6. you (*pl.*) will walk

(*a*) **amāte**
(*b*) **ambulābitis**
(*c*) **erō**
(*d*) **laudābimus**
(*e*) **laudābis**
(*f*) **laudāte**
(*g*) **nārrābunt**
(*h*) **sēparat**
(*i*) **temptābit**
(*j*) **temptābimus**

LATIN LIVES TODAY

In the following story you will find a number of italicized words. Can you give a Latin word with which each is connected?

"May we have less *clamor*, ladies," the chairman of the meeting said *timidly*. "After a *multitude* of suggestions, the question now is whether to present the play '*Sylvia* Achieves *Fame*.' Are there any comments?"

A *magnificently* dressed woman offered to take the *stellar* part. While she was talking, someone behind her began making *invidious* remarks about conceited people.

"The *spectators* won't like a play in which there are no masculine characters," shouted a *feminine* voice.

"Furthermore," *exclaimed* another, "this play will require too much *labor*."

"Madam Chairman," said a woman in *clarion* tones, "this undertaking seems of too great *magnitude* for us. I move that we have moving *pictures* instead."

Without more *oratory*, the motion was carried.

XVIII. AGRICOLA LABORAT

Cornēlia. Quis labōrat?

Fulvia. Galba labōrat; est agricola.

Anna. Spectāte agricolam, puellae. Quid facit?

Fulvia. Agricola terram colit.

Cornēlia. Galba bene labōrat. Quis cum Galbā labōrat? 5

Fulvia. Puella Galbam juvat. Puella lēniter labōrat, sed Galba celeriter labōrat.

Anna. Quis est puella?

Fulvia. Puella est Tullia; Tullia est fīlia agricolae.

Cornēlia. Spectāte parvam puellam! 10

Anna. Parvam puellam videō. Estne parva puella quoque fīlia agricolae?

Fulvia. Minimē, parva puella est cōnsōbrīna Tulliae.

Cornēlia. Quid portat parva puella?

Fulvia. Parva puella urnam portat. Est aqua in urnā. 15

Anna. Ubi est amita parvae puellae?

Cornēlia. Amitam nōn videō; amita est in vīllā.

Anna. Labōrābitne amita cum agricolā?

Fulvia. Minimē, terram nōn colit.

Anna. Quid facit amita? 20

Fulvia. Amita in vīllā bene labōrat; amita parvae puellae est bona fēmina.

Cornēlia. Labōrābitne parva puella interdum cum amitā?

Fulvia. Ita, parva puella interdum cum amitā in vīllā labōrābit; interdum aquam in urnīs portābit et Galbam juvābit; interdum 25 cum Tulliā labōrābit.

co′lit, cultivates, tills
cōnsōbrī′na, -ae, cousin (a girl or woman)
fa′cit, does, is doing
i′ta, so, thus; yes
ju′vō, -āre, help
lē′niter, slowly
mi′nimē, no, not at all
quid, what
quis, who
ur′na, -ae, jar, pitcher

The Roman farmer knew nothing of tractors; oxen pulled his plow.

THE PRONOUN

In the following sentence notice that the word *him* is used instead of *boy.*

The man saw the boy and warned him.

A word which is used instead of a noun is called a *pronoun.*

The noun to which a pronoun refers is called its *antecedent.* In the sentence given above, *boy* is the antecedent of *him.*

The pronouns *I, you, he, she, it, we,* and *they* are called *personal pronouns.* In Latin you have already met forms of some personal pronouns: **mē,** *me;* **mihi,** *to me;* **nōs,** *we, us;* **tē,** *you;* and **tibi,** *to you.*

When the words *who, which,* and *what* are used to introduce questions, they are called *interrogative pronouns.*

In the vocabulary of this lesson there are two interrogative pronouns, **quis** and **quid.**

Quis cum Galbā labōrat? *Who is working with Galba?*
Quid agricola facit? *What is the farmer doing?*

FORMS OF QUESTIONS

In each of the following Latin sentences the syllable **-ne** has been added to the first word.

Habetne poēta fīliam? *Has the poet a daughter?*
Estne Sicilia magna īnsula? *Is Sicily a large island?*

The syllable **-ne** indicates that these sentences are questions. There is no separate English word for **-ne.** In English we indicate that a sentence is a question by the order of words and by the punctuation.

You have had questions introduced by **cūr** and **ubi.** When we use such interrogative words or interrogative pronouns, **-ne** is not used.

The shape of the plowshare has not changed much through the centuries.

ANSWERS TO QUESTIONS

In Latin one generally answers *yes* to a question by repeating the words of the question in the form of a statement.

Estne Sicilia magna īnsula? Sicilia est magna īnsula.

One may answer *no* by repeating the words of the question as a statement with **nōn**.

Habetne poēta fīliam? Poēta fīliam nōn habet.

Sometimes **minimē** is used for *no* and **ita** for *yes*.

1. Habetne Tullia parvam cōnsōbrīnam? Ita, Tullia parvam cōnsōbrīnam habet. 2. Quis terram colit? Agricola terram colit. 3. Quid amita tua facit? Amita mea in ōrā maritimā iterum ambulat. 4. Portābitne parva puella magnam urnam? Minimē, parvam urnam portābit. 5. Quid fēmina puellae dabit? Fēmina puellae urnam dabit. 6. Labōratne puella celeriter? Minimē, puella lēniter labōrat. 7. Quis Galbam juvat? Fīlia Tullia Galbam juvat. 8. Ambulatne cōnsōbrīna mea lēniter? Ita, lēniter ambulat.

1. Is your aunt now in the province of Spain? 2. Does Italy have many forests? 3. Will the girls carry the water from the farmhouse? 4. What will the girls give your cousin? 5. Why is the sailor walking fast on the shore?

Each numbered paragraph describes a person mentioned in "Agricola Labōrat." Answer the questions in Latin.
Sample: 1. Amita sum.

1. In vīllā labōrō. Tullia est mea fīlia. Interdum cōnsōbrīna Tulliae mē juvat. Quis sum?

2. Agricolam juvō. Lēniter labōrō. Parva puella est mea cōnsōbrīna. Quis sum?

3. Cum Fulviā et Annā sum. Minimē labōrō. Agricolam et Tulliam spectō. Quis sum?

4. Celeriter labōrō. Tullia est mea fīlia. Amita parvae puellae nōn sum. Quis sum?

5. Aquam in urnā portō. Interdum fēminam bonam in vīllā juvō. Interdum cum Tulliā labōrō. Quis sum?

6. Cornēliae et Annae dē agricolā et puellīs nārrō. Galbam et puellās spectō. Quis sum?

HONOR WORK After you have translated the five English questions in the middle of the page, answer them in Latin.

XIX. CORNELIA ET URSA

Cornēlia, fīlia agricolae, in parvā casā habitat. Casa est silvae propinqua. Cornēlia in silvā saepe ambulat.

Sed ōlim Cornēlia in magnā et obscūrā silvā ē viā errāvit. Subitō magnam ursam vīdit. Ursa stetit et Cornēliam expectāvit. Ursa 5 Cornēliam spectāvit; Cornēlia ursam spectāvit.

Territa Cornēlia clāmāre dēsīderāvit, sed nōn clāmāvit. Viam nōn vīdit, sed celeriter ambulāre temptāvit. Ursa quoque celeriter ambulāvit! Cornēlia lēniter ambulāvit. Ursa quoque lēniter ambulāvit! Dēnique ursa pede (*with her paw*) Cornēliae viam mōnstrāvit.

10 Subitō Cornēlia casam vīdit. Laeta puella properāvit et mox agricolae dē ursā benignā nārrāvit.

Agricola dīxit, "Ursa fuit Callistō. Ōlim Callistō fuit fēmina pulchra; nunc est ursa pulchra. Saepe agricolae ursam necāre temptāvērunt, sed ursa semper effūgit (*has escaped*)."

15 Cornēlia dīxit, "Sum laeta quod agricolae ursam nōn necāvērunt. Ursa benigna mē jūvit; mihi viam mōnstrāvit. Itaque erō ursae benigna; ursae cibum (*food*) dabō."

Sed Cornēlia ursae benignae cibum nōn dedit quod ursam iterum nōn vīdit.

dē′nique, finally, at last
dī′xit, said
er′rō, -āre, -āvī, wander
obscū′ra, dim, dark, obscure
ō′lim, some day, sometimes; once upon a time, formerly
pro′perō, -āre, -āvī, hasten, hurry
su′bitō, suddenly
ter′rita, frightened
vī′dit, saw, did see

Beginning with this lesson, verbs of the first conjugation will have the first person of the perfect given in the vocabulary.

PERFECT TENSE

You are familiar with the English present perfect tense, which indicates action that took place just before the present time.

I have walked a mile. He has come.

The Latin tense which corresponds to our present perfect is the *perfect*. In the following sentence, **laudāvit** is translated as representing action that took place just before the present time.

Agricola puellam laudāvit, *The farmer has praised the girl.*

The Latin perfect is sometimes used where English uses a simple past tense.

Agricola puellam laudāvit, *The farmer praised the girl.*

In this instance the action is represented as happening at any time in the past, and as being a single past act, not continuous. The meaning of the whole sentence or paragraph will help you decide whether to translate a Latin perfect by an English present perfect or by a simple past tense.

STEM OF THE PERFECT

The present and the future tenses belong to the present system; that is, they use the present stem.

The perfect tense belongs to the *perfect system* and has a different stem, called the *perfect stem.* The perfect stem is found by dropping the **-ī** from the first person singular of the perfect.

Perfect: **portāvī** *Perfect Stem:* **portāv-**

PERSON ENDINGS

The person endings for the perfect are different from those you have seen with the other tenses. They are used only for this one tense.

	SINGULAR	PLURAL
First Person:	**-ī** (*I*)	**-imus** (*we*)
Second Person:	**-istī** (*you*)	**-istis** (*you*)
Third Person:	**-it** (*he, she, it*)	**-ērunt** (*they*)

To conjugate a verb in the perfect tense you add the perfect endings to the perfect stem.

PERFECT OF THE FIRST CONJUGATION

The verb **portō** is conjugated as follows in the perfect tense:

SINGULAR	PLURAL
portā'vī, I carried, I have carried	**portā'vimus,** we carried, we have carried
portāvis'tī, you carried, you have carried	**portāvis'tis,** you carried, you have carried
portā'vit, he carried, he has carried	**portāvē'runt,** they carried, they have carried

Most first-conjugation verbs have a perfect stem like **portō,** but a few verbs of this conjugation do not. Some of these are listed below.

PRESENT INDICATIVE	PRESENT INFINITIVE	PERFECT INDICATIVE
dō	**dare**	**dedī**
stō	**stāre**	**stetī**
juvō	**juvāre**	**jūvī**

PERFECT OF *sum*

The verb **sum** is conjugated in the perfect: **fuī, fuistī, fuit, fuimus, fuistis, fuērunt.** This tense of **sum** is not often used.

1. Ōlim rēgīnae urnam dedistī; fuitne urna magna? 2. In silvā obscūrā subitō puella ursam mōnstrāvit. 3. Ōlim ursa puellam jūvit. 4. Errāvitne ursa ex silvā ubi puellae territae clāmāvērunt? 5. Lēniter ursa ex silvā errāvit. 6. Agricola dīxit, "Dēnique ursam necāvimus."

Give the present, future, and perfect of the Latin verb in the person and number indicated.

Sample: carry, *first singular* *Answer:* **portō, portābō, portāvī**

1. walk, *first singular*
2. work, *second singular*
3. try, *third singular*
4. hurry, *first plural*
5. point out, *second plural*
6. kill, *third plural*

Did you ever read about a knight-*errant* who wandered about in search of adventure? An *erroneous* statement has wandered away from the truth. One who makes an *error, errs.* Use *err, error,* and *erroneous* each in a sentence.

XX. REGINA SUPERBA

Cassiopēa, rēgīna nōta terrae antīquae, erat superba quod erat pulchra. Andromeda, fīlia rēgīnae, erat quoque pulchra, sed nōn erat superba.

Ōlim rēgīna et fīlia in ōrā maritimā stetērunt. Rēgīna aquam quiētam mōnstrāvit et dīxit, "Nymphae habitant in aquā, fīlia mea. Sunt pulchrae, sed invidiōsae sunt quod sum pulchrior (*more beautiful*)."

"Spectā!" Andromeda clāmāvit. "Spectā! Nunc aqua nōn est quiēta."

Subitō Neptūnus, deus (*god*) aquārum, rēgīnam vocāvit. "Fēmina superba nymphīs nōn grāta est," dīxit. "Nymphae sunt īrātae, et nymphae mihi cārae sunt. Mox multa aqua erit in terrā tuā, et mōnstrum (*monster*) erit in aquā. Mōnstrum incolās terrae necābit." 5

Mox erat multa aqua in terrā. Posteā mōnstrum erat in aquā; incolās—fēminās et puellās et agricolās et nautās—necāvit.

Dēnique incolae clāmāvērunt, "Quid Neptūnus dēsīderat? Gemmās pulchrās?"

Neptūnus Cassiopēae dīxit, "Gemmās tuās nōn dēsīderō. Fīliam 10 tuam, Andromedam, sacrificium (*as a sacrifice*) postulō. Fīlia tua erit misera quod es superba. Mōnstrum fīliam tuam necābit; nymphae īrātae nōn erunt; incolās terrae servābō."

Rēgīna fīliam servāre temptāvit, sed incolae terrae Andromedam sacrificium dare dēsīderāvērunt. 15

Subitō Perseus ē caelō mōnstrum et puellam miseram vīdit. Celeriter mōnstrum necāvit et fīliam pulchram rēgīnae servāvit.

antī′qua, old, ancient
e′rant, were
e′rat, was
mi′sera, unhappy, miserable
nō′ta, known, well-known, noted
post′eā, afterward, later
pos′tulō, -āre, -āvī, demand
rēgī′na, -ae, queen
super′ba, proud, haughty

This artist had never heard of moving pictures, but he suggested motion by showing Perseus both approaching and in the act of killing the monster.

ENGLISH NOUNS FROM LATIN NOUNS OF THE FIRST DECLENSION

On pages 28 and 47 you met some Latin nouns which give us English nouns similar in form and meaning. All these Latin nouns end in **-a** and belong to the first declension.

You have also had the noun **Sicilia,** which has become *Sicily.* From other Latin words ending in **-ia** come English words ending in *-y:* **injuria,** *injury.*

What is the English word for each of the following nouns?

victoria	**controversia**	**gloria**

Among the nouns which you have already met are words alike in Latin and English except that the English nouns end in *-e,* while the Latin nouns end in **-a: fama,** *fame.*

Sometimes there is more than one change. In addition to the **-a** at the end which changes to *-e,* some Latin nouns have an internal vowel which does not appear in the English noun: **fabula,** *fable.*

These two changes occur in the word *table.* What is the Latin for this word?

Many English nouns end in *-nce* where the Latin nouns end in **-tia:** *abundance,* **abundantia;** *eloquence,* **eloquentia.**

What do you think is the English for the Latin word **prudentia?** For **pestilentia?**

What is the English noun coming from each of the Latin nouns listed below?

epistula	**machina**	**pirata**
figura	**magnificentia**	**temperantia**
ignorantia	**natura**	**vigilantia**
Italia	**patientia**	**vipera**

When in your Latin reading you meet a first-declension noun that is similar in form and meaning to an English noun, you will know its meaning. Hence, such words will not be included in the lesson vocabulary. They will, however, be found in the review list for the unit and in the reference vocabulary at the back of the book.

1. Posteā aquam postulāvimus. 2. Rēgīna superba in ōrā maritimā stetit. 3. Mox rēgīna erat misera. 4. Posteā pecūniam postulāvistis. 5. Fīliam rēgīnae nōtae servāvērunt.

Ancient worshipers of Neptune dedicated this temple to the sea god.

Change each verb in the six sentences below, (1) to future, (2) to perfect; (3) translate each sentence you make.

Sample: **In jānuā stāmus,** *We are standing in the door.*
In jānuā stābimus, *We shall stand in the door.*
In jānuā stetimus, *We stood in the door.*

1. Sagittās postulāmus.
2. Amitae tuae epistulam dās.
3. Puellae in silvā errant.
4. Agricola sum.
5. In silvā errātis.
6. Rēgīna rānās spectat.

HY

In "Rēgīna Superba" there are perfect forms of **mōnstrō, stō,** and **vocō.** Of what are these forms made up?

LLT

Complete the sentences below with English words related to Latin words. The first and last letters of each omitted word are given, and the number of dashes shows the number of letters in the word.

1. He was n _ _ _ d for his generosity.
2. The child was t - - - - - - - d by the sudden noise.
3. A person with a s _ _ _ _ e mind is not e _ _ _ _ _ c.
4. The shipwrecked people looked cold and m _ _ _ _ _ _ _ e.
5. There were some interesting curios in the a _ _ _ _ _ e shop.
6. The cottage was almost entirely o _ _ _ _ _ _ d by the trees.
7. The teacher had written "e _ _ _ _ _ _ _ s statement" opposite a sentence on my paper.

(If you have difficulty with any of these, review pp. 70-81.)

The pirates who attacked Roman ships may have sailed in such boats as these.

XXI. ARCA PIRATARUM

Lūcrētia in Siciliā habitābat. Erat fīlia nautae et in casā albā habitābat. Casa erat ōrae maritimae propinqua. Noctū Lūcrētia saepe in ōrā maritimā stābat et nautam expectābat.

Sed ōlim noctū quattuor pīrātās in ōrā vīdit. Pīrātae magnam
5 arcam portābant. Arca erat longa et angusta. Lūcrētia territa pīrātās diū spectābat, sed nōn clāmāvit. Pīrātae terram celeriter effōdērunt (*dug up*) et arcam cēlāvērunt. Tum ab ōrā maritimā properāvērunt.

Mox Lūcrētia nautam vīdit; nautae dē quattuor pīrātīs et dē arcā novā nārrāvit.

10 Nauta fīliam laudāvit et dīxit, "Incolae īnsulae nostrae multam pecūniam habent; interdum pecūniam in magnīs arcīs cēlant. Pīrātae saepe incolās Siciliae necant, quod gemmās et pecūniam dēsīderant. Arcam incolīs īnsulae dabō."

Tum nauta et puella arcam longam et angustam invēnērunt (*found*).
15 In arcā erant gemmae et urnae et pecūnia.

Nauta incolīs īnsulae arcam mōnstrāvit. Incolae nautam et fīliam laudāvērunt et nautae multam pecūniam dedērunt. Posteā incolae Siciliae pīrātās expectāvērunt et necāvērunt.

ar′ca, -ae, box, chest
cē′lō, -āre, -āvī, conceal, hide
diū, long, for a long time
no′va, strange, new
quat′tuor, *not declined,* four
tum, then

IMPERFECT TENSE

You are familiar with the Latin perfect tense, which represents an act as happening at any time in the past, and as being a single past act, not continuous.

Nauta Siciliam mōnstrāvit, *The sailor pointed out Sicily.*

There is also another Latin tense that expresses past time: the imperfect. The imperfect tense represents an act as happening in the past time and as going on, or continuing, in the past.

Nauta arcam cēlābat, *The sailor was hiding the chest.*

In English we sometimes use the simple past tense of a verb to represent an act or situation as continuing. Here also the Latin uses the imperfect.

Agricola fīliam amābat, *The farmer loved his daughter.*

You will often find the imperfect and the perfect tenses used in the same sentence or in successive sentences. Here the perfect tells what happened, and the imperfect describes or tells something about the circumstances connected with the act.

Agricolae pīrātās necāvērunt, quod pīrātae īnsulās occupābant, *The farmers killed the pirates, because the pirates were seizing the islands.*

This Roman arca *is made of wood covered with bronze.*

TENSE SIGN OF THE IMPERFECT

The syllable **-bā-**, which is seen in all forms of the imperfect, is called the tense sign of the imperfect. The forms all have **-bā-** before the person endings. Notice that in the conjugation of **portō** the **-a-** becomes short before **-m, -t,** and **-nt.**

PERSON ENDINGS

The person endings for the imperfect are the same as those for the present, except that **-m** instead of **-ō** is used for the first person singular, just as it is in the present of **sum.**

IMPERFECT OF *portō*

The verb **portō** is conjugated as follows in the imperfect:

SINGULAR	PLURAL
portā'bam, I was carrying, I carried	**portābā'mus,** we were carrying, we carried
portā'bās, you were carrying, you carried	**portābā'tis,** you were carrying, you carried
portā'bat, he was carrying, he carried	**portā'bant,** they were carrying, they carried

PRESENT SYSTEM

The imperfect tense, like the present and future, is formed on the present stem of the verb, which is found by dropping the **-re** of the infinitive. These three tenses make up the *present system.*

As you have seen (pp. 35, 69, and above), in the first conjugation the tenses of the present system are formed as follows:

Present = present stem + person endings
Future = present stem + **bi** (**b, bu**) + person endings
Imperfect = present stem + **bā** (**ba**) + person endings

IMPERFECT OF *sum*

The irregular verb **sum** is conjugated as follows in the imperfect:

SINGULAR	PLURAL
e'ram, I was	**erā'mus,** we were
e'rās, you were	**erā'tis,** you were
e'rat, he, she, it was	**e'rant,** they were

1. Cēlat, cēlābit, cēlāvit, cēlābat; est, erit, fuit, erat. 2. Clāmās, clāmābis, clāmāvistī, clāmābās; es, eris, fuistī, erās. 3. Spectant, spectābunt, spectāvērunt, spectābant; sunt, erunt, fuērunt, erant. 4. Stō, stābō, stetī, stābam; sum, erō, fuī, eram. 5. Properātis, properābitis, properāvistis, properābātis; estis, eritis, fuistis, erātis. 6. Quattuor pīrātae novam arcam hīc cēlāvērunt. 7. Tum puella pīrātās ab ōrā spectābat. 8. Puella erat territa, sed nōn clāmāvit. 9. Incolae īnsulae nōtae arcās ex silvā portābant. 10. Diū pecūniam postulābāmus.

In each group give the form of the Latin verb called for.

1. Poēta (*pres.*)	walk	1. I (*pres.*)	hide	1. Dea (*pres.*)	watch
2. Agricola (*fut.*)		2. I (*perf.*)		2. Deae (*perf.*)	
3. Puella (*perf.*)		3. I (*impf.*)		3. Puella (*impf.*)	
4. Nauta (*impf.*)		4. I (*fut.*)		4. Puellae (*fut.*)	

HW

In the last paragraph of "Arca Pīrātārum" change the perfect verbs to imperfect.

HELP YOURSELF

Find in "Arca Pīrātārum" an imperfect form of **habitō, portō, spectō, stō,** and **sum.** Find a perfect form of **cēlō, clāmō, dō, mōnstrō, necō.** How can you always tell the imperfect? The perfect?

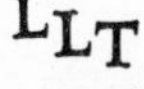

LLT

Below the sentences is a list of English words. Some of these are related to Latin words and others are not. Find the Latin derivative that completes each sentence.

1. His invention is a ___.
2. The beggar looked ___.
3. The ___ was crowded with travelers.
4. The bright ___ leaped high in the air.
5. Noah took all the animals into the ___.
6. The mind of an ___ thinker often wanders.
7. From a humble and ___ artist, he became a very ___ one.

ark	erratic	gifted	novelty
boat	field	gun	obscure
dirty	fish	miserable	station
earnest	flame	noted	starving

The center of family life in this Pompeian house was the atrium. Here are shown servants at work, a child playing, and master and mistress directing the household.

THE ROMAN HOUSE

The heart of a Roman house was the *atrium*. Just above is shown a rich man's house, with the atrium in the foreground as the center of the family's activities. Gradually the atrium lost its character as the *living* room of the house and became a reception hall used for formal occasions. There the master received his guests; there, too, he greeted his bride; and there, upon his death, his body lay in state.

The distinctive feature of the atrium was the *impluvium*, a large rectangular opening in the roof through which came practically all the light in the room. Rain also came through this opening and was caught in a shallow pool for use in the household.

In the *tablinum*, a smaller room opening off the rear of the atrium, the master had his office. It could be closed off from the atrium by curtains and from the back of the house by folding doors. A passageway at one side of the tablinum made it possible for the servants to go from the front of the house to the back without disturbing their master.

An ancient house cut in two from front to back to show the arrangement of the most important rooms

These walls and pillars, once a part of the atrium and court of a house in Pompeii, still stand. They were the basis of the artist's picture shown on the opposite page.

Beyond the tablinum was an open court, with pillars on three sides, which was in effect the living room of the family. The Romans were great lovers of the out-of-doors, and the court with its gay flowers and softly splashing fountain was the most delightful part of the house.

Rooms opening off the court or off the atrium were used as dining room, library, bedrooms, and bathrooms. The servants' quarters were usually among the rooms reached from the court, and the kitchen and bakery were also entered from the court.

Lavish sums were spent in the decoration of a fine Roman house. The floors were often bright with mosaics like those shown on pages 44 and 46. Even the ceilings were gaily colored, and the walls were painted with scenes from the lives of the gods and goddesses or in other elaborate designs. (See pp. 33, 43, 74.) The walls which are still standing in the house pictured above show colorful decorations of this kind.

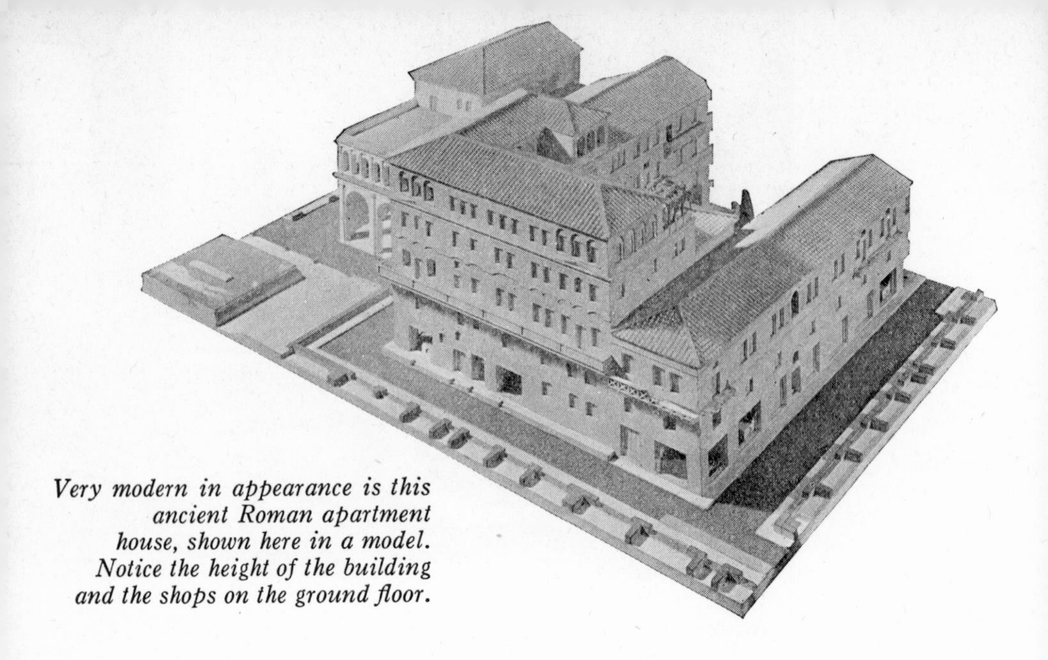

Very modern in appearance is this ancient Roman apartment house, shown here in a model. Notice the height of the building and the shops on the ground floor.

But only wealthy Romans could afford to live in large and richly decorated houses. People of moderate means lived in small houses of few rooms similar to the house whose plan is shown below. Others lived in one-room houses.

In the cities many poor people lived in apartments. The Romans called these apartments *insulae* because each one occupied an entire block and was surrounded by streets, as an island is by water. Some tenements were six or seven stories high and poorly constructed of cheap materials, so that the owner might make quick money from his rentals without much investment of capital. Each of these tenements had hundreds of inhabitants, and often a large family would live in one crowded room.

There was a great contrast between the home of a poor Roman and the home of a wealthy Roman in size and in decoration, but the main features were the same for all classes.

This insula *was in Ostia, the seaport of Rome.*

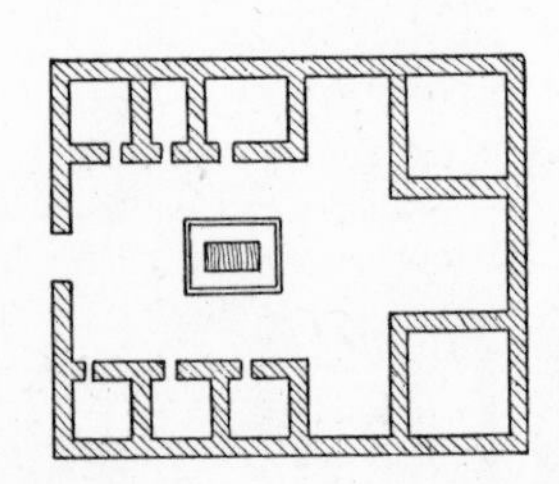

In this plan of a simple Roman house, notice the atrium and the small rooms at each side. The rooms next to the tablinum in the rear may have been kitchen and dining room.

REVIEW OF UNIT V LESSONS XVIII-XXI

Nouns		*Verbs*	*Adjectives*	*Other Words*
arca, -ae	**cēlō, -āre**	**facit**	**antīqua**	**dēnique**
cōnsōbrīna, -ae	**colit**	**juvō, -āre**	**misera**	**diū**
***nympha, -ae**	**dīxit**	**postulō, -āre**	**nōta**	**ita**
rēgīna, -ae	**erat**	**properō, -āre**	**nova**	**lēniter**
urna, -ae	**erant**	**vīdit**	**obscūra**	**minimē**
Pronouns	**errō, -āre**		**quattuor**	**ōlim**
quid			**superba**	**posteā**
quis			**territa**	**subitō**
				tum

I. From the list above, select the Latin word that translates each parenthesis in the sentences below. Be sure every word has the correct form.

1. (*What*) (*cousin*) misera mea postulat?
2. Quis fēminam (*proud*) (*will aid*)?
3. Quid (*the frightened nymph*) cēlāvit?
4. (*Who*) ab ōrā (*hastened*)?

II. Below are given a number of statements, each followed by three words or syllables, only one of which is correct. Find the one which completes the statement and makes it true.

1. The infinitive of **juvō** is (**juvat, juvā-, juvāre**).
2. The perfect stem of **properō** is (**properāre, properā-, properāv-**).
3. The present stem of **postulō** is (**postulāre, postul-, postulā-**).
4. The tense sign of the future is (**-bā-, -bi-, -āre**).
5. The tense sign of the imperfect is (**-ō, -bā-, -bi-**).

III. If the following paragraph were in Latin, which of the verbs would be imperfect and which perfect?

As I was walking down the street with my mother, I saw a friend who was hurrying home. People were coming toward us, but no one spoke to us. Then we saw Father. He was walking very fast.

IV. Find in group B the English equivalent of each Latin word in group A.

A		**B**		
1. celeriter	5. minimē	(*a*) *afterward*	(*e*) *finally*	(*i*) *slowly*
2. dēnique	6. posteā	(*b*) *at night*	(*f*) *formerly*	(*j*) *so*
3. ita	7. subitō	(*c*) *by day*	(*g*) *here*	(*k*) *suddenly*
4. lēniter	8. tum	(*d*) *by no means*	(*h*) *quickly*	(*l*) *then*

UNIT VI

XXII. DEAE NOTAE

Mārcus. Ubi incolae Ītaliae et Graeciae templa aedificābant?

Lūcius. Templa in oppidīs et in ōrā maritimā et in silvīs aedificābant. Interdum erant ārae prō templīs, sed multae erant in viīs et in casīs. Saepe dōna incolārum erant in ārīs.

5 *Mārcus.* Cūr erant dōna in ārīs?

Lūcius. Deae dōna amābant et saepe praemia incolīs dabant.

Mārcus. Nōnne erant multae deae in Ītaliā?

Lūcius. Ita, erant multae deae. Cerēs et Minerva erant deae nōtae. Cerēs erat dea agricultūrae. Cerēs 10 templa in Ītaliā et in Siciliā habēbat. Cerēs Siciliam amābat, quod incolae Siciliae erant agricolae.

Mārcus. Eratne Minerva quoque dea agricultūrae?

15 *Lūcius.* Minimē, Minerva oppida amābat et multa templa in oppidīs habēbat.

Mārcus. Nōnne spectāvistī templum Minervae?

20 *Lūcius.* Ita, templum Minervae spectāvī. In templō erat statua deae. Fāma templī est magna.

A modern artist's portrayal of Ceres

aedi'ficō, -āre, -āvī, build
ā'ra, -ae, altar
dō'num, -ī, gift
habē'bat, had
nōn'ne, *a word used to introduce a question which expects the answer "yes"*
op'pidum, -ī, town
prae'mium, praemiī, reward
prō, *prep. with abl.,* in front of, on behalf of, for
tem'plum, -ī, temple

Beginning with this lesson, nouns of the second declension have the genitive ending in the vocabularies, e.g., **dōnum, -ī.**

The Roman Forum contained many temples.

DECLENSION OF *templum*

The different case forms of the noun **templum,** *temple,* are as follows:

SINGULAR

Nominative:	**tem′plum,** a temple (*as subject or predicate noun*)
Genitive:	**tem′plī,** of a temple, a temple's (*possessive*)
Dative:	**tem′plō,** to a temple, a temple (*as indirect object*)
Accusative:	**tem′plum,** a temple (*as direct object*)
Ablative:	**tem′plō,** (from, with, in, on) a temple

PLURAL

Nominative:	**tem′pla,** temples (*as subject or predicate noun*)
Genitive:	**templō′rum,** of temples, temples' (*possessive*)
Dative:	**tem′plīs,** to temples, temples (*as indirect object*)
Accusative:	**tem′pla,** temples (*as direct object*)
Ablative:	**tem′plīs,** (from, with, in, on) temples

ENDINGS

You see that the case endings differ from those of **silva** and other first-declension nouns everywhere except in the dative and ablative plural.

SECOND DECLENSION

Nouns with the genitive singular ending in **-ī** are of the *second declension.* The second-declension nouns are not all alike in the nominative. Some have the nominative ending in **-um,** others in **-us,** and others in **-er.** Those ending in **-um** are declined like **templum.** Later you will see the declension of nouns ending in **-us** and **-er.**

FORMS OF QUESTIONS

You have already learned about the use of the ending **-ne** in questions. In this lesson you meet questions of another form.

Nōnne patriam tuam amās? *Do you not (Don't you) love your native country?*

Nōnne implies the answer *yes,* but with **-ne** the answer expected is not indicated.

Amāsne patriam tuam? *Do you love your native country?*

You have seen that **-ne** is not used in questions which have such interrogative words as **cūr, quis, quid,** and **ubi.** The word **nōnne** is likewise not used with questions which have such interrogative words.

1. Ex templō properāvī; prō ārā stetī. 2. Dōnum Diānae dedistī. 3. Templum in īnsulā aedificāvistī; nōnne templa in īnsulīs aedificāvimus? 4. In oppidō labōrāvistī; in oppidīs labōrāvistis. 5. Nōnne amita tua tibi praemium dabit?

Supply the correct forms of the Latin words.

1. In īnsulā __ aedificābimus. (*temples and altars*)
2. In templīs deae erant __. (*many statues*)
3. Nōnne pictūrās __ mōnstrāvimus? (*of the temples*)
4. __ pictūram templī? (*Did you* [sing.] *point out*)
5. Prō casā meā __. (*you* [pl.] *were standing*)

HY

In the next to last line of the story in what case is **statua?** How do you know? What is the gender of **statua?** What proves this?

LLT

Select the proper words to complete each sentence. In each case give the Latin word that proves your choice.

1. An edifice is { a city official. / a large building. / a light lunch. }

2. A donation is { a gift. / a song. / a speech. }

Diana, as goddess of the forests, is hunting with her maidens, but she wears a crescent in her hair because she is also goddess of the moon.

XXIII. TEMPLUM ANTIQUUM

Olim in Ītaliā erat templum antīquum Diānae in silvā. Propinqua erat casa ubi hieme nauta cum agricolā habitābat. Aestāte nauta ab Ītaliā nāvigābat et multās terrās spectābat.

Agricola templum amābat quod Diāna, dea lūnae, agricolīs cāra erat. Sed nauta dīxit, "Dea in templō antīquō nōn habitat." 5

Ōlim noctū nauta in silvā ambulābat. Lēniter ambulābat quod via erat obscūra. Subitō jānuam apertam templī antīquī et flammās clārās in ārā vīdit. Prō ārā stābat dea pulchra cum multīs puellīs. Puellae parvās lucernās portābant, sed dea sagittās clārās portābat.

Diāna āram et flammās diū spectābat. Dēnique dea dīxit, "Multa 10 templa habeō, sed incolae terrae ārās meās nōn servant. Mihi dōna nōn dant. Dea nōn manet in terrā ubi incolae āram deae nōn servant. Date mihi lucernās, puellae; eritis stellae in caelō. Erō lūna in caelō."

Puellae deae lucernās dedērunt. Templum antīquum erat obscūrum; 15 flammae nōn erant in ārā. Sed lūna erat clāra; stellae erant clārae.

Tum nauta ex silvā properāvit. Celeriter ambulāvit, quod nunc via nōn erat obscūra. Diāna et puellae erant in caelō.

aestā'te, in summer
ha'beō, I have
hi'eme, in winter
lucer'na, -ae, F., lamp
ma'net, remains, stays
nā'vigō, -āre, -āvī, sail

Beginning with this lesson the gender of each new noun is indicated in the lesson vocabulary. M. means masculine; F., feminine; and N., neuter. Be sure to learn the gender of each noun as you study the vocabulary.

Up to this point all words of more than one syllable have had the accent marked in the lesson vocabularies. But the accent of Latin words is fixed by definite rules. If you know these rules, you will not have to learn the accent of each new word as you do in English. Words of two syllables are accented on the first syllable, for example, **ma'net.**

GENDER

In English we use the pronoun *he* when referring to a man, a boy, or a male animal, the pronoun *she* when referring to a woman, a girl, or a female animal, and the pronoun *it* when referring to a thing. *He* is in the *masculine gender*, *she* is in the *feminine gender*, and *it* is in the *neuter gender*.

Small altars stood on Roman street corners.

Nouns also are said to have gender. Thus, *brother* is masculine, *sister* is feminine, and *house* is neuter.

In Latin, gender does not depend entirely on meaning, as it does in English. For example, most first-declension nouns are feminine, even though we should expect many of them to be neuter from their meanings. Those denoting males, however, are masculine. Thus, **agricola, nauta, pīrāta,** and **poēta** are masculine; **incola** may be either masculine or feminine. All other nouns of this declension which have been given are feminine.

You have learned the forms of second-declension nouns ending in **-um,** such as **templum.** All nouns ending in **-um** in the nominative singular are neuter.

AGREEMENT OF ADJECTIVES IN GENDER

An adjective agrees with its noun in gender, as well as in case and number. The adjectives which you have learned with the ending **-a** have also a neuter form in **-um** declined like **templum.**

magna īnsula, *a large island* **magnum templum,** *a large temple*

The different forms of **magnum** with a neuter noun are as follows:

SINGULAR

Nom. **mag′num tem′plum,** a large temple (*as subj. or pred. noun*)
Gen. **mag′nī tem′plī,** of a large temple, a large temple's (*possessive*)
Dat. **mag′nō tem′plō,** to a large temple, a large temple (*as ind. obj.*)
Acc. **mag′num tem′plum,** a large temple (*as direct obj.*)
Abl. **mag′nō tem′plō,** (from, with, in, on) a large temple

PLURAL

Nom. **mag′na tem′pla,** large temples (*as subj. or pred. noun*)
Gen. **magnō′rum templō′rum,** of large temples, large temples' (*possessive*)
Dat. **mag′nīs tem′plīs,** to large temples, large temples (*as ind. obj.*)
Acc. **mag′na tem′pla,** large temples (*as direct object*)
Abl. **mag′nīs tem′plīs,** (from, with, in, on) large temples

In such small boats the Romans sailed through the Mediterranean, out into the Atlantic, and north to Britain.

1. Quid videō? Quid habeō? Ubi habitās? 2. Hieme Fulvia in Britanniā manet; aestāte ā Britanniā nāvigābat. 3. Dēnique pīrātae ab Hispāniā nāvigāvērunt. 4. In tuō oppidō habitābit; in tuā casā habitābimus. 5. Hieme puella diū in parvō oppidō manet, sed aestāte in ōrā maritimā habitat.

Supply the correct form of each adjective.

1. Templum __ oppidī est antīquum. (*large*)
2. Templa magnōrum oppidōrum sunt __. (*old*)
3. Āra in __ templō est. (*small*)
4. Templum __ laudābimus. (*famous*)
5. Mihi __ praemium dabunt. (*great*)
6. In oppidō __ habitāvērunt. (*beautiful*)

HELP YOURSELF

Remember that a noun with the ending **-um** may be in either the nominative or the accusative singular. In the sentence **In oppidō est magnum templum,** what is the case of **templum?** In the sentence **In oppidō magnum templum videō,** what is the case of **templum?** Give your reason for each decision.

LLT

Complete each sentence with one or more of these words related to **manet:** *permanent, remained, remainder.*

1. If you take 8 from 15, the __ is 7.
2. When Sally got a __ job, she had a __ wave.
3. Harry went abroad for two months and __ a year.

XXIV. HERCULES ET LEO

In Ītaliā antīquā hieme incolae oppidōrum multās et nōtās fābulās nārrābant. Ōlim Mārcus et amīcus bonus domī fābulās nārrābant. Mārcus amīcō dīxit, "Nārrā mihi fābulam bonam."

"Tibi fābulam nōtam nārrābō," amīcus dīxit.

5 Ōlim aestāte in silvīs Graeciae leō validus habitābat. Interdum noctū leō equōs agricolārum necābat; interdum agricolās quoque necāre temptābat. Dēnique leō malus fīlium agricolae necāvit. Tum incolae oppidī propinquī leōnem necāre temptābant, sed leō semper effūgit (*escaped*).

10 Itaque agricola clāmāvit, "Nūllus leō in silvīs habitābit et fīliōs nostrōs et equōs nostrōs necābit! Vocāte Herculem! Herculēs est satis validus. Leōnem necābit et nōs servābit!"

Itaque Herculēs ex terrā propinquā properāvit. Nūllās sagittās portābat, sed magnam clāvam (*club*) portābat. Quod silva erat 15 obscūra, lēniter ambulābat. Tum subitō lūna clāra magnum leōnem mōnstrāvit.

Diū Herculēs et leō pugnābant. Dēnique Herculēs ex silvā properāvit et agricolīs dīxit, "Clāva mea leōnem malum necāvit. Leō nūllōs fīliōs et nūllōs equōs amīcōrum meōrum necābit."

amī'cus, -ī, M., friend
do'mī, at home
e'quus, -ī, M., horse
fī'lius, fī'liī,[1] M., son
le'ō, M., lion; *acc.* **leō'nem**
ma'lus, -a, -um, bad, wicked
nūl'lus, -a, -um, no, none
pug'nō, -āre, -āvī, fight
sa'tis, sufficiently, enough
va'lidus, -a, -um, strong, well

Remember that **qu** (pronounced like English *qu* in *queer*) is treated as a single consonant. Hence **equus** consists of only two syllables: **e'quus.**

Now that you have learned the rule for accenting two-syllable words, only words of more than two syllables will have the accent marked in the lesson vocabularies.

Nūllus is declined like **bonus,** except in the genitive and dative singular, which are irregular. These forms are not used in this book.

A Roman emperor wearing a lion skin and carrying a club like Hercules

[1] TO THE TEACHER: In this book **fīliī**, the uncontracted form of the genitive, is used.

DECLENSION OF *amīcus*

The noun **amīcus** is of the second declension. It has the same endings as **templum**, except in the nominative singular and the nominative and accusative plural. It is declined as follows:

SINGULAR

Nom. **amī'cus**, a friend (*as subject or predicate noun*)
Gen. **amī'cī**, of a friend, a friend's (*possessive*)
Dat. **amī'cō**, to a friend, a friend (*as indirect object*)
Acc. **amī'cum**, a friend (*as direct object*)
Abl. **amī'cō**, (from, with, by) a friend

PLURAL

Nom. **amī'cī**, friends (*as subject or predicate noun*)
Gen. **amīcō'rum**, of friends, friends' (*possessive*)
Dat. **amī'cīs**, to friends, friends (*as indirect object*)
Acc. **amī'cōs**, friends (*as direct object*)
Abl. **amī'cīs**, (from, with, by) friends

All second-declension nouns which end in **-us** are declined like **amīcus.** Most of them are masculine.

ADJECTIVES IN *-us*

Such adjectives as **bona** and **magna** have a masculine form ending in **-us** in the nominative. The other case endings are also like those of the noun **amīcus.**

SINGULAR

Nom. **amī'cus bo'nus**, a good friend (*as subj. or pred. noun*)
Gen. **amī'cī bo'nī**, of a good friend, a good friend's (*poss.*)
Dat. **amī'cō bo'nō**, to a good friend, a good friend (*as ind. obj.*)
Acc. **amī'cum bo'num**, a good friend (*as dir. obj.*)
Abl. **amī'cō bo'nō**, (from, with, by) a good friend

PLURAL

Nom. **amī'cī bo'nī**, good friends (*as subj. or pred. noun*)
Gen. **amīcō'rum bonō'rum**, of good friends, good friends' (*poss.*)
Dat. **amī'cīs bo'nīs**, to good friends, good friends (*as ind. obj.*)
Acc. **amī'cōs bo'nōs**, good friends (*as dir. obj.*)
Abl. **amī'cīs bo'nīs**, (from, with, by) good friends

You will see the difference between the forms of the adjective used with **amīcus** and the forms of the same adjective used with a feminine noun, as for example **puella.**

	SINGULAR	PLURAL
Nominative:	**puel′la bo′na**	**puel′lae bo′nae**
Genitive:	**puel′lae bo′nae**	**puellā′rum bonā′rum**
Dative:	**puel′lae bo′nae**	**puel′līs bo′nīs**
Accusative:	**puel′lam bo′nam**	**puel′lās bo′nās**
Ablative:	**puel′lā bo′nā**	**puel′līs bo′nīs**

1. Fīlius agricolae domī est; amita agricolae aestāte domī est; fīlia agricolae tum nōn est domī. 2. Nōn diū fīlius meus hieme in oppidō manet. 3. Multī amīcī ab Hispāniā nāvigābant. 4. Fīliōs amīcōrum meōrum expectō. 5. Amīcus tuus fīlium habet.

1. Cornelia praised the farmer's friend; Galba was praising the farmer's friends. 2. I shall give no gift to the sailor's wicked son. 3. The cottage of the poet's friend was near the old town. 4. In winter the sailor remains at home. 5. There he sees many friends.

Choose the correct word to complete each sentence and give a reason for your choice.

1. Equus meus est (mala, malus, malae).
2. Hieme et aestāte in (īnsulam, īnsula, īnsulā) habitō.
3. Cum amīcīs (tua, tuīs, tuārum) ambulās.
4. Equus amīcī (bonīs, bonam, bonī) nōn ibi est.
5. Cum fīliō (tuam, tuus, tuō) in casā es.
6. (Nūllīs, Nūllum, Nūllōs) equōs habeō.
7. Fīliī (meus, meī, meum) pugnābant.

Supply the Latin word which will complete each sentence. Be sure the form of the word is correct.

1. (*The farmers*) arcam cēlāvērunt.
2. (*The daughters*) amīcī meī expectō.
3. (*The sons*) rēgīnae servāvistī.
4. (*The rewards*) erant magna.
5. (*Gifts*) fēminīs dabimus.
6. (*The horses*) in viā stābant.

LLT

At a peace conference would it be better to have *amicable* or *pugnacious* delegates? Why?

What is *domestic* science? What is your *domicile?*

What is an *equestrian* statue?

Name a *valid* excuse for absence from school. Name one that would be *invalid*. Would an *invalid* have a *valid* excuse?

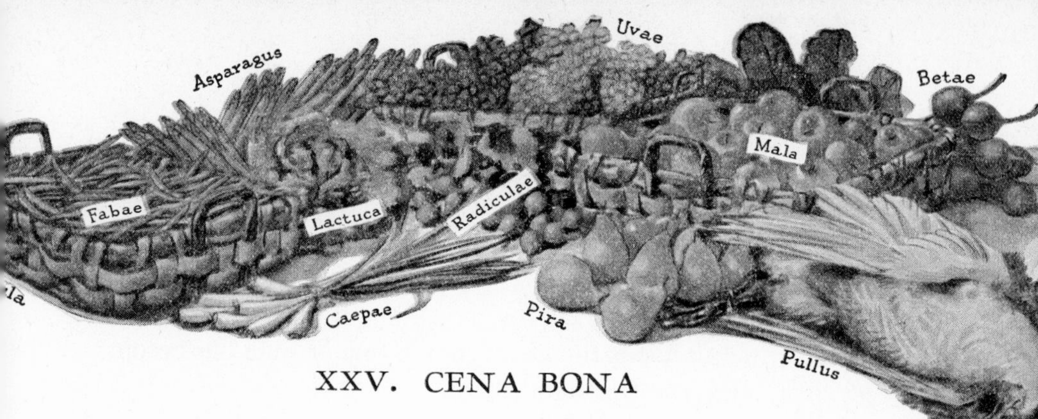

XXV. CENA BONA

Anna et Mārcus in magnō macellō (*market*) stant; fēminās et puellās et puerōs spectant.

Anna. Ecce! Agricolae ex agrīs et ex hortīs properant; corbulās portant.

Mārcus. Quid agricolae in corbulīs portant? Cūr properant?

Anna. Agricolae corbulās ūvārum portant. Properant quod fēminās et puellās et puerōs in macellō vident.

Mārcus. Corbulās in magnā mēnsā videō. Nōnne sunt corbulae mālōrum?

Anna. Ita, māla videō. Pira quoque videō. Ūvae sunt parvae sed māla et pira sunt magna.

Mārcus. Quid servus facit?

Anna. Servus agricolam juvat; in mēnsā lactūcam et rādīculās et caepās videō.

Mārcus. Lactūcam et rādīculās amō, sed caepās nōn amō.

Anna. Nunc asparagum et bētās et carōtās videō. Amāsne carōtās et bētās?

Mārcus. Minimē, carōtās et bētās nōn amō, sed asparagum amō.

Anna. Parvam mēnsam videō. Sunt pullī in parvā mēnsā.

Mārcus. Ecce! Amita tua pullum et ōva emit (*is buying*). Fabās et māla quoque habet.

Anna. Hodiē amita mea bonam cēnam parābit. Amitam meam juvābō, et mihi et tibi bonam cēnam dabit.

ager, agrī, M., field
cēna, -ae, F., dinner, meal
ecce, look!
hortus, -ī, M., garden
mēnsa, -ae, F., table
parō, -āre, -āvī, prepare, get ready, obtain
puer, pu′erī, M., boy
servus, -ī, M., servant, slave

In any word the syllable before the last is called the *penult*. In a word of more than two syllables the accent falls on the penult if it has a long vowel: **parā′re.**

ENGLISH NOUNS AND LATIN NOUNS

On pages 28, 47, and 82 you met some common English nouns much like Latin nouns of the first declension. There are also English nouns like second-declension Latin nouns: *auditorium, forum.*

Some English nouns do not have the Latin ending: *sign,* **signum.**

What is the Latin for *fact?*

In other English nouns the Latin ending **-um** or **-ium** has become *-e: temple,* **templum;** *domicile,* **domicilium.**

What is the Latin for *fate?*

Some English words have *e* where Latin had **ae.** What is the usual English spelling of **Aetna**? What two changes do you see in *edifice,* from **aedificium**?

Give the English for each Latin noun listed below.

Aethiopia	**fragmentum**	**meritum**	**praejudicium**
exilium	**impedimentum**	**officium**	**sacrificium**

What is the Latin for each of these English nouns?

college (like *exile*)	*pendulum* (like *forum*)
monument (like *merit*)	*testament* (like *fragment*)

SECOND-DECLENSION NOUNS IN *-er*

In this book you will use few second-declension nouns ending in **-er.** Two of these, **puer,** *boy,* and **vesper,** *evening,* keep the **-e-** in cases other than the nominative singular. You can remember this by means of English words derived from them: *puerile, vespers.* The words **ager,** *field,* **liber,** *book,* and **magister,** *teacher,* do not keep the **-e-.** You can remember this by the words *agriculture, library, magistrate.*

Second-declension nouns ending in **-er** are masculine, and their forms, except the nominative singular, are the same as those of **amīcus.**

1. Quis cēnam parābat? 2. Quis fenestram apertam videt? 3. Quid Mārcus hieme facit? Mārcus hieme in oppidō labōrat. 4. Quid Mārcus in hortīs facit? Mārcus multās rosās spectat. 5. Labōrāvistīne in hortō? 6. Graecīne ārās prō templō aedificant? 7. Suntne dōna in mēnsā? 8. Quis servōs jūvit? 9. Nōnne puerī servōs jūvērunt? 10. Nōnne puer mē juvābit?

1. Why did you not help the boys? 2. I did not help the boys because they did not work. 3. Shall we not give a reward to the boys?

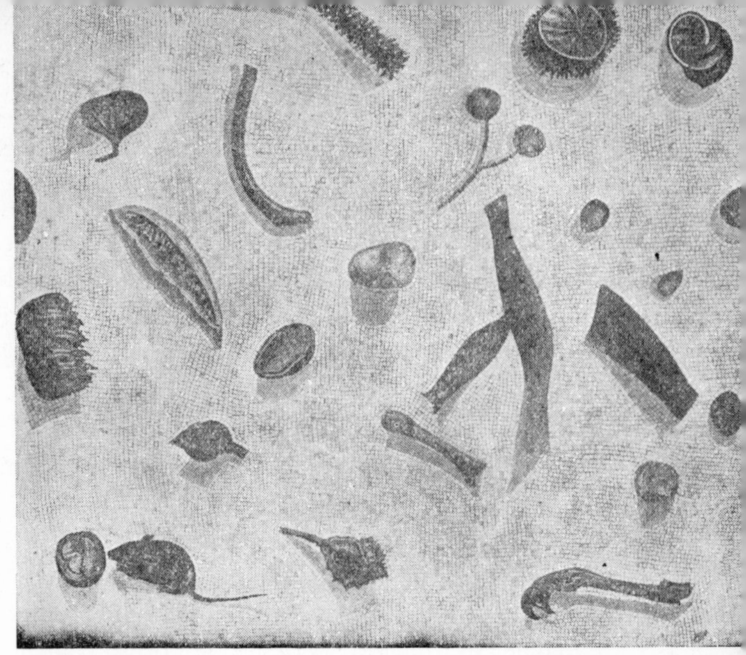

The mosaic floor of a Roman dining room

Make two sentences from each Latin sentence by translating the English phrases.

1. Amīcus servī { *in a large field* / *with the happy boys* } labōrābat.
2. Praemium { *of the good boy* / *of the boy's friend* } erat in mēnsā.
3. Fīlius amīcī { *out of the garden* / *in the town* } ambulābat.
4. Praemia { *of the good boys* / *of the kind friends* } erant magna.
5. { *In the small fields* / *With the boy's friend* } ambulābō.

LLT

Find, in the list below, a word that completes each sentence correctly, and give the corresponding Latin word.

exiles *fragments* *impediment* *merits* *sacrifice*

1. How long were they __ from their country?
2. Twelve baskets full of __ remained.
3. The judge will decide the case on its __.
4. He will sell his house at a __.
5. A crutch is an __ to one who is not lame.

XXVI. AMICUS FIDUS

Sextus et Mārcus erant amīcī. Sextus in magnā vīllā habitābat. Mārcus sōlus in silvā in parvā casā habitābat.

Saepe aestāte Mārcus in hortīs amīcī Sextī labōrābat, et agricolās in agrīs juvābat. Mārcus equōs amābat, et aestāte erant multī equī 5 in agrīs Sextī. Interdum hieme Mārcus servōs juvābat; frūmentum equīs dare amābat.

Ōlim equī Sextī ab agrō errāvērunt.

Territī servī Sextum vocāvērunt et clāmāvērunt, "Nūllī equī sunt in agrīs tuīs! Ubi sunt equī tuī?"

10 Sextus īrātus clāmāvit, "Cūr equōs in agrīs nōn spectābātis, servī? Nunc equī in silvā sunt. Ursae equōs meōs necābunt!"

Tum Sextus ē vīllā properat. In agrō propinquō agricolam videt. Agricolae dē magnō perīculō equōrum nārrat. Celeriter agricola Sextō hastam dat.

15 Via est obscūra in silvā; sed Sextus celeriter ambulat quod equōs servāre dēsīderat. Subitō Mārcum videt. Mārcus dēfessus cum magnā ursā pugnat. Est in magnō perīculō quod nūllum gladium et nūllam hastam habet.

Sextus clāmat, "Tē juvābō, Mārce! Hastam habeō!"

20 Celeriter ursam necat et Mārcum amīcum servat. Tum Mārcus Sextō equōs territōs mōnstrat.

Sextus laetus equōs spectat, et dīcit, "Equōs meōs servāvistī, Mārce; es amīcus fīdus!"

dēfes'sus, -a, -um, tired, weary
fīdus, -a, -um, faithful
frūmen'tum, -ī, N., grain
gla'dius, -ī, M., sword
hasta, -ae, F., spear
perī'culum, -ī, N., danger, peril
sōlus, -a, -um,[1] alone, only

In a word of more than two syllables the accent falls on the penult if its vowel is followed directly by two consonants: **frūmen'tum, angus'tus.**

IMPERFECT OF *dō*

You will remember that **dō** has short **a** in all forms of the present, except the second person singular, **dās**. In the imperfect, all forms have the short **a** before the tense sign.

[1]**Sōlus** is declined like **bonus,** except in the genitive and dative singular, which are not used in this book.

An ancient Roman house as it looks today

SUMMARY OF SECOND-DECLENSION NOUNS

You have now learned four classes of second-declension nouns. The four nouns you have had as examples are given below. If you will read each line across, you will see just where the classes differ.

	NEUTER	MASCULINE		
		SINGULAR		
Nominative:	**templum**	**amīcus**	**ager**	**puer**
Genitive:	**templī**	**amīcī**	**agrī**	**puerī**
Dative:	**templō**	**amīcō**	**agrō**	**puerō**
Accusative:	**templum**	**amīcum**	**agrum**	**puerum**
Ablative:	**templō**	**amīcō**	**agrō**	**puerō**
		PLURAL		
Nominative:	**templa**	**amīcī**	**agrī**	**puerī**
Genitive:	**templōrum**	**amīcōrum**	**agrōrum**	**puerōrum**
Dative:	**templīs**	**amīcīs**	**agrīs**	**puerīs**
Accusative:	**templa**	**amīcōs**	**agrōs**	**puerōs**
Ablative:	**templīs**	**amīcīs**	**agrīs**	**puerīs**

The following is a summary of important facts regarding the second declension:

(1) The genitive singular ends in **-ī**.

(2) Nouns ending in **-um** are neuter.

(3) Nouns ending in **-er** are masculine.

(4) Most nouns ending in **-us** are masculine.

(5) The nominative plural of **-us** and **-er** nouns ends in **-ī**.

(6) The nominative and accusative plural of all neuter nouns (in all declensions) end in **-a**.

ENDINGS OF THE SECOND DECLENSION

	SINGULAR		PLURAL	
	MASC.	NEUT.	MASC.	NEUT.
Nominative:	**-us, -er (-ir)**	**-um**	**-ī**	**-a**
Genitive:	**-ī**	**-ī**	**-ōrum**	**-ōrum**
Dative:	**-ō**	**-ō**	**-īs**	**-īs**
Accusative:	**-um**	**-um**	**-ōs**	**-a**
Ablative:	**-ō**	**-ō**	**-īs**	**-īs**

VOCATIVE CASE OF THE SECOND DECLENSION

In Lesson XV you learned that the vocative case of most Latin nouns has the same form as the nominative. An exception is the class of nouns in the second declension ending in **-us.** The vocative singular of these nouns ends in **-e.**[1]

Nominative: **Mārcus, amīcus** *Vocative:* **Mārce, amīce**

In all nouns the vocative plural is the same as the nominative plural.

1. Hodiē Mārcus sōlus in hortō ambulāvit. 2. Suntne Sextus et Mārcus amīcī? 3. Cūr, Mārce, in viā pugnābās? 4. Cūr, amīce, nōn labōrāvistī? 5. Cūr, puerī, sunt equī in hortō? 6. Puerī erant dēfessī, et amīcos nōn jūvērunt.

Make three sentences from each Latin sentence by translating the English phrases.

1. Nauta est { *with a faithful friend.* / *in great danger.* / *with Marcus alone.* }

2. Puerī sunt { *in a beautiful garden.* / *with faithful friends.* / *with strong sailors.* }

3. Sum { *with Marcus.* / *with many boys.* / *in the town.* }

4. Properābant { *with our friends.* / *out of the garden.* / *from the temple.* }

Translate the nouns: 1. The boy is the faithful friend of my son. 2. I did not praise my son, but I shall praise my son's friend. 3. The farmers were carrying grain from the field. 4. The boy's friends will be alone in the forests. 5. We helped the tired woman today; she was preparing dinner.

HY

You have met many words in which the accent is on the penult. Tell why the penult is accented in **dēfessus** and **frūmentum.**

LATIN LIVES TODAY

Choose the correct word or phrase to complete each sentence and give the reason for your choice.

1. A *bona fide* offer is made __.
   (*a*) deceitfully (*b*) in good faith (*c*) jokingly
2. The leaves of gladioli are shaped like __.
   (*a*) arrows (*b*) hearts (*c*) swords
3. A person in peril is __.
   (*a*) gay (*b*) in danger (*c*) safe
4. When you are satisfied, you have __.
   (*a*) enough (*b*) too little (*c*) too much
5. A pilot making a solo flight is flying __.
   (*a*) alone (*b*) for the first time (*c*) in a monoplane.

[1]To the Teacher: The lessons of this book do not use the vocative in -ī of proper nouns ending in -ius.

These Roman diners had spoons for liquids, but used their fingers as forks. After each course slaves brought hot water and towels.

FROM EGG TO APPLE

In imagination let us go back two thousand years and visit a wealthy family in Rome. You already have an idea of what their house is like, but you are curious about the food they eat.

You arrive in time for evening dinner—the most elaborate meal of the day—and find guests already present. When everyone is settled on his couch at the table, slaves serve appetizers. There are fresh oysters, pickled and salted seafoods, lettuce, bread, and sliced eggs. You expected the eggs because of the expression *ab ovo ad mala*, the equivalent of our "from soup to nuts."

When the slaves bring the main part of the dinner, you wish that you had not eaten so many appetizers. You had not expected to have fish, ham, and roast chicken all at the same meal! Each of them is served as a separate course with vegetables.

Most of the vegetables look familiar—peas, beans, carrots, and asparagus—but they taste different. They are seasoned with olive oil. Butter is sometimes used as a salve, but never as a food.

A loaf of bread from Pompeii

No butter, and no sugar! Honey is used for sweetening. Your host has never heard of potatoes. He has never seen a tomato, either, nor a leaf of spinach, nor an orange.

There is no hot drink like coffee, tea, or cocoa. Wine mixed with water is the Roman beverage, and a little is served with each course and at the end of the meal.

Dessert consists of a variety of pastries, sweets, olives, nuts, and fruits, usually including apples. No one is in a hurry to leave the table. Just as the guests have already lingered over the other courses as they talked of the happenings in the Forum that day, they now leisurely eat their dessert as they discuss a new comedy at the theater.

Soon after dinner you go to bed, for the Romans are early risers. For breakfast they usually have only a piece of bread dipped in wine or sprinkled with salt. Because you are a guest, however, you may have cheese, olives, or raisins in addition, if you wish.

By eleven o'clock you are ready for the bread, cold meat, salad, olives, cheese, nuts, and fruit served then. The salad is delicious, for the Romans have many green vegetables and are fond of salads.

You are impressed by the variety and quantity of the food. Of course you know that not all Romans are so well fed. The poorer people have simple meals of bread, vegetables, fruit, and olives, with almost no meat except goats' flesh. You have been fortunate in being a guest in a home where they have everything "from egg to apples."

In this wall painting from Pompeii Cupids are picnicking, with a salad as the main dish.

REVIEW OF UNIT VI LESSONS XXII-XXVI

Nouns		*Verbs*	*Preposition*
ager, agrī	**mēnsa, -ae**	**aedificō, -āre**	**prō**
***agricultūra, -ae**	**oppidum, -ī**	**habēbat**	
amīcus, -ī	**perīculum, -ī**	**habeō**	*Other Words*
āra, -ae	**praemium, -ī**	**manet**	**aestāte**
cēna, -ae	**puer, puerī**	**nāvigō, -āre**	**domī**
dōnum, -ī	**servus, -ī**	**parō, -āre**	**ecce**
equus, -ī	***statua, -ae**	**pugnō, -āre**	**hieme**
fīlius, -ī	**templum, -ī**		**nōnne**
frūmentum, -ī		*Adjectives*	**satis**
gladius, -ī		**dēfessus, -a, -um**	
hasta, -ae		**fīdus, -a, -um**	
hortus, -ī		**malus, -a, -um**	
leō		**nūllus, -a, -um**	
lucerna, -ae		**sōlus, -a, -um**	
		validus, -a, -um	

I. Give the Latin for each phrase.

before the altar — *for the slave*
for the boys — *in the temples*

II. Choose the word that fits each sentence and tell why you chose it.

1. Cēna / Fīlius / Frūmentum / Lucerna } est sōlus.
2. Ārae / Amīcī / Templa / Mēnsae } sunt fīdī.
3. Sunt nūllae { equī. / cēnae. / dōna. / agrī.
4. Aedificābunt { perīculōrum. / ārās. / dōnīs. / gladiōs.

III. Make the direct object plural in each of the following sentences.

1. Puer amīcum laudat.
2. Puella epistulam scrībit.
3. Fēmina dōnum habet.
4. Portā praemium, serve.
5. Parāte cēnam, servī.

IV. Which of the following forms represent only one case? Which represent two or more cases? Justify your answers.

agrī	**cēna**	**hortōrum**	**praemia**
amīcum	**fēminam**	**mēnsae**	**praemium**
casārum	**equō**	**oppidī**	**puellae**
casīs	**fīliī**	**oppidum**	**puerīs**

V. Select an adjective from Group B that agrees in case with each noun in Group A. Be sure the adjective has a suitable meaning.

A		B	
templī	āra	**nōtōrum**	**pulchra**
praemia	amīcō	**dēfessīs**	**antīqua**
equīs	oppidōrum	**laetō**	**angustīs**
		fīdae	**bonus**
		nōtī	**quiēta**

VI. Make each sentence into a question.

1. Amīcus puerum laudābat.
2. Servus equō frūmentum dabat.
3. Fēminae bonae praemium dabās.
4. Oppidum novum aedificābant.
5. Lucernam fīliō meō dabam.

LATIN LIVES TODAY

Select a word or phrase to complete each statement and give the Latin word that justifies your choice.

1. In an aquarium you would expect to find { elephants. / lions. / rabbits. / trout.

2. A friendly girl is well named if she is called { Amy. / Clara. / Rose. / Stella.

3. A lunar month is measured { by days. / from new moon to new moon. / by the stars.

4. Because they are nocturnal creatures, you seldom see { bluejays. / chickens. / owls.

5. A good scholastic record shows { application to studies. / athletic standing. / social popularity.

Before the invention of printing, the Bible was copied and recopied by hand. Much of this copying was done by monks, who often beautified their manuscripts with ornate initials. The initial at the left shows a monk at work; at the right is a beautiful initial for the first Psalm. For centuries the Bible was written in Latin. The story of Gideon is taken from an old Latin Bible.

UNIT VII

XXVII. DOLUS BELLI

Olim Isrāēlītae cum Midianītīs pugnābant. Midianītae erant multī, sed Isrāēlītae magnās cōpiās nōn habēbant. Isrāēlītae bonōs gladiōs et scūta valida habēbant et bene pugnābant, sed Isrāēlītae cōnsilia bellī satis bona nōn habēbant.

Dēnique Gideōn, Isrāēlīta, dolum bonum habēbat. Ubi cōnsilium Isrāēlītīs nārrāvit, cōnsilium laudāvērunt. Virī dēfessī erant, sed laetī erant quod dolus erat bonus.

Gideōn virīs tubās et urnās et lucernās dedit. Noctū cum virīs dēfessīs ā tabernāculīs celeriter properāvit. Virī lucernās in urnīs portābant. Nūllus Midianīta Isrāēlītās vīdit, quod lūna nōn erat clāra.

Subitō Gideōn tubam īnflāvit et clāmāvit. Virī tubās īnflāvērunt, clāmāvērunt, urnās frēgērunt (*broke*). Subitō erant lūmina (*lights*). Cōpiae Isrāēlītārum nōn erant magnae, sed lūmina erant multa et clāra. Midianītae erant territī et celeriter fūgērunt (*fled*).

Itaque Isrāēlītae oppida et agrōs pulchrōs Midianītārum miserōrum occupāvērunt.

bellum, -ī, N., war
cōnsi′lium, cōnsi′ liī, N., plan, advice
cō′pia, -ae, F., plenty, abundance; *pl.*, forces, troops
dolus, -ī, M., trick, scheme
habē′bant, they had
īnflō, -flāre, -flāvī, blow into, blow
scūtum, -ī, N., shield
tabernā′culum, -ī, N., tent
tuba, -ae, F., trumpet
vir, virī, M., man

The syllable before the penult is called the *antepenult.* In a word of more than two syllables, if the penult is short, the accent falls on the antepenult: **cōn si′li um, gla′di us.**

DECLENSION OF *bonus* IN ALL GENDERS

You have now learned the three genders of adjectives like **bonus.** The complete declension is as follows:

SINGULAR

	MASCULINE	FEMININE	NEUTER
Nominative:	**bo′nus**	**bo′na**	**bo′num**
Genitive:	**bo′nī**	**bo′nae**	**bo′nī**
Dative:	**bo′nō**	**bo′nae**	**bo′nō**
Accusative:	**bo′num**	**bo′nam**	**bo′num**
Ablative:	**bo′nō**	**bo′nā**	**bo′nō**

PLURAL

	MASCULINE	FEMININE	NEUTER
Nominative:	**bo′nī**	**bo′nae**	**bo′na**
Genitive:	**bonō′rum**	**bonā′rum**	**bonō′rum**
Dative:	**bo′nīs**	**bo′nīs**	**bo′nīs**
Accusative:	**bo′nōs**	**bo′nās**	**bo′na**
Ablative:	**bo′nīs**	**bo′nīs**	**bo′nīs**

The following adjectives, of which one or more forms have previously been given, are declined like **bonus:**

albus, -a, -um
amoenus, -a, -um
angustus, -a, -um
antīquus, -a, -um
apertus, -a, -um
benignus, -a, -um
cārus, -a, -um
clārus, -a, -um
dēfessus, -a, -um
fīdus, -a, -um
grātus, -a, -um
invidiōsus, -a, -um
īrātus, -a, -um
laetus, -a, -um
longus, -a, -um
magnus, -a, -um
malus, -a, -um
maritimus, -a, -um
meus, -a, -um
multus, -a, -um
nōtus, -a, -um
novus, -a, -um
obscūrus, -a, -um
parvus, -a, -um
perīculōsus, -a, -um
propinquus, -a, -um
quiētus, -a, -um
superbus, -a, -um
territus, -a, -um
tuus, -a, -um
validus, -a, -um

Notice that the words **meus** and **tuus** are included in this list of adjectives. Like other adjectives, they agree in gender, number, and case with nouns they modify.

ADJECTIVES WITH MASCULINE IN *-er*

You have already met the adjectives **pulchra** and **misera.** These forms are feminine. The masculine form of these words in the nominative singular ends in **-er** instead of **-us: pulcher, miser.**

Some adjectives in **-er** keep **-e-** throughout the declension: **miser, misera, miserum,** etc. In this book you will meet only three such adjectives: **alter, līber,** and **miser.** English words derived from them —*alteration, liberation, miserable*—will help you remember them.

Other adjectives in **-er** drop the **-e-** before **-r** in all forms except the nominative singular masculine: **pulcher, pulchra, pulchrum.** In this book you will meet only six adjectives which drop the **-e-: aeger, impiger, noster, piger, pulcher,** and **vester.**

Remember that only in the nominative singular is there any difference between the declension of these adjectives and that of **bonus.**

ADJECTIVES WITH MASCULINE NOUNS OF THE FIRST DECLENSION

An adjective must agree with its noun in gender, but its endings are not necessarily the same as those of the noun. Since **agricola, nauta, pīrāta,** and **poēta** are masculine, an adjective modifying one of them will be masculine. The words for *a good sailor* are declined as follows:

	SINGULAR	PLURAL
Nominative:	**nauta bonus**	**nautae bonī**
Genitive:	**nautae bonī**	**nautārum bonōrum**
Dative:	**nautae bonō**	**nautīs bonīs**
Accusative:	**nautam bonum**	**nautās bonōs**
Ablative:	**nautā bonō**	**nautīs bonīs**

DECLENSION OF *vir*

In "Dolus Bellī" there are several forms of the noun **vir.** Its declension is like that of **amīcus** except for the nominative singular. There are no other words like **vir** in Latin.

1. Parvī puerī magnās tubās portāvērunt. 2. Virī dēfessī parvās lucernās portābunt. 3. Erant nūllae lucernae in tabernāculīs obscūrīs. 4. Isrāēlītae bona cōnsilia et multōs dolōs bellī habent. 5. Gladiī erant satis longī; scūta nōn erant satis valida. 6. Ubi Isrāēlītae tubās īnflāvērunt, cōpiae Midianītārum pugnāre temptāvērunt.

XXVIII. MIDAS ET AURUM

Mīdās in magnā rēgiā habitābat, ubi erant multae arcae, urnae, lucernae, statuae. Sed Mīdās nōn erat laetus, quod multum aurum dēsīderābat.

Ōlim Mīdās deum jūvit, et deus dīxit, "Tibi praemium dabō. Quid dēsīderās?" 5

Itaque Mīdās dīxit, "Multī multum aurum habent; aurum quoque amō. Dā mihi contāctum (*touch*) aureum. Multa mūtābō; tum erit multum aurum in rēgiā meā."

Deus dōnum virō laetō dedit. Statim Mīdās multa mūtāre temptāvit. Per (*through*) hortum ambulāvit; rosae erant aureae. Per 10 rēgiam ambulāvit; lucernae, mēnsae, urnae, arcae, statuae erant aureae. Mīdās erat vir laetus, quod aurum spectāre amābat. Vesperī multōs incolās convocāvit; aurum incolīs mōnstrāvit.

Dēnique magnam cēnam postulāvit. "Parāte cēnam bonam," dīxit.

Posteā Mīdās cēnam edere (*to eat*) temptāvit, sed cēna erat aurea! 15 Aquam bibere (*to drink*) temptāvit, sed aqua quoque aurea erat! Mīdās erat territus. Contāctum aureum nōn dēsīderābat; cēnam dēsīderābat. Multum aurum nōn dēsīderābat; aquam dēsīderābat.

Mīdās miser deum vocāvit. "Juvā mē! Juvā mē!" clāmāvit.

Deus erat benignus et virum miserum servāvit. Iterum Mīdās 20 magnam cēnam postulāvit. Cēna erat bona; nōn erat aurea. Aqua quoque erat bona.

Mīdās erat laetus et dīxit, "Nunc sum līber; contāctum aureum nōn habeō. Nunc laetus sum, quamquam multum aurum nōn habeō."

aureus, -a, -um, golden, of gold
aurum, -ī, N., gold
convocō, -āre, -āvī, call together
deus, -ī, M., a god; *nom. pl.*, **dī,** the gods
mūtō, -āre, -āvī, change
quamquam, *conj.*, although
rēgia, -ae, F., palace
statim, *adv.*, immediately, at once

Since you have now had the rules for accent, you will be able to determine for yourself where the accent falls in any new word. Therefore the accent of words is not marked in this and the following lesson vocabularies. For further help, consult the summary on page 428.

Perhaps an urn in the palace of Midas was similar to this Greek jar.

ADJECTIVES USED AS NOUNS

The masculine plural of some adjectives may be used without a noun to denote persons. Thus **multī** means *many (persons)* and **bonī** means *the good (persons)*. In descriptions of war or military operations of any kind, **nostrī** means *our men* or *our soldiers.*

The neuter form of some adjectives may be used in the plural to denote things. Thus **multa** means *many things.*

1. Virī fīdī tubās longās īnflāvērunt. 2. Fīliī poētārum bonōrum mihi sunt nōtī. 3. Nauta validus bene pugnat; agricola dēfessus nōn bene labōrat. 4. Deus virō laetō dōnum aureum dedit. 5. Statim Mīdās multa mūtāre temptāvit quod multum aurum dēsīderāvit. 6. In hortō erant rosae aureae; in mēnsīs erant urnae aureae et lucernae aureae. 7. Quamquam Mīdās incolās convocāvit, nōn multī erant in rēgiā.

Translate the italicized words. 1. *Tired men* do not like a *long war.* 2. We see the *long swords* and *strong shields of the faithful men.* 3. Midas *often called* the inhabitants *together.* 4. The man *will want* food; he will not want *gold.*

In each sentence insert the correct form of the Latin words for *tired sailor* or *tired sailors.*

1. Aurum __ (*sing.*) grātum est.
2. Fēmina cum __ (*sing.*) ambulābat.
3. __ in rēgiā est.
4. Lucerna __ (*sing.*) est aurea.
5. Poētae cum __ (*pl.*) pugnant.
6. __ in viīs ambulābant.
7. Convocāte __ (*pl.*)

HW In the seven sentences just above, insert the correct form of the Latin words for *strong man* or *strong men.*

HY Explain the use of **mihi** in Latin sentence 2. Make a Latin sentence of your own, containing the same kind of dative.

LATIN LIVES TODAY By using information gained from the last two vocabularies, complete these sentences correctly.

1. The counselors at a camp give __ to the campers.
2. There was a __ supply of food at the picnic.
3. A garment with the trademark *Aquascutum* must be a __.
4. A large crowd went to the meeting in the __.
5. The Romans worshiped many __.

At the upper left are two sides of a small silver coin with a picture of Roma as a person. The silver coin below them shows the head of Julius Caesar. At the right are the two sides of a copper coin showing an emperor's head. On the reverse, notice the letters S P Q R, which stand for Senatus Populusque Romanus, *the People and the Senate of Rome.*

ROMAN COINS

In early days the Romans had no money, but traded grain or oxen for what they needed. The inconvenience of this way of doing business led to the use of rough, unmarked pieces of copper of various weights for trading. Later, bars of copper were cast with the figures of an ox, a pig, or a fowl on both sides, like the large rectangular plate shown below. These plates were Rome's first real money (**pecunia**), named for the cattle (**pecus**) which they represented.

As the commerce of Rome grew, there arose a need for an even more convenient form of money, and round coins came into use. At first these were made only from copper, like the one shown at the upper right, but gold and silver coins also were minted.

Large numbers of coins have been found throughout the regions which were once under Roman control. Some of these have figures of gods and goddesses worshiped by the Romans; some show the pictures of great men of the state, such as emperors or generals. Others commemorate a victory or other important event.

Coins are like footprints left behind by passing generations. Often they lead us to a discovery of interesting facts about the past.

In the early days of Rome, values were estimated at so many oxen. That is why an ox is shown on this crude piece of metal.

XXIX. LIBRI PRETIOSI

Tarquinius Superbus, vir clārus et validus, rēgnum Rōmānum occupāvit. Rōmānī virum superbum nōn amābant; itaque Tarquiniō fīdī nōn erant.

Ōlim Tarquinius prō rēgiā fēminam sōlam vīdit. Fēmina rēgiam 5 spectābat. Vesperī Tarquinius fēminam in rēgiā vīdit. Jam fēmina novem librōs in parvā arcā portābat. Tarquiniō librōs mōnstrāvit, et magnum pretium postulāvit.

Tarquinius rīsit (*laughed*) et dīxit, "Cūr librī tuī sunt pretiōsī? Tibi magnum pretium nōn dabō. Librōs pretiōsōs nōn dēsīderō."

10 Statim fēmina īrāta ē rēgiā Tarquiniī properāvit, sed postrīdiē in rēgiā iterum Tarquiniō librōs mōnstrāvit.

"Nōn jam novem, sed sex librōs habeō," dīxit. "Trēs librōs dēlēvī (*I have destroyed*). Dā mihi pretium novem librōrum, et tibi sex librōs dabō."

15 Tarquinius iterum rīsit, et iterum fēmina īrāta ē rēgiā properāvit.

Postrīdiē fēmina Tarquiniō trēs librōs mōnstrāvit et dīxit, "Aut dabis mihi pretium novem librōrum aut trēs librōs quoque dēlēbō (*I will destroy*)."

Tarquinius erat territus; jam librōs dēsīderābat. Itaque fēminae 20 dīxit, "Dā mihi trēs librōs et tibi pretium novem librōrum dabō."

Posteā Rōmānī templum pretiōsum aedificāvērunt; semper librī pretiōsī erant in templō. Librī Rōmam ē perīculō servābant, quod Rōmānīs arcāna (*secrets*) mōnstrābant. Erant librī Sibyllīnī.

Many artists have painted the Cumaean Sibyl. This is Michelangelo's picture.

aut, *conj.*, or; **aut . . . aut**, either . . . or
jam, *adv.*, now, already; **nōn jam**, no longer
liber, librī, M., book
novem, *not declined*, nine
postrīdiē, *adv.*, on the next day
pretiōsus, -a, -um, expensive, costly
pretium, -ī, N., price
rēgnum, -ī, N., kingdom
sex, *not declined*, six
trēs, M. *and* F. *nom. and acc. pl.*, three

THE ADVERB

We often use a word with a verb to tell how or when an action is done.

He runs swiftly. *They came today.*

The word *swiftly* tells how the act of the verb *runs* is done; the word *today* tells when the act of the verb *came* was done. Such words are called *adverbs.*

Adverbs are also used to tell something about adjectives and even about other adverbs.

too small *very swiftly* *probably right*

In this lesson you meet the Latin adverbs **jam** and **postrīdiē,** which tell when the action of a verb is done. You have already met the adverbs **celeriter, hodiē, ibi, nōn, saepe, satis, ubi,** and many others, which tell something about verbs, adjectives, or other adverbs.

The Latin adverb regularly precedes the word it modifies.

DISTINCTION BETWEEN *nunc* AND *jam*

Both **nunc** and **jam** may be translated *now.* But **nunc** merely indicates a point of time.

Nunc pugnat, *He is fighting now* (*at this moment*).

Jam indicates that something is now true which was not true before.

Jam novem pīrātās necāvit, *He has now* (*by this time* or *already*) *killed nine pirates.*

1. In librīs erant multae fābulae. 2. Quamquam praemia erant magna, nautae hieme nāvigāre nōn dēsīderābant. 3. Virī lēniter ambulābant; celeriter labōrābant. 4. Lūna erat satis clāra, sed vir aurum nōn vīdit. 5. Librī aut in rēgiā aut in templō sunt. 6. Rēgīna in rēgnō pulchrō habitābat, sed nōn erat laeta. 7. Cūr mihi sex librōs dedistī? 8. Postrīdiē fēmina diū ambulābat. 9. Jam puellae ex silvīs ambulābant; erant dēfessae.

1. I shall no longer try to work. 2. The slave is faithful; we will give the faithful slave a reward. 3. A dangerous road is near our house; it is narrow. 4. There are no lamps in the cottage; the cottage is already dark. 5. Either give me the money or give me the books!

What is the date on this building?

For each blank in the sentences below, substitute **nunc** or **jam** and explain your choice.

1. Puella fābulam domī ___ nārrat.
2. Agricola validus sex ursās ___ necāvit.
3. Virī in ōrā maritimā ___ ambulant.
4. Terrae līberae ___ sunt quiētae.
5. Pīrāta gemmās pulchrās nōn ___ habet.
6. Fēmina trēs librōs Tarquiniō ___ dat.

HELP YOURSELF

Write the following words, adding the long marks, dividing each into syllables, and marking the accent.

aedificare	**invidiosorum**	**pretiosus**
consilium	**postridie**	**vesperi**

LATIN LIVES TODAY

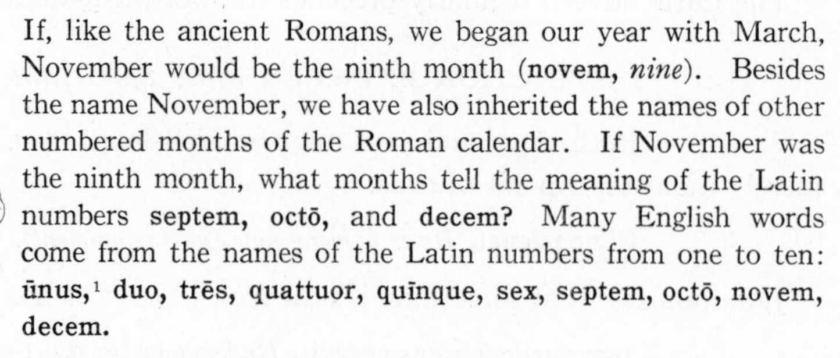

If, like the ancient Romans, we began our year with March, November would be the ninth month (**novem**, *nine*). Besides the name November, we have also inherited the names of other numbered months of the Roman calendar. If November was the ninth month, what months tell the meaning of the Latin numbers **septem, octō,** and **decem?** Many English words come from the names of the Latin numbers from one to ten: **ūnus,**[1] **duo, trēs, quattuor, quīnque, sex, septem, octō, novem, decem.**

The *United* States is *one* nation; its motto is **E pluribus unum,** *From many* (*states*) *one* (*country*).

In a *duet,* how many people are singing? What is a *duel?*

When you have one dollar, if you *triple* the amount, how much money will you have?

What is a *quadruped?*

What are *quintuplets?* What is the difference between a *quintet* and a *sextet?*

How many notes are there in an *octave?* How many sides does an *octagon* have?

You know that it takes twelve to make a *dozen,* but do you know that the word *dozen* comes from the Latin word **duodecim** (from **duo** and **decem**), *two* plus *ten?*

[1] **Ūnus, duo,** and **trēs** are declined; until you learn their declensions you can use **ūnus** only in the nominative singular masculine, **duo** only in the nominative plural masculine and neuter, and **trēs** only in the nominative and accusative plural masculine and feminine. **Quattuor, quīnque, sex, septem, octō, novem,** and **decem** are indeclinable; you can use them with a plural noun in any case.

ROMAN DRESS

Man in toga

For more than a thousand years the *toga* was the characteristic dress of a Roman citizen. Men wore it proudly as a sign of citizenship; no foreigner was permitted to don this garment.

The color was dull white—the natural shade of the wool from which it was woven. A border of crimson or purple on a toga indicated that its wearer was an important official.

The toga was made of a semicircular piece of cloth, and took several yards of material. It was draped about the body and thrown over the left shoulder so that it hung in graceful folds at the back. Since the toga was difficult to adjust, its wearer needed help in putting it on. A wealthy man often had a slave trained to drape his toga.

Under his toga the Roman wore a loose tunic, also of wool, and a pair of shorts. At home a man usually laid aside the toga and wore only his tunic, which was then sometimes belted so that it could be shortened.

In the wardrobe of the Roman woman the outdoor wrap which corresponded to the toga was known as a *palla*. Though it was also a draped, one-piece garment, the palla was less elaborate than the toga. Frequently it was dark colored. A woman wore a tunic similar to a man's and over her tunic she wore a longer garment called a *stola*, which was belted at the waist and hung in folds to her feet. If the tunic had sleeves, the stola was likely to be sleeveless.

While the garments of the Roman woman were not so colorful as women's clothes are today, variety in tint was supplied by the wool of different breeds of sheep. In addition to cloth made from the natural shades of wool in brown, yellow, gray, and black, the Romans had materials that were

Woman in stola and palla

dyed in brighter colors. Among these were several shades of red, violet, and purple.

Although most of the clothing was made of wool, linen was sometimes used for undergarments. In later times, the Romans used cotton and silk as well as linen for some of their outer garments.

A necklace many hundreds of years old and a man's heavily carved seal ring

As a rule, men went bareheaded and, in case of a sudden shower, drew their togas up over their heads. In cold or rainy weather a man wore a wrap with an attached hood. When traveling, a Roman of the upper classes protected his head with a broad-brimmed felt hat. A workingman wore a kind of cap. There were no hats in the wardrobe of a Roman woman. When necessary, she covered her head with a veil or with a fold of her palla.

The chief article of clothing worn by Roman children was the tunic. If they belonged to noble or wealthy families, both boys and girls wore togas with a colored border. When a boy outgrew his childhood, he exchanged his bordered garment for the plain toga of the adult Roman; a girl wore her toga until her marriage.

The shoes worn out-of-doors were made of leather and covered the upper part of the foot as well as the sole. Their color and style varied with the rank and social position of the wearer. Sandals or slippers, with soles of leather or matting, were worn in the house. Some of these were beautifully decorated. The ancients had no socks or stockings.

Such shoes as these were worn by Romans of the upper classes.

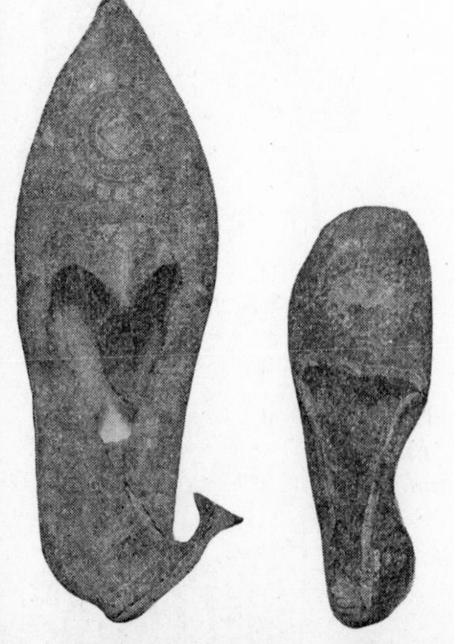

For centuries the Romans scarcely changed the style of their clothing, but they wore their hair in a variety of ways. In early times the men let their hair and their beards grow long. Later, clean-shaven faces and short hair were customary; and then once more it was fashionable to wear full beards. We have portrait busts and statues of distinguished men of Rome with different styles of hair and beard.

Women dressed their hair in many ways and did not hesitate to use plenty of false hair. Most women of fashion wore their hair in waves (see p. 121), but curls were also modish. In those days, too, brunettes who longed to become blondes sometimes had their hair bleached, while others changed the color of their hair with dyes. Make-up also was used; rouge and the Roman equivalent of the eyebrow pencil were part of the beauty kit. There were no beauty parlors in Rome, but the women had slaves to apply their make-up and to dress their hair.

This Roman lady looks as if she might have visited a modern beauty shop.

A Roman man displayed no jewelry except a ring of iron or gold. His ring might be set with a precious stone, but usually it was decorated with a design which could be pressed into soft wax and used as a seal. On the opposite page an ancient seal ring is shown.

Roman women loved jewelry and owned as much of it as they could afford. Their rings, earrings, bracelets, brooches, and necklaces were set with many precious stones and were very costly. The value of the jewels of one Roman empress was equal to about three million dollars in our money. She was described as "covered with emeralds and pearls, gleaming all over her head, hair, ears, neck, and fingers." Some of the skill of ancient craftsmen is revealed in the necklace and bracelet shown here.

Although fashions in hairdressing changed, the toga and stola lasted for centuries. They were the characteristic Roman clothes.

A Roman bracelet rich with jewels

XXX. RAMUS AUREUS

Olim in cavernā propinquā oppidō Cūmīs Sibylla nōta habitābat. Post bellum Trōjānum Aenēās multīs cum virīs ad oppidum Cūmās nāvigāvit.

Hīc Aenēās ante jānuam cavernae Sibyllae stetit et clāmāvit, "Ē 5 rēgnō mortuōrum Anchīsēs, pater (*father*) meus, mē vocat. Mōnstrā mihi viam!"

Sibylla dīxit, "Noctū et interdiū jānua est aperta. Multī in terram mortuōrum properant, sed nōn iterum patriam spectant."

"Māter (*mother*) mea est dea. Dī mē juvābunt," Aenēās clāmāvit.

10 "In silvā propinquā est rāmus aureus," Sibylla dīxit. "Prīmō portā ad mē rāmum aureum. Deinde tibi jānuam terrae mortuōrum mōnstrābō."

Statim Aenēās cum amīcō fīdō in silvam obscūram properāvit. Subitō Aenēās per rāmōs aurum clārum vīdit.

15 "Ecce!" dīxit. "Est rāmus aureus! Dī nōs juvant!"

Laetus rāmum aureum ad cavernam portāvit.

Tum Sibylla clāmāvit, "Dī tē amant. Ecce! Jānua cavernae est aperta; nunc rāmum aureum ad Prōserpinam, rēgīnam mortuōrum, portābimus."

20 Aenēās et Sibylla in cavernam properāvērunt et prīmō per viās perīculōsās et obscūrās ambulāvērunt. Deinde Sibylla rēgiam Prōserpinae mōnstrāvit, et Aenēās rāmum aureum ad jānuam rēgiae portāvit. Dōnum erat rēgīnae grātum.

Itaque trāns agrōs amoenōs ambulāvērunt. Ibi erat pater Anchīsēs. 25 Tum Anchīsēs multa fīliō nārrāvit, et multa in terrā mortuōrum mōnstrāvit.

ad, *prep. with acc.*, to, toward, near
ante, *prep. with acc.*, before, in front of
deinde, *adv.*, then, next
mortuus, -a, -um, dead; M. *as noun*, dead man
per, *prep. with acc.*, through
post, *prep. with acc.*, behind, back of, after
prīmō, *adv.*, at first
rāmus, -ī, M., branch, bough
trāns, *prep. with acc.*, across

When a new preposition is given in the vocabulary, the case with which it is used will be indicated. (For case use with prepositions, see pp. 352-53.)

When the object of a preposition is modified by an adjective, the preposition sometimes stands between the adjective and the word it modifies. Thus, in the second line of the story you see **multīs cum virīs** instead of **cum multīs virīs.**

When Brueghel painted Aeneas and the Sibyl entering the land of the dead, he represented the lower world as full of strange monsters.

CASE USE WITH PREPOSITIONS

The prepositions **ab, cum, dē, ex,** and **in,** as you know, take the ablative case. There are, however, many prepositions with which the accusative is used. In fact, the number of prepositions taking the accusative is larger than the number taking the ablative.

Thus you see that the accusative not only is the case of the direct object of a verb, but is also found with some prepositions. Here you meet five prepositions which take the accusative: **ad,** *to, toward;* **ante,** *before, in front of;* **per,** *through;* **post,** *behind, after;* and **trāns,** *across.*

Per viam ad scholam properat, *He hurries to school through the street.*

Trāns viam est casa, *Across the street is a cottage.*

Hortus est ante templum; nōn est post templum. *The garden is in front of the temple; it is not behind the temple.*

This ancient sculpture shows Aeneas escaping from Troy with his father and his son.

PHRASES WITH *to*

We have seen that the Latin indirect object is in the dative case without a preposition. In English a phrase with the preposition *to* is often used to express the same idea.

Rosam puellae dō, *I give the rose to the girl.*

But when the Latin shows to what place a person or thing moves, it does not use the dative, but the preposition **ad,** followed by the accusative.

Ad silvam properat, *He hastens to the forest.*

In WITH THE ACCUSATIVE

Thus far you have seen the preposition **in** used only with the ablative. The ablative with **in** (meaning *in* or *on*) denotes the place where something is or where some act occurs. The accusative with **in** (meaning *into* or *in*) denotes the place to which motion is directed.

Ablative: **In oppidō habitās,** *You live in the town.*
Accusative: **In oppidum properās,** *You hasten into the town.*

1. Ante bellum; post bellum; per silvam. 2. In templum deī; ante templa deōrum; ante ārās deārum. 3. Per viās; trāns īnsulam; per caelum. 4. Multa bella; bona cōnsilia bellī; ad oppidum; in oppidō. 5. Mūtābō; mūtābit; mūtāvit. 6. Ante jānuam templī; ad oppida; ex oppidīs. 7. Ad silvam nunc properāmus. 8. Sibylla prīmō rāmum aureum postulābit. 9. Deinde vir in terram mortuōrum properābit.

Write each word with an accent and give your reason for placing the accent.

aperta	**postrīdiē**	**sēparat**	**scūtōrum**
Messāna	**properant**	**Sicilia**	**subitō**

Tell which of the phrases with *to* in these sentences will be translated by **ad** with the accusative and which by the dative case alone.

1. I gave the letter to the boy.
2. He is walking to the town.
3. We hurried to the window.
4. The book is not pleasing to your daughter.
5. The boy walked to the house.

Make three sentences of each one by translating the phrases.

1. Virī { *into the forests* / *through the forests* / *in the forests* } ambulābant.
2. Fēmina { *in front of the cottage* / *in the cave* / *back of the temple* } erat.
3. Servus { *into the cavern* / *through the town* / *to the farmhouse* } properāvit.
4. Fīlius { *to the door of the cave* / *through the dim caves* / *to the land of the dead* } ambulābit.

LATIN LIVES TODAY

For each italicized word or phrase below, substitute a word connected with a Latin word that you know.

Jack and Clarence were *strolling* through the park. Since Jack was interested in *farming* and *gardening*, he wanted to *stay* and *look at* the flowers. Clarence wished to visit the zoo. The *water* animals were Clarence's favorites, because of his interest in ships. When the boys saw the sign above the hippopotamus, they laughed. Her name was *Star!*

"What a name for a *beast* with a mouth *like a cave!*" exclaimed Jack.

There was nothing malicious in the *boyish* laughter, but the hippopotamus's face took on a *fighting* look. The boys decided they had *stayed* long enough and hurried away to look at a *figure of a man on horseback*, which was the *gift* of a *well-known* citizen.

XXXI. DAPHNE ET APOLLO

Daphnē, nympha, in silvīs habitābat. Multī nympham amābant quod fōrmam pulchram habēbat, sed Daphnē mātrimōnium nōn probābat.

Daphnē dīxit, "Lībera esse dēsīderō; sōla in silvīs errāre dēsīderō; 5 mātrimōnium nōn probō."

Ōlim deus Apollō in silvā ambulābat. Daphnēn pulchram vīdit, et statim nympham in mātrimōnium dūcere dēsīderābat.

"Tē amō, Daphnē," deus dīxit, "quod Cupīdō mē sagittā vulnerāvit. Sum deus medicīnae, sed jam mē nūlla medicīna juvat. Tē in 10 mātrimōnium dūcere dēsīderō."

Daphnē territa per silvam celeriter properāvit; sed Apollō quoque properāvit. Post multās hōrās Daphnē dēfessa nōn jam properāre temptāvit.

Ōrāvit, "Mē servāte, dī benignī. Mūtāte fōrmam meam. Tum 15 Apollō mē nōn dēsīderābit."

Statim auxiliō deōrum nympha fōrmam mūtāvit. Nōn jam comam sed folia habēbat. Nōn jam bracchia sed rāmōs habēbat. Pulchra Daphnē erat laurus (*laurel tree*).

Deinde Apollō dīxit, "Quamquam nōn jam es nympha, semper tē 20 amābō, Daphnē. Quod es laurus, laurus semper erit arbor (*tree*) mea."

auxilium, -ī, N., help, aid
bracchium, -ī, N., arm
coma, -ae, F., hair
folium, -ī, N., leaf
hōra, -ae, F., hour
mātrimōnium, -ī, N., marriage; **in mātrimōnium dūcere,** to marry (*literally,* to lead into matrimony)
probō, -āre, -āvī, approve, approve of
vulnerō, -āre, -āvī, wound

ENGLISH NOUNS AND LATIN NOUNS

Latin nouns ending in **-um** take various forms in English, but keep much the same meaning. On page 102 you met three kinds of these: nouns alike in the two languages; nouns that do not have the **-um** in English; nouns that end in *-e* where the Latin has **-um** or **-ium.** There are also other kinds.

Some English nouns ending in **-er** are related to Latin nouns ending in **-um:** *sepulcher,* **sepulchrum.**

What is the Latin for *member?*

Non jam bracchia sed ramos habebat.

Some English nouns end in *-y* where the Latin has **-ium**: *matrimony*, **matrimonium.**

What is the Latin for *patrimony?*

Some English nouns from Latin nouns ending in **-ula** or **-ulum** omit **-u-** and have *-e* instead of **-um**: **clavicula,** *clavicle;* **oraculum,** *oracle.*

For each Latin noun give the corresponding English word and explain its meaning.

candelabrum	**fragmentum**	**stabulum**	**tormentum**
decorum	**lamentum**	**tabernaculum**	**vallum** (*v* becomes *w*)
domicilium	**monstrum**	**testimonium**	**vehiculum**

For each English noun give the corresponding Latin noun.

lily (like *matrimony*) *cuticle* (like *clavicle*) *receptacle* (like *oracle*)

ABLATIVE OF MEANS

In the preceding lessons the ablative has been used as the object of certain Latin prepositions. Sometimes, however, the ablative is used without a preposition.

Virī gladiīs pugnābant, *The men were fighting with swords.*

Puer leōnem sagittā necāvit, *The boy killed the lion with an arrow.*

In these sentences **gladiīs** and **sagittā** denote *the means by which* or *with which* an act is done. This use is called the *ablative of means.*

1. Multa folia hīc sunt. 2. Dī fōrmam nymphae probābant. 3. Vir bracchia longa habēbat. 4. Auxiliō amīcī vir dēfessus puerum in casam portāvit. 5. Prīmō vir ursam hastā vulnerāvit; deinde ursam gladiō necāvit. 6. Deus medicīnae nympham amābat, sed Daphnē mātrimōnium nōn probābat. 7. Coma nymphae erat longa et pulchra. 8. Post multās hōrās virī iterum rāmum aureum ad cavernam portāvērunt. 9. Aenēās erat amīcus virī.

Make two sentences of each sentence below, by translating the phrases.

1. Servī (*with swords, with pirates*) pugnābunt.
2. Puer (*with a spear, with the help of a friend*) ursam necāvit.
3. (*With an arrow, In summer*) Cupīdō deum vulnerāvit.
4. Vir vītam fīliī (*with medicine, with the aid of the gods*) servāvit.

HY Find in "Daphnē et Apollō" two ablatives used with a preposition and two ablatives of means.

REVIEW OF UNIT VII LESSONS XXVII–XXXI

Nouns

aurum, -ī
auxilium, -ī
bellum, -ī
bracchium, -ī
*caverna, -ae
coma, -ae
cōnsilium, -ī
cōpia, -ae
deus, -ī
dolus, -ī
folium, -ī
*fōrma, -ae
hōra, -ae
liber, librī
mātrimōnium, -ī
*medicīna, -ae
pretium, -ī
rāmus, -ī
rēgia, -ae
rēgnum, -ī
*rosa, -ae
scūtum, -ī
tabernāculum, -ī
tuba, -ae
vir, virī

Verbs

convocō, -āre
habēbant
īnflō, -āre
mūtō, -āre
probō, -āre
vulnerō, -āre

Adjectives

aureus, -a, -um
mortuus, -a, -um
novem
pretiōsus, -a, -um
sex
trēs

Adverbs

deinde
jam
postrīdiē
prīmō
statim

Conjunctions

aut
quamquam

Prepositions

ad
ante
per
post
trāns

I. Translate the italicized words:

1. They were fighting *with swords.*
2. He is walking *with our friends.*
3. They called the troops together *with a trumpet.*
4. *With the aid of the gods,* the nymph changed her form.
5. *With many troops* he hurried to the town.

II. In the following paragraph find at least five words or phrases that can be translated by Latin adverbs.

Immediately he called together his friends and told them about his plan. At first they did not approve because they were already tired. And so on the next day only nine men wanted to fight. Afterward he again demanded aid. Then many were ready to help, and finally the troops were sufficiently strong.

III. For each blank supply an adjective in the correct form.

1. Scūtum est ___.
2. Pretium erat ___.
3. Cavernae ___ sunt in Ītaliā.
4. Cōnsilia virōrum erant ___.
5. Rāmī ___ sunt aureī.
6. Virī scūta ___, tubās ___, gladiōs ___ habent.
7. Virī ___ sunt in tabernāculīs ___.

IV. Complete each sentence with the correct Latin form.

1. Parvus puer lūnam per ___ videt. (*the branches*)
2. Ursae territae in ___ errābant. (*the woods*)
3. Statua deī ante ___ stat. (*the temple*)
4. Agricola invidiōsus ad ___ properābit. (*the house*)
5. Gladius aureus post ___ erat. (*the tent*)

UNIT VIII

XXXII. DEUCALION ET PYRRHA

Olim virī malī in terrā habitābant. Deōs nōn timēbant; templa deōrum nōn cūrābant.

Itaque Juppiter deōs convocāvit et dīxit, "Quamquam virōs et fēminās monēmus, tamen dōna deīs nōn dant. Nōn jam incolae 5 malī in terrā manēre dēbent."

Tum multa aqua in terrā erat. Diū aqua in terrā manēbat. Mox aqua alta agrōs cēlāvit; in agrīs nūllī virī erant. Aqua alta oppida quoque cēlāvit; in oppidīs nūllī virī et nūllae fēminae erant. Incolae malī erant mortuī.

10 Deucaliōn sōlus erat vir bonus et impiger, et Pyrrha sōla erat fēmina bona et impigra. Itaque dī virum bonum et fēminam bonam servāvērunt.

Dēnique aqua alta nōn jam terram cēlāvit, sed Deucaliōn et Pyrrha nūllōs virōs, nūllās fēminās in terrā vidēbant. Lēniter ambulābant. 15 Caelum et aquam spectābant. Maximē auxilium dēsīderābant.

Templum erat propinquum et Deucaliōn dīxit, "In templum properābimus. Ibi manēbimus et dī nōs juvābunt."

Subitō ōrāculum dīxit, "Jacite (*throw*) ossa mātris (*the bones of your mother*) post terga."

20 Deucaliōn et Pyrrha maximē timēbant. Tum Deucaliōn dīxit, "Dī bonī sunt. Terra est māter (*mother*) nostra. Saxa sunt ossa mātris nostrae."

Ita terra iterum incolas habebat.

Itaque Pyrrha saxa post tergum jēcit (*threw*) et dī saxa in fēminās mūtāvērunt.

Deucaliōn quoque saxa post tergum jēcit et dī saxa in virōs mūtāvērunt. Ita terra iterum incolās habēbat.

altus, -a, -um, deep; high, tall
cūrō, -āre, -āvī, care for, take care of
dēbeō, -ēre, owe, ought; must
impiger, -gra, -grum, industrious
maximē, *adv.*, very much, especially
moneō, -ēre, warn, advise
saxum, -ī, N., stone, rock
tamen, *adv.*, nevertheless
tergum, -ī, N., back, rear

SECOND CONJUGATION

You are familiar with a number of verb forms of the first conjugation.

portat, *he carries* **portābit,** *he will carry*
portābat, *he was carrying, he carried*

Verb forms of the *second conjugation* differ slightly from these.

monet, *he warns* **monēbit,** *he will warn*
monēbat, *he was warning, he warned*

Notice that these second-conjugation forms have **-e-** before the person ending and before the tense sign, where the first conjugation has **-a-**.

The verb **moneō**, of the second conjugation, has the infinitive **monēre.** It is conjugated as follows:

PRESENT

SINGULAR	PLURAL
mo′neō, I warn	**monē′mus,** we warn
mo′nēs, you warn	**monē′tis,** you warn
mo′net, he, she, it warns	**mo′nent,** they warn

FUTURE

SINGULAR	PLURAL
monē′bō, I shall warn	**monē′bimus,** we shall warn
monē′bis, you will warn	**monē′bitis,** you will warn
monē′bit, he, she, it will warn	**monē′bunt,** they will warn

IMPERFECT

SINGULAR	PLURAL
monē′bam, I was warning, I warned	**monēbā′mus,** we were warning, we warned
monē′bās, you were warning, you warned	**monēbā′tis,** you were warning, you warned
monē′bat, he, she, it was warning, he, she, it warned	**monē′bant,** they were warning, they warned

Notice that the person endings are the same as those in the corresponding forms of **portō.**

All verbs which have the infinitive ending in **-ēre** are of the second conjugation and are conjugated like **moneō.** Thus **videō, habeō, maneō,** and **timeō,** forms of which have been used in previous lessons, are of the second conjugation, as well as **moneō** and **dēbeō,** which occur in the vocabulary of this lesson.

PRESENT SYSTEM OF THE SECOND CONJUGATION

As in the first conjugation, the tenses of the present system are formed as follows:

Present = present stem + person endings
Future = present stem + **bi** (**b, bu**) + person endings
Imperfect = present stem + **bā** (**ba**) + person endings

PRESENT IMPERATIVE OF *moneō*

You are familiar with the present imperative of the first conjugation. The imperative of the second conjugation is formed in the same way, using the present stem for the singular and the present stem with the ending **-te** for the plural.

	FIRST CONJUGATION	SECOND CONJUGATION
Singular:	**portā**	**monē**
Plural:	**portāte**	**monēte**

1. Habeō; habitō; habēbam; habēbō; habitābō. 2. Nārrā fābulam, Cornēlia; nārrāte fābulās, puellae. 3. Vidē ursam, Mārce; vidēte ursās, agricolae. 4. In tabernāculō altō manēbimus. 5. Oppida post terga nostra vidēmus; saxa vidēbimus. 6. Amīcōs habēbimus; erimus amīcī. 7. Puerum malum monēre dēbēmus. 8. Amīcī nostrī erunt impigrī. 9. Mē monētis; tamen nōn bene labōrō. 10. Cūrāte rāmōs aureōs et folia aurea.

Find in the list a verb to complete each sentence below.

ambulō dēbēmus manēbunt manēre monēbit necābant necābunt portāte vidēbant vidēbis vidēbunt vident videt

1. Ā tergō vīllam vidēre (*we ought*).
2. Multōs virōs et multās fēminās (*you will see*).
3. Hieme hīc (*they will remain*).
4. Puerōs bonōs (*he will warn*).
5. In vīllā (*to remain*) dēbēmus.
6. Tamen puerī templa deōrum (*see*).
7. Fēminae Americam, patriam pulchram, (*saw*).
8. Virī Britanniam et Eurōpam (*will see*).

Translate the verbs: 1. Bears were wandering in the forests; the farmers were warning the boys about the bears. 2. The industrious slave ought to care for the temple. 3. My friends were very much frightened. 4. I shall stay in the tent; I shall not see the rocks. 5. The large stones are in the water.

HELP YOURSELF

How can you tell first-conjugation verbs from second-conjugation verbs?

Find in "Deucaliōn et Pyrrha" three verbs in the future and tell to what conjugation each belongs.

Find four different verbs in the imperfect and give the person and number of each.

LLT

Complete these sentences with words connected with Latin words new in this lesson.

1. The war — is tremendous.
2. Max was driving at the — speed limit.
3. Her asthma was — by a change of climate.
4. The plane had reached an — of ten thousand feet.
5. People who did not pay their — used to be imprisoned.
6. What can't be — must be endured.

The front seats in a Roman theater were reserved for important persons. Women usually sat in the upper rows.

THE ROMAN THEATER

Rome had only three permanent theaters where plays were presented. These were so large, however, that their combined seating capacity was about fifty thousand. Roman theaters were built in a semicircular form and were open to the sky, as shown in the picture above.

The stage of a Roman theater was large enough to be used for great spectacles with many actors. The scenery for nearly all plays was the same. The high background of the stage usually represented two or three houses, with windows and doors which could be opened or closed. In the late days of the Empire, changes in scenery were possible, but the Roman plays that have come down to us seldom require a shift of scene.

A curtain was used to hide the stage from view before the play began. At the proper time it was rolled down or dropped through a slot in the floor. Thus, for the Roman theater-goer, the falling curtain marked the beginning of the play instead of the end.

All performances were in the daytime, since theaters had no lighting facilities. At one time the plays began in the early afternoon and lasted from two to four hours. Later the morning was sometimes given over to them.

Although the characters in a play naturally included women as well as men, all parts were taken by male actors, who wore masks and costumes to indicate their rôles. Sometimes women appeared on the stage, but only in dances or in pantomimes given between the acts.

Both tragedies and comedies were presented. The comedies were crude and would not please modern people of good taste, but they amused the Romans, who preferred them to tragedies.

Rome had no commercial theaters with regular performances such as our large cities have. Plays were given under the direction of state officials, who hired professional producers. Along with public games and sports, plays were presented on holidays set aside for religious festivals or for the celebration of victories. During the Empire there were about one hundred such holidays in a year. Romans looked forward to festivals and holidays largely because of the public entertainments which marked them.

A Roman actor wore a mask to show the type of rôle he was playing. At the left is a tragic mask, and at the right, a comic one.

XXXIII. PERSEUS ET MEDUSA

Polydectēs fēminam pulchram amābat et in mātrimōnium dūcere dēsīderābat, sed fīlium fēminae timēbat. Fīlius erat Perseus clārus, et Perseus mātrimōnium nōn probāvit quod erat maximē invidiōsus.

5 Amīcī Polydectem monuērunt, "Perseus tē necābit. Perseus prope rēgiam tuam manēre nōn dēbet; in rēgnō tuō habitāre nōn dēbet."

Itaque, quod Polydectēs cum virō perīculōsō in rēgiā habitāre nōn dēsīderāvit, Perseō dīxit, "Hodiē nauta mē dē Medūsā, mōnstrō malō, monuit. Mala Medūsa vīperās habet ubi coma esse dēbet, et 10 faciēs (*face*) Medūsae virōs in saxum mūtat. Validus es; Medūsam necāre dēbēs."

Perseus dīxit, "Medūsam nōn timeō. Mōnstrum necābō."

Deinde auxiliō deōrum Perseus ad terram longinquam ubi Medūsa habitābat properāre parābat. Mercurius tālāria (*winged sandals*) et 15 gladium dedit; Plūtō galeam magicam dedit; Minerva scūtum clārum dedit.

Minerva Perseō dīxit, "Tālāria tē trāns terram et aquam celeriter portābunt; galea magica tē obscūrum faciet (*will make*); scūtum tē ā perīculō servābit. Medūsa tē in saxum nōn mūtābit. Tē nōn vidē- 20 bit, sed Medūsam in scūtō clārō vidēbis. Gladiō Medūsam necābis."

Medusa viperas habet ubi coma esse debet.

Perseus dōna probāvit et statim ad terram longinquam Medūsae volāvit. Ibi mōnstrum in scūtō clārō vīdit. Gladiō Medūsam 25 celeriter necāvit.

Deinde iterum ad rēgiam volāvit ubi Polydectēs habitābat. Perseus caput (*head*) Medūsae portāvit. Polydectēs caput spectāvit. Nōn 30 jam vir sed statua erat quod statim faciēs mōnstrī Polydectem in saxum mūtāvit.

galea, -ae, F., helmet
longinquus, -a, -um, distant
magicus, -a, -um, magic
prope, *prep. with acc.*, near
volō, -āre, -āvī, fly

PERFECT TENSE OF THE SECOND CONJUGATION

In Lesson XIX we saw that the forms of the perfect are made up of the perfect stem, with special endings which are used in no other tense. The formation of this tense is the same for all Latin verbs.

To make the perfect tense of the second conjugation, we simply add the perfect endings to the perfect stem, as we did for **portō**.

The verb **moneō** is conjugated as follows in the perfect tense:

SINGULAR	PLURAL
mo′nuī, I warned, have warned	**monu′imus,** we warned, have warned
monuis′tī, you warned, have warned	**monuis′tis,** you warned, have warned
mo′nuit, he, she, it warned, *etc.*	**monuē′runt,** they warned, *etc.*

The perfects of **timeō** and **habeō** are like that of **moneō.** The perfect of **maneō** is **mānsī, mānsistī,** etc.; that of **videō** is **vīdī, vīdistī,** etc.

1. Multōs pīrātās vīdimus; pīrātae galeās et scūta habuērunt. 2. Vir malus prope tabernāculum mānsit. 3. Mē dē perīculō monuistī. 4. Post multās hōrās oppidum iterum vīdistis. 5. Cōnsilium bellī erat bonum, sed nautae perīculum timuērunt. 6. Multī statim ex oppidō longinquō ad templum properāvērunt. 7. Nautās dē perīculō monēre dēbētis. 8. In vīllā manēre nōn dēbēmus. 9. Perseus ad terrās longinquās volāvit. 10. Auxiliō galeae magicae fēminam malam necāvit.

Translate the verbs: 1. The man had a magic helmet. 2. We saw many farmers in the distant fields, but they did not see us. 3. You warned the boys. 4. With the aid of the gods he flew to a distant land. 5. We ought to warn our friends. 6. The farmer feared the slave. 7. The girl has beautiful hair. 8. Your friends were standing near the water.

HY Name the tense of each verb in "Perseus et Medūsa" and give the reason for your decision.

LLT What does a *magician* do? Perhaps someone you know has a *magic* lantern. Why is it so called?

Do you know what *volatile* gases are and what safety rules to observe when near them? A recent word in our language is *volplane,* meaning to glide toward the earth in an airplane without using motor power. In tennis what is a *volley?*

XXXIV. CENTUM PIRATAE!

Pīrātae semper ab incolīs prōvinciārum timentur. Saepe parva oppida ā pīrātīs oppugnantur; agrī agricolārum vāstantur. Fābula ā Sextō, agricolā prōvinciae Siciliae, saepe nārrātur.

Pīrātae frūmentum Siciliae dēsīderant; magna castra in ōrā maritimā 5 īnsulae nostrae habent. In castrīs est Seleucus, pīrāta malus.

Quamquam dē magnō perīculō monēmur, tamen in agrīs labōrāmus; sed puerī et puellae vigilant. Castra pīrātārum ab agricolīs et ā puerīs nōn videntur.

Fīlia mea sōla pīrātās videt et clāmat, "Pīrātās videō. Properāte, 10 puerī, ad agrōs; vocāte agricolās!"

Ex agrīs properāmus. Ab incolīs oppidī propinquī et ā nautīs juvāmur. Incolae bona arma, scūta lāta, galeās validās habent. Bona arma portāmus, sed nūllās galeās et nūlla scūta habēmus. Cum pīrātīs diū et ācriter pugnāmus.

15 Dēnique clāmō, "Ubi est Seleucus? Mihi Seleucum mōnstrāte! Sōlus Seleucum necābō."

Sed Seleucus abest (*is absent*). Pīrātae male pugnant; multī necantur. Sōlus centum pīrātās necō.

Posteā castra ā Rōmānīs occupantur et Seleucus gladiō necātur. 20 Dux (*general*) mē laudat. Dīcit, "Siciliam, Sexte, servāvistī!"

ācriter, *adv.*, fiercely
arma, -ōrum, N. *pl.*, arms, weapons, tools
castra, -ōrum, N. *pl.*, camp
centum, *not declined*, one hundred
lātus, -a, -um, wide, broad
male, *adv.*, badly
oppugnō, -āre, -āvī, attack
vāstō, -āre, -āvī, destroy, devastate
vigilō, -āre, -āvī, watch, keep awake

USE OF PASSIVE VOICE

The following two sentences both have the word *boy* as subject, since in each sentence we assert something about the boy.

The boy helps his friend. The boy is helped by his friend.

In the first sentence the subject does the act, that is, he helps someone; in the second sentence something is done to the subject. A verb which denotes something that the subject does is in the *active voice.* A verb which denotes something done to the subject by another person or thing is in the *passive voice.* In the illustrative sentences given above, *helps* is in the active voice and *is helped* is in the passive voice.

Today the blue water of the Bay of Naples looks much as it did in Roman times.

PRESENT PASSIVE OF *portō* AND *moneō*

Thus far all the verb forms you have met have been in the active voice. In Latin, just as in English, there is a passive voice. The verbs **portō** and **moneō** are conjugated as follows in the present passive:

SINGULAR

por′tor, I am carried	**mo′neor,** I am warned
portā′ris,[1] you are carried	**monē′ris,** you are warned
portā′tur, he, she, it is carried	**monē′tur,** he, she, it is warned

PLURAL

portā′mur, we are carried	**monē′mur,** we are warned
portā′minī, you are carried	**monē′minī,** you are warned
portan′tur, they are carried	**monen′tur,** they are warned

These forms may also be translated *I am being carried, I am being warned,* etc.

[1]To the Teacher: The form of the second person singular ending in -re is not used in the exercises of this book.

PASSIVE ENDINGS

As you see from the conjugations above, the person endings used in the passive voice are as follows:

	SINGULAR	PLURAL
First Person:	**-or (-r)**[1]	**-mur**
Second Person:	**-ris**	**-minī**
Third Person:	**-tur**	**-ntur**

In the active voice we have seen that the vowel **-ā-** or **-ē-** of the stem becomes short before the person endings **-t** and **-nt.** The **-ā-** disappears before **-ō,** and the **-ē-** becomes short. In the passive voice the **-ā-** and **-ē-** become short before the ending **-ntur.** The **-ā-** disappears before **-or,** and the **-ē-** becomes short.

ā OR *ab* MEANING *by*

In Lesson XIV you met the word **ā** or **ab,** used to mean *from.* But *from* is not the only meaning of this preposition. In "Centum Pīrātae!" you find **ā** or **ab** used to mean *by.*

Pīrātae semper ab incolīs prōvinciārum timentur, *Pirates are always feared by the inhabitants of the provinces.*

With passive verbs the person by whom the act is done is expressed by the ablative with the preposition **ā** or **ab,** meaning *by.*

Epistulae ā puerō portantur, *The letters are carried by the boy.*

This use is called the *ablative of agent.*

1. Magnum templum ā pīrātīs vāstātur; agricolae nōn vigilant. 2. Scūtum lātum ab agricolā validō portātur; agricola ā servō impigrō nōn timētur. 3. Ab amīcīs meīs laudor; ab amīcō meō nōn timeor. 4. Ā virīs validīs nōn timēris; ā virō validō laudāris. 5. Bona arma ā nautīs portantur; pīrātae ab amīcīs monentur. 6. Castra pīrātārum sunt oppidō propinqua. 7. Ā puerīs monēmur; ā fēminīs territīs vocāmur. 8. Cūr male labōrās? Male labōrō quod sum dēfessus. 9. Ā cōpiīs pīrātārum timēminī; ab incolīs īnsulārum laudāminī. 10. Oppida ā pīrātīs ācriter oppugnantur; centum oppida vāstantur.

[1] The use of the person ending **-r** instead of **-or** will be seen later.

These silver plates, recently dug up in England, were used by Romans about sixteen hundred years ago.

Change the verbs to passive and make other necessary changes: 1. Pīrātae terrās nostrās saepe vāstant. 2. Centum virī castra vāstant. 3. Virī castra Rōmāna ācriter oppugnant. 4. Virī praemia puerīs et puellīs dant. 5. Cōpiae nostrae arma bona portant.

HELP YOURSELF

Find in the story two uses of **castra.** When **castra** is the subject of a verb, what is the number of the verb? What is the number of an adjective modifying **castra?**

Nearly all the verbs in "Centum Pīrātae" are in the present tense. As used in this story, these forms are said to be the *historical,* or *vivid, present.* Can you see why each of these names fits?

LLT

We have several English words related to **arma:** (*to*) *arm, army, armament,* war equipment and supplies, *armor, armory,* place where weapons are kept, *armadillo,* the little burrowing animal that was so named because of its *armor*-like outer covering. (*Arm,* a part of the body, is not connected with **arma.**)

In England, there are many place names dating back to the Roman occupation, which started in 43 A.D. These appear in the names of towns that grew up around military camps (**castra**), as *Chester, Colchester, Manchester, Winchester, Gloucester, Worcester, Lancaster.*

XXXV. ARACHNE ET MINERVA

Arachnē erat puella pulchra. Haec puella pallās mīrās texēbat (*used to weave*). In hīs pallīs erant multae pictūrae.

Ōlim nymphae hās pictūrās spectābant et clāmāvērunt, "Es puella beāta. Dea Minerva tibi auxilium dat!"

5 Sed Arachnē superba clāmāvit, "Nūllum auxilium ab hāc deā mihi datur. Minervam superābō. Hanc deam ad certāmen (*contest*) prōvocō."

"Arachnē deam timēre dēbet," Minerva ācriter dīxit. "Ad tēctum hujus puellae superbae properābō et cōnsilium mūtāre temptābō."

10 Sed ubi Minerva ante jānuam tēctī stetit, Arachnē nōn deam, sed fēminam miseram vīdit.

"Deam nōn prōvocāre dēbēs; Minerva īrāta est," fēmina dīxit.

Sed Arachnē clāmāvit, "Haec dea mē timet. Populus meās pallās et pictūrās laudat. Populusne deam Minervam laudat?"

15 Nōn jam fōrma fēminae miserae deam cēlāvit. "Dea Minerva sum," dīxit.

Tamen Arachnē superba nōn erat territa, et cōnsilium nōn mūtāvit.

Itaque Minerva et Arachnē pallās texuērunt (*wove*). In pallā deae erant pictūrae bonōrum factōrum deōrum et deārum. Sed in
20 pallā puellae superbae erant pictūrae malōrum factōrum deōrum et deārum.

Minerva īrāta clāmāvit, "Palla tua est pulchra, sed es mala et superba. Quod mala es, tē in arāneam mūtābō."

Dea puellam pulchram in arāneam mūtāvit. Itaque hodiē arāneae semper texunt (*are weaving*).

arānea, -ae, F., spider
beātus, -a, -um, happy
factum, -ī, N., deed
hic, haec, hoc, this
mīrus, -a, -um, remarkable, strange
palla, -ae, F., cloak, robe; curtain
populus, -ī, M., people
prōvocō, -āre, -āvī, challenge
tēctum, -ī, N., house

The diphthong **ui** as in **huic** is pronounced almost like *ui* in *ruin*, but the **u** is shorter and the two sounds are more closely blended.

DECLENSION OF *hic*

The English word *this* has only two forms: *this*, singular, and *these*, plural. The Latin **hic**, *this*, has different forms for the different cases and genders.

	SINGULAR			PLURAL		
	MASC.	FEM.	NEUT.	MASC.	FEM.	NEUT.
Nom.	**hic**	**haec**	**hoc**	**hī**	**hae**	**haec**
Gen.	**hu'jus**	**hu'jus**	**hu'jus**	**hō'rum**	**hā'rum**	**hō'rum**
Dat.	**huic**	**huic**	**huic**	**hīs**	**hīs**	**hīs**
Acc.	**hunc**	**hanc**	**hoc**	**hōs**	**hās**	**haec**
Abl.	**hōc**	**hāc**	**hōc**	**hīs**	**hīs**	**hīs**

1. Hī puerī; cum hōc puerō; cum hīs puerīs. 2. In hōc oppidō; in hīs oppidīs. 3. Hae fēminae; hārum fēminārum; cum hāc fēminā. 4. Haec via est perīculōsa. 5. Hoc factum amāmus; hanc fābulam amātis; hunc librum amās. 6. Populus pallam mīram hujus deae laudāvit. 7. Huic puellae benigna est. 8. Praemium huic puerō beātō dedī. 9. Haec puella deam beātam prōvocāvit. 10. Puella deam superāvit. 11. Arāneae in hōc tēctō parvō erant. 12. Pallae hujus deae sunt mīrae.

In each phrase or sentence supply a form of **hic**: 1. Cum __ pallā; cum __ amīcīs; cum __ nautā. 2. __ amīcī; __ amīcōrum; __ puellae. 3. In __ tēctum; in __ tēctīs; ex __ tēctō. 4. __ populus __ rānās superābat. 5. __ palla nova __ deae grāta nōn est. 6. __ erat magnum factum; populus __ terrae factum laudāvit.

Arachnida

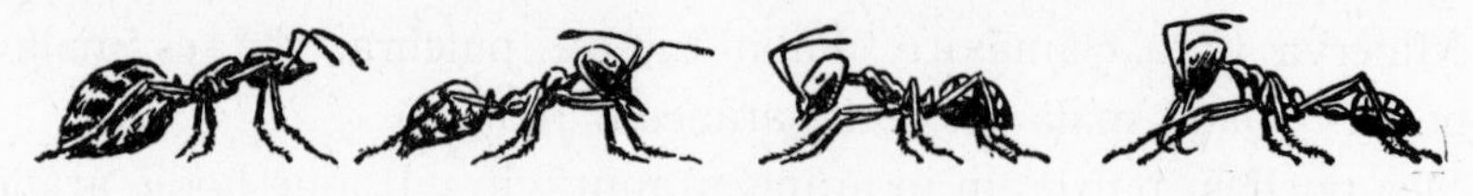

Formicidae

XXXVI. AEACUS ET FORMICAE

Aeacus rēx (*king*) erat bonus vir; semper populum juvāre dēsīderābat. Populus Aeacum benignum amābat et laudābat. Quamquam incolae oppidōrum multam pecūniam nōn habēbant, tamen bene labōrābant et laetī erant.

5 Sed subitō magna pestilentia terram invāsit (*swept over*). Incolae aegrī erant et nōn jam in agrīs labōrābant. Dēnique haec pestilentia virōs, fēminās, puerōs, puellās necāvit. Jam terra nūllōs incolās habēbat.

Aeacus benignus maximē dolēbat. Sine morā ad templum Jovis 10 properāvit. Ante āram ita ōrāvit: "Ō Juppiter, magna pestilentia populum meum necāvit. Aut dā mihi populum novum aut necā mē quoque!"

Prope templum erat alta quercus (*oak tree*). In rāmīs erant multae formīcae; hae formīcae ad tēcta sua (*their*) cibum portābant.

15 Aeacus diū formīcās spectābat et dīxit, "Quam multae sunt hae formīcae! Sed oppida mea nūllōs incolās habent."

Tum ad rēgiam lēniter ambulāvit.

Noctū Aeacus in somniō quercum iterum videt. Iterum formīcās videt, sed nunc formīcae cibum nōn portant. Per rāmōs ambulant et 20 ā rāmīs cadunt (*are falling*).

Tamen in terrā fōrmam formīcārum nōn diū habent; lēniter in virōs et in fēminās mūtantur.

Postrīdiē Aeacus sonum novum prō rēgiā audīvit. Statim rēx ē rēgiā properāvit. Ante tēctum multī virī et multae fēminae 25 stābant.

Ubi Aeacum vīdērunt, clāmābant, "Erimus incolae agrōrum tuōrum et oppidōrum tuōrum. Rēx noster eris."

aeger, -gra, -grum, sick, ill
audīvit, heard
cibus, -ī, M., food
doleō, -ēre, -uī, grieve, grieve for
formīca, -ae, F., ant
mora, -ae, F., delay
quam, *adv.*, how, as, than
sine, *prep. with abl.*, without
somnium, -ī, N., dream
sonus, -ī, M., sound, noise

ENGLISH NOUNS AND LATIN NOUNS

Some English nouns come from second-declension Latin nouns in **-us**.

Many of these nouns are alike in English and Latin: *campus, discus.*

Other English nouns do not have the **-us**: *digit,* **digitus.** What is the Latin for *elephant?*

Some nouns have *-e* instead of **-us**: *mode,* **modus.** What is the Latin for *captive?*

Give the English for each Latin noun listed below. In some cases the meaning, though closely related, is not quite the same. If you are in doubt as to the exact meaning of a Latin word, look it up in the reference vocabulary at the back of this book; for an English word, see an English dictionary.

alienus	**architectus**	**fumus**
angelus	**circus**	**Neptunus**

1. Quam saepe facta bona Aeacī ab hīs amīcīs laudantur! 2. In hōc somniō Aeacus sonum mīrum audīvit. 3. Virī dolēbant quod populus erat aeger. 4. Haec scūta in bellō ā cōpiīs portantur. 5. Hoc oppidum viās lātās habet; in hīs viīs nautae saepe videntur. 6. Castra nostra sunt lāta et longa. 7. In hōc rēgnō populus pestilentiā mīrā necātur. 8. Sine sonō hic cibus ē tēctō ā formīcīs portātur. 9. Dea ab hāc puellā prōvocātur. 10. Noctū multī pīrātae ā nautīs videntur, sed sine morā superantur.

Complete each sentence with the correct verb form or forms: 1. Saepe ab amīcīs meīs (*you* [*pl.*] *are being praised*). 2. Ab amīcīs meīs nōn (*you* [*sing.*] *are being warned*). 3. Oppida nostra ā pīrātīs saepe (*are being devastated*). 4. Pīrātae ab incolīs (*are being warned*). 5. Pīrāta in oppidō nostrō interdum (*is seen*). 6. Magnum praemium ā nautīs (*is expected*) quod pīrātās (*they killed*).

HW

In the first four sentences which you completed with verb forms, change the verbs from passive to active voice and make other necessary changes.

LLT

Connected with **doleo** is the adjective *doleful.* How do you look when you feel *doleful?*

The word *unison* is a combination of **unus** and **sonus.** When several people say the same thing at the same time, they speak in *unison.*

XXXVII. VICTORIA PYRRHI

Olim Pyrrhus cum cōpiīs Graecīs ad Ītaliam nāvigāvit. Ad oppidum Graecum, Tarentum, auxilium portābat, quod Tarentīnī cum populō Rōmānō pugnābant. Quamquam Tarentum erat in Ītaliā, tamen incolae Tarentī erant Graecī.

5 Tarentīnī cum Rōmānīs saepe pugnābant. Nunc auxilium maximē dēsīderābant.

Itaque Pyrrhus ad Ītaliam cōpiās Graecās portāvit. In cōpiīs Graecōrum erant multī sagittāriī et funditōrēs (*slingers*). Virī gladiōs longōs, hastās, scūta, galeās habēbant.

10 Rōmānī quoque bona arma—jacula, pīla, galeās, scūta, gladiōs—habēbant, sed gladiī Rōmānōrum nōn erant longī. Rōmānī multōs equōs habēbant, et interdum in proeliō equitēs (*cavalrymen*) ā dextrā et ā sinistrā stābant.

In magnō proeliō Rōmānī cum Pyrrhō ācriter pugnāvērunt, sed 15 dolus novus Pyrrhum in hōc proeliō jūvit. Pyrrhus multōs elephantōs habuit. Elephantī erant magnī; in tergīs elephantōrum erant parva tēcta ubi virī stābant. Virī in dextrīs longās et acūtās hastās et longās sagittās habēbant.

Rōmānī hastās et sagittās minimē timēbant, sed elephantōs maximē 20 timēbant. Equī Rōmānōrum quoque novōs elephantōs timēbant. Itaque equī territī fūgērunt (*fled*); multōs Rōmānōs equī territī et elephantī necāvērunt.

Quamquam dolus novus Pyrrhō victōriam dedit, tamen in hōc proeliō Rōmānī quoque multōs Graecōs necāvērunt. Itaque Pyrrhus 25 magnam victōriam nūntiāvit; tamen victōria Pyrrhī fuit pretiōsa.

acūtus, -a, -um, acute, sharp
dextra, -ae, F., right hand; **ā dextrā,** on the right
jaculum, -ī, N., javelin
nūntiō, -āre, -āvī, announce
pīlum, -ī, N., spear
proelium, -ī, N., battle
sagittārius, -ī, M., archer
sinistra, -ae, F., left hand; **ā sinistrā,** on the left

This ancient plate commemorates the victory of Pyrrhus.

Give the correct form of **hic** for each blank in the following sentences and translate the completed sentences.

1. ___ pīlum est longum et acūtum.
2. Cūr in ___ proeliō sine pīlō pugnās?
3. Interdum ___ sagittārium in oppidō vidēmus.
4. Vīta ___ virī est maximē perīculōsa.
5. Puerō ___ jaculum dedī; sagittāriō ___ jacula dedistī.
6. ___ pīlum, ___ sagittam, ___ gladium vīdimus.

Find in the list of Latin phrases one that completes each sentence correctly.

ā dextrā	**haec jacula**	**hōrum poētārum**	**in silvīs**
ā sinistrā	**hujus morae**	**in proeliō**	**virī et puerī**

1. Sagittāriī ā sinistrā stetērunt; elephantī ___ stetērunt.
2. Prīmō ___ Pyrrhus Rōmānōs elephantīs superāvit.
3. Hodiē librī ___ nōn laudantur.
4. Amīcus tuus causam ___ nūntiābit.
5. ___ sunt viae lātae; ā dextrā sunt hortī.
6. Quam longa et acūta ___ sunt!

By translating the phrases which follow, make three sentences of each one.

1. Hodiē ___ ad scholam properābunt.
   these boys *these girls* *these women*
2. Populus ___ benignus erat.
   to this girl *to this poet* *to these spiders*
3. Pallae ___ pulchrae sunt.
   of these goddesses *of this girl* *of these women*
4. Magna victōria ___ nūntiātur.
   by this man *by these Romans* *by this boy*
5. ___ proelium maximē timēbant.
   These elephants *These archers* *These men*

LLT

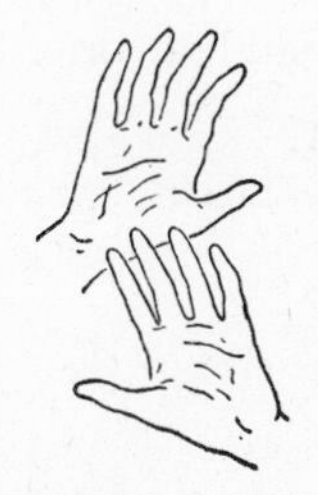

The English word *acute* comes from the Latin **acutus.** Do dogs have an *acute* sense of smell? What is an *acute* headache?

Our English words *dexterity* and *sinister* have an interesting story. It used to be thought that one could do things correctly only with the right hand; hence the word *dexterous*, meaning "skillful." Accordingly, what was done with the left hand was considered unskillful. From this reasoning came the word *sinister*, meaning, first, "left," then "evil," and now "threatening." What is a *sinister* expression?

REVIEW OF UNIT VIII LESSONS XXXII-XXXVII

Nouns	*Nouns*	*Verbs*	*Adjectives*
arānea, -ae	proelium, -ī	audīvit	acūtus, -a, -um
arma, -ōrum	sagittārius, -ī	cūrō, -āre	aeger, -gra, -grum
castra, -ōrum	saxum, -ī	dēbeō, -ēre	altus, -a, -um
cibus, -ī	sinistra, -ae	doleō, -ēre	beātus, -a, -um
dextra, -ae	somnium, -ī	moneō, -ēre	centum
*elephantus, -ī	sonus, -ī	nūntiō, -āre	hic, haec, hoc
factum, -ī	tēctum, -ī	oppugnō, -āre	impiger, -gra, -grum
formīca, -ae	tergum, -ī	prōvocō, -āre	lātus, -a, -um
galea, -ae	*victōria, -ae	vāstō, -āre	longinquus, -a, -um
jaculum, -ī	*vīpera, -ae	vigilō, -āre	magicus, -a, -um
*monstrum		volō, -āre	mīrus, -a, -um
mora, -ae	*Adverbs*		
*ōrāculum, -ī	ācriter		
palla, -ae	male		
*pestilentia, -ae	maximē	*Prepositions*	
pīlum, -ī	quam	prope	
populus, -ī	tamen	sine	

I. Choose the ending which completes each sentence correctly.

1. The infinitive of a second-conjugation verb has the ending { -ere. / -ēre. / -āre. }
2. The present stem of a first-conjugation verb ends in { -ē-. / -e-. / -ā-. }
3. The plural imperative of a second-conjugation verb ends in { -āte. / -ete. / -ēte. }
4. The singular imperative of a first-conjugation verb ends in { -ete. / -ā. / -āte. }

II. Give the correct Latin phrase for each English one.

1. Populus beātus (*to these houses*) properābat.
2. Galeae (*to these archers*) nōn grātae sunt.
3. Hic sonus (*to sick people*) nōn grātus est.
4. Haec pīla et jacula (*to this man*) dantur.
5. Volāte celeriter (*to the distant kingdom*).

III. For each blank substitute **ā, ab, ē, ex,** or **dē.**

1. Tamen sagittāriī ___ proeliō properāre dēbuērunt.
2. Cum ___ tergō castra ācriter oppugnantur, populus ___ oppidīs properat.
3. Monēte populum ___ hōc somniō.
4. Arma acūta ___ hōc virō portantur.
5. Centum agrī ___ virīs malīs vāstantur.

IV. Select the correct form and tell why you chose it.

1. Sine morā populus ā servō impigrō
   - moneor.
   - monentur.
   - monētur.
2. Cibus ā populō maximē
   - postulābat.
   - postulātur.
   - postulāvit.
3. Sagittārius prope saxum lātum et altum
   - prōvocāvī.
   - prōvocātur.
   - prōvocantur.
4. Quam male hoc tēctum ā fīliīs
   - aedificāris!
   - aedificātur!
   - aedificābit!
5. Ubi vir haec facta mīra nūntiābat, fēminae
   - dolēbat.
   - doluērunt.
   - dolētur.

LATIN LIVES TODAY

Read the following story and tell to what Latin word each italicized word is related.

One day *Beatrice* and *Clara* went to the movies. They paid forty *cents* for a double feature. The travel *picture* showed scenes in *Argentina* and in *Manchester*, England. The *people* of *Argentina* were dressed like those in the *United* States. In *Manchester* it seemed as if the entire *population* had turned out to watch a circus parade. Beside a *magnificent elephant* ran a clown, balancing balls with great *dexterity*. The *elephant* was followed by *six* white horses.

The main feature of the movie was a *superb* picture in which appeared two *famous* stars. Other actors were a *sinister*-looking villain and a *dexterous janitor*, who did *magic* tricks with his tools. He pretended his dust mop was a *tuba*. He also talked in a strange *lingo*. A *popular* actor finally brought about the downfall of the villain, and the story ended happily.

FURNISHINGS OF A ROMAN HOUSE

While this kitchen stove is built of stone, iron cookstoves have also been found.

The Romans were faced with problems of providing heat, water, and light for their homes just as we are today. That they were able to solve at least two of these problems in ways which we consider quite modern is shown by a study of the houses in which they lived and the furnishings which they used.

For example, we know that in the colder provinces large houses had furnaces which supplied heat to the rooms by means of hollow tiles in the floors and walls. Such furnaces were not in general use in Italy because of the milder climate. A common source of heat was a small charcoal stove, made of metal, which could be carried from room to room. In the homes of the wealthy, small furnaces were used to heat the bathrooms and occasionally a few other rooms.

Like a modern electric heater, this Roman stove could be carried where warmth was needed.

The plumbing which supplied the houses with running water was surprisingly modern. Lead pipes have been found in Rome inscribed with the names of the men into whose homes they ran. From a main in the street, water was brought to the kitchen and baths and to fountains in the courtyard and atrium. Only well-to-do Romans, however, had the convenience of running water in their homes. Those who lived in small houses or in apartments usually had to carry water from public fountains in the streets.

By our standards, the problem of providing light was not solved satisfactorily by the Romans. They used lamps which were merely containers holding olive oil or animal fat, with wicks of loosely twisted thread. Some lamps had handles by which they were carried; others were suspended from the ceiling by chains. Often several lamps were hung on a tall stand, giving the effect of a modern floor lamp. A Roman lamp probably supplied about as much light as a small candle.

This strongly built table was probably intended to support a marble statue.

According to our ideas, the rooms in a Roman house would seem bare, for there was little furniture. However, what furniture there was—mostly chairs, couches, tables, lamps, chests—was of fine quality. In addition a rich man might spend a fortune in decorating his house—the walls with paintings and marble panels, the floors with mosaics, and the rooms with statues, glassware, and articles of silver and gold (p. 37).

Although the Romans had fine chairs of wood, bronze, iron, and marble, none of them would be considered comfortable today. Their only easy chair was armless, but its back fitted the curve of the body. The ordinary seat for one person was a stool, one style of which folded up like a modern camp chair and was portable.

Since a Roman reclined not only at meals but also when engaged in tasks at which a modern man would sit, there were a number of couches in his house. Couches were used, too, as beds, but these were much larger than the others and often so high that it was necessary to use a stool to climb into one of them. There were mattresses on the couches, and cushions and coverings on both chairs and couches, but there was no such upholstering as we have.

Roman tables were of different shapes and materials, according to the purpose for which they were used. In addition to dining tables, there were tables on which dishes, lamps, toilet articles, or pieces of statuary were placed. Some of our modern tables resemble these tables of long ago.

It must have taken a great deal of water to fill this seven-foot bronze bathtub.

At the left is an old Roman lamp on a bronze stand. The pieces of glassware at the right are good examples of the beautiful objects of art to be found in the home of a rich Roman.

Much of our knowledge about the furnishings and decorations of the Roman house has been gained from the excavations in Pompeii and Herculaneum. Metal furniture has survived, and utensils of bronze and earthenware which have been found show that the Roman kitchen was equipped for different kinds of cookery. Many wall paintings (pp. 33, 74, 109, 176, 308, 310), beautiful mosaics (pp. 13, 44, 46, 47, 185), and numerous objects of art (pp. 85, 123) have been uncovered. In a villa near Pompeii over one hundred silver dishes were found.

From time to time, other treasures have been discovered in different parts of the Roman Empire. A few years ago some fine pieces of Roman silverware (p. 143) were plowed up in England on a farm which must have been the site of a Roman villa.

The ancient Roman seldom did much to beautify the outside of his house. A person walking down a street would see for the most part only plain stucco walls. But once he crossed the threshold of a fine house, he found beautiful decorations and furnishings.

Twelve eggs could be served in the silver dish at the right. This egg dish and the goblets at the left look quite modern.

The ant and the grasshopper as a modern artist drew them

UNIT IX

XXXVIII. FORMICA ET CICADA

In Americā formīcae sunt parvae, sed in Āfricā multae formīcae sunt magnae et validae. Illae formīcae interdum sunt perīculōsae quod magna spīcula (*stings*) habent. Formīcae nostrae nōn sunt perīculōsae quod sunt parvae et spīcula parva habent.

Interdum formīcās in tēctīs nostrīs vidēmus. Cum hās formīcās vidēmus, īrātī sumus. Sunt multae formīcae in agrīs et in hortīs. Multae formīcae tēcta sub terrā habent. Formīcae sunt impigrae; aestāte frūmentum ex agrīs in haec tēcta portant. 5

Fābula nōta dē formīcā et cicādā saepe nārrātur.

Aestāte formīca bene labōrābat; multum cibum ad tēctum portābat. Prope tēctum formīcae cicāda pulchra in agrīs habitābat. Aestāte cicāda nōn labōrābat; semper cantābat. Itaque hieme formīca impigra cibum habēbat; erat laeta. Sed jam cicāda pigra cibum nōn habēbat; erat misera. 10

Dēnique cicāda misera sub terram ad tēctum formīcae properāvit; formīca domī erat. Cicāda clāmāvit; lacrimāvit; auxilium ōrāvit. Sed formīca impigra cicādam pigram in tēctum nōn invītāvit. In illō tēctō erat magna cōpia cibī, sed formīca cicādae nūllum cibum dedit. 15

Formīca cicādam miseram spectāvit et dīxit: "Quam pigra es! Aestāte labōrō; aestāte nōn labōrās. Hieme cibum habeō; hieme cibum nōn habēs." 20

cantō, -āre, -āvī, sing
cicāda, -ae, F., grasshopper, locust
ille, illa, illud, that
invītō, -āre, -āvī, invite
lacrimō, -āre, -āvī, weep, cry
piger, -gra, -grum, lazy
sub, *prep. with acc. or abl.*, under, below

THE PREPOSITION *sub*

When used in expressions which denote motion, **sub** takes the accusative. When used in expressions where there is no idea of motion, but only rest or existence, it takes the ablative.

Formīca sub terram ad tēctum properat, *The ant is hastening under the ground to her house.*

Tēcta formīcārum sub terrā sunt, *The houses of ants are under the ground.*

THE DEMONSTRATIVE *ille*

You have already learned how to decline the word **hic,** *this.* This word points out something, and so it is called a demonstrative adjective.

Another Latin demonstrative is **ille,** *that* (plural, *those*). It is declined as follows:

	SINGULAR			PLURAL		
	MASC.	FEM.	NEUT.	MASC.	FEM.	NEUT.
Nom.	il′le	il′la	il′lud	il′lī	il′lae	il′la
Gen.	illī′us	illī′us	illī′us	illō′rum	illā′rum	illō′rum
Dat.	il′lī	il′lī	il′lī	il′līs	il′līs	il′līs
Acc.	il′lum	il′lam	il′lud	il′lōs	il′lās	il′la
Abl.	il′lō	il′lā	il′lō	il′līs	il′līs	il′līs

A demonstrative adjective, like any other adjective, must agree in number, gender, and case with the noun it modifies.

You have already learned that an adjective can be used as a noun.

multī, *many men* **multa,** *many things*

In the same way a demonstrative may be used as a pronoun.

ille, *that man* **illa,** *those things*

The demonstratives **hic** and **ille** both point out persons or things. Usually **hic** refers to a person or thing near the speaker, while **ille** indicates a person or thing farther away. Sometimes **hic** and **ille** are used in the same sentence.

Hic liber est bonus; ille liber est malus, *This book is good; that book is bad.*

1. Hae puellae et illī puerī lacrimant; hī virī et illae fēminae nōn lacrimant. 2. Illī nautae prope ōram perīculum nōn timent. 3. Illōs amīcōs invītāre dēbēmus. 4. Cūr in illā terrā manēs? 5. Illa formīca cibum sub terram portābat. 6. Cicāda sub tabernāculō erat. 7. Illud templum antīquum prope viam aedificāvērunt; hoc templum novum est in oppidō. 8. Incolae Eurōpae cibum nōn habent; quam miserī sunt! 9. Illī puerō aegrō cibum dabimus; illī puellae aegrae aquam dabitis. 10. Illa fēmina hās puellās nōn invītābat.

Complete each sentence with the correct Latin words.

1. (*That dream*) erat longum.
2. Dā mihi (*that book*).
3. Quam misera (*that girl*) est!
4. Fāma (*of that war*) magna est.
5. Oppidum pulchrum est (*on this island*).
6. Virī (*in those fields*) erant.
7. Viam (*near that farmhouse*) aedificant.
8. Vir (*to that boy*) librum dedit.
9. Aestāte (*those grasshoppers*) cantābant.
10. Aurum (*of those men*) est (*under the ground*).

HY Compare the declension of **ille** with that of **bonus.** In what cases are the endings alike? In what cases are they different?

LATIN LIVES TODAY

Complete these sentences with English words connected with **canto.** The first and last letters of each word are given, and the number of blanks shows the number of missing letters in the word.

1. A c _ _ _ _ _ a is a story or play set to music to be sung by a chorus, but not acted.
2. A c _ _ _ _ r is a man who leads a choir or congregation in singing, or a soloist in a synagogue.
3. The church choir c _ _ _ _ _ d the Psalm.
4. E _ _ _ _ _ t means to charm by looks, actions, manners, talking, or singing.
5. The tourists were e _ _ _ _ _ _ _ d with the mountain scenery.
6. There was a look of e _ _ _ _ _ _ _ _ _ t on the child's face as she listened to the fairy story.

Statim Appius Claudius in senatum properavit.

XXXIX. FAMA APPII CLAUDII

Appius Claudius, vir clārus, in Rōmā antīquā habitābat. Quod Rōma satis magnam cōpiam aquae bonae nōn habēbat, Appius longum aquaeductum (*aqueduct*) aedificāvit. Hic nōtus aquaeductus, Aqua Appia, aquam ab altīs locīs ad populum oppidī Rōmae 5 portābat.

Appius quoque longam viam ab oppidō Rōmā ad oppidum Capuam aedificāvit. Haec via erat Via Appia.

Fāma Appiī Claudiī erat magna propter hunc aquaeductum et hanc viam, sed in senātū (*senate*) Rōmānō quoque Appius erat nōtus. 10 Tamen post multōs annōs Appius nōn saepe in senātū aderat quod jam caecus erat.

Ōlim Pyrrhus, Graecus, contrā Rōmānōs pugnābat, et populus Rōmānus propter magnam victōriam Pyrrhī dolēbat. Jam nūntius Graecus in senātū aderat et dēditiōnem (*surrender*) multōrum op- 15 pidōrum Rōmānōrum postulābat. Multī Rōmānī Graecōs timēbant et oppida Pyrrhō dare dēsīderābant.

Quamquam Appius aberat, tamen dē nūntiō audīvit. Statim auxiliō servōrum in senātum (*acc.*) properāvit, ubi nūntius Pyrrhī aderat.

20 Ibi dīxit, "Interdum amīcī meī dolent quod sum caecus. Sed hodiē sum laetus quod illum nūntium in hōc locō nōn videō. Quam caecī estis, Rōmānī! Rōma erit tūta; illa oppida erunt tūta! Rōmānī in terrā Rōmānā nōn superābuntur!"

Propter Appium Claudium Rōmānī cōnsilium Pyrrhī nōn probāvērunt. Posteā cōpiae Rōmānae ācriter pugnāvērunt et Pyrrhum superāvērunt. Itaque Appius Claudius magnam fāmam habēbat quod Rōmae fīdus erat.

absum, abesse, āfuī, be absent, be away
adsum, adesse, adfuī, be present, be here
annus, -ī, M., year
caecus, -a, -um, blind
contrā, *prep. with acc.*, against
locus, -ī, M., place; *pl.* **loca,**[1] **-ōrum,** N.
nūntius, -ī, M., messenger; message, news
propter, *prep. with acc.*, on account of; because of
tūtus, -a, -um, safe, unharmed

In the division of a compound verb into syllables, the prefix is separated from the simple verb. Thus the second and third persons of **adsum** in the singular are **ad'es** and **ad'est.**

ENGLISH ADJECTIVES AND LATIN ADJECTIVES

Many English adjectives come from Latin adjectives ending in **-us.** Sometimes the meaning is somewhat different, but you can always see the connection.

Some English adjectives have dropped the **-us** of the Latin: **validus,** *valid;* **rapidus,** *rapid.*

What is the Latin word for each of the following English adjectives?

civic *long* *timid*

Some English adjectives have *-e* instead of **-us: obscurus,** *obscure.* What is the Latin word for each of the following English adjectives?

antique *fortunate* *private*

Some English adjectives have *-y* instead of **-ius: ordinarius,** *ordinary.* What is the Latin word for each of the following English adjectives?

contradictory *imaginary* *peremptory*

Explain the formation of an English adjective from each Latin adjective in the list below and use the English word in a sentence.

acutus	**frigidus**	**quietus**	**solus**
amplus	**magicus**	**secretus**	**superbus**
contrarius	**perfectus**	**severus**	**temporarius**

[1]To the Teacher: The masculine plural locī is not used in the exercises of this book.

THE VERBS *adsum* AND *absum*

The verb **adsum** is made from **sum** and the prefix **ad.** The verb **absum** is made from **sum** and the prefix **ab.** Such verbs are called *compound verbs.*

Adsum and **absum** are conjugated like **sum: ad'sum,** *I am present;* **ad'es,** *you are present,* etc.; **ab'sum,** *I am absent, am away from;* **ab'es,** *you are absent, are away from,* etc.

1. Multī agricolae aberant, sed nūntiī aderant. 2. Hic locus est altus; haec loca sunt alta. 3. Aqua ab altīs locīs ad oppidum nostrum portātur. 4. Auxiliō deōrum prō patriā pugnābimus. 5. Post multōs annōs in patriā meā tūtus aderō. 6. Quam validī illī virī caecī sunt! 7. Hic adfuit; ille āfuit. 8. Hodiē illae puellae hanc fēminam invītant. 9. Tum cōpiae Rōmānae contrā hunc virum pugnābant. 10. Nūntiī propter amīcōs mortuōs dolēbant.

1. The blind women are here. 2. How blind you are, Romans! 3. These places are not safe. 4. The Romans were grieving on account of the news. 5. Great forces were fighting against our men.

HELP YOURSELF

Account for the tenses used in the first two paragraphs of "Fāma Appiī Claudiī."

In this story find **in** used once with the ablative and once with the accusative and explain each use.

How do you translate **ad oppidum Rōmam? Ab oppidō Rōmā? Rōmānī? Cōpiae Rōmānae?**

LATIN LIVES TODAY

Find in each sentence an English word related to a Latin word in the vocabulary of this lesson. What is the meaning of each English word?

1. The high-school annual is published in the spring.
2. We celebrate Labor Day annually.
3. Name some anniversaries we celebrate.
4. Absentee voting is permitted in our state.
5. An annuity is a specified sum of money received each year.
6. Our newspaper has a column headed "Local Happenings."
7. Her absence from three rehearsals almost ruined the senior play.
8. Half a block from the lake he found a perfect location for the cottage.
9. Why must Julia always act in such a contrary manner?

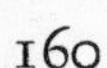

This scabbard, in which some Roman officer carried his sword, was found in Spain.

XL. VIR TIMIDUS

Locus est Hispānia, prōvincia Rōmāna. Virī, fēminae, puerī, puellae in viā parvī oppidī stant aut ambulant. Galba, vir timidus, cum Titō ā sinistrā stat. Nūntius dēfessus ā dextrā celeriter venit.

Galba. Quis est ille vir? Epistulās portat. Estne nūntius? 5

Titus. Ille vir est Pūblius, fīlius Sextī. Sextus in Galliā pugnat.

Nūntius. Epistulās ē Galliā portō. Sextus hās epistulās ad incolās hujus oppidī mittit. Barbarī Galliam oppugnant. Fortūna bellī est dubia. Perīculum est magnum!

Galba. Habēbantne Gallī sociōs? Nōnne Gallī auxilium postulā- 10 vērunt?

Nūntius. Ita, Gallī auxilium postulāvērunt, sed multōs sociōs nōn habēbant.

Titus. Quī Gallīs auxilium dedērunt?

Nūntius. Incolae Britanniae Gallīs auxilium dedērunt. Gallī et 15 Britannī fortiter pugnāvērunt, sed barbarī—

Galba. Quī oppida Gallōrum occupāvērunt? Quōrum agrōs vāstā- vērunt?

Nūntius. Noctū barbarī agrōs Gallōrum vāstāvērunt et oppida occupāvērunt et— 20

Virī et fēminae. Gallī sunt sociī nostrī. Gallōs juvāre dēbēmus!

Galba. Timentne Britannī barbarōs?

Nūntius. Minimē, aqua Britanniam ā Galliā sēparat. Sed jam perīculum Hispāniae est magnum. Mox barbarī oppida nostra oppugnābunt. 25

Galba. Heu! Aqua Hispāniam ā Galliā nōn sēparat. Gallōs timeō. Britannōs timeō. Barbarōs timeō. Heu! Heu!

barbarus, -a, -um, barbarous; M. *as noun,* a barbarian
dubius, -a, -um, doubtful
fortiter, *adv.*, bravely
heu, oh me! alas!
mittit, sends, is sending
quis, quid, who, what
socius, -ī, M., ally, companion
venit, comes

The diphthong **eu** is pronounced about like short *e* and *oo* combined in one syllable.

INTERROGATIVE PRONOUN

In Lesson XVIII you met the words **quis,** *who,* and **quid,** *what.* These words are forms of the *interrogative pronoun.*

The interrogative pronoun is declined as follows:

	SINGULAR	
	MASC. AND FEM.	NEUT.
Nom.	**quis,** who	**quid,** what
Gen.	**cu'jus,** whose, of whom	**cu'jus,** of what
Dat.	**cui,** to whom, whom (*as indirect object*)	**cui,** to what
Acc.	**quem,** whom (*as direct object*)	**quid,** what (*as direct object*)
Abl.	**quō,** (from, with, by) whom	**quō,** (from, with, by) what

	PLURAL		
	MASC.	FEM.	NEUT.
Nom.	**quī,** who	**quae,** who	**quae,** what
Gen.	**quō'rum,** whose, of whom	**quā'rum,** whose, of whom	**quō'rum,** of what
Dat.	**qui'bus,** to whom, whom (*as ind. obj.*)	**qui'bus,** to whom, whom (*as ind. obj.*)	**qui'bus,** to what (*as ind. obj.*)
Acc.	**quōs,** whom (*as dir. obj.*)	**quās,** whom (*as dir. obj.*)	**quae,** what (*as dir. obj.*)
Abl.	**qui'bus,** (from, with, by) whom	**qui'bus,** (from, by, with) whom	**qui'bus,** (from, with, by) what

In the singular the same forms of the interrogative pronoun are commonly used for the masculine and feminine, but the plural is regularly declined in the three genders.

CASE OF THE INTERROGATIVE

The case of an interrogative pronoun is, of course, determined by its use in the sentence. In the following sentence the English interrogative, *whom,* is in the objective case, and the accusative will be required in the Latin. This can be seen still more clearly by supplying an answer to the question.

Whom did you see? I saw your aunt.

In the answer, *aunt* replaces the *whom* of the question. The word *aunt* is the object in the answer. Hence you may be sure that *whom* is also the object and will be translated by the accusative.

Quem vīdistī? Amitam tuam vīdī.

Using information given in "Vir Timidus," answer these questions in Latin.

1. Quī in viā stant?
2. Quis est nūntius?
3. Quid Pūblius portat?
4. Quis epistulās mittit?
5. Ad quōs epistulās Sextus mittit?
6. Quī Galliam oppugnant?
7. Quī sunt sociī Gallōrum?
8. Quōrum agrōs barbarī vāstant?
9. Quibus Britannī auxilium dabant?
10. Quid Britanniam ā Galliā sēparat?

Translate the interrogative pronouns: 1. Whose son are you? 2. Whose (*pl.*) daughters are those girls? 3. To whom (*sing.*) was Titus giving food? 4. Whom (*sing.*) do you see in the street? 5. Whom (*pl.*) do our allies fear? 6. Who was working in the field? 7. Who were demanding money? 8. By whom are the towns being attacked? 9. To whom (*pl.*) were those men giving money?

HW Translate completely the first five of the English sentences above.

LATIN LIVES TODAY

To the ancient Romans **barbarus** originally meant any foreigner. Later *barbarian* came to mean an uncivilized person. What feminine name is related to **barbarus?**

How do **dubius** and its English equivalent differ in spelling? Should we be *dubious* of the success of a team that shows *timidity?*

In ancient Rome, Fortuna was the goddess of luck or *fortune.* Therefore a person blessed with good luck would be a *fortunate* person. Wealth gained through *fortunate* circumstances became a *fortune.* A *fortune*teller pretends to foresee the good and bad luck in our lives.

Complete these sentences with words related to **socius.**

1. The __ Party supports __.
2. I especially enjoy the __ of Andrew.
3. In college my older brother is studying __.
4. We have __ workers, __ security, and __ science.
5. It was a purely __ meeting; no business was transacted.
6. I like to go to the home of the Joneses because they are a __ family.

Vesuvius before a recent eruption

XLI. VESUVIUS ET POMPEII

Plīnius sum; cum avunculō meō habitābam. Vīlla nostra erat in locō altō inter oppidum Mīsēnum et ōram maritimam.

Ōlim māter (*mother*) mea in hortō vīllae ambulābat. Subitō illa clāmāvit, "Spectā flammās clārās! Spectā caelum! Quam obscūrum 5 est caelum! Quod perīculum est propinquum?"

Caelum spectāvī. Circum Vesuvium flammae erant clārae et fūmus erat dēnsus. Statim Plīnium, avunculum meum, vocāvī.

Avunculus Vesuvium spectāvit. Tum jussit, "Vocā servōs! Vīllae amīcōrum nostrōrum sunt in magnō perīculō; nōn longē ā Vesuviō 10 absunt. Amīcōs nostrōs juvāre dēbeō. Quī servī mē juvābunt?"

Avunculus meus cum multīs servīs ad ōram maritimam properāvit. Diū in hortō avunculum expectābam. Noctū quoque avunculum meum expectābam.

Postrīdiē erat magnus tremor terrae (*earthquake*); fūmus dēnsus 15 caelum cēlāvit; cinis (*ashes*) erat dēnsus in hortō et circum mūrōs.

Nōs ā vīllā per viās Mīsēnī properāvimus. Propter fūmum dēnsum viae erant obscūrae; multī incolae territī per viās angustās errābant.

Post multās hōrās iterum ad vīllam lēniter ambulābāmus. Ibi avunculum meum expectābāmus.

20 Postrīdiē nūntius vēnit et mihi nūntiāvit, "Vesuvius Pompeiōs et Herculāneum vāstāvit. Avunculus tuus est mortuus."

avunculus, -ī, M., uncle
circum, *prep. with acc.*, around
inter, *prep. with acc.*, between, among
jubeō, -ēre, jussī, order
longē, *adv.*, far, at a distance
mūrus, -ī, M., wall
quī (quis), quae, quod, which, what
vēnit, came

The diphthong **ei** is pronounced like **ei** in **vein.**

INTERROGATIVE ADJECTIVE

You are familiar with interrogative pronouns, used to ask questions.

Quid **videō?** *What do I see?*

Sometimes an interrogative word is used to modify a noun.

Quod **oppidum videō?** *What city do I see?*

In the sentence above, **quod** modifies **oppidum.** **Quod** is therefore an *interrogative adjective.* Like any other adjective, an interrogative adjective must always agree in number, gender, and case with the noun it modifies.

	MASC.	FEM.	NEUT.	
	SINGULAR			
Nom.	**quī, quis**	**quae**	**quod**	which, what
Gen.	**cu′jus**	**cu′jus**	**cu′jus**	of which, what
Dat.	**cui**	**cui**	**cui**	to which, what
Acc.	**quem**	**quam**	**quod**	which, what
Abl.	**quō**	**quā**	**quō**	(from, with, by, in, on) which, what
	PLURAL			
Nom.	**quī**	**quae**	**quae**	which, what
Gen.	**quō′rum**	**quā′rum**	**quō′rum**	of which, what
Dat.	**qui′bus**	**qui′bus**	**qui′bus**	to which, what
Acc.	**quōs**	**quās**	**quae**	which, what
Abl.	**qui′bus**	**qui′bus**	**qui′bus**	(from, with, by, in, on) which, what

A Roman street

1. Quod oppidum ā vīllā nōn longē aberat? 2. Quid Plīnius in caelō vīdit? 3. Quōs avunculus vocāvit? 4. Quōrum vīllae erant in perīculō? 5. Ad quem locum avunculus et servī properāvērunt? 6. Per quās viās Plīnius properāvit? 7. Quis Plīniō dē Vesuviō nūntiāvit? 8. Quae oppida Vesuvius vāstāvit?

Translate the italicized words: 1. *Who* has my book? 2. *By whom* (*sing.*) is the money demanded? 3. *By whom* (*pl.*) are the towns being seized? 4. *Whose* (*sing.*) son is Marcus? 5. *To what* boy did you give these books?

HW Find in "Vesuvius et Pompeiī" the answers to the eight questions asked above.

HELP YOURSELF Compare the declension of the interrogative adjective on page 165 with that of the interrogative pronoun on page 162. What slight differences are there?

Notice that questions in which an interrogative pronoun or interrogative adjective is used—like those introduced by an interrogative adverb (**cūr, ubi,** etc.)—keep the normal word order. In sentences requiring **-ne,** the **-ne** is usually attached to the verb, which comes at the beginning of the sentence. Find examples of different types of interrogative sentences in "Vir Timidus" (p. 161) and "Vesuvius et Pompeiī."

LLT Choose the word or phrase that completes each sentence correctly, and give the Latin word that justifies your choice.

1. A century plant blooms (*a*) annually (*b*) every month (*c*) once in a hundred years.
2. The cantata was attended by a large crowd of (*a*) cicadas (*b*) landscape architects (*c*) music-lovers.
3. When Magellan circumnavigated the globe, he sailed (*a*) all the way around the earth (*b*) halfway around the earth (*c*) ten miles and went back.
4. The density of the forest (*a*) enabled us to see far ahead (*b*) made it open and sunny (*c*) prevented us from seeing far ahead.
5. A mural is a (*a*) kind of monkey (*b*) girl (*c*) wall-painting.
6. I felt dubious about passing because (*a*) I had often been absent (*b*) I had worked hard (*c*) my grades were all good.
7. The fumes from the burning building (*a*) blinded him (*b*) enabled him to go fast (*c*) made him sharp-eyed.
8. An interscholastic contest is one between (*a*) airplane mechanics (*b*) laboratories (*c*) schools.
9. Local affairs relate to (*a*) a group of states (*b*) a single community (*c*) the world.

In Arles, France, once a Roman town, this ancient amphitheater is still in use today.

ROMAN SPORTS

Watching the contests of the amphitheater and the exciting chariot races of the circus were favorite pastimes of the Romans.

Almost every city in the Empire had an amphitheater, and in Rome there was the famous Colosseum (see p. 21). In these amphitheaters men fought with each other or with wild animals. Gladiators—men specially trained for such combats—fought in pairs or with several on each side. In spite of the name, gladiators did not always use swords; they fought with spears and with their fists. If not killed in combat, a defeated gladiator was at the mercy of the spectators, who

The walls of the amphitheater at Arles echo the cheers of people watching a modern bullfight. Just so the Romans must have cheered the gladiators in the arena.

The low wall running down the center of the race course is the spina *on which are statues, small temples, and obelisks. At each end are the goals, called* metae. *How can you tell whether this race is nearly over?*

might vote for his death. So certain was death for most of them that gladiators appearing in the arena greeted their sponsor with *Morituri te salutamus*, "We who are about to die salute you!"

Even more popular among the Romans than the fights of the arena was chariot-racing. Its popularity made it necessary to increase the seating capacity of the Circus Maximus, Rome's oldest race course, from sixty thousand to two hundred thousand. Usually four-horse teams were used, although teams of two, three, six, and seven also competed. Seven large marble eggs placed on pedestals stood for the seven laps of the race. As a lap was completed, one egg was taken down. There was plenty of excitement for the spectators as one charioteer tried to get ahead of another. The excitement was increased by the fact that there were heavy bets on favorite drivers and teams.

This Roman mosaic shows charioteers in their racing dress. Each man is wearing the colors of the syndicate for which he raced.

Victims for the Minotaur

XLII. THESEUS ET MINOTAURUS

Crēta, īnsula nōta, ā Graeciā nōn longē abest. In hāc īnsulā Daedalus, vir ēgregius, magnum Labyrinthum aedificāvit. Hīc Mīnōtaurus habitābat et per multās et caecās viās hujus Labyrinthī errābat. Hoc mōnstrum nōn cibum, sed virōs, fēminās, puerōs, puellās edēbat (*used to eat*). 5

Ōlim populus Athēnārum fīlium rēgis (*of the king*) Crētae necāvit. Propter hoc factum malum, sacrificium postulābātur. Itaque puerī et puellae saepe ab oppidō Athēnīs ad hunc Labyrinthum portābantur, ubi ā mōnstrō necābantur.

Thēseus, fīlius rēgis Athēnārum, puer ēgregius et validus, maximē 10 dolēbat.

Ita dīxit, "Populus puerōs et puellās Mīnōtaurō dare nōn dēbet. Sum validus; Mīnōtaurum superābō. Hodiē puerī ad Crētam nāvigant; cum cēterīs nāvigābō."

Itaque Thēseus cēterīs cum puerīs ad Crētam nāvigāvit. Perīculum 15 vidēbātur magnum, sed ab Ariadnā, fīliā rēgis Crētae, Thēseus juvābātur. Ariadna Thēseō viam sēcrētam in Labyrinthum mōnstrāvit, et Thēseō fīlum (*thread*) longum dedit.

Noctū Thēseus sēcrētō hoc fīlum ad jānuam Labyrinthī alligāvit (*tied*). Taedam quoque in Labyrinthum portāvit quod via erat obscūra. Mīnōtaurus īrātus Thēseum vīdit et statim puerum necāre temptāvit.

Sed Thēseus erat validus et parātus; gladiō mōnstrum necāvit. Deinde sine perīculō cēterōs puerōs cum multīs et miserīs virīs, fēminīs, puellīs servāvit.

Dēnique auxiliō fīlī ad jānuam Labyrinthī tūtus iterum vēnit, ubi ab Ariadnā expectābātur.

cēterī, -ae, -a, *pl.*, the rest of, the other
ēgregius, -a, -um, excellent, distinguished, unusual
parātus, -a, -um, ready, prepared
sēcrētō, *adv.*, secretly
taeda, -ae, F., torch
videor, -ērī, seem

The adjective **cēterī** is used chiefly in the plural. Its forms in the singular may be disregarded.

The verb **videor** is merely the passive of **videō.** It is usually translated *seem,* rather than *be seen.* The form **vidērī** is translated like a present active infinitive, *to seem.*

IMPERFECT PASSIVE

You have already met the imperfect active of the first and second conjugations. As you know, the tense sign of the imperfect is **-bā-**. The imperfect passive differs from the imperfect active only in having passive endings instead of the active endings you met on page 86. The vowel **-ā-** becomes short before the endings **-r** and **-ntur.**

The imperfect passive of the first and second conjugations is given below. Notice that the vowel preceding the tense sign is **-ā-** in the first conjugation and **-ē-** in the second conjugation.

SINGULAR

portā′bar, I was being carried	**monē′bar,** I was being warned
portābā′ris, you were being carried	**monēbā′ris,** you were being warned
portābā′tur, he, she, it was being carried	**monēbā′tur,** he, she, it was being warned

PLURAL

portābā′mur, we were being carried	**monēbā′mur,** we were being warned
portābā′minī, you were being carried	**monēbā′minī,** you were being warned
portāban′tur, they were being carried	**monēban′tur,** they were being warned

The imperfect passive is frequently translated by a simple past: *I was carried,* etc.

1. Interdum sociī Rōmānīs auxilium in bellīs sēcrētō dabant. 2. Sociī nostrī ōlim superābantur quod nōn parātī erant. 3. Agrī vāstābantur et oppida ācriter oppugnābantur. 4. Auxilium postulābātur, sed magnās cōpiās tum nōn habēbāmus. 5. Sed nunc cōnsilia tua nōn bona videntur. 6. Populus Rōmānus sociōs ēgregiōs habēbat. 7. In hōc bellō Rōmānī sociōs sēcrētō juvābant. 8. Sine taedā trāns viam sēcrētam vēnit.

This mythical Minotaur had a bull's head and a man's body.

1. The rest of the arrows were being carried by Theseus without help. 2. Formerly our allies were not feared by the Gauls, but now they are feared. 3. I see my friend; he seems to me to be a good man. 4. Formerly your native country was not praised by our allies, but now it is often praised. 5. The other boys were in danger and help was secretly demanded. 6. The rest of the allies seemed to be ready. 7. The torches were carried through the town.

HELP YOURSELF

In the sentence "Amīcum meum videō; mihi vir bonus esse vidētur," what is the meaning of **videō?** Of **vidētur?** Since **videor** is the passive of **videō**, it usually has the meaning *seem.*

The Latin **et** means *and*, as you know. In English the common Latin expression, **et cetera** (*and other things*), became one word, and was then abbreviated. How does Latin help you remember the correct spelling of the abbreviation?

LATIN LIVES TODAY

With what Latin verb that you have had is the Latin adjective **paratus** connected? The motto of the United States Coast Guard is **Semper Paratus** (*Always Ready*). The name of the Women's Reserve of the Coast Guard is SPAR (initials of **Semper Paratus,** *Always Ready*).

Most of the mottoes in the different branches of the armed services have been taken from the Latin. Here are a few: **Auxilium Semper Adest; Parati Defendere; Sine Mora; Monstrat Viam.**

The mottoes of many colleges, universities, and high schools are also in Latin: **Esse Quam Videri; Sum Americanus; Scientia et Disciplina.** What Latin mottoes do you know?

Subito cera a pennis separabatur.

XLIII. PRIMUS AVIATOR

Olim Daedalus in īnsulā Crētā cum fīliō Īcarō habitābat. Quamquam Daedalus erat vir ēgregius, tamen līber nōn erat. Captīvus in eā īnsulā servābātur, sed semper viam fugae parāre temptābat. Neque terra neque aqua eī auxilium dedit.

Deinde in caelō avēs (*birds*) vīdit. Diū avēs spectābat. 5

Dēnique fīliō dīxit, "Illae avēs ālīs volant. Nōs quoque volābimus. Hās avēs necābimus et pennīs eārum ālās parābimus."

Itaque Daedalus et Īcarus sagittīs multās avēs necāvērunt et pennās eārum servāvērunt. Auxiliō cērae magnās ālās parāvērunt.

Dēnique ālae erant parātae. Statim Daedalus eās temptāvit et 10 Īcarum ālās temptāre invītāvit. Mox Īcarus cum Daedalō volābat.

"Ālae sunt validae, sed propter cēram prope sōlem (*sun*) volāre nōn dēbēmus," Daedalus fīlium monuit.

Prīmō Īcarus erat timidus et prope terram manēbat, sed nōn diū prope terram manēbat. Daedalus territus fīlium appellāvit et eum 15 dē perīculō iterum monuit. Sed Īcarus longē ā terrā et ab aquā per caelum altum volābat. Prope sōlem volābat.

Daedalus fīlium spectābat et propter audāciam ejus lacrimābat. Subitō cēra ā pennīs sēparābātur et bracchia Īcarī erant sine ālīs. In aquam puer cecidit (*fell*), et aqua eum cēlāvit. 20

Posteā Daedalus propter fīlium mortuum semper dolēbat et iterum in caelō nōn volāvit.

āla, -ae, F., wing
appellō, -āre, -āvī, name, call
audācia, -ae, F., boldness, daring
cēra, -ae, F., wax
fuga, -ae, F., flight
is, ea, id, that, this, *pl.*, those, these; *as pronoun*, he, she, it, *pl.*, they
neque, *conj.*, nor, and not; **neque . . . neque,** neither . . . nor
penna, -ae, F., feather
prīmus, -a, -um, first
Aviātor was not a Latin word, but is formed like many Latin words. It is from **avis,** *bird.*

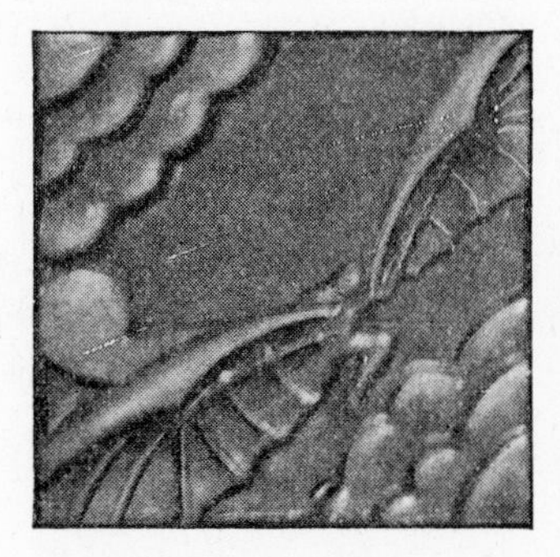
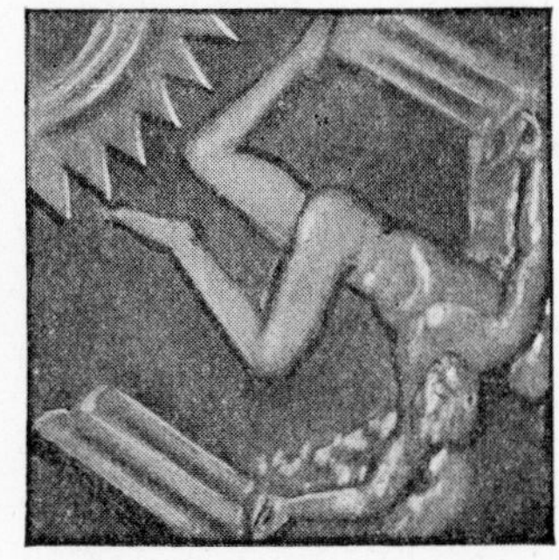

Two panels from a steel door in the memorial to the Wright Brothers, at Kitty Hawk, North Carolina.

THE DEMONSTRATIVE *is*

You have learned two demonstratives: **hic,** *this,* and **ille,** *that.* There is also another important demonstrative, **is.**

When used as adjectives, the forms of **is** may be translated either *this* or *that,* as the sense requires, since **is** does not emphasize that the thing is near, as does **hic,** or that it is some distance away, as does **ille.**

Is puer nauta est, *This boy* (or *that boy*) *is a sailor.*

PRONOUN USE OF *is*

The forms of **is** are very commonly used as pronouns, meaning *he, she, it, his, her, its,* etc., as shown in the translation below.

When **is** is used as a pronoun, it must agree with its antecedent in number and gender, but its case depends on the use in the sentence.

Ager est magnus. Vidēsne eum? *The field is large. Do you see it?*

In the example above, **eum,** a masculine singular form, is used, because the antecedent, **ager,** is masculine singular. In this instance, the masculine form, **eum,** is translated *it,* because in English *field* is neuter. **Eum** is accusative because it is the object of the verb **vidēs.**

The forms of **is** with its meanings as a pronoun are as follows:

	SINGULAR		
	MASC.	FEM.	NEUT.
Nom.	**is,** he	**e′a,** she	**id,** it
Gen.	**e′jus,** his	**e′jus,** her (*possessive*)	**e′jus,** its
Dat.	**e′ī,** to him, him (*as indirect object*)	**e′ī,** to her, her (*as indirect object*)	**e′ī,** to it, it (*as indirect object*)
Acc.	**e′um,** him (*as direct object*)	**e′am,** her (*as direct object*)	**id,** it (*as direct object*)
Abl.	**e′ō,** (from, with, by) him	**e′ā,** (from, with, by) her	**e′ō,** (from, with, by) it
	PLURAL		
Nom.	**e′ī, iī** } they	**e′ae,** they	**e′a,** they, those things
Gen.	**eō′rum,** their	**eā′rum,** their	**eō′rum,** their
Dat.	**e′īs, iīs** } to them, them (*as ind. obj.*)	**e′īs, iīs** } to them, them (*as ind. obj.*)	**e′īs, iīs** } to them, them (*as ind. obj.*)
Acc.	**e′ōs,** them (*as dir. obj.*)	**e′ās,** them (*as dir. obj.*)	**e′a,** them (*as dir. obj.*)
Abl.	**e′īs, iīs** } (from, with, by) them	**e′īs, iīs** } (from, with, by) them	**e′īs, iīs** } (from, with, by) them

The forms **iī** and **iīs** are pronounced in one syllable as if spelled **ī** and **īs.**

hic AND *ille* AS PRONOUNS

The forms of **hic** and **ille** are sometimes used instead of the forms of **is** as pronouns meaning *he, she, it, his, her, him,* etc. The plural forms **hī, illī,** etc., mean *these* or *those* (*persons*); the neuter **haec, illa,** etc., mean *these things* or *those things.*

1. Neque puer neque amīcus ejus est impiger. 2. In hōc oppidō sagittāriōs et fīliōs eōrum vidēmus. 3. Puerōs expectāmus, sed eōs nōn vidēmus; puellās quoque expectāmus, sed eās nōn vidēmus. 4. Eī puellae et eī puerō fābulās nārrāmus. 5. Illōs captīvōs prīmōs saepe vidēbātis. 6. Propter audāciam nautārum īnsula nostra erat tūta. 7. Daedalus viam fugae sēcrētō parābat. 8. Pennīs et cērā ālās parābant; ālīs volābant. 9. Appellā eōs puerōs; adesse dēbent. 10. Magna audācia ejus fīliī laudābātur.

Translate the italicized words: 1. I often walk *with him.* 2. The first man gives *them* a reward. 3. We live *with his friend;* I work *with their friend.* 4. I was calling *him.* 5. I was *with those girls;* I was helping *them.* 6. We often see *your son and his friend.* 7. *These women and their daughters* do not remain on the island in winter. 8. The *man's* boldness was famous.

Give the Latin for each phrase.

of her book	of this boy	of that farmer
of his news	of this reward	of that girl
of its wing	of this woman	of that temple
to this house	to his friend	to that ally
to this man	to her uncle	to that ant
to this tent	to its wall	to that place

HW Translate completely the eight English sentences above.

LLT Find in the vocabulary of this lesson a Latin word with which each of the following English words is connected.

aileron	*appellation*	*audacious*
fugitive	*pen*	*prime*

Use each of these English words in a sentence.

REVIEW OF UNIT IX LESSONS XXXVIII-XLIII

Nouns

āla, -ae
annus, -ī
audācia, -ae
avunculus, -ī
*captīvus, -ī
cēra, -ae
cicāda, -ae
*fortūna, -ae
fuga, -ae
*fūmus, -ī
locus, -ī
mūrus, -ī
nūntius, -ī
penna, -ae
*sacrificium, -ī
socius, -ī
taeda, -ae

Verbs

absum, abesse
adsum, adesse
appellō, -āre
cantō, -āre
invītō, -āre
jubeō, -ēre
lacrimō, -āre
mittit
venit
vēnit
videor, -ērī

Pronouns

ille, illa, illud
is, ea, id

Adjectives

barbarus, -a, -um
caecus, -a, -um
cēterī, -ae, -a
*dēnsus, -a, -um
dubius, -a, -um
ēgregius, -a, -um
parātus, -a, -um
piger, -gra, -grum
prīmus, -a, -um
quī (quis), quae, quod
*sēcrētus, -a, -um
*timidus, -a, -um
tūtus, -a, -um

Adverbs

fortiter
longē
sēcrētō

Prepositions

circum
contrā
inter
propter
sub

Conjunction

neque

Other Word

heu

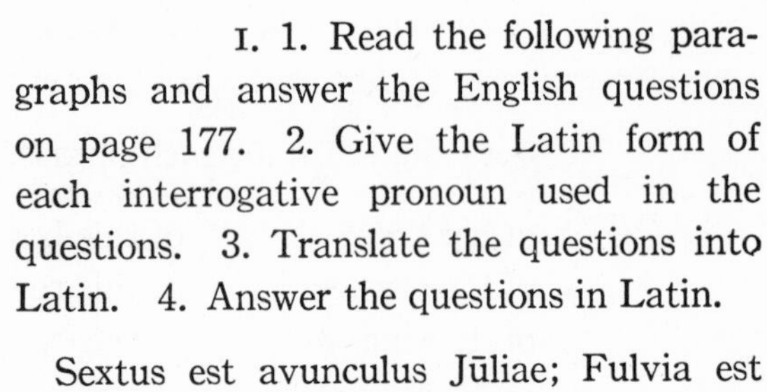

I. 1. Read the following paragraphs and answer the English questions on page 177. 2. Give the Latin form of each interrogative pronoun used in the questions. 3. Translate the questions into Latin. 4. Answer the questions in Latin.

Sextus est avunculus Jūliae; Fulvia est amita Jūliae; Cornēlia est cōnsōbrīna Jūliae. Jūlia in casā Sextī et Fulviae habitat.

Sextus multōs amīcōs habet; Sextus saepe eōs amīcōs in viīs videt. Mārcus est amīcus Sextī, et Sextus saepe Mārcum ad casam invītat. Sed hodiē Mārcum nōn videt.

Jūlia saepe Cornēliam ad casam amitae invītat. Interdum amita Jūliae dōna Cornēliae dat. Interdum Sextus dōnum Mārcō dat. Mārcus saepe cum Jūliā et Cornēliā ambulat. Interdum Fulvia cum Sextō et Mārcō ambulat.

This painting decorated the wall of a Roman house.

1. *Whose* friend is Marcus?
2. *Whose* cousin is Cornelia?
3. *By whom* is Marcus often invited?
4. *By whom* is Cornelia invited?
5. *What* does Sextus give to Marcus?
6. *What* does Julia's aunt give to Cornelia?
7. *Whom* does Sextus often see in the streets?
8. *Whom* does he not see today?
9. *With whom* does Marcus often walk?
10. *To whom* does Sextus sometimes give a present?
11. *To whom* does Fulvia give presents?

II. 1. Hī virī sunt sociī nostrī; illī virī sunt barbarī.
2. Fuga eōrum tūta esse nōn vidēbātur.
3. Mūrus ab eīs circum illud oppidum aedificābātur.
4. Eī captīvī pigrī taedās sub terram portāre jubēbantur.
5. Quamquam cēterī nōn parātī erant, tamen ille nūntius aberat.
6. Propter fūmum dēnsum neque mūrum neque hortum vīdit.
7. Poēta caecus audāciam ēgregiam habēre vidēbātur; sēcrētō erat timidus et dubius.
8. Heu! Cēra inter pennās ālārum nōn manēbat.
9. Īcarus ā Daedalō appellābātur et dē perīculō ab eō monēbātur.
10. Puer lacrimābat quod avunculus ejus longē āfuit.

LATIN LIVES TODAY

Complete each sentence by supplying an English word connected with a Latin word in the review vocabulary on page 176.

1. How many pupils are __ today?
2. A feminine name from Latin is __.
3. In a __ forest one could easily be lost.
4. My uncle was a bold man and showed great __.
5. On February 22 we celebrate the __ of George Washington's birthday.
6. Thomas Jefferson said, "We mutually pledge to each other our lives, our __, and our sacred honor."
7. We are all interested in __ events.
8. Some wild animals are happy in __.
9. On the walls of the auditorium were several __.
10. Two firemen were overcome by the dense __.

A portion of a Roman wall still standing in Britain

UNIT

X

XLIV. DOLUS ANNAE

Anna erat puella Rōmāna, sed in Britanniā cum avunculō prope magna castra Rōmāna habitābat. Quamquam Britannia erat prōvincia Rōmāna, tamen multī incolae Britanniae Rōmānōs nōn amābant. Terram līberam dēsīderābant et jam bellum parābant. 5 Gallī eīs sēcrētō auxilium dabant.

Ōlim Anna rāmōs ē dēnsā silvā portābat. Avunculus, quamquam erat caecus, tamen Annam juvābat. Subitō erat sonus armōrum; deinde Anna virōs novōs undique vīdit. Virī erant armātī, et arma eōrum erant nova. Prīmō virī Annam et avunculum nōn vīdērunt. 10 Anna avunculō nārrāvit, "Virōs novōs in silvā videō; eōrum arma sunt nova. Virī sunt Gallī."

Jam dux (*leader*) ad locum vēnit ubi Anna et avunculus stābant. Silvam undique circumspectāvit. Deinde Annam et avunculum ejus salūtāvit.

Dē viā rogāvit et dīxit, "Ad oppidum propinquum properāmus. Rōmānī in illō oppidō habitant et nōs sumus amīcī Rōmānōrum. 5 Nōs juvāre dēbētis."

Avunculus respondit, "Sum caecus, sed Anna tibi viam mōnstrābit."

Anna nōn timida erat; virōs per silvam dēnsam dūxit. Sed eōs nōn ad oppidum dūxit; eōs ad castra Rōmāna dūxit. Ibi Rōmānī Gallōs cēpērunt (*seized*). Anna patriae fīda erat; Rōmānōs juvāre audēbat. 10

armātus, -a, -um, armed; M. *pl. as noun,* armed men, soldiers
audeō, -ēre, (*irreg. in perf.*), dare
circumspectō, -āre, -āvī, look around, look around at
dūxit, (he, she) led, did lead
respondeō, -spondēre, -spondī, answer, reply
rogō, -āre, -āvī, ask, request
undique, *adv.*, on all sides

ENGLISH VERBS AND LATIN VERBS

You have met many English nouns like Latin nouns and numerous English adjectives similar to Latin adjectives. There are also Latin verbs which give us English verbs with much the same meaning.

Some English verbs related to Latin verbs are spelled like the first principal part without the **-o**: *expect,* **expecto**; *move,* **moveo.**

What is the Latin verb for *labor?* For *remove?*

Some English verbs end in *-e* instead of **-o**: *adore,* **adoro**; *induce,* **induco.**

What is the Latin word for *explore?* For *invite?* For *compare?*

Some English verbs end in *-ate* instead of **-o**: *navigate,* **navigo.**

What is the Latin for *narrate?* For *communicate*?

Give the English verb that is related to each Latin verb in the list below and explain any differences in meaning.

adorno	**contendo**	**excito**	**observo**
attendo	**defendo**	**libero**	**saluto**
commemoro	**erro**	**migro**	**tempto**

1. Cūr ab eō nōn monēbāris? Cūr ab eā nōn monēbāminī? 2. Propter sonum in hōc locō manēre nōn audeō. 3. Fulvia avunculum meum domī vīdit et eum salūtāvit. 4. Armātī dē viā rogāvērunt.

Metal helmets were part of a Roman soldier's armor.

5. Cornēlia respondit, "Nōn caeca sum." 6. Illī virī sunt armātī, et eōs timēmus. 7. Anna silvam dēnsam undique circumspectāre dēbet quod avunculus ejus longē abest. 8. Cōnsilium est bonum; id probāmus. 9. Parvās fīliās tuās et cōnsōbrīnam eārum in vīllā saepe vīdimus. 10. Anna ad silvam avunculum caecum dūxit.

Translate the italicized words: 1. Cornelia is a good woman; we salute *her*. 2. I do not dare to give *him* a big reward. 3. *These* armed men are *our* allies. 4. We *were looking around* on all sides because there was a loud (great) noise. 5. *This* man asks about the wax and the feathers. 6. *Your* uncle used to praise *these* boys, and so they saluted *him*. 7. *Who* dares to remain *here?* 8. *Who* led the blind man?

HW Translate completely the eight English sentences above.

LLT Complete each of the following sentences with a word connected with **respondeo.**

1. Her __ was an emphatic "No!"
2. Sometimes the teacher and class have __ reading.
3. His father said that Clark must be __ for Sandy.
4. Clark agreed to accept the __ for feeding the dog.

XLV. ROMANI VEIOS OCCUPANT.

Quamquam Veiī, magnum oppidum Etrūscōrum, erant prope Rōmam, tamen populus Veiōrum saepe cum Rōmānīs pugnābat. Rōmānī Veiōs oppugnābant et mūrōs eōrum vehementer dēlēre temptābant. Sed mūrī erant altī et validī, et diū incolae Veiōrum tūtī vidēbantur. 5

Sed post multōs annōs incolae magnam cōpiam cibī nōn habēbant; multī erant aegrī; tamen cēterī incolae oppidum vehementer dēfendēbant.

Dēnique incola Veiōrum in mūrō oppidī stābat. "Haec sunt verba ōrāculī," clāmāvit. "Veiōs nōn occupābitis, Rōmānī, dum aqua erit in lacū (*lake*) Albānō. Semper erit aqua in lacū. Dī semper Veiōs 10 cūrābunt, et Veiī semper erunt tūtī."

Rōmānī respondērunt, "Es stultus! Oppidum tuum occupābitur; templa tua dēlēbuntur; dī Veiōrum ad oppidum nostrum portābuntur; dī tuī Rōmānōs cūrābunt."

Statim Rōmānus Camillus bonum cōnsilium mōnstrāvit. Cēterī 15 virī id cōnsilium probāvērunt.

Noctū Camillus multōs Rōmānōs ē castrīs ad lacum Albānum sēcrētō dūxit. Sēcrētō hī virī magnum cunīculum (*tunnel*) sub terrā fodiēbant (*dug*). Celeriter labōrābant quod populus Veiōrum in tēctīs erat. Dēnique per hunc cunīculum aqua ē lacū trāns campōs 20 flūxit (*flowed*). Jam erat nūlla aqua in lacū Albānō.

Iterum multī Rōmānī Veiōs fortiter oppugnāvērunt. Iterum mūrōs vehementer dēlēre temptābant. Quamquam incolae Veiōrum diū et ācriter pugnāvērunt, tamen nōn jam tūtī erant. Nūlla aqua in lacū erat; itaque Rōmānī oppidum occupāvērunt. Verba ōrāculī 25 erant vēra.

The people of Veii used such shields of bronze.

campus, -ī, M., level plain, plain
dēleō, -ēre, dēlēvī, destroy
dum, *conj.*, while, as long as
stultus, -a, -um, stupid, foolish
vehementer, *adv.*, violently, strongly
verbum, -ī, N., word
vērus, -a, -um, true

Notice that **Veiī,** like **Pompeiī,** is the name of a town. Since it is plural in form, it requires a plural verb and a plural adjective.

FUTURE PASSIVE OF *portō* AND *moneō*

You have already met the future active of verbs of the first and second conjugations. In the future passive **portō** and **moneō** are conjugated as follows:

SINGULAR

portā'bor, I shall be carried	**monē'bor,** I shall be warned
portā'beris, you will be carried	**monē'beris,** you will be warned
portā'bitur, he, she, it will be carried	**monē'bitur,** he, she, it will be warned

PLURAL

portā'bimur, we shall be carried	**monē'bimur,** we shall be warned
portābi'minī, you will be carried	**monēbi'minī,** you will be warned
portābun'tur, they will be carried	**monēbun'tur,** they will be warned

The syllable **-bi-** is the tense sign of the future in the first and second conjugations. Notice that this tense sign has the form **-bu-** in the third person plural of both voices, **-b-** in the first person singular of both voices, and **-be-** in the second person singular of the passive.

1. Haec loca ā nūntiīs vidēbuntur. 2. Mūrī hujus oppidī ā sociīs vehementer oppugnābuntur. 3. In hortō vidēberis; in campō vidēbiminī. 4. Servus stultus cēnam parābit. 5. Perīculum ā cōpiīs nostrīs nōn timēbitur. 6. In tabernāculum vocābiminī. 7. Sunt multa verba in linguā Latīnā. 8. Id oppidum ā cōpiīs nostrīs in magnō bellō dēlētur. 9. Nōnne amīcus vērus librōs meōs cūrābit? 10. Auxilium ā sociīs nostrīs postulābimus.

Translate the verbs: 1. While a man has (*fut.*) weapons, danger will not be feared by him. 2. Your stupid friend has much money as long as he works well. 3. These girls will not dare to remain in this place. 4. You (*sing.*) are not feared by these men because you fight with words alone. 5. These true words will be announced by the messenger.

HELP YOURSELF

In the first line of "Rōmānī Veiōs Occupant" why is **erant** (and not **erat**) used with **Veiī?** What is the construction of **oppidum?** Why is it singular?

Find in the story a form of **campus** and a form of **castra.** What is the meaning of each word? Does **campus** ever mean *camp?* How would you say in Latin, "The camp of the Romans was on a plain"?

Give the tense and voice of each verb in the Latin sentences above. How do you recognize the future? The imperfect? How do you tell a passive form?

A present-day view of the river Cloelia swam

XLVI. CLOELIA

Porsena, rēx (*king*) superbus Etrūscōrum, Rōmam dēlēre dēsīderābat. Etrūscī multōs Rōmānōs vulnerāvērunt et necāvērunt. Itaque Rōmānī pācem (*peace*) rogāvērunt.

Porsena dīxit, "Date decem fīliās et decem fīliōs Rōmānōrum mihi obsidēs (*as hostages*); tum Rōmānīs pācem dabō." 5

Rōmānī miserī respondērunt, "Tibi hās fīliās et hōs fīliōs dabimus."

Inter obsidēs erat Cloelia, puella magnae audāciae. Quod castra Porsenae in rīpā Tiberis erant et nōn longē ab oppidō Rōmā aberant, Cloelia cēterīs puellīs et puerīs dīxit, "Cōnsilium bonum erit trāns Tiberim natāre." 10

Māne puellae et puerī trāns Tiberim natāvērunt. Quamquam Etrūscī eam et sociōs ejus sagittīs vulnerāre temptābant, mox Cloelia tūta cum cēterīs in rīpā stābat. Herī fuērunt captīvī; hodiē erant iterum līberī.

Tamen iterum Rōmānī puellās et puerōs Porsenae dedērunt quod 15 esse fīdī dēsīderābant. Tum Porsena Cloeliae lībertātem (*liberty*) dedit quod magnā audāciā ejus movēbātur. Eī equum dedit et eam ad oppidum Rōmam properāre jussit. Sed Cloelia lībertātem quoque prō cēterīs postulāvit.

Itaque, quod rēx Porsena verbīs et magnā audāciā Cloeliae movē- 20 bātur, multōs sociōs puellae servāvit et Cloelia nōn sōla in oppidum Rōmam vēnit.

decem, *indecl.*, ten
herī, *adv.*, yesterday
māne, *adv.*, in the morning
natō, -āre, -āvī, swim
rīpa, -ae, F., bank (*of a stream*)

1. Eōs servābimus, quod amīcī nostrī sunt. 2. Haec terra ab eīs vāstābitur. 3. Cōpiae nostrae post hunc mūrum manēbunt. 4. Fuga decem puellārum stulta vidētur. 5. Vir ā rīpā natābit. 6. Māne oppidum dēlēbitur. 7. Herī captīvī ad rīpam Tiberis movēbantur.

Choose the correct verb form to complete each sentence.

1. Sagittārius in hōc proeliō (*will be wounded*).
   vulnerābitur vulnerābātur vulnerābat vulnerātur
2. Vir ā servō (*will be feared*).
   timēbat timēbitur timēbit timēbuntur
3. Herī illa puella trāns Tiberim (*was swimming*).
   natābit natābunt natābat natat
4. Decem oppida (*will be destroyed*).
   cūrābitur dēlēbat movēbitur dēlēbuntur
5. Magna castra Rōmāna māne (*will be moved*).
   movēbitur oppugnābuntur manēbunt movēbuntur
6. Captīvī natāre ad rīpam (*will try*).
   temptābuntur temptābit temptābunt temptābant
7. Rōmānī dare decem puerōs et decem puellās (*were ordered*).
   jubēbantur jubēbuntur jubēbant jubēbunt

Translate the verbs: 1. In the morning this wall will be destroyed; that camp will be destroyed. 2. The men were swimming in the water. 3. We shall help our allies, and their country will be saved. 4. The Roman forces will fear us on the plains. 5. We were moving this camp. 6. Yesterday an armed man attacked me on this bank.

LLT

Which of our months is called to mind by a word in the vocabulary? Another derivative of this word is *decimal*. What is a *decimal* point?

What is the difference between an *aquarium* and a *natatorium?*

Complete each of the following sentences with a word related to **moveo.**

1. Don't ___ or you will fall.
2. All his ___ were quick and jerky.
3. ___ furniture is hard work.
4. Although heavy, this box is ___.
5. A small phonograph can easily be ___.
6. I ___ that we adjourn.

XLVII. MANLIUS CAPITOLIUM SERVAT.

Gallī erant barbarī, et Rōmānī eōs maximē timēbant. Jam Gallī ā portīs Rōmae nōn longē aberant. Propter magnum perīculum multī incolae Rōmae manēre ibi nōn dēsīderābant; itaque ad oppida propinqua fūgērunt.

Virī validī sōlī in oppidō manēbant. Tamen in tēctīs nōn manēbant, 5 sed in Capitōliō. Hīc Juppiter et Jūnō et Minerva templa habēbant. In templō Jūnōnis erant ānserēs (*geese*) sacrī.

Quamquam Capitōlium propter templa ab hīs virīs dēfendēbātur, tamen oppidum tōtum erat minimē tūtum. Portae Rōmae erant apertae, et mox Gallī ferī adfuērunt; mox tēcta et templa et ārās 10 dēlēbant.

Dēnique noctū Gallī viam sēcrētam vīdērunt. Via erat dūra sed eōs ad mūrum Capitōliī dūxit. Quamquam Rōmānī Capitōlium vigilābant, tamen Gallōs nōn vīdērunt. Nūllus sonus erat; Gallī erant maximē quiētī. 15

Sed in templō Jūnōnis sacrī ānserēs strepuērunt (*cackled*), et eōrum clangor Mānlium excitāvit. Statim Mānlius cēterōs Rōmānōs vocāvit et ad mūrum properāvit.

Prīmus Gallus jam in mūrō stābat. Sē servāre temptāvit, sed celeriter Mānlius eum gladiō necāvit. Post prīmum Gallum erant 20 multī sociī ejus, sed statim ā Gallō cadentī (*falling*) dē viā angustā dēpulsī sunt (*were knocked off*). Mox hī Gallī quoque ā Mānliō et ab amīcīs ejus necābantur et Capitōlium servābātur.

dūrus, -a, -um, hard, difficult
excitō, -āre, -āvī, arouse, alarm
ferus, -a, -um, fierce, wild
fūgērunt, (they) fled
porta, -ae, F., gate
sacer, -cra, -crum, sacred
suī, of himself, herself, itself, themselves
tōtus, -a, -um, whole

Tōtus is declined like **bonus,** except in the genitive and dative singular, which are irregular. You will not need to learn these forms now, because they are not used in this book.

Though venerated because they saved Rome, geese were also pets of Roman children.

REFLEXIVE PRONOUN

As you have already learned, the demonstratives **is, hic,** and **ille** are sometimes used as pronouns. One use of such a pronoun is as the object of a verb whose subject refers to a different person or thing.

> **Mānlius virōs excitāvit et eōs servāvit,** *Manlius aroused the men and saved them.*

In the following sentence the object, *himself*, means the same person as the subject, *he*.

> **Sē servat,** *He saves himself.*

A pronoun which is thus used is called a *reflexive pronoun.*

The Latin reflexive pronoun is used in the genitive, dative, accusative, or ablative case to denote the same person as the subject of the sentence in which it stands.

The Latin reflexive pronoun meaning *himself, herself, itself,* or *themselves* is declined as follows:

	SINGULAR	PLURAL
Genitive:	**su'ī**	**su'ī**
Dative:	**si'bi**	**si'bi**
Accusative:	**sē, sē'sē**	**sē, sē'sē**
Ablative:	**sē, sē'sē**	**sē, sē'sē**

1. Herī ab oppidō āfuī; hodiē adfuī. 2. Ōlim fuērunt portae sacrae in templō, sed barbarī eās dēlēvērunt. 3. In longō et dūrō proeliō virī contrā barbarōs ferōs fortiter prō patriā et prō sē pugnābant. 4. Gallī fūgērunt et sē servāre temptāvērunt. 5. Rōmānī ā Mānliō excitābuntur et ad mūrum properābunt. 6. Puella in aquā sē spectābat, sed nōn erat sibi grāta.

This picture of a triumphal procession shows the splendor of Rome's buildings. Notice the temples and arches.

1. Yesterday I was near the gate of the camp with my uncle. 2. Boys, you are present today; why were you absent yesterday? 3. Today the boys will keep watch; yesterday we kept watch. 4. The whole town will be destroyed, but the people will save themselves. 5. The Romans fled from the fierce barbarians to the gates of a nearby town.

From your reading of the stories of Lessons XLVI and XLVII, answer these questions with Latin sentences.

1. Erantne portae Rōmae apertae?
2. Quī trāns Tiberim natāvērunt?
3. Quis erat Cloelia?
4. Quī multōs Rōmānōs vulnerāvērunt?
5. Quid erat cōnsilium Cloeliae?
6. Quid Porsena Cloeliae dedit?
7. Quis Rōmānōs vocāvit et excitāvit?
8. Quī ex oppidō fūgērunt?

HY LLT

What is the meaning of **dē** in "dē viā angustā" in the last paragraph of "Manlius Capitolium Servat"? With what meanings of **dē** are you familiar?

Complete the following sentences with words related to words in the vocabulary of this lesson.

1. Jack was too used to the tame creatures to feel any ___.
2. At the sudden appearance of the bears some of the campers ___.
3. The ___ children ran from the picnic, because they thought that the bears were ___.
4. Soon the bears were gone, and the ___ was over.
5. The picnic was ___ ruined, because the bears had eaten all the food.

Illa est sagitta Trojana!

XLVIII. ASCANIUS ET CERVUS ALBUS

Postquam Graecī Trōjam dēlēvērunt, Trōjānus Aenēās ad Ītaliam cum fīliō suō et multīs sociīs nāvigāvit. Hīc erat Latium, rēgnum Latīnī. Aenēās prō sē et suīs sociīs agrōs rogāvit. Latīnus Aenēae et ejus virīs benignus erat et eīs agrōs dedit. Tamen multī incolae
5 Latiī Trōjānīs inimīcī erant.

Prope castra Trōjāna agricola Tyrrhus habitābat; trēs fīliōs et fīliam, Silviam, habēbat. Ōlim Tyrrhus et ejus fīliī cervum album paene mortuum ē silvā portāvērunt. Cervum Silviae dedērunt.

Silvia suum cervum cūrābat et amābat. Māne per silvās cervus
10 errābat sed vesperī semper ad Silviam redībat (*came back*).

Ōlim Ascanius, fīlius Aenēae, cum sociīs suīs in silvā errābat et cervum album vīdit. Quod prō sē glōriam dēsīderābat et nōn quod Silviae inimīcus erat, Ascanius cervum necāre temptābat. Itaque eum sagittā suā vulnerāvit.

15 Cervus ad casam Silviae fūgit. Ubi Silvia cervum paene mortuum vīdit, vehementer lacrimāvit.

Sed ubi Tyrrhus sagittam vīdit, īrātus erat. Dīxit, "Illa est sagitta Trōjāna! Perfidī Trōjānī! Cervum fīliae meae sagittīs vestrīs vulnerāvistis; sagittīs nostrīs, igitur, Ascanium et sociōs ejus vulnerābimus."

Itaque Tyrrhus cum fīliīs suīs et amīcīs eōrum castra Trōjāna vehementer oppugnāvit; hoc erat initium bellī.

cervus, -ī, M., stag; **cerva, -ae,** F., deer
fūgit, fled
igitur, *adv.*, therefore
inimīcus, -a, -um, unfriendly; M. *and* F. *as noun*, enemy
initium, -ī, N., beginning
paene, *adv.*, almost
perfidus, -a, -um, treacherous
postquam, *conj.*, after
suus, -a, -um, his, her, its, their; his own, etc.
vester, -tra, -trum, your, yours; (*of more than one person*)

USE OF *SUUS*

In the first sentence below, the word *his* refers to the subject. In the second sentence the word *their* refers to the subject.

The boy praises his friends.

The boys praise their friends.

In both sentences the possessors are the same persons as the subjects. The Latin word for *his, her, its,* or *their* when referring to the subject is **suus.**

Puer amīcōs suōs laudat.

Puerī amīcōs suōs laudant.

To decide whether **suōs** in such a sentence means *his, her, its,* or *their*, notice whether the subject is singular or plural and whether it is masculine, feminine, or neuter. In the first sentence above, **suōs** is translated *his*, because **puer** is masculine singular; in the second sentence above, **suōs** is translated *their*, because **puerī** is plural. In the following sentence **suōs** is translated *her*, because **puella** is feminine singular.

Puella amīcōs suōs laudat, *The girl praises her friends.*

DECLENSION OF *SUUS*

Suus is an adjective declined like **meus** and **tuus.** Since it is an adjective, it must agree in number, gender, and case with the noun it modifies. Thus, in the sentence above, **suōs** is masculine plural accusative, to agree with **amīcōs.**

ejus AND *eōrum*

Sometimes *his, her,* or *their* does not refer to the subject of the sentence.

They praise his friends. *He praises their friends.*

In the sentences above, the possessors are not the same persons as the subjects. When thus used, *his, her, its* are expressed by **ejus**; and when *their* is similarly used, it is expressed by **eōrum** (or **eārum**).

Amīcōs ejus laudant. **Amīcōs eōrum laudat.**

Ejus is the genitive singular of **is,** and **eōrum** (**eārum**) is the genitive plural. Since they are pronouns in the genitive case, their forms are not affected by the nouns which they modify.

Sometimes a possessive word is omitted in Latin when the meaning is clear, even though the corresponding English sentence requires a possessive. Possessives are to be supplied in translation whenever the sense requires.

Fēmina fīliam amat, *The woman loves her daughter.*

1. Librum suum habet; librum ejus habeō; librum tuum habet. 2. Librōs vestrōs habent; librōs suōs habent; librōs eōrum habēmus. 3. Postquam arma eōrum vīdimus, eōs nōn timēbāmus. 4. Ante initium proeliī virī perfidī fūgērunt; cōpiae nostrae, igitur, sine perīculō eōs superāvērunt. 5. Postquam amīcus tuus suam epistulam scrībit, fīlius meus ejus epistulam legit. 6. Pīrāta amīcīs suīs arcam pulchram mōnstrat; amīcī ejus arcam maximē laudant. 7. Ā dextrā est via lāta; ā sinistrā sunt mūrī altī. 8. Cervus vester est paene mortuus.

Find a phrase that correctly completes each sentence.

casae suae	**fīliam ejus**	**fīlium suum**	**in oppidum**
castra eōrum	**fīliam suam**	**fīlius ejus**	**oppida eōrum**
fīlia sua	**fīlium ejus**	**in agrō suō**	**oppida sua**

1. Agricola (*in his own field*) labōrat.
2. (*His son*) quoque in agrō labōrat.
3. Barbarī (*their own towns*) dēlēbant.
4. Vir (*his son*) laudat.
5. (*His son*) nōn laudō.
6. Ab hōc locō (*their camp*) vidēmus.
7. (*Their towns*) oppugnābuntur.
8. Fēmina saepe (*her daughter*) monet.
9. (*Her daughter*) monēmus.

REVIEW OF UNIT X LESSONS XLIV–XLVIII

Nouns	*Verbs*	*Adjectives*	*Conjunctions*
campus, -ī	audeō, -ēre	armātus, -a, -um	dum
cerva, -ae	circumspectō, -āre	decem	postquam
cervus, -ī	*dēfendēbant	dūrus, -a, -um	
*clangor	dēleō, -ēre	ferus, -a, -um	*Adverbs*
*glōria, -ae	dūxit	inimīcus, -a, -um	
initium, -ī	excitō, -āre	perfidus, -a, -um	herī
porta, -ae	fūgērunt	sacer, -cra, -crum	igitur
rīpa, -ae	fūgit	stultus, -a, -um	māne
verbum, -ī	*moveō, -ēre	suus, -a, -um	paene
	natō, -āre	tōtus, -a, -um	undique
Pronoun	respondeō, -ēre	vērus, -a, -um	vehementer
suī	rogō, -āre	vester, -tra, -trum	
	*salūtō, -āre		

I. Give the Latin for the missing word.

1. Puella librum (*her*) habet.
2. Puella librum (*their*) habet.
3. Puella librōs (*her*) habet.
4. Puella librōs (*his*) habet.
5. Puerī librōs (*their own*) habent.
6. Puellae librōs (*their own*) habent.
7. Puella cum amīcīs (*her*) vēnit.
8. Puella cum amīcīs (*their*) vēnit.
9. Puella cum amīcō (*her*) vēnit.
10. Puella cum amīcō (*their*) vēnit.

II. Choose the correct Latin pronoun for each English pronoun.

1. Tōtum oppidum nōn dēlēbitur; (*it*) vigilāmus. { illum / id / sē }

2. Vir ferus (*himself*) vulnerāvit. { sē / suī / eum }

3. Haec verba erant dūra sed vēra; populus (*them*) audīvit. { sibi / ea / sē }

4. Portae movēbuntur, sed (*them*) dēlēre nōn audēbimus. { eās / sēsē / ea }

5. Hic puer (*to himself*) cārus est, sed cēterīs nōn grātus est. { suī / eī / sibi }

III. Explain the grouping of these words, all of which refer to time.

herī	**interdum**	**aestāte**	**interdiū**	**deinde**
hodiē	**saepe**	**hieme**	**māne**	**dēnique**
	semper		**noctū**	**mox**
nunc		**ante**	**vesperī**	**ōlim**
tum		**post**		**prīmō**

IV. From the following list of adverbs select one that replaces each blank in the sentences below.

ācriter	**fortiter**	**iterum**	**maximē**	**posteā**	**statim**
bene	**hīc**	**lēniter**	**minimē**	**postrīdiē**	**tum**
celeriter	**igitur**	**longē**	**nunc**	**quam**	**undique**
diū	**ita**	**male**	**paene**	**satis**	**vehementer**

1. Prīmō puerī pigrī ___ ambulāvērunt; deinde, territī, ___ ambulāvērunt.
2. Puerī impigrī ___ labōrant; puerī pigrī ___ labōrant.
3. Oppidum ā silvā dēnsā ___ abest.
4. ___ eram armātus; ___ nōn armātus sum; ___ armātus erō.
5. Amāsne hunc campum? Respondē "___" aut "___."
6. Nūntium ___ expectāvistī; nūntius ___ nōn vēnit; tamen ___ aderit.
7. ___ perfidī estis!

LATIN LIVES TODAY

In the following story, try to connect each italicized word with a Latin word you have met.

On their wedding *anniversary* Mr. and Mrs. *Porter* started on a motor trip with *Max* and *Vera*. *Fido*, the *terrier*, looked very *doleful* because he could not go. As the family drove away, he began to bark *vehemently*. Max *responded* to the barks with, "We'll be back soon, Fido. *Expect* us on *September* sixth. It's a *bona fide* promise. High *school* starts the eighth."

The Porters found an excellent *location* to make *camp* that night. The place was so *quiet* that they all slept soundly in their *novel* surroundings.

In the morning Max started a fire in the *primitive* way. His *initial* attempt failed, but he was more *fortunate* the second time.

Mrs. Porter began to *prepare* breakfast. When she got out the *cereal*, Vera said, "Please save the box top, Mother. For a *total* of ten tops and ten *cents* I can get a *premium*."

As soon as the family had had their *vitamins*, they set out.

After a trip through the most *picturesque* part of *Pennsylvania*, they started home. The *unanimous verdict* concerning the trip was "perfect."

These mills at Ostia ground grain from Egypt and Sicily.

ROMAN INDUSTRIES

In early days all Romans were shepherds or farmers. Even the leaders of Rome tilled the land with their own hands. Each man owned his farm of a few acres and produced the food his family used. From his sheep came the wool which was woven into cloth for the garments of his household.

The Cupids in this wall painting are preparing newly woven cloth for use.

Specialty shops were common in Rome just as they are in our country. In this shop cushions and scarves were sold.

Later, some of these small farms came into the possession of rich men and were parts of large estates. On these larger farms, as on the smaller ones, many varieties of crops were raised, some of which were sent to market. The most important products were grain, olives, and grapes, for these furnished food for the people of the cities as well as for those of the country.

Nearly everything the Romans used was made by hand, usually by slaves working in the household. Strangely enough, most Romans did not make their own bread, finding it cheaper and more practical to buy loaves from a baker. In his small shop the baker ground the wheat, made the dough, baked the bread, and sold it. Loaves were also sold in street markets.

Working at a small forge, a smith is pounding metal into shape. Some of his tools hang above the forge.

Household slaves, sometimes with the aid of hired laborers, made many articles requiring skilled workmanship. Carpenters, masons, mechanics, smiths, spinners, and weavers worked in the home. In many cases all their products were used in the house where they were made; sometimes surplus articles were sold in small shops.

There were also a few factories where large numbers of men were employed. In the city of Arretium, which was near a supply of fine potter's clay, a kind of red-glazed pottery

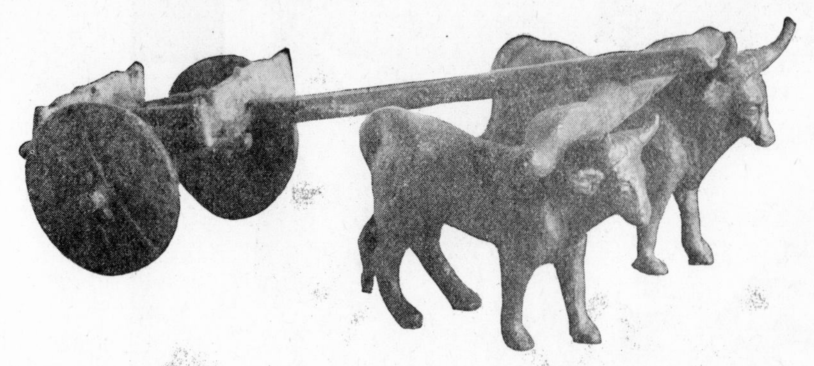

Carts like this carried the Roman farmer's grain to the granary, his grapes to the wine press, and his olives to the crusher (p. 103).

was produced. Numerous pieces of this pottery with the manufacturer's trademark on them have been found. Bronze and copper utensils were also made in factories.

One brick-making plant, employing several thousand workers in its yards and kilns, made most of the bricks used in Rome. The bricks were stamped with the name of the manufacturer and the date of production.

Even in factories the work was done in much the same way as in individual households. There could not have been many large industries, however, in days when there was neither machinery nor quick transportation for goods.

A grove of old olive trees—the source of olive oil, a valuable item in the Roman diet

Spanish boys learned Latin in school.

UNIT

XI

XLIX. SERTORIUS ET CERVA DIANAE

Olim in Ītaliā Sulla, dux Rōmānus, cōpiās Mariī, cōnsulis Rōmānī, superāvit. Posteā Sertōrius, amīcus Mariī, ad Hispāniam fūgit.

Tum Hispānī rēgēs nōn habēbant, sed ducēs bonōs et bona cōnsilia bellī habēbant. Quamquam Hispānī multīs Rōmānīs inimīcī erant, 5 tamen Sertōrium amābant, quod mātribus et patribus lēgēs bonās dedit; līberīs eōrum scholās bonās dedit. Magistrī Rōmānī in scholīs Hispāniae labōrābant. Līberī Hispānōrum togās Rōmānās habēbant et in scholīs linguam Rōmānam discēbant (*learned*).

Posteā Sertōrius pācem ōrāvit, sed ducēs Rōmānī eī respondērunt, 10 "Rōma pācem virīs perfidīs nōn dat."

Sertōrius igitur in silvīs Hispāniae contrā cōpiās Rōmānās pugnāre parābat.

Ōlim Hispānus cervam albam Sertōriō dedit. Hoc dōnum Sertōriō erat grātum. Cervam cōpiīs suīs mōnstrāvit et dīxit, "Haec cerva est 15 dōnum Diānae. Dum ea est tūta, Diāna cōpiīs nostrīs auxilium dabit."

Posteā Sertōrius dīxit, "Per hanc cervam Diāna mihi dīcit et mē dē perīculīs nostrīs monēbit."

Multae vōcēs clāmāvērunt, "Sertōrius est frāter noster! Diāna frātrī nostrō auxilium dabit. Rōmānōs superābimus."

20 Diū haec cerva alba Sertōrium juvābat; Rōmānī saepe superābantur. Dēnique cerva in silvam errābat, neque Hispānī eam iterum vīdērunt. Nōn jam fortūna Sertōriō benigna erat. Dēnique ejus inimīcī eum necāvērunt.

cōnsul, -ulis, M., consul, *a Roman magistrate*
dux, ducis, M., leader
frāter, frātris, M., brother
lēx, lēgis, F., law
līberī, -ōrum, M., *pl.*, children
magister, -trī, M., teacher, master
māter, mātris, F., mother
pater, patris, M., father
pāx, pācis, F., peace
rēx, rēgis, M., king
vōx, vōcis, F., voice

THIRD DECLENSION

The declension to which a Latin noun belongs can always be determined from the ending of the genitive singular. First-declension nouns have the ending **-ae** in the genitive, and second-declension nouns have **-ī**. All third-declension nouns have the genitive singular ending in **-is**, but the endings of the nominative singular are of many kinds. Examples of the various types will be given in the following lessons.

Roman soldiers wore such leather and metal corselets and helmets as the ones shown below. The banner at the right and the shield below belonged also to the Roman army, as did the spears.

MASCULINE AND FEMININE NOUNS OF THE FIRST CLASS

Nouns of the third declension may be divided into two classes. Those of the first class have the genitive plural ending in **-um.** Masculine and feminine nouns of this class are declined as follows:

	māter, F., *mother*	**rēx**, M., *king*	**dux**, M., *leader*	**prīnceps**, M., *chief*
		SINGULAR		
Nom.	**mā'ter**	**rēx**	**dux**	**prīn'ceps**
Gen.	**mā'tris**	**rē'gis**	**du'cis**	**prīn'cipis**
Dat.	**mā'trī**	**rē'gī**	**du'cī**	**prīn'cipī**
Acc.	**mā'trem**	**rē'gem**	**du'cem**	**prīn'cipem**
Abl.	**mā'tre**	**rē'ge**	**du'ce**	**prīn'cipe**
		PLURAL		
Nom.	**mā'trēs**	**rē'gēs**	**du'cēs**	**prīn'cipēs**
Gen.	**mā'trum**	**rē'gum**	**du'cum**	**prīn'cipum**
Dat.	**mā'tribus**	**rē'gibus**	**du'cibus**	**prīnci'pibus**
Acc.	**mā'trēs**	**rē'gēs**	**du'cēs**	**prīn'cipēs**
Abl.	**mā'tribus**	**rē'gibus**	**du'cibus**	**prīnci'pibus**

ENDINGS

You will observe that the case endings in this class of the third declension are as follows:

	SINGULAR	PLURAL
Nominative:	—	**-ēs**
Genitive:	**-is**	**-um**
Dative:	**-ī**	**-ibus**
Accusative:	**-em**	**-ēs**
Ablative:	**-e**	**-ibus**

1. Cōpiae hōrum ducum in magnō proeliō pugnābunt. 2. Illa fēmina est māter rēgum. 3. Is rēx togam pretiōsam frātrī vestrō dedit. 4. Rōmānī bonās lēgēs habēbant. 5. Ducēs eōrum bonōs magistrōs laudant. 6. Gallī huic rēgī auxilium dedērunt. 7. Patrem meum magnā vōce vocāvī. 8. Dux perfidus hīs rēgibus pācem nōn dedit. 9. Magistrī nostrī et patrēs nostrī līberōs laudant, quod in scholā bene labōrant.

Translate the italicized words: 1. The *king's* brother was the leader. 2. Your *father's* letter was long and good. 3. *The king* is praised *by the good leader.* 4. We are praised *by good leaders.* 5. I will give the letter *to my teacher.* 6. My teacher will show the letters *to our fathers.*

HELP YOURSELF

In earlier units of this book you have met nouns belonging to the first and second declensions. Most of the nouns in this unit belong to the third declension. Compare the nouns in the columns below and then answer the questions at the foot of the columns.

	FIRST DECL.	SECOND DECL.	THIRD DECL.	
		SINGULAR		
Nom.	**silva**	**magister**	**pater**	**vōx**
Gen.	**silvae**	**magistrī**	**patris**	**vōcis**
Dat.	**silvae**	**magistrō**	**patrī**	**vōcī**
Acc.	**silvam**	**magistrum**	**patrem**	**vōcem**
Abl.	**silvā**	**magistrō**	**patre**	**vōce**
		PLURAL		
Nom.	**silvae**	**magistrī**	**patrēs**	**vōcēs**
Gen.	**silvārum**	**magistrōrum**	**patrum**	**vōcum**
Dat.	**silvīs**	**magistrīs**	**patribus**	**vōcibus**
Acc.	**silvās**	**magistrōs**	**patrēs**	**vōcēs**
Abl.	**silvīs**	**magistrīs**	**patribus**	**vōcibus**

What is the genitive singular ending of first-declension nouns? Of second-declension? Of third-declension?

Nouns of which declension have **-em** in the accusative singular? **-um? -am?**

In which declension do you find **-ibus** in the dative plural? In what other case do you find **-ibus?**

LATIN LIVES TODAY

As you have already observed, the English equivalents of many Latin words are almost identical with the Latin: *antique, form, invite, long, move, rose.*

Other Latin words have the same meaning as English words that look entirely different: **frater,** *brother.* In such cases we sometimes have two groups of words, one group made from the Latin word, and the other from its English equivalent: **frater,** *fraternal, fraternity; brother, brotherly, brotherhood.*

In the following list find (1) words connected with **lex, mater, pater, rex;** (2) words connected with the English equivalent of each of these words.

lawmaker	fatherly	kingly	fatherhood
motherhood	legal	motherly	lawful
maternal	legislator	paternity	maternity
paternal	regal		

Caesar's army was highly organized and each soldier had his appointed duties. This man sounded his trumpet at regular intervals during the day, as the watches changed.

L. FRATER PERFIDUS

Ariovistus, rēx Germānus, cum magnīs cōpiīs in Galliam vēnit. Cōnsilium ejus erat occupāre tōtam Galliam. In Galliā erant multī mercātōrēs Rōmānī.

Jūlius Caesar, dux Rōmānus, legiōnēs suās in Galliā trāns Rhodanum 5 habēbat.

Dīviciācus, igitur, amīcus Caesaris, et cēterī prīncipēs Gallōrum Caesarī nūntiāvērunt, "Ariovistus, rēx Germānōrum, et ejus mīlitēs magnam regiōnem Galliae jam occupāvērunt et oppida nostra vāstant. Est homō perfidus et malus. Fēminae nostrae et līberī nostrī erunt servī Germānōrum; magna erit calamitās. Sumus amīcī Rōmānōrum, et Rōmānī Gallīs et mercātōribus suīs auxilium dare dēbent."

Caesar nūntiīs prīncipum respondit, "Magnum perīculum vidēmus et hominēs Galliae juvāre dēsīderāmus, sed satis magnam cōpiam frūmentī nōn habēmus." 5

Tum nūntius ā Dīviciācō ad Caesarem vēnit, "Frūmentum Rōmānīs dabimus et cum Rōmānīs contrā Germānōs pugnābimus. Dumnorīx, frāter meus, est dux equitum; ille Rōmānīs frūmentum et auxilium quoque dabit."

Itaque Caesar cum legiōnibus suīs in Galliam properāvit, sed 10 Dumnorīx perfidus auxilium Germānīs sēcrētō dabat neque Rōmānīs frūmentum dedit. Dumnorīx equitēs Gallōrum in proelium dūxit sed ante initium proeliī equitēs perfidī fūgērunt.

The Roman soldier is buying some delicacy to supplement his rations, which were largely grain. The man is writing down the amount to be paid later.

Tamen Caesar cōpiās Ariovistī in magnō proeliō superāvit, quamquam Ariovistus trāns Rhēnum fūgit.

Caesar igitur Dīviciācum dē frātre ejus perfidō monuit. Diū Dumnorīx perfidus ā mīlitibus Rōmānīs spectābātur; sed, quod Dīviciācus erat amīcus Caesaris, mīlitēs Dumnorīgem nōn necāre jubēbantur.

calamitās, -tātis, F., disaster, calamity, misfortune

eques, equitis, M., horseman; *pl.*, cavalry

homō, hominis, M., man, human being

legiō, -ōnis, F., legion, *a Roman company of soldiers (4000 to 6000 men)*

mercātor, -ōris, M., trader, merchant

mīles, mīlitis, M., soldier

prīnceps, prīncipis, M., chief, prince, leader

regiō, -ōnis, F., region

Both **vir** and **homō** are sometimes translated *man;* **vir** may also mean *hero,* while **homō** may refer to any human being. With an adjective of favorable meaning, as, for example, **bonus,** we usually find **vir** rather than **homō.**

MASCULINE AND FEMININE NOUNS OF THE THIRD DECLENSION

Other masculine nouns and feminine nouns in the first class of the third declension are declined as follows:

mīles, M., *soldier* **mercātor,** M., *trader* **homō,** M., *man*
legiō, F., *legion* **calamitās,** F., *calamity*

			SINGULAR		
Nom.	mī'les	mercā'tor	ho'mō	le'giō	cala'mitās
Gen.	mī'litis	mercātō'ris	ho'minis	legiō'nis	calamitā'tis
Dat.	mī'litī	mercātō'rī	ho'minī	legiō'nī	calamitā'tī
Acc.	mī'litem	mercātō'rem	ho'minem	legiō'nem	calamitā'tem
Abl.	mī'lite	mercātō're	ho'mine	legiō'ne	calamitā'te
			PLURAL		
Nom.	mī'litēs	mercātō'rēs	ho'minēs	legiō'nēs	calamitā'tēs
Gen.	mī'litum	mercātō'rum	ho'minum	legiō'num	calamitā'tum
Dat.	mīli'tibus	mercātō'ribus	homi'nibus	legiō'nibus	calamitā'tibus
Acc.	mī'litēs	mercātō'rēs	ho'minēs	legiō'nēs	calamitā'tēs
Abl.	mīli'tibus	mercātō'ribus	homi'nibus	legiō'nibus	calamitā'tibus

1. Legiōnis; legiōnum; cum mīlite; cum mīlitibus. 2. Frātris tuī; patris tuī; cum patre tuō. 3. Amīcus ejus hominis est;

amīcus eōrum hominum erat. 4. Rēx ā duce laudātur; dux ā rēge laudātur. 5. Ā quō mīles vocātur? 6. Ā quibus equitēs timentur? 7. Postrīdiē initium magnae calamitātis vīdimus. 8. Erant multī prīncipēs perfidī in hāc regiōne. 9. Mercātōrēs dēfessī viās hujus regiōnis nōn laudāvērunt. 10. Legiōnēs Rōmānae bona arma habent.

Make three sentences from each one by translating the phrases.

1. Fīlius { *of the soldier* / *of the leader* / *of the king* } fortiter pugnābat.

2. Homō { *with your brother* / *with the king* / *with those horsemen* } aderat.

3. Vīllae { *by the tired soldiers* / *by a Roman legion* / *by the cavalry* } occupābantur.

4. Frāter { *of this chief* / *of the merchants* / *of that man* } in Galliā nunc est.

5. Praemium { *to these traders* / *to the good teachers* / *to the treacherous leaders* } dabō.

From the words in Group B select an adjective that will fit each noun in Group A.

A		B	
calamitātum	mīlitibus	**angustōrum**	**multae**
ducī	patrem	**apertō**	**multārum**
hominum	prīncipis	**bonī**	**multōrum**
legiōnis	regiō	**bonō**	**nostra**
magister	rēgēs	**decimae**	**perfidōs**
mātrem	vōcēs	**fīdus**	**suīs**
		longīs	**suum**
		meam	**tūtārum**

LI. DANIEL ET LEONES

Olim rēx Babylōnius cum Isrāēlītīs pugnāvit et eōs facile superāvit. Deinde paucōs puerōs Isrāēlītārum ad rēgiam suam dūxit. Inter eōs puerōs erat Daniēl. Quamquam ā rēge tenēbātur, tamen Daniēl Deum Isrāēlītārum adōrābat; deōs Babylōniōs nōn adōrābat. Rēx Babylōnius Daniēlem amābat et eī multa praemia et multōs honōrēs dabat. Comitēs rēgis erant invidiōsī et Daniēlem necāre dēsīderābant.

Rēgī dīxērunt, "Ō rēx, Daniēl deōs Babylōniōs nōn adōrat neque tē, rēgem hujus terrae, adōrat. Contrā lēgem Deum Isrāēlītārum adōrat."

Propter haec verba comitum, rēx miser Daniēlem in spēluncam cum leōnibus injēcit (*threw*).

Etiam tum Daniēl nōn territus erat. Clāmāvit, "Deus mē servābit."

Tum rēx Daniēlī dīxit, "Es nōn perfidus, Daniēl. Deus tuus, quod eum semper adōrās, tē juvābit et tē ā bēstiīs servābit."

Deinde servī rēgis magnum saxum prō portā spēluncae sine morā mōvērunt.

Prīmā lūce ad spēluncam leōnum rēx properāvit et Daniēlem magnā vōce vocāvit, "Ō Daniēl, servāvitne tē Deus tuus?"

Ē spēluncā Daniēl respondit, "Ō rēx, angelus ex caelō vēnit; in hāc spēluncā aderat. Nūllus leō mē vulnerāvit. Deus mē servāvit."

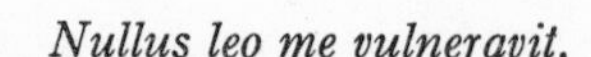

Nullus leo me vulneravit.

bēstia, -ae, F., beast, animal
comes, comitis, M., companion, attendant
etiam, *adv.*, even, also
facile, *adv.*, easily
lūx, lūcis, F., light; **prīmā lūce,** at daybreak
paucī, -ae, -a, *pl.*, few, a few
spēlunca, -ae, F., cave, den
teneō, -ēre, -uī, hold, keep

LATIN NOUNS AND ENGLISH NOUNS

Many Latin nouns of the third declension give us English nouns which have the same spelling and similar meanings: **animal,** *animal;* **labor,** *labor.*

What is the Latin word for each of the following nouns?

color *error* *honor* *omen* *victor*

Some English nouns come from Latin nouns ending in **-io.** Such nouns end in *-n* because they are made from the stem of the Latin noun, which ends in **-n: educatio,** *education;* **opinio,** *opinion.*

What, then, is the Latin word for each of the following nouns?

accommodation *description* *expectation* *inflation*

Some English nouns ending in *-y* come from Latin nouns ending in **-tas: calamitas,** *calamity;* **infirmitas,** *infirmity.*

What is the Latin word for each of the following nouns?

antiquity *dignity* *liberty* *security*

Give the English noun which comes from each Latin noun.

clamor	**dictator**	**humanitas**	**regio**	**suspicio**
collectio	**difficultas**	**recitatio**	**religio**	**terror**

1. Illī hominēs hunc rēgem adōrābant. 2. Prīncipēs bēstiam in spēluncā obscūrā tenuērunt. 3. Etiam nunc in illā terrā sunt malae lēgēs. 4. Sine morā populus eōs leōnēs facile necābit. 5. Magnā vōce mīlitēs illīus legiōnis pācem postulāvērunt. 6. Lūcem clāram prope casam mātris tuae vīdimus. 7. Prīnceps hārum regiōnum paucōs comitēs facile superāvit. 8. Rōmānī multōs deōs adōrābant. 9. Rēx virō validō magnum honōrem dabit.

LLT Find some other English nouns like *color, description,* or *infirmity* and look them up to see if they come from Latin.

LII. EPISTULA ROMANA

Mārcus Sextō salūtem dīcit. Sī valēs, bene est; valeō. Sumus in magnā silvā Galliae, et legiō nostra castra in rīpā magnī flūminis posuit (*pitched*). Hoc flūmen lātum et altum est.

Mīlitēs bene labōrāvērunt et circum castra mūrum aedificāvērunt. 5 Multī rāmōs et saxa ex silvā portābant, multī equōs cūrābant, multī tabernācula parābant, sed cum illīs mīlitibus nōn labōrābam. Cum paucīs mīlitibus cibum in dēnsā silvā petēbam (*was seeking*).

In hāc regiōne sunt multa genera bēstiārum. Sunt nūllī leōnēs in Galliā, sed in silvā ursās paucās et multōs cervōs vīdimus. Multōs 10 cervōs necāvimus et corpora eōrum ad castra portāvimus.

Hodiē cum sociīs paucīs iterum in silvam ambulāvī. Nōn longē ā castrīs nostrīs parvum flūmen vīdimus. Silvam circumspectāvimus, sed nūllōs Gallōs vīdimus. In mediō flūmine erat magnum saxum. Cum sociīs meīs ad hoc saxum natāvī. In hōc saxō diū sēdimus et 15 mīlitēs in dextrā rīpā flūminis spectāvimus. Paucī in flūmine natābant; capita eōrum in aquā vīdimus.

Laetus sum quod in hāc regiōne diū manēbimus. Germānī magnās cōpiās trāns Rhēnum habent et hanc regiōnem vāstāre parant, sed eōs nōn timēmus. Gallī Germānōs timent quod corpora valida habent 20 et sunt barbarī. Dux Germānus est perfidus, sed ducēs nostrī bona cōnsilia bellī habent.

Nōnne legiō tua mox erit in Galliā? Tum tē vidēbō et tibi multa dē hāc regiōne nārrābō. Valē.

A Roman bridge in France which is still used

caput, capitis, N., head
corpus, corporis, N., body
flūmen, flūminis, N., river
genus, generis, N., kind, sort
medius, -a, -um, middle, the middle of
salūs, salūtis, F., safety; **salūtem dīcit,** gives greetings
sedeō, -ēre, sēdī, sit, be seated; settle down, settle
sī, *conj.*, if
valeō, -ēre, -uī, be well; **valē** (*at end of a letter*), farewell

NEUTER NOUNS OF THE FIRST CLASS

Many neuter nouns of the third declension belong to the same class as the masculine and feminine nouns you studied in Lesson XLIX, that is, they have the genitive plural in **-um.** Neuter nouns of this class are declined as follows:

	flūmen, N., *river*	**caput,** N., *head*	**corpus,** N., *body*	**genus,** N., *kind*
		SINGULAR		
Nom.	**flū'men**	**ca'put**	**cor'pus**	**ge'nus**
Gen.	**flū'minis**	**ca'pitis**	**cor'poris**	**ge'neris**
Dat.	**flū'minī**	**ca'pitī**	**cor'porī**	**ge'nerī**
Acc.	**flū'men**	**ca'put**	**cor'pus**	**ge'nus**
Abl.	**flū'mine**	**ca'pite**	**cor'pore**	**ge'nere**
		PLURAL		
Nom.	**flū'mina**	**ca'pita**	**cor'pora**	**ge'nera**
Gen.	**flū'minum**	**ca'pitum**	**cor'porum**	**ge'nerum**
Dat.	**flūmi'nibus**	**capi'tibus**	**corpo'ribus**	**gene'ribus**
Acc.	**flū'mina**	**ca'pita**	**cor'pora**	**ge'nera**
Abl.	**flūmi'nibus**	**capi'tibus**	**corpo'ribus**	**gene'ribus**

These words illustrate different formations of the nominative singular, but they are all declined in the same way.

1. Sunt magna flūmina in patriā meā, sed in magnīs flūminibus natāre nōn amō. 2. Prō salūte mīlitum suōrum dux bonus semper labōrat. 3. Hī barbarī magna corpora habent, sed nōn erunt mīlitēs bonī. 4. In hōc flūmine saepe natāmus; interdum in magnīs saxīs in mediō flūmine sedēmus. 5. Sī multa genera bēstiārum sunt in hīs regiōnibus, castra nostra nōn sunt tūta. 6. Hieme in flūmine nōn natābimus, sed mūrōs prope rīpam aedificābimus.

Change the italicized words to plural and make any other necessary changes.

1. Parvum *caput* vīdī.
2. Temptā nārrāre dē *bellō* Rōmānō.
3. *Corpus mīlitis* validum erat.
4. Mīlitēs trāns illud *flūmen* properābant.
5. *Mīles* in rīpā *flūminis* lātī sedēbat.
6. *Eques* in *rīpā* illīus flūminis tenēbātur.
7. Aut in flūmine *natō* aut in rīpā *sedeō.*

LIII. POETA CAECUS

Vir in summō colle ambulat; lyram portat. Quamquam est caecus, celeriter ambulat. Cum virō in viā dūrā est parva puella.

Puella. Nox est et in silvā avēs et bēstiae silent. Via est obscūra; lūnam nōn videō quod nūbēs eam cēlant.

5 *Vir.* Longē ā tēctō nostrō absumus. Es dēfessa et nūllum cibum habēmus.

Puella. Undique collēs et montēs sunt. Neque urbem neque oppidum videō. Tamen nōn longē lūmen videō. Lūmen est in parvō tēctō.

Vir. Appropinquābimus et cibum rogābimus, quod dēfessus sum et 10 nūllam pecūniam habeō. Illī virī nōn barbarī sunt et cibum dabunt. Pecūniam nōn rogābimus.

In tēctō parvō agricola et puer sedent. In fenestrā tēctī est lucerna. Nōn jam via est obscūra quod subitō per nūbēs lūna vidētur.

Puer [*magnā vōce*]. Ecce, pater! Virum et parvam puellam videō. Ad 15 tēctum appropinquant.

Agricola. Virum et puellam appellāre dēbēmus. Eīs cibum dabimus; vir est dēfessus.

Poeta caecus

Puer ad jānuam properāvit; virum et puellam 20 appellāvit.

Vir. Ā tēctō meō longē absum. Caecus sum et nūllam pecūniam habeō.

25 *Agricola.* Sed es homō, et homō hominem juvāre dēbet!

Itaque vir cum puellā in tēctum vēnit. Agricola eīs 30 cibum dedit.

Post cēnam vir caecus lyram suam ōrāvit et dē urbe longinquā et dē bellō Trōjānō cantāvit.

35 Caecus erat Homērus, clārus poēta Graeciae.

appropinquō, -āre, -āvī, approach
avis, avis, -ium, F., bird
collis, collis, -ium, M., hill
lūmen, lūminis, N., light
mōns, montis, -ium, M., mountain
nox, noctis, -ium, F., night
nūbēs, nūbis, -ium, F., cloud
sileō, -ēre, siluī, be silent
summus, -a, -um, highest; highest part of, top of
urbs, urbis, -ium, F., city

In this book the genitive plural ending **-ium** is printed in the lesson vocabulary after each noun which has that ending.

When **b** appears before **s**, it has the sound of *p:* **urbs,** *urps.*

MASCULINE AND FEMININE NOUNS OF THE SECOND CLASS

Nouns of the third declension which make up the second class end in **-ium** in the genitive plural. Practically all masculine and feminine nouns of the second class have (*a*) the same number of syllables in the nominative and the genitive singular or (*b*) two consonants immediately preceding the ending of the genitive singular: **nūbēs,** *gen.*, **nūbis;**[1] **nox,** *gen.*, **noctis.**[2]

collis, M., *hill* — **nox,** F., *night* — **mōns,** M., *mountain*
nūbēs, F., *cloud* — **urbs,** F., *city*

	SINGULAR				
Nom.	col'lis	nū'bēs	nox	urbs	mōns
Gen.	col'lis	nū'bis	noc'tis	ur'bis	mon'tis
Dat.	col'lī	nū'bī	noc'tī	ur'bī	mon'tī
Acc.	col'lem	nū'bem	noc'tem	ur'bem	mon'tem
Abl.	col'le	nū'be	noc'te	ur'be	mon'te
	PLURAL				
Nom.	col'lēs	nū'bēs	noc'tēs	ur'bēs	mon'tēs
Gen.	col'lium	nū'bium	noc'tium	ur'bium	mon'tium
Dat.	col'libus	nū'bibus	noc'tibus	ur'bibus	mon'tibus
Acc.	col'lēs[3]	nū'bēs	noc'tēs	ur'bēs	mon'tēs
Abl.	col'libus	nū'bibus	noc'tibus	ur'bibus	mon'tibus

1. Nox erat et in collibus et montibus avēs et bēstiae silēbant. 2. Lūmen lūnae obscūrum erat propter nūbēs, quamquam paucās stellās vidēbam. 3. Longē ab urbe aberam; nox erat et territus eram. 4. Homō dēfessus ad flūmen appropinquat; hominēs

[1]Two exceptions are **canis,** *dog,* and **juvenis,** *young man;* both have the genitive plural ending in **-um.**
[2]Exceptions are **frāter, pater,** and **māter.**
[3]To the Teacher: The **-ēs** ending is regularly used in this book in preference to the **-īs** ending.

ad rīpās flūminis appropinquābant. 5. Hieme hōrae noctium longae videntur. 6. In summō colle avēs cantābant. 7. Hic puer est amīcus avium, et saepe eīs cibum dat. 8. Ā viā properāmus, quod nūbēs obscūrās vidēmus. 9. Hominēs hominem dēfessum juvāre dēbent. 10. Hominēs appropinquāre nōn audent.

Translate the italicized words: 1. *Of the long night; of many nights; of this night.* 2. *From a high hill; from the top of the hill* (not genitive); *through the clouds.* 3. *The nights* are *long* in winter. 4. I see a *bright light* in the window of the cottage. 5. The man sees a light *on the high mountain.* 6. We saw *many birds* in this forest.

HELP YOURSELF

Remember that the Latin words for "middle of" and "top of" are adjectives declined like **bonus** and modify nouns in the same way. What is the Latin for: *middle of the street, middle of the night, top of the hill, top of the mountain, top of the head?*

LATIN LIVES TODAY

In the aviary of a zoo, would you expect to find bees, canaries, or goldfish?

If you wanted to buy a watch with a luminous dial, would the jeweler show you a watch with a diamond-studded case, gold hands, or numerals that glow in the dark?

What is the summit of a mountain?

LIV. ERROR CONSIDII

A Roman standard

Olim mīlitēs Rōmānī in proeliīs īnsignia habēbant. Nāvēs in marī īnsignia quoque habēbant. Sīc hostēs et amīcī erant nōtī. Signa quoque habēbant. Interdum haec signa erant figūrae, exemplāria avium et animālium.

Cōnsidius erat mīles Rōmānus, dux cōpiārum Rōmānārum. Caesar, prīnceps Rōmānus, hunc ducem ad collem propinquum mīsit.

Cōnsidiō Caesar dīxit, "Properā sine morā ad collem propinquum. Castra hostium sub hōc colle sunt, sed Labiēnus hunc collem occupāvit. Hostēs nōs nōn expectant; auxiliō Labiēnī eōs oppugnāre dēsīderō, sed proelium perīculōsum erit sī hostēs collem jam habent."

Cōnsidius, cum paucīs comitibus, per campum properāvit. Labiēnus jam collem occupābat, et Caesarem et cōpiās ejus expectābat. Hostēs Labiēnum nōn vīdērunt. Sed Cōnsidius, propter timōrem, mīlitēs in colle nōn bene vīdit. Īnsignia hostium et īnsignia amīcōrum suōrum satis bene nōn cognōvit (*did not know*).

Itaque clāmāvit, "Illa īnsignia sunt Gallica! Hostēs collem occupāvērunt!"

Cōnsidius ad Caesarem properāvit et eī nūntiāvit, "Perīculum magnum est! Gallī sunt in summō colle!"

Propter haec verba Cōnsidiī, Caesar cōpiās suās in castrīs tenuit, quamquam, auxiliō Labiēnī, hostēs facile superāre potuit (*he was able*).

exemplar, -āris, -ium, N., example, likeness
hostis, hostis, -ium, M., enemy; **hostēs,** *pl.*, the enemy
īnsigne, īnsignis, -ium, N., decoration, badge, insigne
mare, maris, -ium, N., sea, ocean
nāvis, nāvis, -ium, F., ship, boat
sīc, *adv.*, thus, so
timor, -ōris, M., fear

The word **hostis** is applied to an enemy of one's country, while **inimīcus** means a personal enemy.

NEUTER NOUNS OF THE SECOND CLASS

The second class of third-declension nouns has a number of neuters. These end in **-e, -al,** or **-ar** in the nominative. They are declined as follows:

	īnsigne, N., *badge*	**animal,** N., *animal*	**exemplar,** N., *example*	**mare,** N., *sea*
		SINGULAR		
Nom.	**īnsig'ne**	**a'nimal**	**exem'plar**	**ma're**
Gen.	**īnsig'nis**	**animā'lis**	**exemplā'ris**	**ma'ris**
Dat.	**īnsig'nī**	**animā'lī**	**exemplā'rī**	**ma'rī**
Acc.	**īnsig'ne**	**a'nimal**	**exem'plar**	**ma're**
Abl.	**īnsig'nī**	**animā'lī**	**exemplā'rī**	**ma'rī**
		PLURAL		
Nom.	**īnsig'nia**	**animā'lia**	**exemplā'ria**	**ma'ria**
Gen.	**īnsig'nium**	**animā'lium**	**exemplā'rium**	**ma'rium**
Dat.	**īnsig'nibus**	**animā'libus**	**exemplā'ribus**	**ma'ribus**
Acc.	**īnsig'nia**	**animā'lia**	**exemplā'ria**	**ma'ria**
Abl.	**īnsig'nibus**	**animā'libus**	**exemplā'ribus**	**ma'ribus**

These nouns differ from neuter nouns of the first class in that the genitive plural ends in **-ium,** the ablative singular ends in **-ī,** and the nominative and accusative plural end in **-ia.** As with all neuter nouns, the nominative and accusative singular are alike, and the nominative and accusative plural are alike.

GENDER IN THE THIRD DECLENSION

You can remember the gender of third-declension nouns in this way. Nouns ending in **-tor** are usually masculine; in **-iō, -tās,** or **-tūs,** feminine; in **-al, -ar, -e,** or **-t,** neuter.

Modern insignia

1. Illōrum animālium; illōrum flūminum; hōrum hostium; hōrum mīlitum. 2. Exemplāria nōta sunt; īnsignia nōta sunt; erant flūmina pauca in illā terrā. 3. Signum Gallōrum erat figūra animālis. 4. Ē nāvibus signa Rōmāna nōn facile vidēbantur. 5. Cūr īnsignia vestra sīc cēlātis? 6. Avēs noctū in silvīs silēbant. 7. Haec animālia in marī natant; magna corpora et parva capita habent. 8. Sīc semper amīcōs habēbitis.

1. Of this animal; of that badge; of our ships. 2. The decorations of the enemy are being concealed. 3. There are many animals in the sea. 4. We see examples of the insignia of our soldiers in the pictures of this book. 5. This place is well known on account of a great battle. 6. Thus the words of Considius warned his leader.

LLT

Most of the words in the vocabulary are related to English or Latin words that you already know.

exemplar, *example, exemplary*
hostis, *hostile*
insigne (in + signum), *insigne, insignia*
mare (ora maritima), *marine, mariner*
navis (navigo), *naval*
timor (timeo, timidus), *timorous*

Give some English derivatives from **maritima, navigo, signum, timeo, timidus.**

REVIEW OF UNIT XI LESSONS XLIX–LIV

Nouns

*angelus, -ī
*animal, animālis, -ium
avis, avis, -ium
bēstia, -ae
calamitās, -tātis
caput, capitis
collis, collis, -ium
comes, comitis
cōnsul, cōnsulis
corpus, corporis
dux, ducis
eques, equitis
exemplar, exemplāris, -ium
*figūra, -ae
flūmen, flūminis
frāter, frātris
genus, generis
homō, hominis
*honor, -ōris
hostis, hostis, -ium
īnsigne, īnsignis, -ium
legiō, -ōnis
lēx, lēgis
līberī, -ōrum
lūmen, -inis
*lyra, -ae
lūx, lūcis
magister, -trī
mare, maris, -ium
māter, mātris
mercātor, -ōris
mīles, mīlitis
mōns, montis, -ium
nāvis, nāvis, -ium
nox, noctis, -ium
nūbēs, nūbis, -ium
pater, patris
pāx, pācis
prīnceps, prīncipis
regiō, -ōnis
rēx, rēgis
salūs, salūtis
*signum, -ī
spēlunca, -ae
timor, -ōris
*toga, -ae
urbs, urbis, -ium
vōx, vōcis

Adjectives

medius, -a, -um
paucī, -ae, -a
summus, -a, -um

Verbs		*Adverbs*	*Conjunction*
*adōrō, -āre	sileō, -ēre	etiam	sī
appropinquō, -āre	teneō, -ēre	facile	
sedeō, -ēre	valeō, -ēre	sīc	

I. Make four sentences of each one by supplying the correct Latin words.

1. Pictūrās (*of bodies, of cities, of heads, of rocks*) habēmus.
2. Fōrma (*of the birds, of the examples, of the hills, of the insignia*) est pulchra.
3. In hortō (*a lion, birds, children, men*) vidēmus.
4. (*To my father, To the animal, To the leader, To your brothers*) signum dabō, sī parātus es.

II. You have already learned the declensions of the nouns in Group A. In Group B are other third-declension nouns that you have met in this unit. Find in Group B one or more words declined in the same way as each word in Group A.

A		B		
calamitās	legiō	avis	hostis	pater
collis	māter	comes	lēx	pāx
dux	mercātor	eques	lūmen	regiō
flūmen	mīles	frāter	lūx	salūs
īnsigne	rēx	honor	mare	vōx

LATIN LIVES TODAY

Answer the following questions. (All the italicized words are related to Latin words you know.)

1. What is meant by national debt *per capita?*
2. Is the *summit* of a mountain at the top or the foot?
3. The syllable *-cide* comes from a Latin word meaning "killing"; who is killed in *fratricide, homicide, matricide, patricide, regicide, suicide?*
4. Did Balboa name the ocean *Pacific* because it looked stormy, green, or peaceful?
5. Which of the following persons has a *sedentary* occupation: carpenter, gardener, typist, housewife?
6. Does *paucity* of material mean much or little?
7. Does a vacuum cleaner *facilitate* housework?
8. Does a *valedictorian* deliver a greeting or a farewell?
9. Is a *vocalist* a dancer, a magician, or a singer?

These pillars, which still stand in Rome, belonged to temples in the ancient Forum.

UNIT

XII

LV. CIVES ROMAM ITERUM AEDIFICANT.

Gallī ferī, ubi Rōmam occupāvērunt, aedificia et templa deōrum per urbem vāstāvērunt. Sed aedificia in arce et in Capitōliō erant tūta.

Prope Rōmam erat oppidum antīquum, Veiī. Mūrī hujus oppidī 5 erant validī, et aedificia erant tūta.

Ducēs populum Rōmānum hīs verbīs excitāvērunt, "Cīvēs miserī, cūr hīc manēmus? Ruīnās urbis vidētis. Cūr iterum urbem nostram aedificāre temptābimus? Veiī sunt nostrī. Mīlitēs nostrī illam urbem bellō superāvērunt. Nunc ad illam urbem mīgrāre dēbēmus."

10 Tum virī et fēminae ruīnās urbis Rōmae circumspectāvērunt.

Multī respondērunt, "Ita, ad urbem Veiōs mīgrāre dēbēmus; in illā urbe Rōmam novam aedificābimus."

Sed Camillus, dictātor et dux ēgregius, cīvēs in forum convocāvit. Diū et vehementer dīxit.

"Quid est, Rōmānī? Estisne ignāvī? Cūr ex hāc urbe jam mīgrāre dēsīderātis? Gēns vestra iterum erit valida, quod dī vōs juvābunt. Mīlitēs vestrī et dī vestrī in arce mānsērunt, quamquam Gallī eam oppugnābant. Collēs Rōmae, campōs, flūmen Tiberim, agrōs nostrōs, hoc caelum Ītaliae amāmus. In urbe Veiīs fortūna erit dubia; hīc 5 calamitās est magna, sed dī auxilium dabunt."

Statim dī eīs signum dedērunt. Populus vōcem ducis mīlitum audīvit. Dux virōs cōnsistere (*to halt*) jubēbat.

"Hic est locus bonus. Hīc manēbimus," dīxit.

Itaque verbīs Camillī et hōc signō cīvēs excitābantur. Nōn jam 10 ignāvī et pigrī, sed impigrī et superbī, in urbe suā mānsērunt et urbem iterum aedificāvērunt.

aedificium, -ī, N., building
arx, arcis, -ium, F., citadel
cīvis, cīvis, -ium, M. or F., citizen
gēns, gentis, -ium, F., nation
ignāvus, -a, -um, cowardly
vōs, you (*nom. and acc. pl.*)

LATIN NOUNS AND ENGLISH NOUNS

Some third-declension nouns ending in **-o** have corresponding English words ending in *-e:* **altitudo,** *altitude.*

What is the Latin for each of the following words?

longitude *magnitude* *multitude*

With what familiar Latin adjective is each of these connected?

Many Latin nouns ending in **-or** have come unchanged into English: *dictator, spectator.* In such cases the **-or** is a Latin suffix and has the same meaning as in English—*one who.*

There is an English word spelled exactly like each of the following words. What does each of these Latin words mean?

curator	**gladiator**	**monitor**	**orator**
educator	**moderator**	**narrator**	**victor**

1. Multae gentēs; multārum gentium; in hāc arce; hae arcēs. 2. Magnae calamitātēs; cīvēs ignāvī; mīlitī ignāvō; in urbe pulchrā. 3. Ruīnae aedificiōrum; mūrī urbium et rīpae flūminum. 4. Vōs in ruīnīs urbis vidēbimus, sed vōs nōn juvābimus. 5. Arcem occupāvimus, sed fortūna bellī est dubia. 6. Ille cīvis est ignāvus; in arce nōn manēbit. 7. Magna calamitās hās gentēs excitāvit. 8. Ruīnās arcis antīquae in summō colle vīdimus. 9. Multa animālia in spēluncīs habitant, sed ea nōn timēmus.

Make three sentences of each one by translating the phrases.

1. Cīvis bonus { *will be safe.* / *was not cowardly.* / *loves his city.* }

2. Virī { *a tall building* / *a new city* / *a citadel* } aedificābant.

3. Puerī { *to the forum* / *to the city* / *to the river* } properābant.

4. { *The citizens* / *Few leaders* / *Bad men* } ignāvī sunt.

5. Cīvēs { *the treacherous leader* / *the nation* / *the evil king* } monuērunt.

Conjugate **moneō** and **maneō** in the perfect active.

Decline **cīvis bonus.**

Give the third person plural of **portō** and **moneō** in the present, imperfect, future, and perfect of the active voice.

HY In "Cīvēs Rōmam Iterum Aedificant," find the name of a town that is always plural in form. Find four uses of this name and explain the case use of each one.

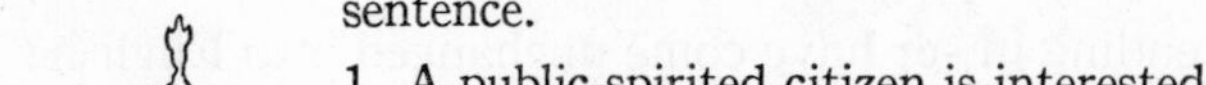

LLT From the list below select the proper word to complete each sentence.

1. A public-spirited citizen is interested in __ activities.
2. The __ at Washington is a beautiful __.
3. The soldier was glad to exchange his __ uniform for __ clothes.
4. The matter was discussed at an open __.
5. It was a __ storm.
6. A __ is not a democratic form of government.
7. If you want this government position, you must pass a __ service examination.
8. Albany is the __ of New York.

capital	civic	civilian	edifice	military
capitol	civil	dictatorship	forum	ruinous

LVI. ANDROCLES ET LEO

Androclēs erat servus dominī Rōmānī in Āfricā. Quod ejus dominus erat malus, Androclēs in loca fera fūgit, ubi in spēluncā obscūrā latēbat.

Sed ōlim leō ferus in hanc spēluncam vēnit ubi Androclēs sedēbat, et fugitīvum magnopere terruit. Tamen servus nōn sē mōvit. Leō lēniter ad Androclem vēnit, et pedem suum, longā spīnā vulnerātum, mōnstrāvit. Androclēs benignus ex pede leōnis spīnam celeriter remōvit.

Jam leō servum benignum amāre vidēbātur. Cum amīcō suō manēre dēsīderābat. Itaque diū homō et leō in spēluncā obscūrā habitāvērunt.

Sed dēnique mīlitēs Rōmānī fugitīvum procul ā spēluncā vīdērunt. Androclēs, sonō pedum monitus, celeriter fūgit, sed mīlitēs eum hastīs vulnerāvērunt. Quod Androclēs erat servus, dux mīlitum eum ad dominum ejus dūxit.

Dominus servum vulnerātum ad Ītaliam portāvit. Hīc vir malus dīxit, "Imperātor Rōmānus est amīcus meus; crās in arēnā ā leōnibus ferīs necāberis."

Postrīdiē mīlitēs armātī Androclem in arēnam portāvērunt. Statim leō ferus ad servum appropinquāvit. Subitō leō stetit et servum spectāvit. Tum ad eum lēniter vēnit et pedem mōnstrāvit. Nōn jam leō erat ferus; Androclēs erat amīcus.

Prīmō populus erat īrātus quod leō servum nōn necāvit. Sed, ubi dē leōne et spīnā audīvit, imperātor, magnopere mōtus, Androclem et leōnem līberāvit.

crās, *adv.*, tomorrow
dominus, -ī, M., master (of slaves or of a household)
imperātor, -ōris, M., commander, emperor
lateō, -ēre, -uī, lurk, hide, be concealed
magnopere, *adv.*, greatly, very much
pēs, pedis, M., foot, paw
procul, *adv.*, at a distance, far
spīna, -ae, F., thorn
terreō, -ēre, -uī, -itum, frighten, terrify

Beginning with the vocabulary of this lesson, four forms are listed for most verbs. They are the first person singular present, the present infinitive, the first person singular perfect, and the perfect passive participle. Some verbs do not have a perfect passive participle. In such cases only three forms are given.

USE OF PARTICIPLES

There are certain verb forms which not only denote action, but also tell something about a person or thing, very much as an adjective does.

The boy, frightened by the noise, called for help.

In the sentence above, the word *frightened* is a form of the verb *frighten,* but it also tells something about the situation or condition of the boy. It is called a *participle,* and it shares something of the character of a verb and of an adjective. It has the character of a verb in that it denotes action, and it has the character of an adjective in that it modifies a noun or pronoun.

FORMS OF THE PERFECT PARTICIPLE

The perfect passive participle of **portō** is **portātus, -a, -um,** translated either *having been carried* or *carried.*

The perfect participle of **juvō** is **jūtus, -a, -um**; of **dō** is **datus, -a, -um** (differing from **portātus** in that the **a** is short). The perfect participles of all the other verbs of the first conjugation which you have met thus far are formed like that of **portō**;[1] for example, **laudātus, amātus.**

The participle of **moneō** is **monitus, -a, -um,** meaning *having been warned* or simply *warned.* Some other second-conjugation verbs form the perfect passive participle like **moneō**; for example, **dēbitus, -a, -um; habitus, -a, -um.**

DECLENSION OF THE PARTICIPLE

The perfect passive participle is declined like **bonus.** Like any adjective, a participle agrees in gender, number, and case with the noun or pronoun it modifies.

Puer, ā patre monitus, ad scholam properābat.	*The boy, having been warned by his father, was hurrying to school,* or *The boy, warned by his father, was hurrying to school.*

The Latin participle is usually placed at the end of the participial phrase.

[1]The verb **stō** has no perfect participle.

In such an arena as the famous Colosseum, Androcles might have met the lion.

1. Urbs, ā Gallīs occupāta, crās dēlēbitur. 2. Dē perīculō monitus, procul ab arēnā manēbō. 3. Etiam imperātōrēs, propter perīculum territī, ex agrīs properant. 4. Salūs mīlitum erat dubia. 5. Sociī, ōlim ab hostibus superātī, in patriā suā manent et auxilium postulātum nōn dabunt. 6. Animal excitātum puerōs terruit. 7. Avēs territae in silvā manēbant. 8. Cūr servus territus in illō locō latet? 9. Androclēs pedem leōnis spīnā vulnerātum vīdit. 10. Crāsne dominus malus magnopere excitābitur?

Translate the italicized words: 1. The *towns, attacked* by the enemy, are in danger. 2. The *book demanded* by Sextus will be given at once. 3. The *king, defeated* by our forces, will not remain in his native country. 4. The *girls, warned*, will not again hide in the forest. 5. The *boys, often called*, do not reply. 6. The *lion, wounded by a spear*, hid in his den.

Arena in "Androclēs et Leō" can be translated by the same word, *arena*. The Latin word **arena,** however, really means "sand." The name was given to the outdoor Roman theater because sand was sprinkled in the central part where contests were held. What uses do we make of the word today?

Only one of the following statements is true. Find the correct statement and tell why each of the others is wrong.

1. We saw many pedestrians on bicycles.
2. If you procrastinate, you will finish the job today.
3. The concert pianist has a latent musical talent.
4. In Latin, a verb that expresses a command is in the imperative mood.
5. A weak man usually dominates his stronger brother.
6. The child was pacified by the terrifying experience.

LVII. PICUS—REX ET AVIS

Pīcus, rēx Latiī antīquī, magnam rēgiam in mediō campō habēbat. Circē, maga clāra, prope rēgiam Pīcī habitābat. Magnam et malam potestātem habēbat; saepe hominēs in bēstiās aut in avēs mūtāvit. Ōlim Circē Pīcum vīdit et statim rēgem amāvit. Sed Pīcus Circam nōn amāvit; nympham pulchram hujus regiōnis amāvit.

Dēnique Pīcus nympham in mātrimōnium dūxit. Postrīdiē cīvēs et uxōrēs cīvium ad magnam cēnam convocāvit. Sed ante cēnam Pīcus cum paucīs comitibus in silvam propinquam vēnit. Circē quoque in silvam sēcrētō properāvit et sub altā arbore stetit. Tum comitēs rēgis, magnopere territī, spectāculum mīrum spectābant. Ubi Pīcus ad hanc arborem appropinquāvit, maga invidiōsa fōrmam ejus mūtāvit.

Nōn jam caput Pīcī corōnā sed cristā (*crest*) adōrnātur; manūs (*hands*) ejus in ālās mūtantur; pedēs ejus in pedēs avis; oculī ejus in parvōs oculōs avis. Nōn jam vōcem hominis habet; ōs (*mouth*) ejus in rōstrum mūtātur. Multī colōrēs in corpore et in ālīs videntur. Pīcus rēx jam est Pīcus avis.

Hōra cēnae vēnit; cīvēs et uxōrēs eōrum aderant; rēgīna aderat; sed Rēx Pīcus aberat. Subitō per apertam portam rēgiae avis pulchra, multīs colōribus adōrnāta, volāvit. Circum magnam rēgiam errāvit; tum ē fenestrā celeriter volāvit.

Jam Pīcus avis in arboribus et in rīpīs flūminis, aut in silvīs aut in hortīs habitat. Semper clāmat, "Ōlim rēx fuī et corōnam habuī; nunc avis sum et rōstrō meō cibum in arbore inveniō (*find*)."

arbor, -oris, F., tree
corōna, -ae, F., crown
maga, -ae, F., witch
oculus, -ī, M., eye
potestās, -tātis, F., power
rōstrum, -ī, N., beak
uxor, -ōris, F., wife

PRINCIPAL PARTS OF THE VERB

There are certain forms of a verb which show important facts regarding its conjugation. These four forms of each Latin verb are commonly listed in a vocabulary. They are called the *principal parts.*

Present Active (*first person singular*):	**portō**
Present Infinitive:	**portāre**
Perfect Active (*first person singular*):	**portāvī**
Perfect Passive Participle:	**portātum**

PRINCIPAL PARTS OF FIRST-CONJUGATION VERBS

Most verbs of the first conjugation form their principal parts like **portō**. Among the verbs given thus far, there are three that do not.

dō, dare, dedī, datum
juvō, juvāre, jūvī, jūtum
stō, stāre, stetī

The verb **stō** has no perfect passive participle; **dō** is different in having the **a** short in the infinitive and in the perfect participle. You will remember that **dō** also has short **a** in all forms of the present tense except the second person singular, **dās**, and in all forms of the imperfect and future.

STEMS OF THE VERB

A Latin verb regularly has three stems: present, perfect, and participial.

PRESENT STEM

The present stem is found by dropping the **-re** of the infinitive.

Infinitive: **portāre** *Present Stem:* **portā-**

The present stem is used to form the tenses of the present system: present, imperfect, and future, both active and passive.

PERFECT STEM

The perfect stem is found by dropping **-ī** from the first person singular of the perfect active.

Perfect Active: **portāvī** *Perfect Stem:* **portāv-**

The perfect stem is used only in the active voice. You have already learned one tense which is formed on the perfect stem: the perfect active. You will learn the others later.

PARTICIPIAL STEM

The participial stem is found by dropping **-um** from the perfect participle.

Perfect Participle: **portātum** *Participial Stem:* **portāt-**

Only a few forms aside from the perfect participle are made on the participial stem. You will learn these later.

1. Corōna rēgis Pīcī multōs colōrēs et multās gemmās habēbat. 2. Sunt altī collēs prope tēctum rēgis. 3. In rāmīs altārum arborum multās avēs vīdimus. 4. In ālīs et in corpore hārum avium sunt multī colōrēs. 5. Uxor ducis magnam potestātem nōn habēbat. 6. Rēx, potestāte magae mūtātus, per portam volāvit. 7. Mūrī, pictūrīs adōrnātī, laudābuntur. 8. Oculī cervī sunt magnī, sed oculī avis sunt parvī. 9. Ea avis parvum rōstrum habet, sed multae avēs magna rōstra habent.

Translate the italicized words: 1. *Many birds* flew among the branches *of the tall trees.* 2. The witch gave a beautiful crown *adorned* with gems *to the king's wife.* 3. The color of the wings *of that bird* is beautiful. 4. The eyes *of those animals* are small. 5. The boy was sitting *on the rock;* he was watching *the birds.*

Write the principal parts of **laudō** and indicate the three stems by drawing vertical lines in such a way as to cut off the final **-re** of the infinitive, the person ending **-ī** of the perfect, and the case ending **-um** of the participle. In the same way indicate the stems of **habeō.**

HW Conjugate **sum, stō,** and **dō** in the perfect.

LLT

Find one Latin derivative in each sentence.

1. Many trees were planted on Arbor Day.
2. The coronation of the king took place in Westminster Abbey.
3. If you are having trouble with your eyes, you should visit an oculist.
4. During the war the queen dressed very simply, without adornment of any kind.

In Lesson LVI you saw the development of the use of the Latin word **arena. Rostrum,** in the vocabulary of this lesson, has had a similar development. From the original meaning "beak" it came to mean a stage decorated with the beaks, or prows, of captured ships. A stage, so decorated, in the Roman Forum was called the *rostrum.* Find this word used in English.

 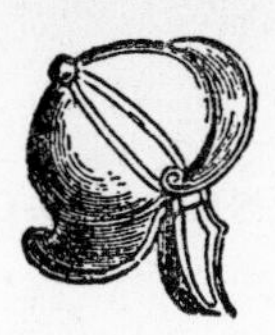  

Such helmets were worn by Roman soldiers to protect the back of the neck as well as the head. (*See also p. 180.*)

LVIII. PRO AMICO

Aenēās Trōjānus cum rēge Rutulōrum pugnābat. Quod ejus castra erant in magnō perīculō, erat necesse auxilium ab urbibus propinquīs rogāre. Itaque Aenēās cum paucīs comitibus ad urbem Evandrī properāvit. Ascanius, fīlius Aenēae, in castrīs mānsit.

Tum Rutulī castra Trōjāna vehementer oppugnāvērunt. Funditōrēs 5 lapidēs in moenia et in vāllum fundīs conjēcērunt (*hurled*). Undique mīlitēs portās ācriter oppugnāvērunt. Dēnique Trōjānī, magnopere excitātī, perīculum Aenēae nūntiāre dēsīderābant.

Nīsus ducibus dīxit, "Hoc iter perīculōsum prope castra hostium cum comite meō, Euryalō, temptābō. Nūntium ad Aenēam por- 10 tābimus. Nōmina nostra erunt clāra."

Ducēs cōnsilium probāvērunt. Ascanius laetus hīs amīcīs bona arma dedit; ducēs eīs epistulās dedērunt.

Sēcrētō Nīsus et Euryalus ad castra hostium appropinquāvērunt. Hīc multōs virōs necāvērunt et sine difficultāte fūgērunt. Jam galeās 15 aureās, in castrīs hostium occupātās, portābant. Lūna et stellae erant clārae, sed comitēs perīculum nōn timēbant.

Subitō agmina hostium novōrum vīdērunt; sociī auxilium ad Rutulōs portābant. Amīcī inter arborēs latēre temptāvērunt, sed hostēs galeās aureās lūce lūnae vīdērunt. Nīsus fūgit et inter arborēs dēnsās 20 latuit, sed Euryalus nōn fūgit. Nīsus ex silvā perīculum vīdit et ad amīcum suum properāvit. Eum servāre temptāvit; sed Euryalus, gladiō ducis vulnerātus, jam mortuus erat.

Tamen Nīsus prō amīcō ācriter pugnāvit et dēnique gladiō ducem hostium necāvit. Sed comitēs hujus ducis mīlitem sōlum facile 25 superāvērunt; et mox capita amīcōrum miserōrum prope castra Trōjāna in hastīs ā sociīs superbīs Rutulōrum portābantur.

agmen, agminis, N., line of march
funda, -ae, F., sling
funditor, -ōris, M., slinger
iter, itineris, N., road, journey
lapis, lapidis, M., stone
moenia, -ium, N. *pl.*, walls, fortifications
necesse, *adj.*, necessary
nōmen, nōminis, N., name
vāllum, -ī, N., rampart

PRINCIPAL PARTS OF SECOND-CONJUGATION VERBS

The principal parts of eight second-conjugation verbs which have appeared in preceding lessons are given below, with their stems.

dēbeō	**dēbēre**	**dēbuī**	**dēbitum**	**lateō**	**latēre**	**latuī**	—
	dēbē-	**dēbu-**	**dēbit-**		**latē-**	**latu-**	
habeō	**habēre**	**habuī**	**habitum**	**sileō**	**silēre**	**siluī**	—
	habē-	**habu-**	**habit-**		**silē-**	**silu-**	
moneō	**monēre**	**monuī**	**monitum**	**teneō**	**tenēre**	**tenuī**	—
	monē-	**monu-**	**monit-**		**tenē-**	**tenu-**	
terreō	**terrēre**	**terruī**	**territum**	**timeō**	**timēre**	**timuī**	—
	terrē-	**terru-**	**territ-**		**timē-**	**timu-**	

The last four verbs in the list above have no perfect passive participle.

DIFFERENT ENDINGS OF THE PERFECT STEM

All the second-conjugation verbs given above have the perfect ending in **-uī**. But this is not true of all verbs of this conjugation. Other ways of forming the perfect are seen in the following:

maneō, manēre, mānsī, mānsum, remain
jubeō, jubēre, jussī, jussum, order, command
moveō, movēre, mōvī, mōtum, move
sedeō, sedēre, sēdī, sessum, sit
videō, vidēre, vīdī, vīsum, see
dēleō, dēlēre, dēlēvī, dēlētum, destroy
respondeō, respondēre, respondī, respōnsum, answer, reply

1. Funditōrēs validās fundās et lapidēs portāvērunt. 2. Multī mīlitēs moenia circum urbem aedificāvērunt. 3. Hī mīlitēs magnās hastās habēbant. 4. Mīlitēs barbarī altum vāllum circum castra sua nōn habēbant. 5. Imperātor, sonō armōrum monitus, inter arborēs latuit. 6. Cīvēs agmina hostium nōn timēbant. 7. Itinera per silvās erant perīculōsa. 8. Nōmina hōrum flūminum sunt clāra.

1. The soldiers were carrying shields and spears, but they were not carrying slings. 2. The slingers stood on the high walls. 3. The friends, much terrified, tried to escape through the camp of the enemy.

Flammae comam Laviniae occupaverunt.

LIX. OMINA MALA

Lāvīnia Turnum, rēgem Rutulōrum, amābat, sed mala ōmina eōrum mātrimōnium prohibuērunt.

In mediō hortō rēgiae ubi Lāvīnia cum patre, rēge Latīnō, habitābat, arbor sacra erat. Ōlim multae apēs ā marī trāns Tiberim volāvērunt et ad urbem appropinquāvērunt. Prīmō circum mūrōs urbis volā- 5 vērunt; dēnique in hortum volāvērunt et in arbore sacrā sēdērunt.

Comitēs rēgis et populus erant territī. Servī apēs terrēre temptāvērunt, sed apēs in arbore mānsērunt. Mīlitēs tubās īnflāre jussī sunt, sed apēs mānsērunt. Ducēs ad rēgiam vocātī sunt et rēx Latīnus ē somnō excitātus est. Tum rēx territus deōs ōrāvit. 10

Vōx magna respondit, "Apēs sunt ōmen. Jam advena appropinquat. Apēs trāns mare ad urbem tuam volāvērunt et in summā arbore sēdērunt; advena in summā arce mox sedēbit."

Postrīdiē Latīnus ōmen iterum vīdit. Lāvīnia prō ārā stābat ubi

Latīnus ignem sacrum incendēbat (*was kindling*). Subitō flammae comam longam Lāvīniae occupāvērunt. Puella territa per rēgiam fūgit. Sed flammae subitō cessāvērunt (*ceased*) et Lāvīnia servāta est.

Rēx, hīs ōminibus magnopere territus, in silvam ad ōrāculum sacrum 5 properāvit. Hīc mediā nocte Latīnus magnās vōcēs audīvit.

Hae vōcēs eī dīcere vidēbantur, "Nōn Turnus, sed advena Lāvīniam in mātrimōnium dūcet (*fut.*). Advenae erunt fīliī tuī, Ō Latīne; advenae nōmen tuum habēbunt. Advenae, Trōjānī nunc appellātī, mox Latīnī appellābuntur. Hī advenae nōmen Latīnum ad stellās 10 portābunt; gēns tua erit clāra."

advena, -ae, M., stranger, foreigner
apis, apis, -ium, F., bee
ignis, ignis, -ium, M., fire
prohibeō, -ēre, -uī, -itum, prohibit, prevent
somnus, -ī, M., sleep

The neuter form of the perfect participle is given in the principal parts because in some verbs this participle has no masculine or feminine form. But most participles are declined in all three genders: **portātus, -a, -um; monitus, -a, -um.**

PERFECT PASSIVE OF *portō* AND *moneō*

The perfect passive, unlike the other tenses which you have met, is not formed by adding person endings to a stem. Instead, the perfect passive participle is used with the present tense of **sum.** Two separate words are used to represent each person and number.

The verbs **portō** and **moneō** are conjugated as follows in the perfect passive:

SINGULAR

portā'tus sum, I was carried, I have been carried	**mo'nitus sum,** I was warned, I have been warned
portā'tus es, you were carried, you have been carried	**mo'nitus es,** you were warned, you have been warned
portā'tus est, he, she, it was carried; he, she, it has been carried	**mo'nitus est,** he, she, it was warned; he, she, it has been warned

PLURAL

portā'tī sumus, we were carried, we have been carried	**mo'nitī sumus,** we were warned, we have been warned
portā'tī estis, you were carried, you have been carried	**mo'nitī estis,** you were warned, you have been warned
portā'tī sunt, they were carried, they have been carried	**mo'nitī sunt,** they were warned, they have been warned

The participle used in forming the perfect passive agrees with the subject in gender and number.

Puella laudāta est, *The girl has been praised.*
Puer laudātus est, *The boy has been praised.*
Puerī laudātī sunt, *The boys have been praised.*

PREDICATE NOUN WITH PASSIVE FORMS

As you have already learned, a noun or pronoun which is used after some form of the verb **sum,** and which means the same thing as the subject, is called a predicate noun. It is in the nominative case.

Like the forms of **sum,** the passive forms of **appellō** and other words of *naming* and *calling* may have a predicate noun.

Virī Gallī appellābantur, *The men were called Gauls.*
Puer Mārcus appellātur, *The boy is called Marcus.*

In the first sentence **Gallī** refers to the same people as the subject **virī.** In the second sentence **Mārcus** refers to the same person as **puer.**

1. Advena rēx appellātus est; virī hujus regiōnis rēgēs appellātī sunt. 2. Coma longa puellae gemmīs adōrnāta est. 3. Puella monita est; advena monitus est. 4. Arbor ā Latīnīs propter apēs sacra appellāta est. 5. Multī ignēs in castrīs vīsī sunt. 6. Auxilium ā mīlitibus nostrīs datum est et castra mōta sunt. 7. Puer ab amīcō suō jūtus est; oppidum ā barbarīs dēlētum est. 8. Āra pulchra prope mare aedificāta est. 9. Ōmina mala rēgem terruērunt. 10. Ducēs, ōminibus monitī, fugam cīvium prohibuērunt.

Translate the italicized words: 1. Our soldiers *have* often *been praised.* 2. The cities of our allies *have been seized* by the enemy (*pl.*). 3. Many bees *were seen* in the garden. 4. The Trojans *settled* near the shore. 5. A message *has not been given* to this man.

HELP YOURSELF Find in the story two participial phrases. In the Latin sentences (1) find five examples of the perfect passive and explain the ending of each participle; (2) point out two examples of a predicate noun with a passive verb.

LLT

From **apis** come *apiarist* and *apiculture.* From **ignis** come *ignite* and *ignition*; from *fire* we have *fireplace, fireworks.*

Give some English derivatives from **mare, princeps, timor, urbs,** and some words made from the corresponding English words *sea, chief, fear, city.*

In large cities there were separate baths for women. In smaller places, rooms were set apart for them or the baths reserved for them at certain hours.

ROMAN BATHS

The public baths of the Romans were more than places for bathing; they were also clubs or community centers for exercise and recreation, where people came to meet each other socially.

In the days of the Empire, every town of any size in Italy or the provinces had its public baths. In Rome itself there were over eight hundred baths. Many of these could truthfully be called palaces, so large were they and so splendidly decorated.

The most famous and elaborate public baths at Rome were the Baths of Caracalla and Diocletian. Sixteen hundred patrons could be accommodated at one time in the former and three thousand in the latter. The Baths of Caracalla were surrounded by a beautiful park made lovely by sparkling fountains and gleaming marble statues. In the extensive grounds there were several swimming pools, a stadium, and places for wrestling, racing, jumping, and ball playing. There were even bowling alleys. The huge structure that housed the baths also included lecture halls, libraries, lounges, and gymnasiums.

These baths were not public in the sense that admission was free. However, the fee was very small—about a quarter of a cent for men and twice that amount for women. Now and then there were "free days," when some person desiring public favor contributed funds so that people could enter the baths without charge.

In all large baths the procedure was much the same. After taking off his clothes in a dressing room and placing them in a locker, the bather entered a warm room. There he remained long enough to start perspiring, in order not to pass too suddenly into the high temperature of the next room, where he took a very hot bath or a sweat bath. From the hot room he entered the cold room, where he plunged into a pool of cold water. Then he went into a room where he was rubbed down by slaves and anointed with oil.

The baths were heated by large furnaces, the heat circulating under the floor and through spaces between the walls. The immense amount of water used in the baths was supplied by aqueducts and stored in huge reservoirs. The reservoirs of one of the largest baths in Rome are said to have had a capacity of several million gallons.

It has been said that the baths were among the greatest achievements of the Romans, making personal cleanliness in surroundings of great beauty possible even for the humblest.

This building at Bath, England, is still in use today, and the mineral water in the pool is brought by a Roman aqueduct.

REVIEW OF UNIT XII LESSONS LV–LIX

Nouns

advena, -ae
aedificium, -ī
agmen, agminis
apis, apis, -ium
arbor, -oris
*arēna, -ae
arx, arcis, -ium
cīvis, cīvis, -ium
*color, -ōris
corōna, -ae
*dictātor, -ōris
*difficultās, -tātis
dominus, -ī
*forum, -ī
*fugitīvus, -ī

funda, -ae
funditor, -ōris
gēns, gentis, -ium
ignis, ignis, -ium
imperātor, -ōris
iter, itineris
lapis, lapidis
maga, -ae
moenia, -ium
nōmen, nōminis
oculus, -ī
*ōmen, ōminis
pēs, pedis
potestās, -tātis
rōstrum, -ī

Nouns

*ruīna, -ae
somnus, -ī
*spectāculum, -ī
spīna, -ae
uxor, -ōris
vāllum, -ī

Adjectives

ignāvus, -a, -um
necesse

Pronoun

vōs

Verbs

*adōrnō, -āre
lateō, -ēre
*līberō, -āre
*mīgrō, -āre
prohibeō, -ēre
*removeō, -movēre
terreō, -ēre

Adverbs

crās
magnopere
procul

I. Give the forms asked for in the present active, imperfect active, future active, and perfect active.

1. Third person singular of **maneō.**
2. Third person plural of **terreō.**
3. Second person singular of **lateō.**

II. Give the form of the perfect passive participle of adōrnō which agrees with: **corōnae, gladiōs, lūx, portīs, puellārum, scūtō, urbem.**

III. In the numbered list find a Latin word equivalent to each English phrase.

1. **fuērunt**
2. **fuistī**
3. **jussērunt**
4. **jussī**
5. **jūvī**
6. **mānsit**
7. **monitī**
8. **monuit**
9. **movent**
10. **mōvērunt**
11. **respondet**
12. **respondit**
13. **terruistī**
14. **timuistī**
15. **vīdimus**

(*a*) he advised
(*b*) he answers
(*c*) he has remained
(*d*) I helped
(*e*) she has answered
(*f*) they have moved
(*g*) they ordered
(*h*) they were
(*i*) having been warned
(*j*) we saw
(*k*) you have been
(*l*) you feared

LATIN LIVES TODAY Give the corresponding English word for each of the starred words in the review vocabulary.

LX. MATER ANTIQUA

Postquam Trōja ā Graecīs vāstāta est, Aenēās, dux Trōjānus, cum sociīs suīs ad Thrāciam nāvigāvit.

In lītore erat tumulus. Hic tumulus parvīs arboribus cēlātus est. Aenēās paucōs rāmōs ab arbore remōvit quod āram adōrnāre dēsīderāvit. Sed ubi sanguinem in rāmīs vīdit magnopere territus erat. 5

Tum vōx ē tumulō clāmāvit, "Ō Aenēās, mē miserum vulnerāvistī. Sum Polydōrus Trōjānus. Rēx hujus terrae mē necāvit et hīc sub hōc tumulō corpus meum cēlāvit. Fuge (*flee*) ab hīs lītoribus perīculōsīs sine morā!"

Hīs verbīs mōtī, Aenēās et sociī ejus ā lītoribus Thrāciae fūgērunt. 10 Īnsula Dēlos, ubi erat templum Apollinis, nōn longē aberat. Hīc Aenēās auxilium deī rogāvit.

Ita Aenēās ōrāvit, "Ō Apollō, dā Trōjānīs domicilium idōneum; dā gentem validam et urbem mānsūram (*lasting*); dā nōbīs ōmen bonum."

Vōx deī respondit, "Exquīrite (*seek*) antīquam mātrem vestram. Ibi 15 Aenēās erit rēx, et līberī ejus erunt rēgēs."

"Ubi est māter nostra antīqua?" rogāvērunt sociī Aenēae.

Tum sine morā Anchīsēs, pater Aenēae, dīxit, "In īnsulā Crētā initium gentis nostrae fuit. Illa īnsula est māter nostra antīqua."

Itaque Trōjānī laetī, ventīs portātī, ad īnsulam Crētam nāvigāvērunt, 20 ubi parvam urbem aedificāvērunt. Sed posteā pestilentia multōs Trōjānōs necāvit.

Tum Aenēās ā deīs suīs ita monitus est, "Crēta nōn est antīqua māter vestra. Longē ab hāc īnsulā in terrā Ītaliā tūtum domicilium vōs expectat." 25

domicilium, -ī, N., home
idōneus, -a, -um, suitable
lītus, lītoris, N., seashore, beach
sanguis, -inis, M., blood
tumulus, -ī, M., mound, tomb
ventus, -ī, M., wind

ABLATIVE WITH *cum*

In Lesson XII you learned that **cum,** meaning *with,* is followed by the ablative.

Cum amīcō ambulō, *I walk with my friend.*

In the sentence above, **amīcō** denotes the *person in company with whom* the act is done. Hence it is called the *ablative of accompaniment.*

There is another common use of the ablative with **cum**, which denotes the way an act is done. This is called the *ablative of manner.*

Ibi magnā cum difficultāte parvum oppidum aedificāvit, *With great difficulty he built a small town there.*

KINDS OF ABLATIVES

You are already familiar with the ablative of agent.

Ursa ā mīlite necāta est, *The bear was killed by the soldier.*

The ablative of agent shows the person by whom the act is done, just as the ablative of means shows the means by which it is done.

Ursa hastā necāta est, *The bear was killed with a spear.*

Remember these points about ablatives:

1. The ablative of accompaniment usually has **cum.**
2. The ablative of agent is used only with the passive voice and always has **ā** or **ab.**
3. The ablative of manner usually has **cum.**
4. The ablative of means never has a preposition.

1. Ventī nāvēs ad lītus portāvērunt. 2. Nāvēs, ad lītus ventīs portātae, dēlētae sunt. 3. Locum idōneum vidēmus; loca idōnea vidēbimus. 4. Hoc domicilium ā rēge malō aedificātum est. 5. Castra, ab hostibus oppugnāta, vāstāta sunt. 6. Prope tumulum erat multus sanguis. 7. Trōjānī domicilia idōnea in lītore aedificābant. 8. Aenēās sanguinem in rāmō videt. 9. Dux Trōjānus, vōce amīcī suī monitus, cum sociīs fūgit. 10. In scholā nōmina multōrum animālium discimus.

Translate the prepositional phrases: 1. The land seen by the sailors was called Crete. 2. The aid asked by our allies was given by our leader. 3. Aided by the wind, the ship sailed swiftly to the shore. 4. We live in a land loved by the inhabitants.

LLT Give the Latin word to which each italicized word is related.

1. Wind is the original *ventilator.*
2. The battle was long and *sanguinary.*
3. We have good *ventilation* in our building.
4. A ruddy complexion is sometimes called *sanguine.*

An ancient ship

LXI. NULLUM DOMICILIUM IDONEUM

Nāvibus parātīs, Aenēās iterum trāns mare ab īnsulā Crētā nāvigāvit. Tamen ubi longē ā lītore āfuit, et caelum undique et undique mare vīdit, magna tempestās eum per undās perīculōsās in vada portāvit. Dēnique Aenēās cum sociīs suīs ad īnsulam vēnit.

Hīc Trōjānī dēfessī multa animālia in lītore vīdērunt. Pauca 5 animālia necāvērunt et cēnam et sacrificia parāvērunt. Sed subitō dē caelō avēs ferae circum eōs volāvērunt. Haec mōnstra habēbant corpora avium, capita fēminārum; Harpyiae appellābantur. Hīs mōnstrīs vīsīs, Trōjānī territī fūgērunt. Posteā, verbīs ducis Aenēae excitātī, contrā Harpyiās pugnāre temptābant, sed haec erat difficultās 10 —etiam gladiīs acūtīs terga dūra avium nōn vulnerāta sunt.

Subitō Harpyia fera magnā cum vōce clāmāvit, "Animālia nostra necāvistis; nōs necāre temptāvistis. In hāc terrā igitur pācem numquam habēbitis. In Ītaliā urbem dēsīderātam habēbitis."

Propter terrōrem mortis Trōjānī in hōc locō manēre nōn jam 15 audēbant. Itaque, mente mūtātā, ab īnsulā celeriter nāvigāvērunt.

Deinde Aenēās prope ōram Graecam nāvigāvit, et dēnique cum Trōjānīs cēterīs ad terram vēnit ubi Helenus erat rēx. Helenus, fīlius rēgis Trōjānī, erat laetus ubi amīcōs vīdit, et eōs ad rēgiam dūxit. Ibi eīs cibum et multa dōna dedit. 20

Tum, auxiliō deī prō Aenēā rogātō, Helenus dīxit, "Magna erunt perīcula et magnae erunt difficultātēs; per multa maria nāvigābitis, sed dēnique in Ītaliā domicilium tūtum et idōneum post itinera perīculōsa habēbitis."

mēns, mentis, -ium, F., mind, purpose
mors, mortis, -ium, F., death
numquam, *adv.*, never
unda, -ae, F., wave
vadum, -ī, N., shoal, ford

THE INDEPENDENT PARTICIPIAL CONSTRUCTION

A phrase consisting of a noun or pronoun and a participle is sometimes used in a sentence without being closely connected with any other word in the sentence.

A new leader having been chosen, we may expect better results.

Here the phrase *A new leader having been chosen* is not directly connected with any word in the rest of the sentence. Such a phrase is said to be independent of the rest of the sentence.

THE ABLATIVE ABSOLUTE

The case which is used in Latin for such independent constructions is the ablative. In the sentence on page 233 as an example the word for *leader* would be put in the ablative in Latin, and the participle for *having been chosen* would agree with it in case as well as in gender and number. This use of the ablative is called the *ablative absolute*—the word *absolute* here meaning virtually "independent."

Duce vocātō, hostēs fūgērunt, *The leader having been called, the enemy fled.*[1]

Fīliīs meīs laudātīs, laetus sum, *My sons having been praised, I am happy.*

Often an adjective or another noun is used instead of a participle as the second part of the ablative absolute.

Amīcō meō aegrō, nōn manēbō, *My friend (being) sick, I shall not remain.*

Sextō duce, mīlitēs semper fortiter pugnābant, *Sextus (being) leader, the soldiers always fought bravely.*

When we translate an ablative absolute of which the second part is an adjective or a noun, we often supply the participle *being*, as in the illustrative sentences above.

FREE TRANSLATION OF THE ABLATIVE ABSOLUTE

In English, independent phrases corresponding to the literal translation of the ablative absolute are not often used. So it is frequently necessary to translate the ablative absolute in other ways.

Sometimes a perfect passive participle in an ablative absolute is best translated by an English perfect active participle.

Nōmine mūtātō, vir fūgit, *Having changed his name, the man fled.*

Frequently the best translation of the ablative absolute is a dependent clause introduced by *when*, *after*, *if*, *since*, or *although*.

monte occupātō, *when the mountain had been seized*
duce vocātō, *after the leader had been called*
Turnō necātō, *if Turnus is killed*
amīcō meō aegrō, *since my friend is sick*
puerō pigrō, *although the boy was lazy*

Sometimes prepositional phrases are used in translating this ablative.

Sextō cōnsule, *in the consulship of Sextus*

[1] The original force of the ablative in this construction may be seen if the preposition *with* is used in the translation of these phrases: *with the leader called; with my sons (having been) praised.*

In the following sentences, first translate each of the ablative absolute phrases *literally;* then consider the relation of the phrase to the rest of the sentence and decide which is better, the literal translation or a clause introduced by *when, after, since,* or *although.* 1. Avibus novīs vīsīs, terror mentēs Trōjānōrum occupāvit. 2. Moenibus aedificātīs, oppidum erat tūtum. 3. Calamitāte hostium nūntiātā, ducēs castra ā tergō oppugnāvērunt. 4. Mentibus mūtātīs, cīvēs fortiter pugnāvērunt. 5. Territī magnā tempestāte, nautae undīs per vada portābantur. 6. Morte prīncipis nūntiātā, mīlitēs doluērunt. 7. Urbe suā dēlētā, Trōjānī mortem numquam timuērunt.

Translate the dependent clauses: 1. After the island was seen, the weary Trojans were happy. 2. After the strange birds were killed, the Trojans fled. 3. Since the girls were frightened, the boys killed the lion. 4. Although the leaders were killed, the soldiers did not fear death. 5. When the boy had been called, the leaders praised the messenger.

HY

Find examples of the ablative absolute in "Nūllum Domicilium Idōneum." Give the gender, number, and case of each participle in the story.

LATIN LIVES TODAY

When you talk about your *mind,* you are using the old English word, but when you use the words that are italicized in the next paragraph, you are using derivatives from Latin.

If Philip's *mental* powers equaled his physical powers, he would be a superman. John Adams had a high degree of *mentality.* I felt *mentally* exhausted after solving the problem.

If a person is *mortally* wounded, will he recover? Does *mortality* mean "death rate" or "accident rate"? Why are human beings described as *mortals?*

To what Latin word are *mental, mentality,* and *mentally* related? *Mortally, mortality,* and *mortals?*

When waves move, they are *undulating.* Their movement is called *undulation.* An *undulant* fever is one that goes and comes.

Aeneas cervos necat.

LXII. AENEAS ET DIDO

Post multa et longa itinera, Aenēās iterum ad Ītaliam nāvigāre temptat. Sed Jūnō, rēgīna deōrum, magnam tempestātem mittit, et nāvēs Aenēae ad lītus Āfricae portantur. Classis Trōjāna inter vada et magna saxa paene vāstātur, sed dēnique Trōjānī tūtī in 5 lītore stant.

Frūmentum portātum ē nāvibus nōn est bonum. Virī dēfessī alium cibum habēre dēbent. Itaque in silvā propinquā Aenēās sagittīs cervōs septem necat, et sociī cēnam in ōrā parant.

Postrīdiē Aenēās et sociī ejus magnam et pulchram urbem, Car-10 thāginem, vident.

Dīdō, ōlim rēgīna Phoenīciae, post mortem conjugis suī trāns mare Mediterrāneum ad Āfricam cum multīs comitibus nāvigāvit et hanc novam urbem aedificāvit.

Calamitāte Trōjānōrum nūntiātā, Dīdō, nunc rēgīna Carthāginis, 15 advenīs benigna est. Aenēās et Ascanius, fīlius ejus, cum multīs prīncipibus ad rēgiam dūcuntur. Cibus quoque et alia dōna ad cēterōs Trōjānōs mittuntur.

Noctū in rēgiā magna cēna parātur. Hīc Aenēās, verbīs rēgīnae mōtus, fābulam Trōjae nārrat. Dux Trōjānus hanc fābulam bene nārrat; Dīdō statim Aenēam maximē amat.

Quod Aenēam et Trōjānōs in Āfricā diū manēre dēsīderat, rēgīna Aenēae et sociīs ejus domicilia in rēgnō suō dat. 5

Dēnique Juppiter, hāc morā vīsā, Mercurium celeriter ad Aenēam mittit.

Mercurius dīcit, "Carthāgō nōn est urbs Trōjānīs ā deīs data. Ītalia tē trāns mare expectat. Ibi urbem clāram aedificābis; ibi Lāvīnia, fīlia rēgis, erit conjūnx tua. Relinque hanc urbem. In 10 Ītaliā pete domicilium tuum."

Tum Aenēās, verbīs deī mōtus, sine morā urbem relinquit. Ē rēgiā Dīdō misera nāvēs Trōjānās videt. Nunc mortem dēsīderat; sine Aenēā vīta nōn jam amoena est.

alius, -a, -ud, another, other
classis, classis, -ium, F., fleet; division, class
conjūnx, -jugis, M., husband; F., wife
petō, -ere, seek
relinquō, -linquere, leave, leave behind

Alius is declined like **bonus** except in the genitive and dative singular, which are not used in this book.

Dido sees Aeneas sailing away.

THIRD CONJUGATION

Verbs of the *third conjugation* have the ending **-ere** in the present infinitive. This ending must be distinguished from that of the second conjugation, which is **-ēre.**

There are two classes of verbs of the third conjugation, one class with the ending **-ō** and the other class with the ending **-iō** in the first person singular of the present active.

PRESENT TENSE OF *-Ō* VERBS OF THE THIRD CONJUGATION

Verbs of the first class are conjugated as follows in the present tense:

SINGULAR	
ACTIVE	PASSIVE
dū'cō, I lead, am leading	**dū'cor,** I am being led, am led
dū'cis, you lead, *etc.*	**dū'ceris,** you are being led, are led
dū'cit, he, she, it leads, *etc.*	**dū'citur,** he, she, it is being led, *etc.*
PLURAL	
dū'cimus, we lead, *etc.*	**dū'cimur,** we are being led, *etc.*
dū'citis, you lead, *etc.*	**dūci'minī,** you are being led, *etc.*
dū'cunt, they lead, *etc.*	**dūcun'tur,** they are being led, *etc.*

In the second person singular of the passive, the vowel before the person ending is **-e-** (not **-i-** as in the active). In the third person plural of both voices it is **-u-.**

You have already met forms of seven verbs which are conjugated like **dūcō, dūcere:**

colō, colere	**discō, discere**	**mittō, mittere**
dēfendō, dēfendere	**legō, legere**	**scrībō, scrībere**
dīcō, dīcere		

IMPERATIVE OF *-Ō* VERBS OF THE THIRD CONJUGATION

As in the first and second conjugations, the singular imperative of most third-conjugation verbs is like the present stem of the verb:

cole dēfende disce lege mitte scrībe

Exceptions are the short forms **dīc** and **dūc.**

In the plural imperative, all third-conjugation verbs have the same ending:

colite dēfendite dīcite discite dūcite legite mittite scrībite

Vergil reading his long poem, the Aeneid

1. Uxor ab Aenēā petitur. 2. Cōpiae in proelium aliud dūcuntur. 3. Propter terrōrem hostium ad mortem ignāvam dūciminī. 4. Auxiliō nōn postulātō, sociī auxilium mittunt. 5. Urbe aedificātā, Trōjānī pācem ab incolīs regiōnis petunt. 6. Fābulā nārrātā, Aenēās urbem relinquit. 7. Lītore novō vīsō, classis Trōjāna ad Ītaliam nāvigāvit. 8. Populō convocātō, rēx aliam calamitātem nūntiāvit. 9. Mercurius dīcit, "Pete urbem aliam."

Translate the phrases which may be ablatives absolute: 1. Because her husband was killed, the wife of Marius wept. 2. When another ship had been destroyed, the leaders saw the danger with their own eyes. 3. Having seen the fleet (the fleet seen), the inhabitants fled. 4. Having given the signal (the signal given), the soldiers left the town.

LLT

Complete the following sentences with English words related to Latin words you have met in this unit.

1. Charles is in the Latin ___ with me.
2. The ___ was pronounced not guilty.
3. A man's residence is his ___.
4. St. Peter's has a magnificent ___.
5. ___ handwriting is easily read.
6. ___ health is as important as physical.
7. When Lincoln was shot, he was ___ wounded.
8. When you sign a ___, you are seeking something.
9. Sadly Philip ___ all hope of being on the football team.

Dona ad regem mittuntur.

LXIII. CONJUNX AENEAE PROMITTITUR.

Post multās difficultātēs et calamitātēs classis Trōjāna ad Ītaliam et urbem Latīnī rēgis venit. Multa et pretiōsa dōna ad rēgem ab Aenēā, prīncipe Trōjānō, mittuntur, et pāx et salūs ā Trōjānīs petuntur.

5 Tum rēx Latīnus comitibus suīs dīcit, "Ille dux Trōjānus est advena ā nōbīs expectātus. Aenēās erit conjūnx fīliae meae. Haec ōmine apium mōnstrantur."

Itaque Aenēās ad rēgiam dūcitur, et Lāvīnia, fīlia rēgis, eī conjūnx prōmittitur. Sed Lāvīnia ā Turnō, rēge Rutulōrum, amātur, et 10 Amāta, uxor Latīnī, Turnum esse conjugem fīliae suae cupit. Itaque Amāta mātrimōnium Aenēae et Lāvīniae prohibēre in animō habet; auxilium Jūnōnis, rēgīnae deōrum, ōrat.

Statim Allēctō, rēgīna Furiārum, ā deā īrātā ad rēgiam mittitur. Allēctō Amātam verbīs īnsānīs excitat.

15 Rēgīna Amāta igitur Latīnum petit et cum lacrimīs dīcit, "Lāvīnia ab Aenēā petitur. Ōminibus territus, dabisne fīliam nostram huic advenae Trōjānō?"

Alia verba quoque ā rēgīnā īrātā dīcuntur; sed Latīnus, ā deīs monitus, mentem suam nōn mūtat. Itaque Amāta sēcrētō fīliam suam capit et noctū in montēs altōs fugit. Ibi Lāvīniam cēlat.

Interim Allēctō mala ad urbem Rutulōrum volat et haec verba Turnō dīcit, "Rēgnum tuum et conjūnx tua ab hōc advenā Trōjānō capiuntur. 5 Convocā comitēs tuōs fīdōs; oppugnā castra hostium; dūc mīlitēs validōs contrā hostēs; pugnā prō virgine; cōnfirmā animum. Dī tē juvābunt; Fortūna tibi victōriam dabit."

Sine morā Turnus populum convocat et clāmat, "Uxōrem meam, Lāvīniam, postulō! Trōjānī sunt perfidī! Ā deīs dūcimur; victōria 10 nōbīs dabitur!"

animus, -ī, M., mind; **in animō habēre,** to intend
capiō, -ere, take, seize
cupiō, -ere, wish, want
interim, *adv.*, meanwhile
lacrima, -ae, F., tear
prōmittō, -mittere, promise
virgō, -inis, F., maiden, girl

PRESENT TENSE OF THIRD-CONJUGATION *-iō* VERBS

The present tense of **-iō** verbs of the third conjugation is as follows:

ACTIVE	PASSIVE
SINGULAR	
ca'piō, I take	**ca'pior,** I am being taken; am taken
ca'pis, you take	**ca'peris,** you are being taken; are taken
ca'pit, he, she, it takes	**ca'pitur,** he, she, it is being taken; is taken
PLURAL	
ca'pimus, we take	**ca'pimur,** we are being taken; are taken
ca'pitis, you take	**capi'minī,** you are being taken; are taken
ca'piunt, they take	**capiun'tur,** they are being taken; are taken

Notice that the **-i-** of the first person singular ending appears also in the third person plural ending, both active and passive. This is the only difference between **-ō** and **-iō** verbs of the third conjugation in the present tense.

You have already met forms of two verbs which are conjugated like **capiō, capere:**

faciō, facere[1] **fugiō, fugere**

[1]**Faciō** has no passive in the present system.

IMPERATIVES OF -iō VERBS

The imperatives of these verbs are:

SINGULAR	**cape**	**fuge**	**fac**
PLURAL	**capite**	**fugite**	**facite**

1. Multī fugiunt; multī servantur. 2. Fugitis, mīlitēs, sed cīvēs perfidī vōs nōn juvābunt. 3. Quamquam flūmen est lātum, ad rīpam natāre temptābimus. 4. Ab hostibus caperis, sed tē servābimus. 5. Propter terrōrem mortis ignāvī mīlitēs fugiunt, itaque ab hominibus aliīs capiuntur. 6. Interim Aenēās Lāvīniam in mātrimōnium dūcere in animō habuit. 7. Puellā captā, populus dolet. 8. Virgō multās epistulās mittere in animō habēbat, sed epistulae ad patrem ejus nōn mittuntur. 9. Auxilium cum lacrimīs petis, sed auxilium prōmissum nōn dabitur. 10. Aurum multī cupiunt, sed paucī id habent.

Translate the italicized words: 1. *I am being seized* by pirates, but I will not scream. 2. You intend *to flee*, but you do not fear death. 3. The king's daughter *is being promised* to the Trojan leader. 4. Many victories *are being promised* by the chiefs. 5. Meanwhile *we are being led* to the camp by traders and horsemen.

HY

What do the verbs **dīcō, dūcō,** and **faciō** have in common?

LATIN LIVES TODAY

In this lesson you have met several words that are related to Latin words you already know.

You can readily see the similarity between the verbs **mitto** and **promitto.**

What is the relationship between the verb **capio** and the noun **captivus?** Between **fugio** and **fuga?** Between **lacrimo** and **lacrima?**

From their relationship to familiar Latin words, tell the meaning of these English words: *admit, captive, fugitive, lacrymose, permit.*

Peto might remind you of *petition* and *repetition*, but would you guess that *appetite* also comes from this Latin word? An *appetite* makes you seek food. When you sign a *petition*, you and others are asking for something. If a saying is *repeated*, we have *repetition.*

LXIV. AENEAS AUXILIUM PETIT.

Turnus sociīque ejus, furōre excitātī, Trōjānōs ex Ītaliā in mare expellere cupiunt. Mīlitēs agricolaeque gentium propinquārum convocantur et contrā Trōjānōs pugnāre parant. Trōjānī quoque castra sua dēfendere vehementer parant; Aenēās maximē labōrat.

Itaque nox est, et dux fīdus est dēfessus. Prope castra Trōjāna flūmen Tiberis fluit; in rīpā ejus flūminis Aenēās jacet. 5

In somniō vōx deī flūminis Aenēae dīcit, "Ā Turnō nōn superāberis. In hāc terrā erit domicilium tuum. Haec ā deīs prōmittuntur. Socius tuus erit Evander. Ante bellum Trōjānum ille ad Ītaliam vēnit, et jam parvae urbis rēx est. Haec urbs, in colle aedificāta, ab eō locō nōn longē abest. Pete auxilium ab Evandrō." 10

Māne Aenēās cum paucīs comitibus castra relinquit et postrīdiē ad urbem Evandrī appropinquat. Nāvibus Trōjānōrum vīsīs, incolae urbis graviter territī sunt et statim arma capiunt.

Pallās, fīlius Evandrī, ad rīpam properat. "Īnsignia armōrum vestrōrum mihi nōn nōta sunt," dīcit. "Cūr ad urbem nostram appropinquātis? Petitisne certāmina?" 15

Aenēās respondet, "Sumus Trōjānī; sum Aenēās, dux Trōjānus. Bellum cum Rutulīs gerimus; auxilium ab Evandrō petimus."

Tum Evander ita dīcit, "Populus meus tibi auxilium dabit. Saepe incolae hujus regiōnis contrā Rutulōs bellum gerunt. Gentēs Etrūriae propinquae quoque vōs juvābunt. Etiam nunc eōrum nāvēs sunt parātae; eōrum mīlitēs sunt in armīs. Sed bella nōn gerimus quod expectāre advenam ducem jussī sumus. Aenēās Trōjānus erit ille dux ēgregius." 20 25

certāmen, certāminis, N., contest, struggle, combat
fluō, -ere, flow
furor, -ōris, M., madness, frenzy
gerō, -ere, wear, carry; carry on, wage
graviter, *adv.*, severely, heavily; greatly, deeply
jaceō, -ēre, -uī, lie, lie down
-que, *conj.* (*attached to a word*), and

Evander showing Aeneas the future site of Rome

ENGLISH AND LATIN NOUNS

What is the English noun related to each of the following Latin nouns? To what declension do they all belong?

diligentia	**indulgentia**	**memoria**	**patientia**
furia	**intelligentia**	**militia**	**perfidia**
herba	**lympha**	**musa**	**sculptura**

What is the Latin noun for each of the following English nouns? To what declension do all these Latin nouns belong?

alumnus	*candelabrum*	*radius*	*stimulus*
auditorium	*dictum*	*stadium*	*stratum*

The Latin nominative plural may be used as the plural of each of the English nouns just above. What is the plural of each noun? Which of these nouns have English plural endings in *-s* or *-es,* as well as Latin endings?

What is the Latin noun for each of the following English nouns? All of these Latin nouns belong to the third declension.

alacrity	*cantor*	*institution*	*liberator*
brevity	*conscription*	*legion*	*severity*

Give the genitive of each of the Latin nouns on this page and tell what you think is the gender of each.

1. Dux graviter vulnerātus est, sed ejus comitēs certāmen gerunt. 2. Lūmine lūnae stellārumque multa animālia in flūmine vidēmus. 3. Relinque haec castra, Turne, et fuge sine morā. 4. Ex eō locō hostēs expellere parātī sumus. 5. Duce ē Thrāciā expulsō, mīlitēs arcem capiunt. 6. Furōre excitātus, Turnus bellum gerere in animō habuit. 7. Interim hastae pīlaque in lītore jacēbant. 8. Magnum flūmen prope castra Trōjānōrum fluit. 9. Numquam cīvēs lacrimās rēgīnae suae vīdērunt. 10. Mīlitēs dēfessī in animō jacēre in castrīs habent.

Choose the word which completes each sentence correctly and translate the sentences.

1. Puer dēfessus in terrā dūrā (jacent, jacēre, jacet).
2. Illudne flūmen in magnum mare (fluitis? fluō? fluit?)
3. Ventīs undīsque territī, mīlitēs lītus (relinquunt, relinquis, relinquuntur).
4. Furōre excitātus, certāmen (gerimus, gerit, gerunt).

REVIEW OF UNIT XIII LESSONS LX-LXIV

Nouns		*Verbs*	*Adjectives*
animus, -ī	**mēns, mentis, -ium**	**capiō, -ere**	**alius, -a, -ud**
certāmen, certāminis	**mors, mortis, -ium**	***cōnfirmō, -āre**	**idōneus, -a, -um**
classis, classis, -ium	**sanguis, -inis**	**cupiō, -ere**	***īnsānus, -a, -um**
conjūnx, -jugis	***tempestās, -tātis**	***expellō, -pellere**	*Adverbs*
domicilium, -ī	***terror, -ōris**	**fluō, -ere**	**graviter**
furor, -ōris	**tumulus, -ī**	**gerō, -ere**	**interim**
lacrima, -ae	**unda, -ae**	**jaceō, -ēre**	**numquam**
lītus, -oris	**vadum, -ī**	**petō, -ere**	*Conjunction*
	ventus, -ī	**prōmittō, -mittere**	**-que**
	virgō, -inis	**relinquō, -linquere**	

I. Find in the list of Latin phrases below, one that translates each English clause.

1. after the city was taken
2. after the monster had been killed
3. on seeing the enemy
4. when many had been wounded
5. when the house was built
6. because his wife had been killed

certāmine temptātō **classe dēlētā** **conjuge necātā** **hostibus vīsīs**
lītore occupātō **mōnstrō necātō** **morte nūntiātā** **multīs vulnerātīs**
tēctō aedificātō **urbe occupātā**

II. Choose the word that completes each sentence correctly and justify your choice.

1. Magna fuit { animus. / calamitās. / domicilium. }

2. { Classem / Undae / Ventum } vīdimus.

3. Trōjānī { certāmina / difficultātis / sanguine } habuērunt.

4. { Animus / Furōris / Vadum } Aenēae erat magnus.

5. Mors { conjugem / mōnstrī / tumulus } erat idōnea.

6. Ventō { classium / nāvēs / pestilentia } ad ōram portātae sunt.

III. Translate the verbs in the following sentences and give the person, number, and voice of each.

1. The ship was being carried to the land.
2. The town was being heavily attacked.
3. The bad omens were being announced.
4. The men of Carthage built a new city.
5. The companions of Aeneas saw the contests.
6. The boy was watching the fleet.

IV. Tell which of the following sentences, if translated into Latin, would contain an ablative absolute, and give your reason.

Warning: No dependent clause may be translated by an ablative absolute unless its subject is different from the subject or object of the independent clause.

1. After messengers had been sent, the enemy made peace.
2. The king fled after the town had been seized.
3. When he was called by his friends, the boy answered.
4. Because she was praised, the girl was happy.
5. When peace had been made, the soldiers left the town.
6. When the man was seen, he fled.
7. When the man was seen, his brother fled.
8. When the message was received, the general hurried to the ships.

Choose the word or words that complete each sentence correctly, and give the English derivative that justifies your choice.

1. An animated person is { dull. / lively. }
2. A tempest causes { laughter and gaiety. / destruction and sorrow. }
3. The mortally wounded man { died in a short time. / recovered his reason. }
4. Ventilation refers to { waves of a river. / circulation of air. }
5. A man's domicile is { his legal residence. / a small gift. }
6. A petition is a { request. / command. }

The poet Vergil, who wrote this story

UNIT

XIV

LXV. AUDACIA TURNI

Nox est, et Trōjānī prope urbem Latīnī castra pōnunt. Rutulī quoque in hōc campō lātō castra pōnunt ubi flūmen Tiberis fluit. Ad hunc locum dēfessī mīlitēs veniunt; aut in grāmine campī aut in rīpā flūminis dormiunt.

Interim Turnus ad rēgiam Latīnī venit. 5

"Māne," Turnus rēgī dīcit, "Aenēam ad certāmen prōvocābō. Aut hāc dextrā ducem Trōjānum necābō aut Aenēās Lāvīniam, fīliam tuam, conjugem habēbit."

Rēx Latīnus respondet, "In Latiō sunt multae virginēs; dēlige conjugem ex hīs virginibus. Aenēae Lāvīniam in mātrimōnium dare 10 dēbeō; ita dī jussērunt. Propter lacrimās conjugis meae hoc bellum injūstum gerō.

"Heu! Fortūnam bellī maximē timeō. Jam Latīnī in proeliō superātī sunt, quamquam moenia urbis mūniuntur et vehementer dēfenduntur. Multī amīcī in campīs, ā Trōjānīs necātī, jacent. 15 Pete pācem ā Trōjānīs!"

Turnus respondet, "Mortem nōn timeō. Vītam sine glōriā nōn cupiō. Gladiō meō Aenēam vincere temptābō."

Interim ā rēgīnā Amātā illa verba audiuntur. "Ō Turne," dīcit, "fortūnam bellī temptāre nōn dēbēs. Necāberis; ubi auxilium ex- 20 pectābimus? Tua perīcula sunt mea. Nōnne meae lacrimae tē movent?"

Sed Turnus ācriter respondet, "Ō rēgīna, lacrimae tuae sunt ōmen malum! Mē nōn vincunt. Mēns mea nōn mūtāta est. Neque Trōjānī neque Rutulī iterum pugnābunt. Cum Aenēā pugnābō; victor Lāvīniam habēbit!"

audiō, -īre, hear, listen
dēligō, -ligere, choose
dormiō, -īre, sleep
grāmen, -inis, N., grass
injūstus, -a, -um, unfair, unjust
mūniō, -īre, fortify
pōnō, -ere, place, put; **castra pōnere,** to pitch camp
vincō, -ere, conquer, overcome

FOURTH CONJUGATION

Verbs of the *fourth conjugation* have the present infinitive ending in **-īre: audiō,** *I hear,* **audīre,** *to hear.* The present of **audiō** is as follows:

ACTIVE	PASSIVE
SINGULAR	
au'diō, I hear	**au'dior,** I am heard
au'dīs, you hear	**audī'ris,** you are heard
au'dit, he, she, it hears	**audī'tur,** he, she, it is heard
PLURAL	
audī'mus, we hear	**audī'mur,** we are heard
audī'tis, you hear	**audī'minī,** you are heard
au'diunt, they hear	**audiun'tur,** they are heard

As you will observe, the characteristic vowel, **ī,** is long, except in the first person singular, active and passive, the third person singular, active, and the third person plural, active and passive.

The present tense, active, of the fourth conjugation is like that of the **-iō** verbs of the third conjugation, except for the long **ī.** The passive differs also in the second person singular.

You have already met forms of **veniō, -īre,** which is conjugated like **audiō, -īre.**

IMPERATIVE OF FOURTH-CONJUGATION VERBS

As in other conjugations, the singular imperative of fourth-conjugation verbs is like the present stem of the verb: **audī, venī.**

In the plural imperative, **-te** is added to the present stem: **audīte, venīte.**

1. Sonus multōrum pedum audītur. 2. Multī mīlitēs nunc castra ā tergō mūniunt. 3. Certāmen injūstum audīmus et vidēmus. 4. Paucī mīlitēs ā duce dēliguntur et castra pōnunt. 5. Multae virginēs ex eō locō celeriter veniunt. 6. Parvum animal in grāmine jacēbat. 7. Mīlitēs nostrī in campō dormiunt. 8. Incolae ejus terrae ab hostibus vincuntur.

Translate the verbs: 1. The town is being fortified. 2. The Trojans did not choose the unjust plan. 3. The weary victor is sleeping in the grass. 4. A new camp is being pitched by the enemy. 5. The good leader is coming to the city.

Complete each sentence with the required form of **audiō** and translate the sentence.

1. Dīcō et ā multīs hominibus (*I am heard*).
2. Vesperī in hortō avem (*I hear*).
3. Nōnne sonum mīlitum (*you* [pl.] *hear*)?
4. Apēs rēgis vidēmus et (*we hear*).
5. Multī mīlitēs ā virīs (*are heard*).
6. Apēsne in hortō (*do you* [sing.] *hear*)?
7. Clāmor mīlitum graviter vulnerātōrum (*is heard*).
8. Sēcrētō ad flūmen properāmus, sed ab hostibus (*we are heard*).

Make two Latin sentences containing a form of **videō** and two with a form of **vincō**.

LATIN LIVES TODAY

Find in "Audācia Turnī" five verbs that are spelled almost the same as English verbs with the same meaning. What other words in the story are much like English words?

Have you ever slept in a *dormitory?* What kind of building was it? What do we mean when we say that a narcissus bulb lies *dormant* during the winter? Is *dormouse* a good name for a little animal that sleeps all winter?

A nation which cannot be conquered is *invincible.* When you *convince* someone you are right, do you overcome his *convictions?*

Munition originally meant "fortification," but now *munitions* means "war materials" or *ammunition.*

Give the Latin word with which each italicized word is connected.

An ancient coin commemorating a treaty

LXVI. FOEDUS FRACTUM

Māne Rutulī et Trōjānī castra sua relīquērunt et sub moenia urbis prōcessērunt ubi locum certāminis parāvērunt.

Tum in medium campum Latīnus et Turnus cum magnō agmine prīncipum suōrum prōcessērunt. Ad eōs Aenēās et Ascanius cum paucīs comitibus appropinquāvērunt. Populus silentium tenēbat.

Prīmō Aenēās ita dīxit, "Foedus aeternum petimus; hoc foedus bellum prohibēbit. Rēx Latīnus arcem suam, urbem suam, rēgnum suum habēbit. Turnō victōre, Trōjānī numquam hoc rēgnum oppugnābunt. Sed, sī erō victor, Latīnī sub potestāte Trōjānōrum numquam erunt. Trōjānī urbem suam aedificābunt, et Lāvīnia huic urbī novae nōmen suum dabit."

Deinde Latīnus ita dīxit, "Haec probō. Hoc foedus sacrum semper erit. Pāx aeterna inter nōs erit."

Hōc foedere probātō ab Aenēā Latīnōque furor mentēs Rutulōrum occupāvit. Eīs hoc foedus nōn erat grātum; bellum, nōn pācem, dēlēgērunt.

Turnus sōlus ad āram silentiō prōcessit. Subitō silentium frāctum est. Soror Turnī, Jūturna, clāmāvit, "Ubi est honor? Ubi est fāma? Capite arma, Rutulī! Pugnāte prō patriā nostrā! Turnus sōlus pugnāre nōn dēbet. Nōs eum juvāre dēbēmus."

Verbīs sorōris ejus audītīs, animus Turnī quoque furōre occupātus est. Etiam mēns ejus jam mūtāta est. Itaque Rutulī foedus frēgērunt. Arma petīta sunt; hastae jactae sunt. Foedere frāctō, mīlitēs cum mīlitibus iterum pugnābant.

aeternus, -a, -um, eternal
foedus, foederis, N., agreement, treaty
frangō, -ere, frēgī, frāctum, break
jaciō, -ere, jēcī, jactum, throw, hurl
prōcēdō, -ere, -cessī, -cessum, proceed, advance, march
silentium, -ī, N., silence; **silentiō,** in silence, silently
soror, -ōris, F., sister

PERFECT ACTIVE OF THE THIRD AND FOURTH CONJUGATIONS

In Lesson XIX we saw that the forms of the perfect active are made up of the perfect stem, with special endings which are used in no other tense. The formation of this tense is the same for all verbs of the Latin language, in all conjugations, and for irregular as well as regular verbs.

There is, therefore, nothing new to learn for the perfect active of the third and fourth conjugations. We simply add the perfect endings to the perfect stem as shown in the principal parts.

SINGULAR

dū'xī, I led, I have led	**audī'vī,** I heard, I have heard
dūxis'tī, you led, *etc.*	**audīvis'tī,** you heard, *etc.*
dū'xit, he, she, it led, *etc.*	**audī'vit,** he, she, it heard, *etc.*

PLURAL

dū'ximus, we led, *etc.*	**audī'vimus,** we heard, *etc.*
dūxis'tis, you led, *etc.*	**audīvis'tis,** you heard, *etc.*
dūxē'runt, they led, *etc.*	**audīvē'runt,** they heard, *etc.*

PERFECT PASSIVE OF THE THIRD AND FOURTH CONJUGATIONS

The perfect passive, like the perfect active, is the same in its method of formation for all Latin verbs. As you learned in Lesson LIX, it consists of the perfect passive participle with the present forms of **sum.** Remember that the participle agrees with the subject in gender and number.

The perfect passive of third- and fourth-conjugation verbs, therefore, is formed like that of first- and second-conjugation verbs.

SINGULAR

duc'tus sum, I was led, I have been led	**audī'tus sum,** I was heard, I have been heard
duc'tus es, you were led, you have been led	**audī'tus es,** you were heard, you have been heard
etc.	*etc.*

PLURAL

duc'tī sumus, we were led, we have been led	**audī'tī sumus,** we were heard, we have been heard
etc.	*etc.*

PRINCIPAL PARTS OF THIRD-CONJUGATION VERBS

The principal parts of **dūcō** and other third-conjugation verbs which have appeared in preceding lessons are as follows:

colō	**colere**	**coluī**	**cultum**	**petō**	**petere**	**petīvī**	**petītum**
dēfendō	**-fendere**	**-fendī**	**-fēnsum**	**pōnō**	**pōnere**	**posuī**	**positum**
dēligō	**-ligere**	**-lēgī**	**-lēctum**	**prōmittō**	**-mittere**	**-mīsī**	**-missum**
dīcō	**dīcere**	**dīxī**	**dictum**	**scrībō**	**scrībere**	**scrīpsī**	**scrīptum**
discō	**discere**	**didicī**	—	**vincō**	**vincere**	**vīcī**	**victum**
dūcō	**dūcere**	**dūxī**	**ductum**	**capiō**	**capere**	**cēpī**	**captum**
fluō	**fluere**	**flūxī**	**flūxum**	**cupiō**	**cupere**	**cupīvī**	**cupītum**
gerō	**gerere**	**gessī**	**gestum**	**faciō**	**facere**	**fēcī**	**factum**
legō	**legere**	**lēgī**	**lēctum**	**fugiō**	**fugere**	**fūgī**	—
mittō	**mittere**	**mīsī**	**missum**				

PRINCIPAL PARTS OF FOURTH-CONJUGATION VERBS

The principal parts of fourth-conjugation verbs which have appeared in preceding lessons are as follows:

audiō	**audīre**	**audīvī**	**audītum**
dormiō	**dormīre**	**dormīvī**	**dormītum**
mūniō	**mūnīre**	**mūnīvī**	**mūnītum**
veniō	**venīre**	**vēnī**	**ventum**

1. Latīnus urbem pulchram et arcem suam habuit. 2. Turnus dīxit, "Foedus frāctum nōn grātum est." 3. Silentium erat, et soror ducis prōcessit. 4. Multae hastae ab hostibus jactae sunt. 5. Trōjānī pācem, nōn bellum dēlēgērunt. 6. Mīlitēs verba ducum suōrum audīvērunt. 7. Rutulī arma cēpērunt et prō patriā suā pugnāvērunt. 8. Ubi verba sorōris audīta sunt, furor mentem Turnī occupāvit. 9. Hoc foedus bellum prohibēbit; pāx aeterna erit. 10. Multī lapidēs jaciuntur et multa corpora sub moenibus jacent.

Translate the verbs: 1. The citadel was never attacked by the enemy. 2. The soldiers advanced; spears were hurled; there was war again; the treaty was broken. 3. When the words of the leader were heard, the plan of the Rutuli was changed. 4. In silence Aeneas and his companions left their camp and marched to the field. 5. Take up arms, Turnus! Fight for your country.

Give the verb that completes each question; then translate the answer.

1. ___ne vir epistulam longam?
   Yes, the man wrote a long letter.
2. Cūr Trōjānī ___?
   The Trojans fought because they had a good leader.
3. Ubi āram ___?
   I placed the altar in the temple.
4. Nōnne Trōjānī et Latīnī foedus ___?
   Yes, they made a treaty.
5. Nōnne fābula ā puerīs ___?
   The story was read in the evening.

LATIN LIVES TODAY Certain Latin verbs are of great importance to English because of the large number of derivatives they yield.

capio, *take*	**moveo,** *move*	**duco,** *lead*
captive	movement	duke
captivate	movable	duchess
captivity	mobile	ductile
captor	motor	aqueduct
capture	motive	conduct
anticipate	motion	conductor
accept	demote	conducive
acceptance	promote	viaduct
acceptable	commotion	abduction
unacceptable	emotion	induce
incipient	remove	induction
intercept	immovable	introduce
receive	automobile	introduction
recipe	automotive	produce
reception	locomotive	reduction

facio, *make, do*	**dico,** *say*	**jacio,** *throw*
fact	diction	abject
faction	dictionary	dejected
factor	dictum	eject
faculty	edict	inject
benefactor	predict	object
manufacture	prediction	objection
confectionery	contradict	project
beneficent	contradiction	projection
deficient	verdict	reject
efficient	valedictory	subject

Be ready to use in a sentence any English word in the lists above.

Make a list of derivatives for each of the following verbs: **defendo, mitto, porto, venio.**

LXVII. IRA AENEAE

Foedere frāctō, Aenēās īrā excitātus Trōjānōs magnā vōce vocāvit. "Cūr bellum iterum geritis?" clāmāvit. "Foedus factum est! Huic foederī fīdus erō. Sōlus cum Turnō pugnāre dēbeō."

Tamen neque Trōjānī neque Rutulī ā proeliō recēdēbant; eum nōn 5 audiēbant. Etiam Turnus in certāmine hastam contrā Trōjānōs vehementer jēcit. Sed ab Aenēā inter agmina Rutulōrum petēbātur, quod dux Trōjānus cum illō sōlō pugnāre cupiēbat.

Undique magnus numerus sociōrum Aenēae, necātus ā Turnō perfidō, in terrā jacēbat. Jam Aenēās, sociīs mortuīs vīsīs, īrā agitābātur; 10 prope urbem Latīnī veniēbat. Urbe vīsā, subitō mēns ejus mūtāta est.

"Oppugnāte moenia!" mīlitēs suōs Aenēās jussit. "Dēbetne haec urbs, causa bellī, manēre, dum nostrī in proeliō injūstō interficiuntur?"

Mox Trōjānī moenia ascendēbant et portās oppugnābant. Nōn sōlum hastae sed etiam taedae in urbem jaciēbantur. Magnus erat 15 terror cīvium; urbs et domicilia eōrum dēlēbantur.

"Ubi est Turnus?" clāmāvit rēgīna Amāta, maximē furōre agitāta. "Urbs nostra vincitur. Turnus sōlus nōs servābit; sine eō superābimur. Sum causa calamitātis; nōn jam vīvere dēbeō."

Statim Amāta sē interfēcit. Propter mortem rēgīnae cīvēs multīs 20 cum lacrimīs dolēbant. Clāmōre audītō, Turnus ad urbem fūmō flammīsque cēlātam properāvit. Undique mīlitēs ab aliīs mīlitibus interficiēbantur.

"Ō Rutulī et Latīnī!" Turnus clāmāvit, "sōlus Aenēam in certāmine petō."

agitō, -āre, -āvī, -ātum, drive on; agitate; pursue
interficiō, -ficere, -fēcī, -fectum, kill, slay
nōn sōlum . . . sed etiam, not only . . . but also
numerus, -ī, M., number
recēdō, -ere, -cessī, -cessum, withdraw, retreat
vīvō, -ere, vīxī, vīctum, live

RELATED LATIN WORDS

Just as we have groups of related words in English, so we have Latin words related in form and meaning. If you get in the habit of associating such words in your mind, you will find it easy to remember their meanings.

As you know, **ager** means *field;* **agricola,** *farmer* (one who cultivates a field); **agricultura,** *farming.*

Give the meaning of **rex, rego, regina, regia.** What do you think is the meaning of **regius, -a, -um?** Of **regnum?** What English words can you think of connected with this group?

You know the meaning of **victoria** and **victor** and also of **vinco, -ere, vici, victum.** When **victi** is used as a noun, what does it mean? Give several English words connected with this group.

Give the meaning of each Latin word in the groups below, and mention some English words connected with each group.

orno	**pugna**	**scribo**	**timeo**
ornatus	**pugno**	**scriptor**	**timidus**
ornamentum	**pugnus**	**scriptum**	**timor**
magnus	**sacer**	**signo**	**vita**
magnanimus	**sacerdos**	**signum**	**vivo**
magnitudo	**sacrum**	**significans**	**vivus**

IMPERFECT OF THE THIRD AND FOURTH CONJUGATIONS

The tense sign of the imperfect in the third and fourth conjugations is **-bā-,** just as in the first and second conjugations. The imperfect tense of **dūcō** is formed in exactly the same way as the imperfect tense of **moneō,** with **-ē-** before **-bā-.** Verbs of the fourth conjugation have **-iē-** before the tense sign.

ACTIVE

SINGULAR

dūcē'bam, I was leading, I led	**audiē'bam,** I was hearing, I heard
dūcē'bās, you were leading, you led	**audiē'bās,** you were hearing, you heard
dūcē'bat, he, she, it was leading; he, she, it led	**audiē'bat,** he, she, it was hearing, *etc.*

PLURAL

dūcēbā'mus, we were leading, we led	**audiēbā'mus,** we were hearing, we heard
dūcēbā'tis, you were leading, you led	**audiēbā'tis,** you were hearing, *etc.*
dūcē'bant, they were leading, they led	**audiē'bant,** they were hearing, *etc.*

PASSIVE

SINGULAR

dūcē'bar, I was being led, I was led	**audiē'bar,** I was being heard, I was heard
dūcēbā'ris, you were being led, you were led	**audiēbā'ris,** you were being heard, you were heard
dūcēbā'tur, he, she, it was being led; he, she, it was led	**audiēbā'tur,** he, she, it was being heard, *etc.*

PLURAL

dūcēbā'mur, we were being led, we were led	**audiēbā'mur,** we were being heard, we were heard
dūcēbā'minī, you were being led, you were led	**audiēbā'minī,** you were being heard, *etc.*
dūcēban'tur, they were being led, they were led	**audiēban'tur,** they were being heard, *etc.*

The imperfect of **-iō** verbs of the third conjugation is just like the imperfect of the fourth conjugation.

ACTIVE	PASSIVE
SINGULAR	
capiē'bam, I was taking, I took	**capiē'bar,** I was being taken, *etc.*
capiē'bās, you were taking, you took	**capiēbā'ris,** you were being taken, *etc.*
capiē'bat, he, she, it was taking; he, she, it took	**capiēbā'tur,** he, she, it was being taken, *etc.*
PLURAL	
capiēbā'mus, we were taking, we took	**capiēbā'mur,** we were being taken, *etc.*
capiēbā'tis, you were taking, you took	**capiēbā'minī,** you were being taken, *etc.*
capiē'bant, they were taking, they took	**capiēban'tur,** they were being taken, *etc.*

1. Rēgīna nōn sōlum furōre agitābātur sed etiam sē interfēcit. 2. Multa animālia ā mīlitibus interficiēbantur. 3. Mīlitēs ad oppidum prōcēdēbant; deinde ab oppidō recēdēbant. 4. In hōc proeliō magnus numerus Trōjānōrum interfectus est. 5. Prīncipēs interficiēbantur et hastae eōrum frangēbantur. 6. Mīlitēs longa itinera saepe faciēbant et in castrīs vīvēbant.

Complete each sentence with one of the following verbs.

audiēbat audiēbātur dūcēbat dūcēbātur jaciēbam jaciēbantur necābant necābantur relinquēbāmur relinquēbant

1. Puerī ursās ___.
2. Ursae ā puerīs ___.
3. Puella caecum ___.
4. Caecus ā puellā ___.
5. Magnus numerus mīlitum vōcem ducis ___.
6. Hastam meam pīlumque meum ___.

Juppiter et Juno e caelo spectabant.

LXVIII. TURNUS RELICTUS A DEIS

Vōce Turnī audītā, Aenēās urbem relīquit et ācriter ad certāmen prōcessit. Hoc certāmen, autem, Juppiter et Jūnō ē caelō spectābant.

Procul Aenēās hastam suam contrā hostem jēcit, sed hasta suprā caput Turnī volāvit et in arbore stetit. Tum gladiīs Aenēās et Turnus vehementer pugnābant. Subitō gladius Turnī scūtō Aenēae frāctus est. Gladiō āmissō, dux Rutulus, captus terrōre, celeriter fūgit. Interim soror ejus, Jūturna, alium gladium invēnit eumque frātrī suō dedit.

Hōc vīsō, Juppiter dīxit, "Quī erit fīnis hujus certāminis, Ō conjūnx mea? Nōnne Aenēās Turnum vincet? Quid in animō facere habēs? Noctū et interdiū, aestāte et hieme, Trōjānōs per terrās et maria agitāvistī. Propter tē, nōn sōlum foedus frāctum est, sed etiam bellum malum iterum inceptum est. Auxiliō tuō, Jūturna gladium invēnit et frātrī suō eum dedit. Jam ad fīnem hoc certāmen veniet. Prohibeō tē haec iterum facere."

Jūnō respondit, "Propter tē, magne Juppiter, Turnum et terram relīquī. Facta Jūturnae probāvī; meō auxiliō illa gladium invēnit. Tamen, potestātem meam āmittam. Nōn jam Turnus vōcem sorōris suae audiet; nūllum auxilium inveniet. Fātīs repulsa, nōn jam fīnem 5 gentis Trōjānae postulō. Mors Turnī fīnem certāminis faciet. Aenēās vītam suam nōn āmittet; is vīvet; sed Turnus interficiētur."

Tum Juppiter haec prōmīsit, "Quamquam Aenēās erit rēx eōrum, Latīnī nōmen suum linguamque suam tenēbunt. Ūnam (*one*) gentem Trōjānī Latīnīque facient; ūnam linguam habēbunt; et ex eōrum 10 līberīs populus clārus veniet."

āmittō, -mittere, -mīsī, -missum, lose, let go

autem, *conj.*, but, however (*never stands first in a clause*)

fīnis, fīnis, -ium, M., end, boundary, limit

incipiō, -cipere, -cēpī, -ceptum, begin

inveniō, -venīre, -vēnī, -ventum, find, discover

repellō, -pellere, reppulī, repulsum, repel, drive back, repulse

suprā, *prep. with acc.*, above, over

FUTURE OF THE THIRD AND FOURTH CONJUGATIONS

Verbs of the third and fourth conjugations are conjugated as follows in the future:

ACTIVE	PASSIVE
SINGULAR	
dū'cam, I shall lead	**dū'car,** I shall be led
dū'cēs, you will lead	**dūcē'ris,** you will be led
dū'cet, he, she, it will lead	**dūcē'tur,** he, she, it will be led
PLURAL	
dūcē'mus, we shall lead	**dūcē'mur,** we shall be led
dūcē'tis, you will lead	**dūcē'minī,** you will be led
dū'cent, they will lead	**dūcen'tur,** they will be led
SINGULAR	
ca'piam, I shall take	**ca'piar,** I shall be taken
ca'piēs, you will take	**capiē'ris,** you will be taken
ca'piet, he, she, it will take	**capiē'tur,** he, she, it will be taken
PLURAL	
capiē'mus, we shall take	**capiē'mur,** we shall be taken
capiē'tis, you will take	**capiē'minī,** you will be taken
ca'pient, they will take	**capien'tur,** they will be taken

ACTIVE	PASSIVE
SINGULAR	
au′diam, I shall hear	**au′diar,** I shall be heard
au′diēs, you will hear	**audiē′ris,** you will be heard
au′diet, he, she, it will hear	**audiē′tur,** he, she, it will be heard
PLURAL	
audiē′mus, we shall hear	**audiē′mur,** we shall be heard
audiē′tis, you will hear	**audiē′minī,** you will be heard
au′dient, they will hear	**audien′tur,** they will be heard

TENSE SIGN OF THE FUTURE

We have seen that in the first and second conjugations the tense sign of the future is **-bi-**. In the third and fourth conjugations the future tense sign is **-ē-**, which is replaced by **-a-** in the first person singular. The **-ē-** becomes short before the person endings **-t, -nt,** and **-ntur.**

1. Cum Jūnō dīcet, tum bellum incipiētur; cum Turnus interficiētur, tum bellum āmittētur. 2. Mors gentis Trōjānae ā deā postulābitur. 3. Dux Trōjānus vīvet; multī advenae, autem, interficientur. 4. Noctū et interdiū, aestāte et hieme, domicilium idōneum petent. 5. Apēs, autem, ā rēge et conjuge ejus suprā hortum vīsae sunt. 6. Mīlitēs dēfessī ab hostibus repellentur. 7. Aenēās Lāvīniam in mātrimōnium dūcet, et līberī eōrum erunt rēgēs. 8. Trōjānī in Latiō tēcta nova aedificāvērunt, sed nōmen eōrum mūtātum est et lingua antīqua āmissa est.

1. The men will discover the limits of the city. 2. The soldiers, seized by terror, were driven back. 3. But will the gods begin a new conflict? 4. Turnus will lose his sword. 5. The leader threw his sword above his enemy's head.

HY

Find in "Turnus Relictus ā Deīs" some verbs ending in **-et** or **-ent** and tell whether each is a future of the third conjugation or a present of the second.

LXIX. FINIS CERTAMINIS

Avis fera, missa ad terram ā deīs, Turnum inter agmina Rutulōrum petēbat. Ante oculōs et circum umerōs ducis Rutulī volābat scūtumque ejus ālīs suīs oppugnābat. Turnus potentiam (*power*) deōrum et ōmen mortis recognōvit.

5 Jūturna hanc avem procul vīdit et clāmāvit, "Certē haec avis missa est quod dī Turnum interficī et Rutulōs superārī cupiunt. Frātre meō interfectō Rutulīsque victīs, nōn jam vīvere dēsīderō."

Hīs verbīs dictīs, Jūturna sē in undās Tiberis jēcit.

Interim Aenēās Turnum agitāre iterum incēpit.

10 "Cūr recēdis, Turne?" dīxit. "Cūr mortem tuam fugere temptās?"

Turnus respondit, "Verba tua mē nōn terrent. Dī et odium deōrum mē terrent. Juppiter est hostis meus."

Tum Aenēās magnam hastam jēcit, et Turnus, graviter vulnerātus, ad terram cecidit (*fell*).

Aeneas Turnum gladio interfecit.

Rutulus victus dīxit, "Vītam meam āmittere prō patriā meā jam diū parātus sum. Satis pugnāvī; nunc mē vīcistī. Lāvīnia erit conjūnx tua. Vītam nōn ōrō, sed certē prō patre miserō meīs amīcīs corpus meum dabis."

Prīmō Aenēās Turnum interficere in animō nōn habēbat. Tum in umerō hostis vulnerātī īnsigne nōtum vīdit. Ōlim fīlius Evandrī illud īnsigne gerēbat; jam ille erat mortuus—necātus ā Turnō. Celeriter Aenēās īrātus Turnum gladiō interfēcit. Ita mors Turnī fīnem certāminis fēcit. 5

certē, *adv.*, surely, certainly
odium, -ī, N., hatred
recognōscō, -cognōscere, -cognōvī, -cognitum, recognize
umerus, -ī, M., shoulder

PRESENT INFINITIVES OF THE FOUR CONJUGATIONS

You have seen the present active infinitives of the four conjugations:

I	II	III	IV
portāre, to carry	**monēre,** to warn	**dūcere,** to lead **capere,** to take	**audīre,** to hear

Each verb has also a present passive infinitive, for instance, **portārī,** *to be carried.* The passive infinitives of the four conjugations of regular verbs are like the following:

I	II	III	IV
portārī, to be carried	**monērī,** to be warned	**dūcī,** to be led **capī,** to be taken	**audīrī,** to be heard

Notice that in the first, second, and fourth conjugations the final **-e** of the active endings (**-āre, -ēre, -īre**) is replaced by **-ī** in the passive; in the third conjugation the entire ending (**-ere**) is replaced by **-ī.**

1. In umerīs tuīs cervum portāre jubēris. 2. Jussitne tē propter odium frātrem tuum interficere? 3. Cūr dī Rutulōs superārī cupiunt? 4. Dux aquam et frūmentum ad equōs in umerīs servōrum portārī jubet. 5. Hī leōnēs ferī ā sagittāriīs timērī nōn videntur. 6. Certē eōs auxilium ad sociōs nostrōs sine morā mittere jubēbō. 7. Urbs ab hostibus recognōscī dēbet. 8. Certē virī malī ā bonīs cīvibus expellī dēbent. 9. Dī Turnum vincī ab Aenēā īrātō cupiunt. 10. Turnus Aenēam vincere in animō habuit.

Make three complete sentences of each of the following by translating the phrases.

1. Mīlitēs frūmentum __ invenient.
   in the city *of the inhabitants* *in the fields*
2. Mīles __ fūgit
   overcome by the enemy *severely wounded* *frightened by trumpets*
3. Sed cōpiae Rōmānae in campō __.
   will sleep *will pitch camp* *will conquer the enemy*
4. Foedus ā Rōmānīs et Latīnīs __.
   will be approved *will be broken* *will be sought*
5. Puer saxum __ jēcit.
   into the water *over the house* *above his friend's head*
6. Turnus __.
   will be killed *will break the spear* *will not be king*

Translate the italicized words: 1. Certainly stories ought *to be written* about good leaders. 2. You (*pl.*) ordered my friends *to listen.* 3. The king will order the captives *to remain.* 4. Aeneas intended *to overcome* Turnus. 5. The leader wanted *to be recognized.* 6. The Trojans wanted *to find* a suitable home.

LATIN LIVES TODAY

Eternal ages are ages without beginning or end. Why is Rome called "the *eternal* city"?

A *fragment* is a broken piece. A *fracture* is a break. *Fragile* describes something that is easily broken. Use each of these words in a sentence.

What does the word *sorority* mean? What is a *fraternity?*

Facilis, facile, factum, and **facultas** are all related to **facio.** What English derivatives do you know from this group of related words?

Each of the following words is related to a Latin word that you recently learned. Give the Latin word and use the English word in a sentence: *agitate, certain, final, finish, incipient, invention, recognize, repel, revive, survive.*

REVIEW OF UNIT XIV LESSONS LXV-LXIX

Nouns	*Verbs*	*Verbs*	*Adverbs*
*causa, -ae	agitō, -āre	prōcēdō, -cēdere	certē
*clāmor, -ōris	āmittō, -mittere	recēdō, -cēdere	nōn sōlum . . .
*fātum, -ī	*ascendō, -ere	recognōscō, -ere	sed etiam
fīnis, fīnis, -ium	audiō, -īre	repellō, -ere	*Preposition*
foedus, foederis	dēligō, -ligere	vincō, -ere	suprā
grāmen, -inis	dormiō, -īre	vīvō, -ere	*Conjunction*
*īra, -ae	frangō, -ere	*Adjectives*	autem
numerus, -ī	incipiō, -cipere	aeternus, -a, -um	
odium, -ī	interficiō, -ere	injūstus, -a, -um	
silentium, -ī	inveniō, -venīre		
soror, -ōris	jaciō, -ere		
umerus, -ī	mūniō, -īre		
*victor, -ōris	pōnō, -ere		

I. Find in the list at the right the Latin verb form corresponding to each English phrase.

1. to begin	6. to fortify	(*a*) dūcere	(*f*) mūnīre
2. to be led	7. to make	(*b*) dūcī	(*g*) scrībere
3. to be broken	8. to lead	(*c*) facere	(*h*) timēre
4. to seem	9. to see	(*d*) frangī	(*i*) vidēre
5. to fear	10. to write	(*e*) incipere	(*j*) vidērī

II. Supply the Latin verbs called for.

1. Magnum oppidum (*is being fortified*).
2. Foedus initiō bellī (*was broken*).
3. Mentēs Trōjānōrum (*were agitated*).
4. Silentiō verba patris ā līberīs ejus (*are heard*).
5. Bellum novum ab hostibus (*will be begun*).
6. Hostēs ā duce bonō (*will be driven back*).

III. Complete each sentence with a form of jaceō or jaciō.

1. Mīles dēfessus in terrā (*lay down*).
2. Certē hostis pīlum suum (*hurled*).
3. Librī Latīnī in mēnsā (*will be lying*).
4. Soror mea lapidem (*will hurl*).
5. Avis necāta in grāmine (*lay*).

IV. Find in the list below, the verb that completes each sentence correctly.

1. Cervum, puerī, (*you have killed*).
2. Bellum in hāc terrā (*has been waged*).
3. Multum grāmen (*has been seen*).
4. Multae virginēs in proeliō (*were slain*).
5. Castra fortiter (*was defended*).
6. In urbe, sorōrēs, (*you have been seen*).
7. Sumus mīlitēs, sed graviter (*we have been wounded*).
8. Silentiō hastae (*were being hurled*).
9. In urbem, Anna, (*you are being led*).
10. Magnum numerum mīlitum (*he recognized*).

dēfendunt **gestum est** **jaciēbantur** **vīsae estis**
dēfēnsa sunt **interfēcistis** **jactae sunt** **vīsum est**
dūceris **interfectae sunt** **recognōvit** **vulnerāmus**
dūciminī **interficiuntur** **vidēbitur** **vulnerātī sumus**

LATIN LIVES TODAY

Choose the word that correctly completes each sentence and give the word in the sentence that influenced you.

1. His agitated manner showed that he was { disturbed. / happy. / odious.

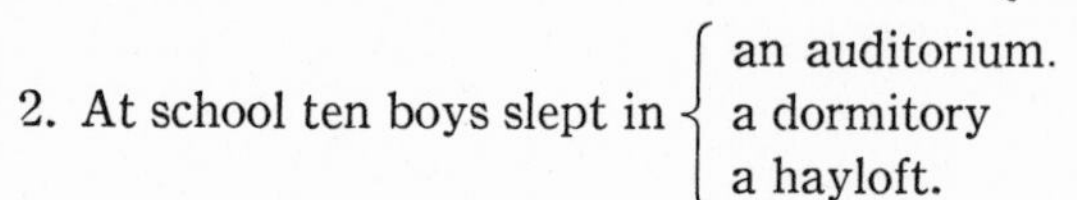

2. At school ten boys slept in { an auditorium. / a dormitory / a hayloft.
3. A fracture is a { cut. / break. / bump.
4. A man whose relatives are numerous has { many relatives. / few relatives. / no relatives
5. A procession usually { moves forward. / moves in a circle. / recedes.
6. The repulsive animal { attracted others. / drove the others away. / pleased everyone.
7. A sorority is a { boyhood. / brotherhood. / sisterhood.

The Romans celebrate a spring festival with flowers, music, and a gay procession.

THE GODS OF THE ROMANS

In honor of Jupiter (left) the Romans built a temple on the Capitoline Hill overlooking the Forum. Juno (right) and Minerva (at right below) were also worshiped in this temple.

The Romans had many gods, each of whom was thought to have a special relationship to mortals. The Romans believed that they could gain the favor of these gods by building beautiful temples (pp. 62, 83) for them and by honoring them with sacrifices and festivals.

Greatest of the deities was Jupiter, king of the gods and ruler of heaven and earth. The Romans believed that he was especially interested in their State, guiding its leaders.

In honor of Jupiter's queen, Juno (p. 257), several annual festivals were celebrated. She was worshiped mostly by women, since their welfare was believed to be in her hands.

Minerva, who sprang, fully grown, from the brain of her father, Jupiter, was the goddess of wisdom. It was she who taught mortals the arts of spinning and weaving.

Mars, the god of war, was venerated by the warlike Romans, who called themselves "Children of Mars" and named the *Campus Martius* after him.

The month of March gets its name from Mars (left), the war god. Since Minerva (right) was goddess of war as well as of wisdom, she was often represented wearing a helmet.

Other major deities worshiped by the Romans were Apollo, the sun god; Diana, goddess of the moon and of hunting; and Venus, goddess of love and beauty. All these divinities watched the lives of mortals from above and sometimes came down to earth to take a hand in their affairs.

To Mercury, another important god, was assigned the task of carrying messages for his fellow deities. Vulcan, husband of Venus, was the god of fire. It was he who bestowed on men the gift of fire and taught them how to use it.

A Lar, stepping lightly and holding a drinking horn

Besides the gods of heaven, there were also earthly divinities, such as Ceres, goddess of grain, who watched over the crops. There were gods of the waters, too, of whom Neptune, god of the sea, was most important. The underworld was likewise under the rule of a special class of deities. Here Pluto, king of the dead, reigned with his kidnaped queen, Proserpina.

Vesta, who ranked among the more important deities, was closely associated with the home and hearth. For her there was a temple in the Forum in which a fire was kept burning day and night by the Vestal Virgins.

In addition to these great gods, whose worship, under different names, the Romans shared with the Greeks, there were several divinities who belonged only to the Romans. Among these was Janus, god of the past and present and of doors and beginnings. He was shown with two faces, since he could look both forward and backward.

A household shrine where a family of Pompeii worshiped

The Lares and Penates were the Roman household gods. The Lares represented the souls of the family's ancestors, while the Penates were the protectors of the storeroom and givers of prosperity. These gods watched over the family, while the State was guarded by the greater deities.

LXX. VELLUS AUREUM

Olim in Colchide erat vellus aureum ā magnō mōnstrō dēfēnsum. Ubi Jāsōn, vir fortis, dē vellere aureō audīvit, statim id invenīre in animō habuit. Magnā nāve aedificātā, Jāsōn cum paucīs comitibus dēlēctīs ad Colchidem nāvigāvit. Statim ad rēgem appropinquāvit 5 vellusque postulāvit.

Rēx respondit, "Sī vellus aureum cupis, haec facere necesse est. Prīmō taurōs jungere dēbēs. Eī taurī sunt ācrēs; ignem expīrant (*breathe out*). Deinde, taurīs jūnctīs, agrum arāre dēbēs. Agrō arātō, in agrō dentēs dracōnis serere (*to sow*) dēbēs. Ē dentibus virī armātī 10 venient et tē necāre temptābunt. Dēnique, omnibus virīs interfectīs, mōnstrum ācre superāre vellusque capere dēbēs."

Haec facta perīculōsa Jāsonī fortī grāta erant, et mox hōra certāminis aderat. Jāsōn in agrō stābat. Perīculum nōn timēbat; in tōtō corpore erat unguentum (*ointment*) magicum datum eī ā Mēdēā, fīliā 15 rēgis. Tamen rēx populusque mortem juvenis fortis expectābant.

In such boats the ancient Greeks and Romans sailed around the Mediterranean and into adjoining waters.

Jason captures the golden fleece.

Taurī in agrum vēnērunt et ad Jāsonem ācriter appropinquāvērunt. Ignem expīrābant, sed Jāsōn nōn vulnerātus erat. Taurīs jūnctīs, sine morā Jāsōn agrum arāvit dentēsque dracōnis serere incēpit. Posteā virī armātī ex dentibus vēnērunt. Magnō saxō captō, Jāsōn id inter hominēs ācrēs jēcit. Mox hominēs stupidī inter sē ācriter 5 pugnābant et nōn jam juvenem necāre temptābant.

Omnibus hominibus mortuīs, Mēdēa Jāsonem in silvam dēnsam dūxit, ubi dracō ācer vellus aureum vigilābat. Celeriter Mēdēa contrā mōnstrum venēnum (*poison*) validum jēcit; statim dracō dormīvit. Tum Jāsōn, vellere captō, ad nāvem fūgit, ubi comitēs laetī ducem 10 fortem salūtāvērunt.

ācer, ācris, ācre, fierce, eager
arō, -āre, -āvī, -ātum, plow
dēns, dentis, M., tooth
dracō, -ōnis, M., serpent, dragon
fortis, forte, brave, strong
jungō, -ere, jūnxī, jūnctum, join, yoke
juvenis, juvenis (*gen. pl.* **-um**), M., young man, youth
omnis, omne, all, every
taurus, -ī, M., bull
vellus, velleris, N., fleece

THIRD-DECLENSION ADJECTIVES

We have seen that many adjectives are declined like nouns of the first and second declensions. There is also a large group of adjectives declined like nouns of the third declension.

ADJECTIVES OF TWO ENDINGS

There are many third-declension adjectives that have two endings in the nominative singular—one for the masculine and feminine and one for the neuter.

In the masculine and feminine, these adjectives are declined like **collis** (p. 209) and in the neuter like **īnsigne** (p. 211), except that the ablative singular of all genders ends in **ī**.

Third-declension adjectives with two endings in the nominative singular are declined as follows:

omnis, *all, every*

	SINGULAR		PLURAL	
	MASC. AND FEM.	NEUT.	MASC. AND FEM.	NEUT.
Nom.	**om′nis**	**om′ne**	**om′nēs**	**om′nia**
Gen.	**om′nis**	**om′nis**	**om′nium**	**om′nium**
Dat.	**om′nī**	**om′nī**	**om′nibus**	**om′nibus**
Acc.	**om′nem**	**om′ne**	**om′nēs,**	**om′nia**
Abl.	**om′nī**	**om′nī**	**om′nibus**	**om′nibus**

ADJECTIVES OF THREE ENDINGS

There are a few third-declension adjectives which have separate forms for the three genders in the nominative singular. In all other respects they are declined exactly like those with two endings.

ācer, *fierce*

	SINGULAR			PLURAL	
	MASC.	FEM.	NEUT.	MASC. AND FEM.	NEUT.
Nom.	**ā′cer**	**ā′cris**	**ā′cre**	**ā′crēs**	**ā′cria**
Gen.	**ā′cris**		**ā′cris**	**ā′crium**	**ā′crium**
Dat.	**ā′crī**		**ā′crī**	**ā′cribus**	**ā′cribus**
Acc.	**ā′crem**		**ā′cre**	**ā′crēs**	**ā′cria**
Abl.	**ā′crī**		**ā′crī**	**ā′cribus**	**ā′cribus**

1. Jāsōn, vir fortis, magna perīcula nōn timēbat. 2. In animō habēbat, taurīs jūnctīs, agrum arāre. 3. Rēx ācer dīcit Jāsonī, "Junge taurōs ācrēs et arā tōtum agrum." 4. Dracōne necātō, Mēdēa ā Jāsone ad nāvem suam dūcitur. 5. Inter hominēs armātōs magnum saxum jaciētur. 6. Dracōnēs sunt magnī et ignem expīrant. 7. Vir validus agrum arāre nōn temptābat. 8. Fēmina fortis perīculum nōn timēbat.

Translate the adjectives: 1. When all the soldiers were dead, Jason was safe. 2. The fierce monster guarded the golden fleece. 3. The brave youth yoked the great bulls and plowed the field. 4. Every dragon will be conquered by the brave youths. 5. From the teeth of the dragon, armed men will come.

Complete each sentence with the correct form of a word in the vocabulary on page 269. Then arrange the sentences in the order of the story.

1. Jāsōn ___ ācrēs jūnxit.
2. Jāsōn magnum agrum ___.
3. ___ vellus cēpit et fūgit.
4. Virī armātī ē ___ vēnērunt.
5. Jāsōn ___ aureum dēsīderābat.
6. Fīlia rēgis ___ fortem amāvit.
7. ___ hominēs armātī mortuī erant.
8. Comitēs laetī Jāsonem ___ salūtāvērunt.
9. Erat in Colchide ___ aureum ā mōnstrō dēfēnsum.

HW Change the verbs to present in the nine Latin sentences above.

HY What is the best translation of **dēbēs** in line 8 of "Vellus Aureum"? Of **ignem** in line 8? Of **aderat** in line 13?

LLT

When you go to a *dentist*, do you expect him to treat your eyes, your feet, or your teeth?

Should a brave man act with *fortitude?*

Why is a railroad *junction* so called? What is a *conjunction?*

What do you find in the *juvenile* department of a clothing store?

Do you know the meaning of the words *omnibus, omnipresent, omniscient,* and *omnivorous?* The bus you ride in was originally called an *omnibus*, "for all (everybody)." *Omniscient* is made up of **omni-** and part of the verb **scio**, *know*, and therefore means "knowing *all.*" *Omnipresent* means "being present in all places at the same time." *Omnivorous* is made from **omni-** and **voro**, *eat*, and means eating all kinds of food.

Use *omnibus, omnipresent, omniscient,* and *omnivorous* each in a sentence.

LXXI. UXOR INFELIX

Nūlla puella uxor Plūtōnis esse dēsīderābat quod ille erat rēx mortuōrum et in Orcō habitābat.

Ōlim, autem, ubi Plūtō in terrā equōs suōs agēbat, Prōserpinam, fīliam Cereris, vīdit. Statim puellam pulchram amāvit et in mātri-
5 mōnium dūcere cupiēbat. Rēx potēns igitur puellam vī (*by force*) capere cōnstituit.

Celeriter Prōserpina īnfēlīx capta est et ā Plūtōne sub terram in Orcum, rēgnum mortuōrum, portāta est. In terrā puella misera vēstīgia nūlla relīquit.

10 Jam Plūtō uxōrem habēbat. Jam Prōserpina erat rēgīna mortuōrum, sed illa erat rēgīna īnfēlīx. Semper magnopere dolēbat quod mātrem vidēre cupiēbat. Lūcem, autem, amābat, et in Orcō erat, ubi neque sōl neque lūna erat.

Diū māter īnfēlīx Prōserpinam fīliam in terrā invenīre temptābat.
15 Mox nūllum frūmentum in agrīs erat et nūlla folia in arboribus erant, quod Cerēs, dea agricultūrae, per multās terrās errābat neque agricultūram cūrābat.

Dēnique Cerēs dē Plūtōne et dē uxōre īnfēlīcī audīvit. Dea īrāta ad Jovem, rēgem potentem deōrum, properāvit et auxilium ab eō
20 postulāvit.

Juppiter respondit, "Fīliam tuam tibi dare cupiō, sed Prōserpina in Orcō manēre dēbet quod cibum gustāvit (*has tasted*). Illa est lēx deōrum."

Mōtus Cereris lacrimīs, autem, Juppiter benignus cōnsilium bonum
25 cōnstituit.

"Annum dīvidam," dīxit. "Per sex mēnsēs Prōserpina in terrā cum mātre suā habitābit; tum in Orcō cum conjuge suō per sex mēnsēs manēbit."

Itaque aestāte, dum Prōserpina est in terrā, Cerēs est fēlīx et ho-
30 minibus frūmentum dat. Hieme, autem, dum Prōserpina est in Orcō, Cerēs est īnfēlīx et hominibus nihil dat.

agō, -ere, ēgī, āctum, do, drive
cōnstituō, -stituere, -stituī, -stitūtum, decide, decide upon, set up
fēlīx, *gen.*, **fēlīcis,** happy, fortunate
īnfēlīx, *gen.*, **īnfēlīcis,** unhappy, unlucky
mēnsis, mēnsis, -ium, M., month
nihil, N., *not declined,* nothing
potēns, *gen.*, **potentis,** powerful
sōl, sōlis, M., sun
vēstīgium, -ī, N., footstep; track, trace

LATIN PREFIXES

In this lesson what two adjectives are there that differ only by a syllable? What does this syllable mean? Such a syllable is called a prefix.

To each of the following Latin words add this prefix and tell what the new word means.

credibilis **sanus** **validus**

Latin verbs also are made from other verbs by the addition of prefixes.

ab + sum = absum, *be away (absent)*
circum + specto = circumspecto, *look around*

Tell what the prefix is in each of the following verbs and give the meaning of the verb.

adsum	**circumvenio**	**expello**	**remitto**
contradico	**desisto**	**pervenio**	**transporto**

THIRD-DECLENSION ADJECTIVES OF ONE ENDING

Some adjectives of the third declension have the same form in the nominative singular for all genders. They are declined as follows:

fēlīx, *fortunate* **potēns,** *powerful*

	MASC. AND FEM.	NEUT.	MASC. AND FEM.	NEUT.
	SINGULAR			
Nom.	**fē'līx**	**fē'līx**	**po'tēns**	**po'tēns**
Gen.	**fēlī'cis**	**fēlī'cis**	**poten'tis**	**poten'tis**
Dat.	**fēlī'cī**	**fēlī'cī**	**poten'tī**	**poten'tī**
Acc.	**fēlī'cem**	**fē'līx**	**poten'tem**	**po'tēns**
Abl.	**fēlī'cī**	**fēlī'cī**	**poten'tī, -e**	**poten'tī, -e**
	PLURAL			
Nom.	**fēlī'cēs**	**fēlī'cia**	**poten'tēs**	**poten'tia**
Gen.	**fēlī'cium**	**fēlī'cium**	**poten'tium**	**poten'tium**
Dat.	**fēlī'cibus**	**fēlī'cibus**	**poten'tibus**	**poten'tibus**
Acc.	**fēlī'cēs**	**fēlī'cia**	**poten'tēs**	**poten'tia**
Abl.	**fēlī'cibus**	**fēlī'cibus**	**poten'tibus**	**poten'tibus**

The neuter is given separately though it differs from the masculine and feminine only in the accusative singular and in the nominative and accusative plural.

Answer each question in a complete Latin sentence.

1. Quis erat Cerēs? (Cerēs erat dea agricultūrae.)
2. Quis erat Plūtō?
3. Ubi Plūtō habitāvit?
4. Quis erat Prōserpina?
5. Quis erat uxor Plūtōnis?
6. Quis erat Juppiter?
7. Ubi Juppiter habitāvit?
8. Quis erat uxor Jovis?
9. Ubi aestāte Prōserpina habitat?
10. Ubi hieme Prōserpina habitat?

Choose the form of the adjective which correctly completes each sentence.

1. Vellus aureum ā juvene { fortī / fortis / fortēs } captum est.
2. Dracōnēs { ācre / ācrēs / ācris } virōs necāre dēsīderābant.
3. Bella ā rēgibus { īnfēlīcibus / īnfēlīcī / īnfēlīcia } geruntur.
4. Praemia puerīs { omnēs / omnibus / omnis } dabantur.
5. Mōnstrum { ācre / ācer / ācria } ā virō { potentī / potentis / potēns } necātur.

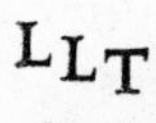

Some everyday English words are related to the Latin word **ago**: *actor, actress, action, active, actual, exact.*

The phrase "Constitution of the United States" contains three words derived from Latin. Two of them you have already met: *United* (from **unus**) and *States* (from **sto**). From what Latin word does the third come?

If someone said your team's chances of winning the game were *nil*, what would he mean? *Nil* is a contraction of **nihil.** The English words *annihilate* and *annihilation* also come from **nihil.** If a regiment is *annihilated,* what happens to it?

A *solarium* is a sunroom. If you carry a *parasol,* you are prepared for the sun. The *solar* system includes the sun and the planets that revolve around it. What is a *solar* year?

LXXII. UXOR AMISSA

Orpheus and Cerberus, famous for his three heads

Per silvam sonus amoenus lyrae audītus est. Avēs, sonō lyrae audītō, cantāre dēstitērunt. Bēstiae ferae quidem stetērunt et nōn jam necāre hominēs temptāvērunt. 5

Orpheus, fīlius Apollinis, lyram habēbat et cantābat. Eurydicē, virgō pulchra, Orpheum cantantem audīvit. Eum vidēre cupiēns, 10 ad eum properāvit. Orpheus eam venientem vīdit et statim eam amāvit. Posteā Eurydicēn in mātrimōnium dūxit.

Ōlim serpēns pedem Eurydicēs 15 ambulantis in agrō momordit (*bit*). Illa statim ē vītā excēdēns sub terram in Orcum, locum mortuōrum, ducta est.

Orpheus, propter uxōrem āmissam dolēns, eam etiam in Orcō 20 petere cōnstituit. Itaque per cavernam sub terram dēscendit.

Sed ubi ad flūmen Stygem vēnit, portitor (*ferryman*) Charōn eum vīventem trāns flūmen nāve suā portāre recūsāvit. Orpheus autem lyram cēpit et cantāvit; tum Charōn libenter eum trāns flūmen portāvit. Ibi Cerberus, magnus canis, eum terrēre temptāvit. Sed 25 Orpheus iterum cantāvit et canis statim dormīvit.

Ita post multa perīcula Orpheus ad rēgiam Plūtōnis vēnit et ā Plūtōne uxōrem petīvit. Plūtō autem Eurydicēn āmittere recūsābat. Tum Orpheus, capiēns lyram, cantāvit.

Dēnique Plūtō sonō lyrae victus Eurydicēn Orpheō dedit, sed sub 30 hāc lēge: "Orpheus ad terram prōcēdet; Eurydicēn post sē venientem nōn respiciet. Sī Orpheus respiciet, Eurydicē in Orcum iterum dūcētur."

Orpheus laetus ad terram ascendere incēpit. Dum sub terrā Orpheus erat, nōn respexit. Subitō prope portam cavernae respexit et uxōrem 35 amātam suam vīdit.

Eurydicē misera clāmāvit, "Valē! Iterum ad mortuōs dūcar. Valē!"
Conjuge suā iterum āmissā, Orpheus dolōre victus est et in terrā nōn diū habitābat. Mox in Orcō Eurydicēn cāram iterum invēnit.

canis, -is (*gen. pl.* **-um**), M. or F., dog
dēsistō, -sistere, -stitī, -stitum, desist from, cease, stop
dolor, -ōris, M., grief, sorrow
excēdō, -cēdere, -cessī, -cessum, go out, depart
libenter, *adv.*, gladly, freely
quidem, *adv.*, certainly, indeed
recūsō, -āre, -āvī, -ātum, refuse, reject
respiciō, -spicere, -spexī, -spectum, look back, look back at
serpēns, -entis, F., serpent, snake

LATIN AND ENGLISH PREFIXES

On page 273 you met the Latin prefixes **ab, ad, circum, contra, de, ex, in, per, re-,** and **trans.** These prefixes occur in English words and have similar meanings. Find the prefix in each of the following words and explain the meaning of the word. If possible, tell from what Latin word it comes.

abduct	**circumstance**	**exalt**	**remove**
admit	**contradict**	**infinite**	**report**
circumnavigate	**demonstrate**	**perambulate**	**transcribe**

PRESENT ACTIVE PARTICIPLE

You are familiar with the perfect passive participle.

portātus, *having been carried*

There are also participles in the active voice.

Present Active Participle: **portāns,** *carrying*

The present participles of regular verbs in the four conjugations are as follows:

I	II	III		IV
(portō)	(moneō)	(dūcō)	(capiō)	(audiō)
portāns	**monēns**	**dūcēns**	**capiēns**	**audiēns**
carrying	*warning*	*leading*	*taking*	*hearing*

As you can see from these examples, the present active participle of a Latin verb ends in **-ns**, and is formed on the present stem.

The present participle of **-ō** verbs of the third conjugation is exactly like that of the second conjugation. In the fourth conjugation and in **-iō** verbs of the third conjugation the stem ending appears as **-iē-**.

DECLENSION OF THE PRESENT PARTICIPLE

Like other participles, the present participle agrees in gender, number, and case with the noun or pronoun it modifies. It is declined as an adjective of the third declension:

	SINGULAR			
	MASC. AND FEM.	NEUT.	MASC. AND FEM.	NEUT.
Nom.	por′tāns	por′tāns	mo′nēns	mo′nēns
Gen.	portan′tis	portan′tis	monen′tis	monen′tis
Dat.	portan′tī	portan′tī	monen′tī	monen′tī
Acc.	portan′tem	por′tāns	monen′tem	mo′nēns
Abl.	portan′te, -ī	portan′te, -ī	monen′te, -ī	monen′te, -ī
	PLURAL			
Nom.	portan′tēs	portan′tia	monen′tēs	monen′tia
Gen.	portan′tium	portan′tium	monen′tium	monen′tium
Dat.	portan′tibus	portan′tibus	monen′tibus	monen′tibus
Acc.	portan′tēs	portan′tia	monen′tēs	monen′tia
Abl.	portan′tibus	portan′tibus	monen′tibus	monen′tibus

1. Fīlius Apollinis, lyram portāns, per silvam vēnit et Eurydicēn vīdit. 2. Lacrimae uxōris lacrimantis numquam dēstitērunt. 3. Vir respexit et canēs necantēs magnam serpentem vīdit. 4. Dum Orpheus, fīlius Apollinis, cantat, avēs parvae quidem cantāre dēsistunt. 5. Juvenēs fortēs taurōs ācrēs jungere nōn recūsāvērunt. 6. Charōn quidem virōs vīventēs trāns flūmen nōn libenter portābit. 7. Dolōre victus, Orpheus sub terram in Orcum dēscendit. 8. Conjūnx laetus respexit et Plūtō iterum conjugem miseram cēpit. 9. Orpheus lyram cēpit et cantāre nōn recūsāvit.

Supply the participle for each blank.

1. Serpēns pedem Eurydicēs __ in hortō vulnerābat. (*walk*)
2. Cerēs, __ fīliam āmissam, in Orcum properāvit. (*grieve for*)
3. Lyram __ et __, Orpheus ad rēgiam Plūtōnis vēnit. (*carry, sing*)
4. Orpheus uxōrem post sē __ respexit. (*come*)
5. Charōn virōs __ trāns flūmen nāve suā nōn portābat. (*live*)

HW Make up five Latin sentences containing participles.

HELP YOURSELF In the next to the last sentence of "Uxor Āmissa," what is the gender of **suā**? Why? In Latin sentence 8 what is the gender of **laetus**? Of **miseram**?

LXXIII. FEMINA CURIOSA

Olim in terrā sōla fēmina erat uxor Epimētheī. Haec fēmina nōn sōlum pulchra erat, sed etiam maximē cūriōsa erat. Multa dōna ā deīs data habēbat. Nōmen ejus igitur erat Pandōra, significāns "dōna omnia." Inter dōna deōrum erat parva arca, dōnum Jovis.
5 "Haec arca," Juppiter dīxit, "magnum sēcrētum tenet; aperīrī nōn dēbet. Sī aperiētur, perīcula gravia in terrā aderunt. Dā arcam clausam tuō conjugī."

Epimētheus arcam libenter cēpit; sed, ā deīs monitus, eam nōn aperuit. Nōn satis sapiēns autem erat conjūnx Pandōrae cūriōsae.
10 Arcam nōn cēlāvit.

Cotīdiē Pandōra arcam spectābat, cupiēns eam aperīre. Timēns autem perīcula gravia ā Jove prōmissa, ab eā procul manēre temptāvit.

Ōlim Pandōra sōla erat in hortō ubi arca erat. Fēmina cūriōsa eam diū spectāvit; scrīpta in arcā haec verba vīdit: "Teneō omnia
15 gaudia deōrum. Aperī mē."

Maximē haec gaudia habēre cupiēns, Pandōra arcam aperuit. Subito mala, nōn gaudia, ex arcā volāvērunt. Prīmō duo mala, deinde tria alia ex arcā vēnērunt. Dēnique omnia mala hominum per terrās volāvērunt. Pandōra territa celeriter arcam clausit.

Pandora as the English artist Rossetti painted her

20 Mox autem Pandōra īnfēlīx audīvit vōcem dīcentem: "Aperī iterum arcam. Summum bonum in arcā relīquistī. Hominēs juvābō. Līberā mē!"

25 Itaque Pandōra cūriōsa parvam arcam iterum aperuit. Ex arcā Spēs (*Hope*), sōlum dōnum bonum deōrum, vēnit.

aperiō, -īre, -uī, apertum, open
claudō, -ere, clausī, clausum, close
cotīdiē, *adv.*, every day, daily
cūriōsus, -a, -um, curious
duo, duae, duo, two
gaudium, -ī, N., joy, delight, pleasure
gravis, -e, heavy, severe, serious
sapiēns, *gen.*, **-entis,** wise
significō, -āre, -āvī, -ātum, mean

LATIN ADJECTIVES AND ENGLISH ADJECTIVES

From some Latin nouns come Latin adjectives, which in turn give us English adjectives. From the meaning of the noun it is easy to see the meaning of both the Latin and English adjectives.

Thus we have Latin adjectives made by adding **-inus** to the base of a noun: **femininus = femin + -inus.** The English adjective with the same meaning has *-ine* instead of **-us.**

Give the Latin noun and adjective from which *aquiline* comes.

What is the English adjective from each of the following pairs of words? What does it mean?

canis, caninus	**felis, felinus**
equus, equinus	**leo, leoninus**

Many of these Latin adjectives are made up of the base of the noun + **-alis**; in the English adjective the **-is** has been dropped. Thus **legalis = leg-** (the base of **lex**) + **-alis,** and the English adjective is *legal.*

With what Latin noun and adjective is each of the following connected?

conjugal	*corporal*	*naval*	*regal*

Give the Latin noun or adjective with which each of the following words is connected. If you can, give both noun and adjective.

local	*natural*	*principal*	*vital*
marine	*nominal*	*Sibylline*	*vocal*

Use each of these eight adjectives in a sentence.

CARDINAL NUMBERS

The cardinal numbers from one to ten in Latin are **ūnus, duo, trēs, quattuor, quīnque, sex, septem, octō, novem, decem.** Of these, only the first three are declined. **Ūnus, -a, -um** is declined like **bonus** except in the genitive and dative singular (which are not used in this book). **Duo** and **trēs** are, of course, always in the plural. They are declined as follows:

	MASC.	FEM.	NEUT.	MASC. AND FEM.	NEUT.
Nom.	du′o	du′ae	du′o	trēs	tri′a
Gen.	duō′rum	duā′rum	duō′rum	tri′um	tri′um
Dat.	duō′bus	duā′bus	duō′bus	tri′bus	tri′bus
Acc.	du′ōs, du′o	du′ās	du′o	trēs	tri′a
Abl.	duō′bus	duā′bus	duō′bus	tri′bus	tri′bus

1. Conjūnx sapiēns Pandōrae cūriōsae arcam nōn aperuit 2. Aperī duās arcās, Pandōra; aperī trēs arcās. 3. Cotīdiē fēminae cūriōsae arcam gravem aperiēbant claudēbantque. 4. Verba sapientia sapientibus virīs grāta sunt. 5. In viā urbis octō puerōs et quīnque puellās vīdī. 6. Aenēās gaudia pauca et dolōrēs multōs habuit. 7. Sex verba in arcā scrīpta sunt. 8. Aperī jānuam, Mārce; claude fenestram. 9. Nōmina multa aut gaudium aut fortūnam bonam significant. 10. Legitisne omnēs fābulās duōrum librōrum?

Ōlim fuērunt decem canēs parvī.
Ūnus canis puerō datus est. Tum fuērunt novem.
Ūnus canis puellae datus est. Tum fuērunt octō.
Ūnus canis ā leōne captus est. Tum fuērunt septem.
Ūnus canis ā fēminā in casam portātus est. Tum fuērunt sex.
Ūnus canis procul errāvit. Tum fuērunt quīnque.
Ūnus canis ē vītā excessit. Tum fuērunt quattuor.
Ūnus canis fūgit. Tum fuērunt trēs.
Ūnus canis āmissus est. Tum fuērunt duo.
Ūnus canis ā virō in silvam portātus est. Tum fuit ūnus.
Ūnus canis in cavernā latuit. Jam fuit nūllus.

1. Two and six are eight. 2. Three and one are four. 3. Eight and two are ten. 4. Four and three are seven. 5. One and nine are ten. 6. Five and four are nine.

REVIEW OF UNIT XV LESSONS LXX-LXXIII

Nouns	*Nouns*	*Verbs*	*Adjectives*
canis, -is	taurus, -ī	*dīvidō, -ere	fortis, forte
dēns, dentis	vellus, velleris	excēdō, -cēdere	gravis, -e
dolor, -ōris	vēstīgium, -ī	jungō, -ere	īnfēlīx, -fēlīcis
dracō, -ōnis	*Verbs*	recūsō, -āre	omnis, omne
gaudium, -ī	agō, -ere	respiciō, -spicere	potēns, -entis
juvenis, juvenis	aperiō, -īre	significō, -āre	sapiēns, -entis
*membrum, -ī	arō, -āre	*Adjectives*	*stupidus, -a, -um
mēnsis, mēnsis, -ium	claudō, -ere	ācer, ācris, ācre	*Adverbs*
nihil	cōnstituō, -stituere	cūriōsus, -a, -um	cotīdiē
serpēns, -entis	*dēscendō, -ere	duo, duae, duo	libenter
sōl, sōlis	dēsistō, -sistere	fēlīx, fēlīcis	quidem

I. Complete each sentence with the correct Latin word.

1. Sex et quattuor sunt —.
2. Quīnque et trēs sunt —.
3. Septem et duo sunt —.
4. Novem et ūnus sunt —.
5. Octō et duo sunt —.

II. First try to understand the following story without looking up any words. Then look up what you need to.

AUDACIA JUVENIS

Phaëthōn erat superbus fēlīxque quod Apollō erat pater ejus. Cotīdiē juvenis Apollinem, deum sōlis, agentem equōs potentēs trāns caelum spectābat. Ōlim ad rēgiam sōlis vēnit.

Fīliō salūtātō, Apollō dīxit, "Quid cupiēns vēnistī? Nihil recūsābō."

Phaëthōn magnō cum gaudiō respondit, "Equōs sōlis trāns caelum 5 agere cupiō."

Apollō cum dolōre dīxit, "Ō Phaëthōn īnfēlīx, es fortis sed neque satis potēns neque satis sapiēns. Tua audācia quidem tibi mortis, mihi dolōris causa erit."

Fīlius, autem, respondit, "Deus hoc prōmissum recūsāre nōn audet. 10 Cōnstituī; mentem nōn mūtābō."

Māne, igitur, equī ācrēs jūnctī sunt, et per portās Aurōrae apertās Phaëthōn eōs libenter ēgit. Equī subitō respicientēs territī erant. Prīmō prope terram, deinde procul inter stellās juvenem īnfēlīcem portantēs, dēsistere recūsābant. In agrīs arātīs flammae frūmentum 15 vāstābant; aquae quidem flūminum mariumque recēdēbant.

Tum Juppiter, perīculō gravī terrae vīsō, fulmen (*thunderbolt*) jēcit. Statim inter flammās Phaëthōn ē caelō in flūmen cecidit (*fell*). Posteā sorōrēs ejus in rīpā flūminis lacrimantēs in arborēs mūtātae sunt, et folia eārum sonum fēminārum dolentium facere numquam dēstitērunt. 20

LLT After you have completed each sentence correctly, give the Latin word or words to which the English key word is related.

1. A conjunction { joins. / modifies. / separates.
2. The K-9 corps was made up of { cooks. / dogs. / nurses.
3. A pedestrian { rides horseback. / takes an airplane. / walks.
4. We procrastinate when we { delay. / hurry. / loaf.
5. Significance is { grief. / meaning. / relationship.
6. A trio is made up of { six. / three. / two.

LXXIV. JUDICIUM PARIDIS

Paris judicium facile non fecit.

Olim dī deaeque ad magnam cēnam invītātī sunt. Discordia erat sōla dea quae nōn invītāta est. Tamen, maximē īrāta, ad cēnam 5 vēnit et jēcit inter deōs deāsque mālum aureum in quō hoc verbum scrīptum est: "Pulcherrimae (*for the most beautiful*)."

Statim erat contrōversia inter deās 10 Jūnōnem et Minervam et Venerem. Omnēs mālum aureum habēre cupiēbant.

Juppiter, quī aderat, dīxit, "In hāc contrōversiā jūdex esse nōn 15 cupiō. In monte Īdā, autem, habitat pāstor, cujus nōmen est Paris. Petite eum; is hoc mālum, īnsigne victōriae, deae 'pulcherrimae' dabit."

Deae, igitur, in montem Īdam convēnērunt. Cum eīs erat Mercurius, 20 cujus auxiliō deae Paridem invēnērunt.

Mercurius pāstōrī mālum aureum mōnstrāvit, et dīxit, "In hōc mālō quod teneō ūnum verbum scrībitur: 'Pulcherrimae.' Magna est contrōversia inter hās deās quibuscum veniō. Juppiter, igitur, tē jūdicem hujus contrōversiae dēlēgit."

25 Itaque Paris, graviter agitātus, verba deārum audiēbat. Prīmō Jūnō dīxit, "Dā mihi mālum aureum, Paris. Rēgīna deōrum sum; dīvitiās potentiamque tibi dabō."

Deinde Minerva jūdicī dīxit, "Dā mihi mālum aureum. Dea sapientiae sum; magnam sapientiam et cōnsilia bona tibi dabō."

30 Dēnique Venus pulchra prō jūdice stetit. "Fīnem hujus contrōversiae facile faciam," dīxit. "Dā mihi mālum aureum. Dea amōris sum; pulcherrimam fēminam quae in orbe terrārum (*the world*) vīvit conjugem tibi dabō!"

Paris, autem, jūdicium facile nōn fēcit. Dīvitiae, potentia, sapi-35 entia—omnēs juvenī grātae erant. Tamen conjugem pulcherrimam prōmissam ā Venere maximē cupiēbat. Itaque deae amōris mālum dedit.

amor, -ōris, M., love
conveniō, -venīre, -vēnī, -ventum, assemble, gather
dīvitiae, -ārum, F., *pl.*, riches, wealth
jūdex, jūdicis, M., judge
jūdicium, -ī, N., judgment, decision
mālum, -ī, N., apple
pāstor, -ōris, M., shepherd
potentia, -ae, F., power
sapientia, -ae, F., wisdom

MEANING AND USE OF THE RELATIVE PRONOUN

In Lesson XIV you met a dependent clause introduced by a *conjunction* to show its relationship to an independent clause.

In the sentence *The boy whom you saw yesterday is my brother,* the dependent clause *whom you saw yesterday* is introduced by the relative pronoun *whom.* The word *whom* connects the dependent clause with the independent clause and is a pronoun with *boy* as its antecedent.

The English relative pronouns are *who, which,* and *that.* We use *who* to refer to persons and *which* to refer to things. We may use *that* for either persons or things. In the following sentence **quem** is a relative pronoun.

> **Homō quem vidēs amīcus meus est,** *The man whom you see is my friend.*

The Latin relative pronouns may be translated *who* (*whom*), *which,* or *that.*

FORMS OF THE LATIN RELATIVE PRONOUN

The forms of the Latin relative pronoun are as follows:

SINGULAR

	MASC.	FEM.	NEUT.	
Nominative:	**quī**	**quae**	**quod**	who, which, that
Genitive:	**cu′jus**	**cu′jus**	**cu′jus**	whose, of whom, of which
Dative:	**cui**	**cui**	**cui**	to whom, to which
Accusative:	**quem**	**quam**	**quod**	whom, which, that
Ablative:	**quō**	**quā**	**quō**	(from, with, by, in) whom, which

PLURAL

	MASC.	FEM.	NEUT.	
Nominative:	**quī**	**quae**	**quae**	who, which, that
Genitive:	**quō′rum**	**quā′rum**	**quō′rum**	whose, of whom, of which
Dative:	**qui′bus**	**qui′bus**	**qui′bus**	to whom, to which
Accusative:	**quōs**	**quās**	**quae**	whom, which, that
Ablative:	**qui′bus**	**qui′bus**	**qui′bus**	(from, with, by, in) whom, which

AGREEMENT OF THE RELATIVE PRONOUN

The relative pronoun agrees with its antecedent in gender and number, but its case depends on its use in its own clause.

Homō quem vidēs amīcus meus est, *The man whom you see is my friend.*

In the sentence above, **quem** is masculine singular to agree with its antecedent, **homō.** It is accusative because it is the object of **vidēs.**

RELATIVE PRONOUN WITH *cum*

When the ablative forms of the relative pronoun are used as objects of the preposition **cum,** they regularly have **cum** added as a final syllable.

quōcum, quācum, quibuscum, *with whom, with which*

This is also true of the interrogative pronoun.

1. Pāstor quī erat jūdex erat fīlius rēgis. 2. Pāstōrēs quī dīvitiās dēsīderant jam in campum convēnērunt. 3. Mālum, quod ā deā īrātā jactum est, erat initium contrōversiae. 4. Māla quae erant in arboribus erant aurea. 5. Fēminae quās in silvā vīdistī erant deae. 6. Propter sapientiam jūdicis lēx bene facta est. 7. Dea cui mālum datum est dea amōris erat. 8. Deae ante tumulum stetērunt in quō jūdex sedēbat. 9. Pāstor ā quō jūdicium audītum est mīlitēs monuit.

Complete each sentence with a form of **quī, quae, quod.** 1. Pāstor __ mālum habet est frāter tuus. 2. Jūdex __ vīdī est amīcus tuus. 3. Fēmina __ mē monuit est māter tua. 4. Fēmina ā __ monitus sum est māter tua. 5. Oppidum __ occupāvimus erat in colle. 6. Oppidum __ occupātum est prope flūmen erat. 7. Deae __ convocāvērunt fuērunt Jūnō et Venus et Minerva. 8. Collis in __ stant nōn est altus.

LLT

In the following sentences find seven words related to Latin words in this vocabulary and give the Latin word to which each is related.

When Congress convenes, important matters are taken up.

Because it is a convenient place in which to meet, many conventions are held in Chicago.

The judges of the Supreme Court belong to the judiciary branch of the government. Their judicial duties include the handing down of decisions on judgments of lower courts.

LXXV. PARIS ET HELENA

Mālō aureō acceptō, Venus Paridī nūntiāvit, "Fēmina pulcherrima (*most beautiful*) in Graeciā habitat. Nōmen ejus est Helena; Helena erit tua conjūnx."

Dea Paridī quoque dīxit patrem et mātrem ejus esse rēgem et rēgīnam Trōjae. "Monitus ōrāculō, pater tuus mortem tuam cupiēbat et tē in silvīs relīquit; pāstor tē servāvit," dīxit.

Dea ostendit Hectorem, frātrem Paridis, in rēgiā Trōjānā habitāre et ā populō propter magnam audāciam laudārī.

Itaque Paris invidiōsus īrātusque ad urbem Trōjam prōcessit. Ubi Priamus rēx pāstōrem vīdit, statim sēnsit eum esse fīlium suum. Nōn jam mortem Paridis cupiēbat. Laetus quod Paris vīvēbat, Priamus juvenem libenter in rēgiam invītāvit.

Posteā cum classe Paris ad Graeciam nāvigāvit, quamquam pater ejus crēdidit eum ad aliam terram iter facere. Hīc audīvit Helenam, fēminam ā Venere prōmissam, Spartae rēgīnam et uxōrem Menelāī esse.

Itaque Paris sōlus ad urbem Spartam prōcessit, sed cum Helenā sēcrētō discessit. Regīna perfida, conjuge relictō, ad urbem Trōjam cum Paride fūgit.

Uxōre āmissā, Menelāus prīncipēs Graeciae convocāvit. Graviter agitātus, rēx in animō bellum contrā Trōjānōs gerere habuit.

accipiō, -cipere, -cēpī, -ceptum, receive, accept
crēdō, -ere, crēdidī, crēditum, believe, trust
discēdō, -ere, -cessī, -cessum, depart, withdraw
ostendō, -tendere, -tendī, -tentum, show, display
sentiō, -īre, sēnsī, sēnsum, feel, believe

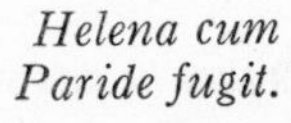

Helena cum Paride fugit.

DIRECT QUOTATIONS

A *direct quotation* is one which repeats the exact words of the speaker.

He said, "I will come."

The exact words of the speaker are inclosed in quotation marks.

INDIRECT QUOTATIONS

An *indirect quotation* is one which repeats the thought, but not the exact words of the original speaker. In English an indirect quotation is often introduced by the conjunction *that,* but sometimes the conjunction is omitted.

He said that he would come, or *He said he would come.*

No conjunction is used to introduce indirect quotations in Latin. An indirect quotation has its verb in the infinitive and its subject in the accusative.

Dīcit puerum in silvā ambulāre, *He says that the boy is walking in the forest.*

In the direct form this quotation would be **Puer in silvā ambulat.** In the indirect quotation **puer,** the subject, becomes **puerum,** and **ambulat** becomes **ambulāre.**

INDIRECT DISCOURSE

The name *indirect discourse* is given to the use of the infinitive with subject accusative in indirect quotations.

Certain other expressions which are not exactly quotations take the same form as indirect quotations.

I heard that you had received a letter.

Everyone thought that the day would be pleasant.

In the sentences above, the clauses introduced by *that* would be in the form of indirect discourse in Latin. Accordingly, their verbs would be infinitives and their subjects would stand in the accusative.

Indirect discourse is used with verbs of *saying, hearing, knowing, thinking, believing, seeing,* and the like.

Crēdō tē librum meum habēre, *I believe* (*that*) *you have my book.*

When the speaker makes a statement about himself in indirect discourse, the reflexive pronoun is used.

Dīcit sē librum tuum habēre, *He says that he has your book.*

PREDICATE NOUN OR ADJECTIVE IN INDIRECT DISCOURSE

A predicate noun or adjective used with an infinitive in indirect discourse is in the accusative, to agree with the subject of the infinitive.

Crēdimus ducem nostrum fortem esse, *We believe (that) our leader is brave.*

PRESENT INFINITIVE IN INDIRECT DISCOURSE

The act expressed by the present infinitive in indirect discourse is represented as occurring at the time shown by the tense of the main verb.

Dīcit sē perīculum timēre, *He says that he fears danger.*
Dīxit sē perīculum timēre, *He said that he feared danger.*

1. Mīles cui arma dedimus discēdet; mīlitēs quibus arma data sunt auxilium nostrum accipient. 2. Urbs ex quā vēnistī est magna; oppidum ex quō vēnī in montibus est. 3. Cīvēs ostendēbant auxilium ā Graecīs libenter mittī. 4. Trōjānī crēdēbant Graecōs ab īnsulā discēdere. 5. Populus videt portās urbis ā mīlitibus mūnīrī. 6. Nūntius dīcit ducem hostium praemia accipere. 7. Cīvēs sēnsērunt jūdicem ēgregiam sapientiam habēre.

Choose the correct verb to complete each sentence.

1. Paris dīcit fēminam in Graeciā (habitāre habitat).
2. Helena dīcit, "In Graeciā (habitāre habitō)."
3. Dea nūntiat juvenem fīlium rēgis (esse est).
4. Priamus dīcit, "Paris (esse est) fīlius meus."
5. Rēgīna dīcit, "Conjugem meum (āmīsī āmittere)."

HY Find in the second paragraph of "Paris et Helena" a direct quotation and an indirect quotation, and explain the forms of the verbs and their subjects.

LLT There are many English words related to Latin words in this vocabulary. From each of the following lists select one word and give a sentence containing it.

accipio: *accept, acceptable, acceptably, acceptance*
credo: *credible, credit, creditable, credulous, creed*
ostendo: *ostentation, ostentatious, ostensible, ostensibly*
sentio: *sentence, sentiment, sense, sensible, sensitive*

LXXVI. DOLI ULIXIS

Convocātī ā Menelāō, multī prīncipēs Graeciae convēnērunt. Parātī ad urbem Trōjam nāvigāre sunt.

Duo ducēs, autem, Ulīxēs et Achillēs, aberant.

Ulīxēs uxōrem suam, Pēnelopam, et fīlium suum, Tēlemachum, 5 relinquere nōn dēsīderābat. Itaque, equō et bove jūnctīs, Ulīxēs ōram maritimam arāre incipiēbat. Ubi nūntius bellī vēnit, prīmō crēdidit Ulīxem esse īnsānum.

Sed nūntius dēnique sēnsit hunc esse dolum Ulīxis. Itaque, Tēlemachō captō, parvum puerum prō equō et bove posuit. Ulīxēs, quī 10 fīlium suum interficere nōn dēsīderāvit, ā dolō dēstitit, et sē cum cēterīs Graecīs jūnxit.

Interim māter Achillis, Thetis, quae fīlium bellum gerere nōn dēsīderābat, Achillem ad rēgiam amīcī mīsit. Ibi Achillēs vestēs fēminae gerēbat. Thetis crēdidit juvenem, inter fēminās cēlātum, 15 tūtum esse.

Multī nūntiī, autem, ad rēgiam vēnērunt et bellum nūntiāvērunt. Nūllōs virōs autem vīdērunt. Tamen Ulīxēs sēnsit dolum latēre. Itaque ad rēgiam iter fēcit, sed vestem mercātōris gerēbat. Fēminīs puellīsque gemmās et vestēs pulchrās et urnās aureās ostendit. 20 Gladium pulchrum quoque ostendit. Fēminae gemmās et vestēs laudāvērunt sed Achillēs gladium statim cēpit.

Tum Ulīxēs clāmāvit, "Achillēs es! Cum aliīs ducibus ad urbem Trōjam nāvigāre dēbēs!"

Mōtus hīs verbīs Ulīxis, Achillēs libenter arma cēpit et cum eō 25 discessit.

Itaque duo ducēs quī pugnāre nōn dēsīderābant sē cum aliīs ducibus jūnxērunt.

bōs,[1] **bovis,** M., ox

vestis, -is, -ium, F., garment, clothing

1. Ulīxēs crēdidit fortem Achillem inter fēminās cēlārī. 2. Nūntius sēnsit Ulīxem īnsānum nōn esse. 3. Achillēs, cujus māter eum cēlāvit, vestem fēminae gerere nōn dēsīderābat. 4. Trēs deae inter quās contrōversia ācris erat mālum cupiēbant. 5. Dīcō Paridem juvenem īnfēlīcem esse. 6. Audīmus omnēs mīlitēs in oppidō capī. 7. Magnus bōs agrum arābat.

[1]In this book, the plural of this word is used only in the nominative and accusative. These forms are regular.

Achilles gladium statim cepit.

Answer in Latin the following questions.

1. Quis erat uxor Ulīxis?
2. Quis erat fīlius Pēnelopae?
3. Quis Tēlemachum prō equō et bove posuit?
4. Quis erat māter Achillis?
5. Quī gemmās et vestēs laudāvērunt?
6. Quis gladium statim cēpit?
7. Quis cum Ulīxe discessit?

Translate the italicized words: 1. I believe that *Helen is running away.* 2. They say that Achilles *is being led* to war *by Ulysses.* 3. *Whose* book is on the table? 4. The man *to whom* I gave the money shows me that *the road is safe.* 5. Do you say that the ox and the horse *are yoked together?* 6. Who said that the brave youth *was wearing* women's garments?

HW Translate completely the six English sentences above.

HY Find three perfect participles and three dependent clauses introduced by relative pronouns in Dolī Ulīxis. Translate the participles as if they were relative clauses and the relative clauses as if they were participles.

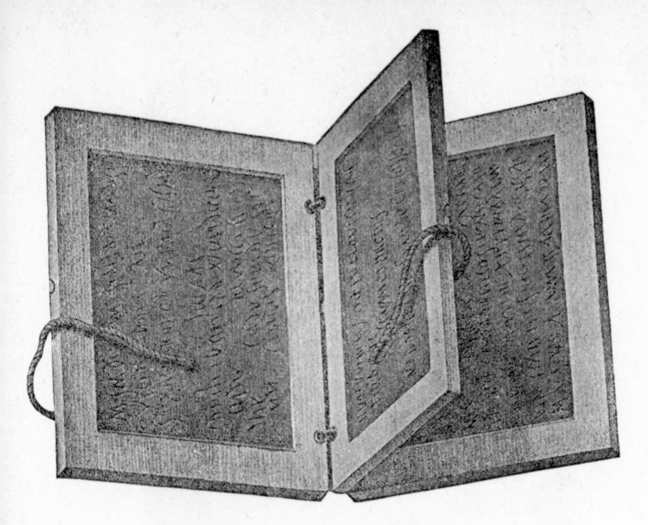

On tablets like the ones at the left, a Roman child practiced writing. If he made a mistake, he smoothed the wax and started again. Above is an ancient letter written on papyrus.

SCHOOLS AND BOOKS

The Romans had no public schools like those in America, which are paid for by taxes and provide free instruction for all. The Roman school was a small, private one, and each pupil paid the teacher a fee. Often the school building was nothing more than a roof on pillars, and the children must have found the passers-by quite distracting.

At the age of seven, children started in what we should call a primary school. Girls usually attended only this first school, receiving no further instruction except in their homes.

In the primary school, the children learned reading, writing, and arithmetic. To teach his pupils to read, the teacher first pronounced the syllables, then the word, and finally the sentence, while the children pronounced them after him. Pupils learned to write on wax-covered tablets, making the letters with a bone or metal tool that had a pointed end (pp. 31, 71). In working simple arithmetic problems, the child counted on his fingers; for harder sums, he might use a reckoning board like the one shown at the left.

Even this reckoning board, or abacus, could not have made arithmetic easy for the boy who had to use Roman numerals.

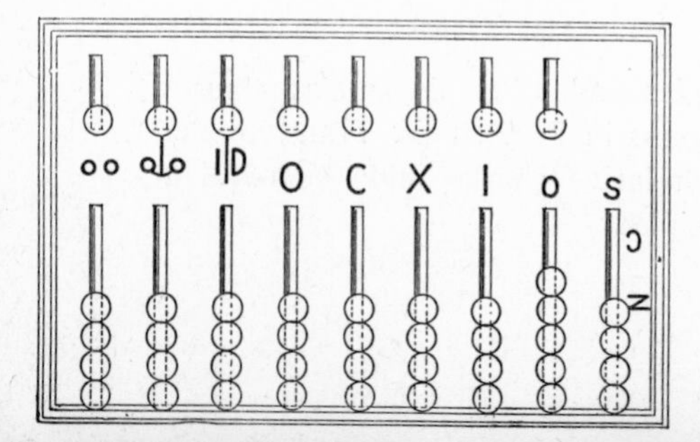

Some boys went on to grammar school, where they studied elocution, music, geometry, and literature—especially the poems of Homer.

The reader is unrolling the book with his right hand and, with his left, rolling up what he has just read.

This Roman schoolboy, wearing a tunic, is apparently practicing his elocution.

Young men sometimes went to schools of rhetoric, where they learned to compose and deliver speeches.

Roman schoolboys had no attractive textbooks such as children in this country have. In fact they had very few books, for all books had to be written by hand.

The Roman book had no pages. Instead, sheets made of papyrus were fastened together, forming a long strip. When a strip was not in use, it was rolled around a stick and put in a cabinet.

If a man wanted a certain book, he might borrow a copy and have it written out laboriously by hand or he might buy it from a "publisher," who kept hundreds of scribes busy copying books.

In early days the Romans did little reading, but during the Empire almost every educated Roman had a library in his home. In time there were as many as twenty-eight public libraries in Rome.

From such papyrus reeds the ancients made paper. The inside of the stem was cut into thin strips which were glued together and pressed into sheets.

LXXVII. HELENA ET MENDICUS

Postquam Paris et Hector ā Graecīs interfectī sunt, magnus dolor mentēs populī Trōjānī occupāvit. In viās urbis Helena exīre nōn audēbat, quod fēminae Trōjānae clāmāvērunt, "Propter tē, fēmina mala, dī nōs nōn jam amant."

5 In templīs sacerdōtēs dīxērunt, "Deōs, Trōjānī, ōrāre dēbētis; in ārīs sacrificia pōnite. Ōmina sunt mala. Fāta nōs nostramque urbem dēlēbunt."

Trōjānī sciēbant sē ducēs bonōs nōn jam habēre.

Jam Helena ad Graecōs trānsīre cupiēbat. Tamen nōn sōlum īram 10 Menelāī timēbat sed etiam portae urbis clausae sunt.

Ōlim Helena in urbe mendicum vīdit. Multī līberī, clāmantēs et lapidēs jacientēs, ad eum ībant. Helena subitō sēnsit hunc mendicum esse Ulīxem, ducem clārum Graecum. Itaque servō suō dīxit, "Vocā mendicum in rēgiam; dā eī cibum et aquam."

15 Hōc factō, Helena servōs suōs expulit et parvā vōce mendicō dīxit, "Tē recognōscō; tū es Ulīxēs. Quid in hāc urbe facis? Nōnne ad Graecōs redībis?"

Ulīxēs respondit sē portās et viās urbis spec- 20 tāre; Graecōs novum cōnsilium habēre. "Certē," dīxit, "urbs Trōja dēlēbitur."

Tum Helena dīxit, "Tē 25 juvābō; tibi viam sēcrētam in mediam urbem mōnstrābō. Ita, meō auxiliō, Graecī Trōjam vāstābunt."

eō, īre, iī (īvī), itum, go
exeō, -īre, -iī, -itum, go out
mendicus, -ī, M., beggar
redeō, -īre, -iī, -itum, go back
sacerdōs, -dōtis, M. *and* F., priest, priestess
sciō, scīre, scīvī, scītum, know
trānseō, -īre, -iī, -itum, go across, cross

Helen at Troy

*Helen being taken to Troy—
an ancient painting*

CONJUGATION OF *eō*

The irregular verb **eō,** *go,* is conjugated in the present system as follows:

PRESENT	IMPERFECT	FUTURE
	SINGULAR	
e'ō, I go	**ī'bam,** I was going, I went	**ī'bō,** I shall go
īs, you go	**ī'bās,** you were going, you went	**ī'bis,** you will go
it, he, she, it goes	**ī'bat,** he, she, it was going; he, she, it went	**ī'bit,** he, she, it will go
	PLURAL	
ī'mus, we go	**ībā'mus,** we were going, we went	**ī'bimus,** we shall go
ī'tis, you go	**ībā'tis,** you were going, you went	**ī'bitis,** you will go
e'unt, they go	**ī'bant,** they were going, they went	**ī'bunt,** they will go

The principal parts are **eō, īre, iī** or **īvī, itum.** The perfect is conjugated as follows:

SINGULAR	PLURAL
i'ī, I went, I have gone	**i'imus,** we went, we have gone
īs'tī, you went, you have gone	**īs'tis,** you went, you have gone
i'it, he, she, it went; he, she, it has gone	**iē'runt,** they went, they have gone

COMPOUNDS OF *eō*

There are many compounds of **eō**, such as **exeō**, *go out*, **redeō**, *go back*, **trānseō**, *go across.* They are conjugated like **eō**, with the syllable **ex-**, **red-**, **trāns-**, etc., prefixed: present, **exeō**, **exīs**, etc.

1. Scīmus Ulīxem fortem ad Graecōs sēcrētō redīre. 2. Sacerdōtēs ad templa deōrum eunt. 3. Rēx potēns in Eurōpam trānsībit. 4. Multī ad urbem eunt quod audīvērunt bellum gerī. 5. Māne ex urbe exiī; crēdidī hostēs ācrēs urbem oppugnāre. 6. Māne mendicus celeriter trānsiit. 7. Achillēs fortis ad urbem Trōjam ībit. 8. Paris et Helena ad urbem ībunt.

By translating the phrases make three sentences of each of the following.

1. Mendicus altus { *went out of the temple.* / *went to the house.* / *went back.* }

2. Canis parvus { *goes across the street.* / *goes back.* / *goes quickly.* }

3. Sacerdōs { *will go into the temple.* / *will go back.* / *will go across the street.* }

4. Nūntius dīxit { *the boys were going across.* / *they were going back.* / *we were going.* }

5. Vir scit { *you* (sing.) *are here.* / *I am going.* / *we are going across the sea.* }

HELP YOURSELF

Redeō is made up of a prefix (**red-**) and the verb **eō**. The prefix **re-** (or **red-**) means *back* or *again.* What is the meaning of **redūcō, refugiō, remittō, removeō, repellō?**

You can also tell the meaning of some unfamiliar verbs by removing a prefix. From **recognōscō** (l. 16 of "Helena et Mendicus"), what is the meaning of **cognōscō?**

Account for the case of **fēmina** in line 4 of "Helena et Mendicus." For that of **Deōs** in line 5.

LLT

What is a mendicant? A priest? A scientist? In the following list find two words or phrases suitable to each man: *church, laboratory, rags, sacerdotal robes, street corner, test tube.*

A Roman lad wearing the bordered toga of boyhood. Around his neck hangs his bulla, *which contains a charm to ward off evil.*

COMING OF AGE

In our country it is determined by law that a boy becomes of age when he is twenty-one. In Rome it was a boy's father who decided when his son should come of age. The date chosen usually fell between the fourteenth and seventeenth birthdays. Instead of being celebrated on the boy's birthday, the event often took place on the March 17 nearest his birthday. March 17 was a feast day known as the *Liberalia.*

The day was a gala one, with gifts and congratulations, ceremonies and festivities. Early in the morning, at the shrine of the household gods, the boy dedicated to the Lares his *toga praetexta,* the bordered garment of boyhood, and also his *bulla,* the charm he had always worn. Then from his father he received a *toga virilis,* the pure white toga of manhood, which only a Roman citizen could wear (p. 121).

Later, relatives and friends accompanied the lad to the registry office in the Forum, where he was enrolled as a Roman citizen. From there they proceeded to the temple of Liber, where offerings were made. The day ended with a feast in honor of the new Roman citizen.

Every Roman child wore a bulla. *Here two sides of a* bulla *are shown.*

LXXVIII. EQUUS LIGNEUS

Hectore mortuō, tamen exercitūs Graecī urbem Trōjam nōn cēpērunt. Quamquam Helena Graecōs juvāre dēsīderāvit, fortēs Trōjānī eam prohibuērunt.

Dēnique Graecī dolum parāvērunt. Magnum equum ligneum 5 fēcērunt in quō paucōs virōs fortēs cēlāvērunt. Noctū cēterī Graecī, equō in cōnspectū Trōjānōrum relictō, ad īnsulam propinquam discessērunt. Relīquērunt ūnum ē comitibus suīs, cujus nōmen erat Sinōn; et is prope urbem sē cēlāvit.

Māne Trōjānī ex urbe magnō cum gaudiō prōcessērunt et in castra 10 Graecōrum dēserta convēnērunt. Equum spectāvērunt. Multī quī dolum nōn sēnsērunt eum in urbem trahere dēsīderāvērunt. Aliī, autem, equum timuērunt eumque dēlēre dēsīderāvērunt.

Deinde Lāocoōn, sacerdōs, clāmāvit in equō latēre dolum. "Timeō Graecōs," dīxit, "etiam dōna dantēs."

15 Hīs verbīs dictīs, statim Lāocoōn hastam contrā equum jēcit. Subitō autem duo serpentēs ē marī vēnērunt et Lāocoontem et ejus duōs fīliōs interfēcērunt.

Tum omnēs dīxērunt Lāocoontem malum esse. Clāmāvērunt, "Dī sunt īrātī. Equum in urbem trahere dēbēmus."

20 Interim Sinōn inventus est et ad rēgem ductus est.

"Graecus sum," dīxit. "Cēterī Graecī mē interficere temptāvērunt. Fūgī, autem, et mē (*myself*) cēlāvī. Jam Graecī in patriam suam sēcrētō rediērunt. Equus est sacer deae Minervae. Pōne eum in arce; ita urbs tua semper tūta erit."

25 Equō in arce positō, deīs sacrificia Trōjānī fēcērunt. In tōtā urbe magnum erat gaudium.

Mediā nocte (*at midnight*) Sinōn ad equum vēnit. Jānuam parvam in corpore equī aperuit; Graecī dēscendērunt et portās urbis aperuērunt. Jam omnēs exercitūs Graecī adfuērunt; signum proeliī cornibus 30 dedērunt; impetum in Trōjānōs fēcērunt. Urbs, capta auxiliō equī ligneī, mox ā Trōjānīs dēserēbātur.

cōnspectus, -ūs, M., sight
cornū, -ūs, N., horn; wing of an army
dēserō, -serere, -seruī, -sertum, desert, abandon
dēsertus, -a, -um, deserted
exercitus, -ūs, M., army
impetus, -ūs, M., attack
ligneus, -a, -um, wooden, of wood
trahō, -ere, trāxī, tractum, drag, draw, pull

Equus ligneus

FOURTH DECLENSION OF NOUNS

In the *fourth declension* the genitive singular ends in **-ūs**. The nominative singular ends in **-us** for the masculine and feminine and in **-ū** for the neuter. Most nouns ending in **-us** are masculine.

exercitus, M., *army* **cornū**, N., *horn*

	SINGULAR		PLURAL	
Nom.	**exer′citus**	**cor′nū**	**exer′citūs**	**cor′nua**
Gen.	**exer′citūs**	**cor′nūs**	**exerci′tuum**	**cor′nuum**
Dat.	**exerci′tuī**	**cor′nū**	**exerci′tibus**	**cor′nibus**
Acc.	**exer′citum**	**cor′nū**	**exer′citūs**	**cor′nua**
Abl.	**exer′citū**	**cor′nū**	**exerci′tibus**	**cor′nibus**

ENDINGS

As you see, the endings of fourth-declension nouns of the two classes are as follows:

	SINGULAR		PLURAL	
Nominative:	**-us**	**-ū**	**-ūs**	**-ua**
Genitive:	**-ūs**	**-ūs**	**-uum**	**-uum**
Dative:	**-uī**	**-ū**	**-ibus**	**-ibus**
Accusative:	**-um**	**-ū**	**-ūs**	**-ua**
Ablative:	**-ū**	**-ū**	**-ibus**	**-ibus**

1. Duo exercitūs impetum in urbem īnfēlīcem faciunt. 2. Vīdimus equum ligneum per mūrōs trahī. 3. In cōnspectū hostium dux duo cornua exercitūs relīquit. 4. Scīmus urbem dēsertam esse; itaque ad patriam nostram redībimus. 5. Numquam amīcōs nostrōs dēserēmus quod sentīmus eōs in perīculō esse. 6. Serpentēs Lāocoontem ab ārā Neptūnī trahēbant. 7. Haec animālia potentia ē marī exiērunt. 8. Impetum fortem in fīliōs quoque fēcērunt.

Find in the list below, a phrase which completes each of the sentences.

1. Hastae mīlitum ___ .
2. Vīdimus ___ per montēs.
3. Mox cum pīrātīs ācribus ___ .
4. Dux ___ in proeliō necātus est.
5. Servus scīvit ___ calamitātis.
6. ___ quī in oppidō manēbant captī sunt.

Graecōrum fortium	**hostēs omnēs**	**sē esse causam**
gravēs sunt	**pugnābimus**	**viam dūram esse**

HELP YOURSELF

How do you translate the phrase "impetum in Trōjānōs fēcērunt" (next to last line of the story)? What other meanings do you know for the word in used with the accusative? What meanings does it have with the ablative?

REVIEW OF UNIT XVI LESSONS LXXIV-LXXVIII

Nouns	*Nouns*	*Verbs*	*Adjectives*
amor, -ōris	pāstor, -ōris	discēdō, -ere	dēsertus
bōs, bovis	potentia, -ae	eō, īre	ligneus
cōnspectus, -ūs	sacerdōs, -dōtis	exeō, -īre	
*controversia, -ae	sapientia, -ae	ostendō, -ere	*Pronoun*
cornū, -ūs	vestis, -is, -ium	redeō, -īre	quī, quae, quod
dīvitiae, -ārum		sciō, -īre	
exercitus, -ūs	*Verbs*	sentiō, -īre	
impetus, -ūs	accipiō, -ere	trahō, -ere	
jūdex, jūdicis	conveniō, -īre	trānseō, -īre	
jūdicium, -ī	crēdō, -ere		
mālum, -ī	dēserō, -ere		
mendicus, -ī			

I. Complete each of the following sentences with a form of the relative pronoun.

1. Vir __ vīdī fuit dux noster.
2. Vestis __ gerēbat alba erat.
3. Hic est lapis __ vir necātus est.
4. Virī __ cum ambulābant jūdicēs sunt.
5. Sacerdōtēs __ vidēbimus convēnērunt.

II. Supply the correct forms of the verb **eō** in the following sentences.

1. Deae ad montem __ (*are going*).
2. Paris ad urbem Trōjam __ (*was going*).
3. Ad urbem Spartam mox __ (*he will go*).
4. Ad ōram maritimam saepe __ (*we have gone*).

III. In the following sentences a form of one of these words should be supplied for each blank. Select the right word and the right form.

cōnspectus	**exercitus**	**mālum**
cornū	**impetus**	**pāstor**

1. Crēdō __ esse fīlium rēgis.
2. Audīmus __ Venerī darī.
3. Dīcit __ exercitūs contrā hostēs __ facere.
4. Crēdō __ ducis mentēs mīlitum cōnfirmāre.
5. Silentium __ proelium parārī ostendit.

IV. By translating the phrases make three sentences out of each of the following sentences.

1. Virī et puerī { *are being called together.* / *are industrious.* / *are watching.* }

2. Oppidum { *is being attacked.* / *is being destroyed.* / *is large and wide.* }

3. Itaque, servī, { *you are being warned.* / *you are watching.* / *you have good weapons.* }

4. Tēctum novum { *is being built.* / *is being prepared.* / *is mine.* }

5. Gladius ā puerō { *is carried.* / *is being destroyed.* / *is being changed.* }

LLT

From the list below the sentences choose the word that correctly fills each blank, and give the Latin word to which each English word is related.

1. This is the first __ in this exercise.
2. In case of fire, look for the nearest __ .
3. The soldier __ the army, and fled to the __ .
4. The United States has produced many noted __ .
5. I __ with pleasure the position you have offered.
6. The __ is the branch of the government that administers justice.
7. He was elected a delegate to the national __ for the nomination of President.

accept	*creed*	*exit*	*judiciary*	*scientists*
convention	*desert*	*impetus*	*legal*	*sentence*
credible	*deserted*	*judgment*	*pastor*	*transit*

UNIT XVII

LXXIX. EPISTULA FALSA

Nox erat, et castra Graecōrum, prope urbem Aulidem posita, silēbant. In tabernāculō Agamemnonis, ducis Graecī, erat lūmen clārum. Subitō rēx ad portam tabernāculī vēnit servumque fīdum ad sē vocāvit.

Servus. Ō domine, vocāvistīne mē?

Agamemnōn. Ita; ego dēsīderō hanc epistulam ad uxōrem meam, Clytemnestram, sine morā portārī.

Servus. Tibi semper fīdus sum. Cūr, domine, per tōtam noctem numquam tū dormīvistī?

Agamemnōn. Magnam causam dolōris habeō. Ventī adversī per trēs mēnsēs nāvēs nostrās nāvigāre prohibuērunt. Calchās sacerdōs mihi nūntiāvit Diānam esse īrātam, magnaque sacrificia postulāre. Meam fīliam, Īphigenīam, sacrificāre jussus sum.

Servus. Certē Calchās est vir malus. Īphigenīa nōbīs cāra est.

Agamemnōn. Sed Menelāus, frāter meus, dīxit, "Hōc sacrificiō ā tē factō, ventī secundī nōs ad urbem Trōjam portābunt. Nōbīscum et auxiliō deōrum Trōjānōs superābis."

Servus. Cūr Menelāus fīliam suam nōn dat? Tū tē tuamque familiam dēfendere dēbēs.

Agamemnōn. Dī fīliam ejus nōn postulāvērunt. Itaque maestus ad uxōrem meam jam mīsī epistulam in quā scrīpsī, "Achillēs fīliam nostram, Īphigenīam, in mātrimōnium dūcere dēsīderat. Mitte eam sine morā ad castra nostra."

Servus. Sed cūr nunc aliam epistulam mittis?

Achilles

Agamemnōn. Mentem meam mūtāvī. In hāc epistulā quam tibi dō scrīpsī, "Ō conjūnx amāta, servā tē et fīliam nostram; perīculum magnum est; tenē eam domī."

Servus fīdus, epistulā acceptā, per noctem fūgit.

ego, I	**secundus, -a, -um,** favorable, second
maestus, -a, -um, sad, gloomy	**tū,** you

USE OF PERSONAL PRONOUNS

Thus far the personal pronouns *I*, *you*, and *we*, as subjects of the verb, have been indicated in Latin by the person endings of the verb, **-ō, -s, -mus, -tis.** But when the importance of the subject is emphasized or a contrast is brought out between subjects which are not in the same person, a personal pronoun in the nominative is used in Latin just as in English. The nominative forms are: **ego,** *I;* **tū,** *you;* **nōs,** *we;* **vōs,** *you* (plural).

The cases other than the nominative are used as we should expect, except that the genitive is not used to indicate possession.[1]

DECLENSION OF *ego* AND *tū*

SINGULAR

Nom.	**e′go,** I	**tū,** you
Gen.	**me′ī,** of me	**tu′ī,** of you
Dat.	**mi′hi,** to me, me (*as indirect object*)	**ti′bi,** to you, you (*as indirect object*)
Acc.	**mē,** me (*as direct object*)	**tē,** you (*as direct object*)
Abl.	**mē,** (from, with, by) me	**tē,** (from, with, by) you

PLURAL

Nom.	**nōs,** we	**vōs,** you
Gen.	**nos′trum, nos′trī,** of us	**ves′trum, ves′trī,** of you
Dat.	**nō′bīs,** to us, us (*as indirect object*)	**vō′bīs,** to you, you (*as indirect object*)
Acc.	**nōs,** us (*as direct object*)	**vōs,** you (*as direct object*)
Abl.	**nō′bīs,** (from, with, by) us	**vō′bīs,** (from, with, by) you

As you have learned (pp. 9 and 189), possession is expressed in the singular by **meus, -a, -um** and **tuus, -a, -um;** in the plural by **noster, -tra, -trum** and **vester, -tra, -trum.**

[1]To THE TEACHER: The genitive forms of ego and tū are not used in the exercises of this book.

REFLEXIVE PRONOUNS OF THE FIRST AND SECOND PERSONS

On the previous page you learned the declension of the personal pronouns **ego** and **tū**. The genitive, dative, accusative, and ablative forms of these words are used as reflexive pronouns.

Examples of the accusative used as reflexive are given below.

Mē nōn laudō, *I do not praise myself.*
Nōs nōn laudāmus, *We do not praise ourselves.*
Tē nōn laudās, *You do not praise yourself.*
Vōs nōn laudātis, *You do not praise yourselves.*

PRONOUNS WITH *cum*

When the ablative forms **mē, tē, nōbīs,** and **vōbīs** are used as objects of the preposition **cum,** they usually have **cum** attached as the final syllable.[1]

mēcum, *with me* **tēcum,** *with you* **nōbīscum,** *with us* **vōbīscum,** *with you*

1. Ego crēdō tē mihi fīdum esse. 2. Nōbīscum bellum secundum bene gessistī! 3. Mēcum contrā fortūnam adversam per multōs mēnsēs contendistī. 4. Sacerdōs maestus crēdit vōs causam ācris dolōris habēre. 5. Tū nōbīs epistulam dedistī. 6. Mīlitēs tēcum impetum in hostēs facient. 7. Prō nōbīs et exercitū nostrō Īphigenīa sacrificābitur.

Complete each sentence in the first column with a word or phrase from the second.

I	II
1. Juvā	(*a*) ad portam
2. Tēcum ībimus	(*b*) ad templum
3. Jūdex, dūc nōs	(*c*) tē
4. Scīmus vōs sacerdōtēs habēre	(*d*) tibi
5. Causam dolōris ducis nārrābō	(*e*) vōbīscum

LLT In "Epistula Falsa" find eight words whose meaning you might know even without having learned any Latin. What gives you the clue to their meaning?

[1]To THE TEACHER: While this is true also of **sē**, **sēcum** is not used in this book.

Iphigenia

LXXX. MATER ET FILIA PERVENIUNT.

Servus portāns epistulam Agamemnonis ā vigilibus captus erat, sed Agamemnōn haec nōn audīverat. Ubi, igitur, audīvit Clytemnestram cum Īphigeniā ad castra appropinquāre, graviter mōtus erat, quod scīvit fīliam suam ad mortem dūcī. Itaque ad Menelāum vēnerat. 5

Agamemnōn. Heu! Uxor mea fīliam nostram mox ad mē dūcet. Ego, rēx potēns sapiēnsque, ad mortem fīliam meam mittō! Jam in vincula Īphigenīa conjiciētur. Numquam iterum fēlīx laetusque erō. Hanc calamitātem timēbam. Fāta mē regunt.

Menelāus. Dīc eīs Achillem ā castrīs abesse; Calchās in tabernāculō 10 manēbit fīliamque nōn vidēbit.

Agamemnōn. Sed Ulīxēs, vir sapiēns, voluntātem deōrum scit. Ego sciō hunc virum potentem cum inimīcīs meīs sē jungere.

Interim Clytemnestra et Īphigenīa, ā mīlite ductae, ad Agamemnonem appropinquāverant. 15

Clytemnestra. Ecce, Īphigenīa, pater tuus! Laeta, Agamemnōn, tē videō. Propter imperāta tua ad castra pervēnimus.

Īphigenīa. Ō pater, iter erat dūrum. Heu! Tū es maestus! Nōnne putās Achillem mē in mātrimōnium dūcere dēbēre? Putō Achillem esse virum potentem, sapientem, fēlīcem. Fēlīx erō, uxor ducis 20 clārī.

Agamemnōn. Ita, Achillēs vir fortis est. Sed Trōja est longinqua.

Īphigenīa. Sciō iter esse longum; bene sciō omne bellum esse ācre. Ubi est Achillēs? Cūr ad mē nōn venit? Cūr nōs nōn salūtat?

Agamemnōn. Achillēs cum cōpiīs suīs in lītore nunc est. Mox 25 aderit.

Hōc dictō, Agamemnōn fēminās in tabernāculum dūcit.

Agamemnōn [tabernāculō relictō]. Heu! Jam miser vīvō! Certē servus meus epistulam ad Clytemnestram nōn portāvit.

conjiciō, -jicere, -jēcī, -jectum, throw, hurl

imperātum, -ī, N., command, order; **imperāta facere,** carry out orders, obey commands

perveniō, -venīre, -vēnī, -ventum, arrive at, reach

putō, -āre, -āvī, -ātum, think

vigil, vigilis, M., watchman, guard, sentinel

vinculum, -ī, N., chain, bond

voluntās, -ātis, F., wish, desire

MEANING OF THE PAST PERFECT

The *past perfect tense* represents an act which took place before some specified or suggested time in the past. The English past perfect has the auxiliary verb *had.*

I had carried. *You had carried.*

FORMATION OF THE PAST PERFECT ACTIVE

The past perfect active of a Latin verb has the tense sign **-erā-**, which is added to the perfect stem. The endings are used as in the imperfect. The **-ā-** of the tense sign is short before the endings **-m**, **-t**, and **-nt**. The past perfect is formed in the same way for all four conjugations.

SINGULAR

portā'veram, I had carried	**monu'eram,** I had warned
portā'verās, you had carried	**monu'erās,** you had warned
portā'verat, he, she, it had carried	**monu'erat,** he, she, it had warned

PLURAL

portāverā'mus, we had carried	**monuerā'mus,** we had warned
portāverā'tis, you had carried	**monuerā'tis,** you had warned
portā'verant, they had carried	**monu'erant,** they had warned

The site of Troy today

PAST PERFECT PASSIVE

The past perfect in the passive voice is formed by combining the perfect participle with the imperfect tense of **sum.** This is true of all four conjugations.

SINGULAR	
portā'tus eram, I had been carried	**mo'nitus eram,** I had been warned
portā'tus erās, you had been carried	**mo'nitus erās,** you had been warned
portā'tus erat, he, she, it had been carried	**mo'nitus erat,** he, she, it had been warned
PLURAL	
portā'tī erāmus, we had been carried	**mo'nitī erāmus,** we had been warned
portā'tī erātis, you had been carried	**mo'nitī erātis,** you had been warned
portā'tī erant, they had been carried	**mo'nitī erant,** they had been warned

1. Īphigenīa nōn audīverat deōs sacrificium postulāre. 2. Imperātum Agamemnonis ad Clytemnestram nōn pervēnerat. 3. Per multa et perīculōsa bella Agamemnōn ducēs exercituum dūxerat. 4. Putāmus nōs ā virō sapientī regī. 5. Mīlitēs hostium in vincula conjectī erant. 6. Certē fīlia rēgis ā sacerdōte interficiētur. 7. Dolor servī bonī magnus erat quod vīderat magnum dolum parārī. 8. Dī jam voluntātem suam nūntiāverant.

Translate the italicized words: 1. The judge *had* not *ordered* the shepherd *to be sacrificed.* 2. The soldier *had dragged* his weary *body* to the shore. 3. We see that the camp *is being attacked* by the enemy. 4. Calchas *had* not *returned* from the altar. 5. I think that *we are being ruled* well. 6. Agamemnon *had feared* the will of the gods. 7. The guards *will be thrown* into chains.

LATIN LIVES TODAY

Several words in this lesson are related to Latin words you know, and to English words. What has each group of related words in common? Give the meaning of each word.

imperatum	**imperator**	*imperative*
rego	**regia regina regio regnum rex**	*regal*
vigil	**vigilo**	*vigilant*

LXXXI. ACHILLES DOLUM INVENIT.

Māne Achillēs, quī nōn audīverat Clytemnestram in castra pervēnisse, prō tabernāculō Agamemnonis stetit.

Achillēs [magnā vōce]. Ubi est Agamemnōn quī exercitūs Graecōs agit? Dīc eī Achillem prō tabernāculō stāre. Omnēs sciunt mē 5 ad hoc bellum ā Menelāō arcessītum esse. Jam pugnāre parātus, exercitus meus propter moram longam graviter dolet.

Clytemnestra ē tabernāculō venit.

Achillēs. Quem videō? Certē tū fēmina nōbilis es.

Clytemnestra. Sum Clytemnestra, conjūnx Agamemnonis. Laeta 10 sum quod tū fīliam meam in mātrimōnium dūcēs.

Achillēs. Quid dīcis? Ego sum Achillēs. Quis dīxit mē fīliam tuam in mātrimōnium petīvisse?

Clytemnestra. Quid? Agamemnōn scrīpserat tē cupere eam in mātrimōnium dūcere.

15 *Achillēs.* Ego fīliam tuam numquam arcessīvī.

Servus territus ad Clytemnestram properat.

Servus. Ō rēgīna, mala sunt ōmina! Agamemnōn in animō magnum scelus habet. In animō habet fīliam suam occīdere! Nōn sōlum āram parātam et gladium sed etiam sacerdōtem vīdī. Jam Calchās 20 sacrificium parāverat; nunc virī animālia ad āram dūcunt. Tua fīlia quoque sacrificābitur.

Clytemnestra. Crēdō conjugem meum īnsānum esse. Quis hoc scelus parāvit? Achillēs, juvā nōs! Servā fīliam meam, quae uxor tua erit!

25 *Achillēs* [graviter excitātus]. Ō Clytemnestra, ego fīliam tuam ab omnī impetū dēfendam! Meōs mīlitēs contrā Agamemnonem agam.

arcessō, -ere, -īvī, -ītum, summon
nōbilis, -e, noble; M. *pl. as noun,* the nobles
occīdō, -cīdere, -cīdī, -cīsum, kill, slay
scelus, sceleris, N., crime; **scelus facere,** to commit a crime

Iphigenia, filia Agamemnonis

LATIN PARTICIPLES AND ENGLISH ADJECTIVES

Present participles of Latin verbs were often used as adjectives: **latens, -entis** (from **lateo**); **vigilans, -antis** (from **vigilo**).

Many such participles have come into English as adjectives which end in *-ant* and *-ent*: *vigilant, latent.* With some exceptions, first-conjugation verbs give us the ending *-ant* and other verbs give *-ent.*

What is the English adjective from **repellens?** From **expectans?**

Perfect passive participles likewise became adjectives in Latin: **temperatus, -a, -um** (from **tempero**); **oppositus, -a, -um** (from **oppono**).

These participles have also become English adjectives in *-ate* or *-ite.* What is the English adjective from **ornatus?** From **finitus?**

Give the Latin verb and the English adjective for each of the following participles.

ambulans	**currens**	**errans**	**separatus**
cogens	**definitus**	**fortunatus**	**significans**
conveniens	**desperatus**	**incipiens**	**silens**

PERFECT ACTIVE INFINITIVES

You have already learned the present active infinitive.

portāre, *to carry*

The perfect active infinitive of **portō** is **portāvisse,** *to have carried.*

This infinitive is formed by adding **-isse** to the perfect stem. The present and perfect active infinitives of the model verbs of the four conjugations are:

	I	II	III	IV
Present:	**portāre**	**monēre**	**dūcere**	**audīre**
Perfect:	**portāvisse**	**monuisse**	**dūxisse**	**audīvisse**

PASSIVE INFINITIVES[1]

You are familiar with the present passive infinitive.

I	II	III		IV
portārī	**monērī**	**dūcī**	**capī**	**audīrī**

The perfect passive infinitive of all verbs is made up of the perfect participle followed by **esse.**

I	II	III		IV
portātus esse	**monitus esse**	**ductus esse**	**captus esse**	**audītus esse**

[1]TO THE TEACHER: Since the future passive infinitive is rarely used, it is omitted from the exercises of this book.

TENSE OF INFINITIVES IN INDIRECT DISCOURSE

The act expressed by the present infinitive in indirect discourse is represented as occurring at the time shown by the tense of the main verb.

Dīcit sē perīculum timēre, *He says that he fears danger.*

Dīxit sē perīculum timēre, *He said that he feared danger.*

The act expressed by the perfect infinitive in indirect discourse is represented as already past at the time shown by the tense of the main verb.

Hostēs fūgisse videō, *I see that the enemy have fled.*

Hostēs fūgisse vīdī, *I saw that the enemy had fled.*

Find in the list below, the equivalent of each English phrase in the Latin sentences and translate the complete sentences.

āctum esse	**dūxisse**	**fuisse**	**parāvisse**
arcessīvisse	**dēsertum esse**	**occīdī**	**trānsīsse**

1. Crēdimus oppidum ā duce (*was abandoned*).
2. Certē fīlia nōbilis (*to be killed*) nōn dēbet.
3. Scīmus bellum causam magnī dolōris (*has been*).
4. Servus dīcit sacerdōtem sacrificium (*has prepared*).
5. Menelāus ostendit Helenam ad Graecōs (*had gone across*).
6. Agamemnōn dīxit sē Īphigenīam ad castra (*had summoned*).
7. Achillēs dīxit exercitum suum ad bellum (*had been driven*).

1. They say that the watchmen have arrived. 2. The general announces that I have summoned an army. 3. Surely you did not believe that we had been killed. 4. He shows that the orders have been sent and that the leader has come to the camp.

A goddess to the rescue

LXXXII. SACRIFICIUM IPHIGENIAE

Puellam ad locum longinquum Diana portavit.

Agamemnōn fīliam suam amātam sacrificāre nōn dēsīderāvit, sed putāvit deōs hoc per Calcham sacerdōtem jussisse.

Diē sacrificiī mīlitēs omnium exercituum Graecōrum in lītore Īphigenīam multās hōrās expectāvērunt; ventōs secundōs et iter fēlīx multōs mēnsēs petīverant; itaque mortem virginis nōn dolēbant.

Achillēs tamen suōs mīlitēs ad tabernācula sua redīre subitō jusserat. Ulīxēs et Menelāus, ubi audīvērunt Achillem hanc rem nōn probāre, graviter mōtī erant.

Clytemnestra, clāmōribus hominum audītīs, sēnsit Īphigenīam ā mīlitibus arcessītam esse. Agamemnōn tōtam noctem doluerat sed fīliam suam ē tabernāculō ad āram dūcere parābat.

Īphigenīa mātrī maestae dīxit, "Māter amāta, nūllō tempore pater meus mē sacrificāre dēsīderāvit; injūriam nōn facit; est voluntās deōrum. Nōn erō ignāva; cupiō mīlitēs nostrōs contrā fortūnam malam dēfendī. Brevī tempore exercitūs Graecī ā portū ventīs secundīs nāvigābunt; Graecī victōriam habēbunt; omnēs scient mē prō patriā occīsam esse." 20

Ubi Agamemnōn fīliam ad āram dūxit, puella fortis mīlitibus dīxit, "Sentiō deōs mortem meam cupere. Mortem nōn recūsābō." 25

Multae rēs ā sacerdōte parātae erant et puella in ārā posita est. Subitō magnus clāmor audītus est magnumque lūmen in caelō apparuit (*appeared*). Dea Diāna aderat. Dea corpus cervae in ārā posuit quod Graecī corpus Īphigenīae esse crēdidērunt. Puellam, nūbe dēnsā tēctam, per caelum ad locum longinquum Diāna portāvit. 30

brevis, -e, short, brief
diēs, diēī, M. *and* F., day
portus, -ūs, M., harbor
rēs, reī, F., thing, affair, fact, matter
tegō, -ere, tēxī, tēctum, cover, protect
tempus, temporis, N., time

FIFTH DECLENSION

Nouns of the fifth declension may be recognized by the ending **-ēī** (**-eī** after a consonant) of the genitive singular. The nominative singular always ends in **-ēs.**

The nouns **diēs,** *day,* and **rēs,** *thing,* are declined as follows:

	SINGULAR	PLURAL	SINGULAR	PLURAL
Nominative:	di'ēs	di'ēs	rēs	rēs
Genitive:	diē'ī	diē'rum	re'ī	rē'rum
Dative:	diē'ī	diē'bus	re'ī	rē'bus
Accusative:	di'em	di'ēs	rem	rēs
Ablative:	di'ē	diē'bus	rē	rē'bus

ENDINGS

Notice that the fifth-declension endings are as follows:

SINGULAR	PLURAL
-ēs	-ēs
-ēī, -eī	-ērum
-ēī, -eī	-ēbus
-em	-ēs
-ē	-ēbus

Diēs, *day,* is sometimes masculine and sometimes feminine in the singular, but always masculine in the plural. The other nouns of this declension are feminine, except one compound of **diēs.**

Diēs and **rēs** are the only nouns which have all the forms. The few nouns in this declension are almost always used in the singular.

ACCUSATIVE OF DURATION OF TIME

In English we sometimes use a noun without a preposition to tell how long an act or a situation continues.

We stayed in the country three days.

Sometimes we use a preposition with the noun to express this idea.

We stayed in the country for three days.

The expressions *three days* in the first sentence and *for three days* in the second mean exactly the same thing.

In Latin a word which is used to denote duration of time is regularly put in the accusative without a preposition.

Multās hōrās in īnsulā mānsī, *I remained on the island many hours* (or *for many hours*).

ABLATIVE OF TIME AT WHICH

The time at which or within which something happens is regularly expressed in Latin by a noun or pronoun in the ablative case without a preposition.

> **Eō annō pater meus tēctum aedificāvit,** *My father built a house that year* (or *in that year*).
>
> **Paucīs hōrīs portum vidēbit,** *In a few hours he will see the harbor.*

Commonly these expressions of time have the preposition *in* or *on* or *at* in English: *in that year; on the same day; at the appointed hour.*

The *ablative of time* answers the question "When?" The *accusative of duration of time* answers the question "How long?"

1. Scit vōs īsse ad portum mēcum. 2. Putō Īphigenīam ā sacerdōte nōn sacrificātam esse. 3. Ad ōram maritimam breve tempus eō diē ierant. 4. Virī quibuscum contendēbās dē hāc rē vigilēs arcessīverant. 5. Certē dux scit nōs in urbe diem tōtum fuisse. 6. Scelus quod brevī tempore vir fēcit stultum fuit. 7. Exercitus expellere advenās vōbīscum recūsāverat. 8. Vir nōbilis decem annōs rēx erat.

Translate the italicized words: 1. *In the first hour* of the night the enemy made an attack on the camp. 2. *On account of this matter* your sister remained in this city *four years.* 3. We watched *all day,* but we saw no animals near the road. 4. The leader says that the citizens *defended* the wall *all night* from every attack of the enemy. 5. *At no time* was the town without guards.

Complete the sentences with English words related to **brevis, nobilis, portus, tempus,** or **voluntas.** All needed words are in the list below.

1. The men who joined the army ___ were called ___ .
2. For the sake of ___, we will use ___ for the names of the states.
3. Although he was not of ___ birth, he was a man of great ___ .
4. The speaker ___ lost his notes; so he had to speak ___ .
5. ___ is a well-known ___ on the Gulf of Mexico.

abbreviate	*temporarily*	*nobleman*	*volunteers*
abbreviations	*temporary*	*voluntarily*	*export*
brevity	*nobility*	*voluntary*	*Gulfport*
extemporaneously	*noble*	*volunteered*	*port*

Nonne es Orestes, frater meus?

LXXXIII. IPHIGENIA INVENTA EST.

Graecī crēdidērunt, Īphigeniā sacrificātā, animum deōrum mūtātum esse. Itaque brevī tempore ad lītora Trōjae nāvigā-
5 verant. Decem annōs pugnāverant; tandem Trōja expugnāta erat victōrēsque Graecī ad patriam redierant.

Quod Agamemnōn imperāta
10 eōrum facere recūsāverat dī erant crūdēlēs. Rēx miser ab uxōre occīsus est quod Clytemnestra crēdidit Īphigenīam fīliam ab eō ad mortem āctam esse. Deinde
15 Orestēs, fīlius eōrum, lēge deōrum, mātrem suam occīdere coāctus est. Propter hoc scelus mentem āmīsit et diū erat īnsānus.

Dēnique sacerdōtēs eī dīxērunt, "In īnsulā Taurōrum est parva statua Diānae; nāvigā ad hanc īnsulam, cape hanc statuam, portā eam
20 ad templum Apollinis. Hōc factō, tū iterum sānus eris."

Īnsula Taurōrum longē aberat. Orestēs nōn scīvit sorōrem suam Īphigenīam vīvam esse et ā Diānā ad hanc īnsulam portātam esse et jam sacerdōtem Diānae in illō locō habitāre.

Orestēs cum amīcō Pylade post multōs mēnsēs in portum hujus
25 īnsulae vēnit. Hīc nāvem cēlāvērunt. Sed duo aliēnī ā pāstōribus captī sunt et ad Īphigenīam ductī sunt.

Statim sacerdōs Īphigenīa aliēnōs sacrificāre parāvit.

Ubi prope āram tenēbantur, Īphigenīa Orestem recognōvit et clāmāvit, "Nōnne es Orestēs, frāter meus? Sum soror tua, Īphigenīa,
30 ā Diānā servāta. Dēbēmus fugere sine morā."

Orestēs respondit, "Prīmō necesse est capere statuam Diānae."

Hāc statuā captā, Orestēs et ejus amīcus cum Īphigenīā ad nāvem fūgērunt. Orestēs nōn jam īnsānus erat. Ventīs secundīs portātī, brevī tempore ad Graeciam pervēnērunt. Ibi magnō cum gaudiō acceptī
35 sunt.

cōgō, -ere, coēgī, coāctum, compel, force

crūdēlis, -e, cruel

expugnō, -āre, -āvī, -ātum, take by storm

tandem, *adv.*, finally, at last

LATIN NOUNS AND ENGLISH NOUNS

Many Latin nouns of the fourth declension give us English nouns. Some of these are spelled just like the Latin: *impetus.*

Some English nouns do not have the **-us: adventus,** *advent.*

Some English nouns connected with Latin fourth-declension nouns end in **-e: magistratus,** *magistrate.*

Give the English noun connected with each of the following Latin nouns.

aquaeductus	**conspectus**	**portus**	**tumultus**
consensus	**lacus** (*c* becomes *k*)	**recessus**	**usus**

Give a Latin noun of the fourth declension for each of the following English nouns.

census *dome* *event* *exit* *senate*

If you do not know the meaning of any English word here, look it up in a dictionary.

1. Nūntiat aliēnōs virōs in castrīs tenērī. 2. Brevī tempore rēx crūdēlis discēdere cōgētur. 3. Scīmus injūriam factam esse, et puellam ad mortem coāctam esse. 4. Nūntiāmus portum propter hanc rem expugnātum esse. 5. Voluntāte rēgis audītā, omnēs putāvērunt eum īnsānum esse. 6. Omnēs eō tempore crēdidērunt sacrificium factum esse. 7. Īphigeniā tandem servātā, tū tē et amīcum tuum servābis.

1. He stayed in the cottage with me for a few days. 2. Then Orestes recognized that Iphigenia had been saved by Diana. 3. For a short time they had refused to go back. 4. For a few hours the city had been ruled by a crazy man.

LATIN LIVES TODAY

Each of the following sentences contains (1) an English derivative of a Latin word you have recently learned, and (2) the exact English translation of a related Latin word. Find the two words in each sentence and explain their relationship to each other.

1. I live with a vivacious person.
2. He had his protégé stay in the house.
3. I am not pugnacious, but I fight when I am attacked.
4. She is an alien because she comes from another country.

REVIEW OF UNIT XVII LESSONS LXXIX-LXXXIII

Nouns	*Verbs*	*Adjectives*	*Pronouns*
diēs, diēī	arcessō, -ere	*adversus, -a, -um	ego, nōs
*familia, -ae	cōgō, -ere	*aliēnus, -a, -um	tū, vōs
imperātum, -ī	conjiciō, -jicere	brevis, -e	
*injūria, -ae	*contendō, -ere	crūdēlis, -e	*Adverb*
portus, -ūs	expugnō, -āre	*falsus, -a, -um	
rēs, reī	occīdō, -cīdere	maestus, -a, -um	tandem
scelus, sceleris	perveniō, -venīre	nōbilis, -e	
tempus, temporis	putō, -āre	*sānus, -a, -um	
vigil, vigilis	*regō, -ere	secundus, -a, -um	
vinculum, -ī	*sacrificō, -āre	*vīvus, -a, -um	
voluntās, -ātis	tegō, -ere		

I. In the following sentences translate the pronouns.

1. He knows that you (*pl.*) have seen the boys on the shore with me.
2. I think that Iphigenia was not sacrificed by the priest.
3. They had gone to the seashore for a short time on that day.
4. The men with whom you (*sing.*) contended about that matter have summoned guards.
5. Surely the leader knows that we have been in the city all day.
6. The goddess by whose order Iphigenia had been seized was Diana
7. The army had refused to drive out the strangers with you (*pl.*).
8. The noble king had ruled for ten years.

II. Translate the following verbs in the sentences above, tell what each form is, and account for the form.

have seen (1) *was sacrificed* (2) *had gone* (3) *have summoned* (4)
have been (5) *had been seized* (6) *to drive out* (7) *had ruled* (8)

III. Translate the following expressions of time in the sentences above: *on that day* (3) *all day* (5) *for ten years* (8)

IV. Complete the translation of the eight sentences above.

LATIN LIVES TODAY

Tell what is wrong with each statement and make it correct.

1. They rode side by side on a tandem bicycle.
2. The egotist did not think highly of himself.
3. The vigilant guard went to sleep at his post.
4. The speaker wearied his audience with his brevity.
5. A man is an alien when he lives in his own country.
6. A permanent employee always has a temporary position.
7. Your character is what others think of you; your reputation is what you are.

LXXXIV. ULIXES AD PATRIAM REDIT.

Decem annōs Ulīxēs circum mūrōs Trōjae pugnāverat. Posteā decem annōs propter īram deōrum in multīs terrīs errāre coāctus erat, quamquam dea Athēna prōmīserat eum ad patriam suam tūtum reditūrum esse.

Dēnique autem post multōs cāsūs Ulīxēs ad Ithacam pervēnit. 5 Nēmō eum recognōvit, quod dea Athēna vestēs ejus et faciem (*features*) mūtāverat. Omnēs crēdidērunt eum esse mendicum.

Itaque Ulīxēs casam Eumaeī, pāstōris fidēlis, petīvit, sed subitō canēs ferī impetum in eum fēcērunt. Magnā cum difficultāte Eumaeus canēs lapidibus reppulit Ulīxemque servāvit. Celeriter 10 eum in casam dūxit et eī cibum vīnumque dedit.

Tum Ulīxēs, acceptūrus haec dōna, dīxit, "Cūr es mihi, hominī miserō, benignus? Nūllam pecūniam habeō, sed mihi cibum vīnumque dedistī. Dominus tuus erit īrātus; tē culpābit."

Eumaeus autem respondit, "Ille benignus erat et semper mendicōs 15 juvābat; tamen nōn jam domī adest. Vīgintī annōs dominum nostrum expectāvimus. Ejus uxor et fīlius Tēlemachus crēdunt eum ad tēctum suum reditūrum esse."

Tum Ulīxēs dīxit, "Suntne Tēlemachus et rēgīna in rēgiā?"

Eumaeus respondit, "Tēlemachus Ithacam relīquit; dīxit sē patrem 20 suum petītūrum esse. Pēnelopē Ulīxem expectat. Cotīdiē in rēgiā texit. Pallā factā, conjugem alium accipere cōgētur. Itaque interdiū texit; noctū pallam textam retexit (*ravels out*).

"Cotīdiē procī hūc veniunt et animālia, frūmentum, vīnum dominī meī cōnsūmunt, sed mihi pecūniam nōn dant. Jam Pēnelopē territa 25 est, quod procī dīcunt ūnum ē numerō suō brevī tempore eam in mātrimōnium ductūrum esse."

cāsus, -ūs, M., fall, accident, disaster
culpō, -āre, -āvī, -ātum, blame, find fault with
fidēlis, -e, faithful
hūc, *adv.*, to this place, here, hither
nēmō (*dat.* **nēminī,** *acc.* **nēminem,** *no gen. or abl.*), M. *and* F., no one
procus, -ī, M., suitor, lover
texō, -ere, -uī, textum, weave
vīgintī, *indecl.*, twenty
vīnum, -ī, N., wine

Telemachus and Penelope

FUTURE ACTIVE PARTICIPLE

Latin verbs have a future active participle formed on the participial stem. It is declined like the perfect passive participle, from which it differs by having **-ūr-** before the case ending.

portātūrus, -a, -um, *about to carry* or *going to carry*
monitūrus, -a, -um, *about to warn* or *going to warn*

Some verbs which have no perfect passive participle have a future active participle. The future active participle of such verbs is given as the fourth principal part. The future participle of **sum** is **futūrus.** The principal parts of **sum** are **sum, esse, fuī, futūrus.** The fourth of the principal parts of **stō** is **stātūrus.**

The future participle is often combined with forms of **sum** to refer to something which someone intends to do or is about to do.

Mānsūrus eram, *I was about to remain,* or *I intended to remain.*
Laudātūrus est, *He is about to praise,* or *He intends to praise.*

FUTURE ACTIVE INFINITIVE

The future active infinitive consists of the future active participle with **esse.**

portātūrus esse monitūrus esse ductūrus esse audītūrus esse

The act expressed by the future infinitive in indirect discourse is represented as future in relation to the time denoted by the main verb.

Puer dīcit frātrem ventūrum esse, *The boy says that his brother will come* or *is going to come.*

Puer dīxit frātrem ventūrum esse, *The boy said that his brother would come* or *was going to come.*

The future infinitive is regularly translated with *shall* or *will* after a main verb in the present tense and with *should* or *would* after a main verb in any past tense.

1. Cotīdiē nauta nūntiāvit sē nēminem in īnsulā invēnisse. 2. Pāstor crēdidit canēs in mendicum impetum factūrōs esse. 3. Post multōs cāsūs ad patriam meam reditūrus sum. 4. Nēmō, autem, mendicum recognōvit quī pāstōrem petēbat. 5. Servus fidēlis dīxit procōs brevī tempore tōtam cōpiam cibī con-

Ulysses

sūmpsisse. 6. Scīmus tē mox dē itineribus Ulīxis audītūrum esse. 7. Nūntius dīxit ducem interfectum esse et ejus corpus hūc portātum esse. 8. Crēdidimus ducēs nostrōs benignōs futūrōs esse; nōn crēdidimus eōs nōs culpātūrōs esse. 9. Pēnelopē scīvit sē pallam numquam textūram esse. 10. Nēmō procīs nūntiāverat pāstōrem fidēlem eōs culpātūrum esse. 11. Hūc vigintī servī ventūrī sunt.

Translate the italicized words: 1. The young man said that *he had hidden* all weapons. 2. *About to sail,* we sent messages to our friends. 3. We knew that the sailors *would sail* at daybreak. 4. I believe that our leader *will drive* us into a dangerous matter. 5. We heard daily that the barbarians *would take* many towns *by storm.*

HELP YOURSELF How should **reditūrum esse** be translated in line 4 of "Ulīxēs ad Patriam Redit"? In line 18? Why do you translate the same word in two ways?

Can you find **in** used with an accusative in this lesson with a meaning different from the one you learned? If necessary, consult the Reference Vocabulary at the back of the book.

LLT Select the proper word or phrase to complete each sentence.

1. Automobile casualties are { accidents. / outings. / trips. }

2. A culprit should be given { blame. / food. / praise. }

3. **Semper fidelis,** the motto of the U. S. Marine Corps, means { always faithful. / always true. / on land and sea. }

LXXXV. TELEMACHUS PATREM VIDET.

Tēlemachus quidem per omnēs urbēs Graeciae iter fēcerat, sed nēmō prō certō dīcere potuerat patrem Ulīxem esse vīvum. Dēnique dea Athēna in somniō Tēlemachum dē perīculō mātris, Pēnelopae, monuerat; itemque dīxerat procōs malōs in animō eum 5 interficere habēre.

Tēlemachus autem ad patriam suam statim redīre cōnstituit. Sed quod sciēbat procōs adventum suum expectāre, in portum nōn intrāre potuit. Nāve relictā, ante prīmam lūcem sōlus ad casam Eumaeī, pāstōris fidēlis, prōcessit.

10 Hīc Eumaeus et mendicus ignem accenderant cibumque parābant. Vōce hominis audītā, Eumaeus ad portam properāvit.

Ubi Tēlemachum vīdit, juvenem magnō cum gaudiō nōmine appellāvit. Tēlemachus dē mātre et dē procīs atque dē rēgnō et dē multīs et aliīs rēbus rogāvit, dolēbatque quod pater ad Ithacam 15 nōn redierat.

Dēnique dīxit, "Ego propter suspīciōnem procōrum in casā tuā tōtum diem manēbō; tū, Eumaee, ī ad tēctum meum et dīc mātrī meae mē tūtum rediisse."

Eumaeus omnēs hās rēs fēcit. Interim Athēna iterum vestem et 20 faciem (*face*) Ulīxis mūtāvit.

Tēlemachus quidem clāmāvit ubi hominem tam mūtātum vīdit, "Tū es deus! Tū nōs juvāre potes! Nōlī nōs relinquere!"

Ulīxēs fīliō suō respondit, "Nōlī timēre! Nōn deus sum; sum pater tuus, quī post multōs cāsūs rediī. Tempus est breve; necesse est nōs 25 procōs interficere et mātrem tuam līberāre. Tū, Tēlemache, ad rēgiam redī; explōrā omnia; es fortis!

"Paucīs hōrīs ego mendicus ad tēctum veniam. Tum tibi signum dabō. Hōc signō vīsō, ī sēcrētō et portā omnia arma ex ātriō. Sed relinque prope portam duo scūta valida, duās hastās, duōs gladiōs; 30 hīs armīs impetum mēcum facere poteris; hodiē procōs occīdēmus."

accendō, -cendere, -cendī, -cēnsum, kindle, set on fire
adventus, -ūs, M., approach, arrival
atque, *conj.*, and, and also
ātrium, -ī, N., atrium, *the principal room of a house*
certus, -a, -um, certain, sure; **prō certō,** certainly
intrō, -āre, -āvī, -ātum, enter
item, *adv.*, likewise
possum, posse, potuī, be able, can
tam, *adv.*, so

CONJUGATION OF *possum*

The verb **possum,** *I am able* or *I can,* is irregular. It is a compound of **sum** and the adjective **potis,** *able.* In the present system in the indicative mood it is conjugated as follows. Notice its similarity to **sum.**

PRESENT

SINGULAR	PLURAL
pos'sum, I am able, I can	**pos'sumus,** we are able, we can
po'tes, you are able, you can	**potes'tis,** you are able, you can
po'test, he, she, it is able; he, she, it can	**pos'sunt,** they are able, they can

IMPERFECT

SINGULAR	PLURAL
po'teram, I was able, I could	**poterā'mus,** we were able, we could
po'terās, you were able, you could	**poterā'tis,** you were able, you could
po'terat, he, she, it was able; he, she, it could	**po'terant,** they were able, they could

FUTURE

SINGULAR	PLURAL
po'terō, I shall be able	**pote'rimus,** we shall be able
po'teris, you will be able	**pote'ritis,** you will be able
po'terit, he, she, it will be able	**po'terunt,** they will be able

The principal parts are **possum, posse, potuī.** The perfect is formed like that of regular verbs: **potuī,** *I have been able,* **potuistī,** *you have been able,* etc.

IMPERATIVE OF *eō* AND *sum*

The imperatives of **eō** are **ī** (*singular*) and **īte** (*plural*). Compounds of **eō** form their imperatives like the simple verb, for example, **trānsī, trānsīte.**

The imperatives of **sum** are **es** (*singular*) and **este** (*plural*).

Es fortis, *Be brave.* **Este fortēs,** *Be brave.*

NEGATIVE COMMANDS

A command not to do an act is expressed by **nōlī** for the singular and **nōlīte** for the plural, followed by the infinitive.

Singular: **Nōlī redīre,** *Do not return.*

Plural: **Nōlīte redīre,** *Do not return.*

1. Īte ad silvam, nautae, et vōs cēlāte. 2. Es fortis, mīles fīde, et urbem dēfende. 3. Este fīdī, mīlitēs fortēs; vōs dēfendere potestis. 4. Nōlī monēre cīvēs dē hostium adventū, quod sunt virī timidī. 5. Nōlīte redīre in portum, nautae; ignem in cōnspectū exercitūs accendite. 6. Perīculō vīsō, ego quidem mē in cavernā longinquā cēlāre potuī. 7. Ego et tū semper amīcī erimus. 8. Gladiōs, mīlitēs, capite et in hostēs impetum facite. 9. Dūc tēcum omnēs mīlitēs tuōs; dūcite vōbīscum omnēs mīlitēs vestrōs.

1. We had decided to kindle a fire on the shore. 2. We knew that the sailors would explore the region at daybreak. 3. Surely you will not be able to remain so long. 4. Friend, do not desert me; friends, do not desert your leader. 5. Come with me, friend; I can show you a remarkable thing. 6. Go with us, suitors, and we will show you a beggar whom nobody recognizes.

HELP YOURSELF What would be the best translation of **dīcere potuerat** in line 2 of "Tēlemachus Patrem Videt"? Of **intrāre potuit** in lines 7-8? Of **facere poteris** in line 30? Notice that forms of **possum** are usually accompanied by an infinitive.

Find two uses of **es** in the story. Which of these is imperative and which is indicative?

LXXXVI. ULIXES RECOGNOSCITUR.

Ulīxēs, mendicus, veste iterum mūtātā, ad rēgiam vēnerat. Jussū patris, Tēlemachus arma parāverat. Ulīxēs ipse in ātriō cum servīs mānsit quod sciēbat Pēnelopam brevī tempore adfutūram esse.

Pēnelopē, ubi in ātrium intrāvit, omnēs servōs servāsque dīmīsit
5 praeter nūtrīcem longaevam, cui dīxit, "Cāra nūtrīx, ubi omnēs servī discesserint, dūc ad mē mendicum. Certē iter fēcit in regiōnibus ipsīs ubi conjūnx meus errāvit."

Jussū nūtrīcis Ulīxēs ad rēgīnam ipsam appropinquāvit. Pēnelopē sine suspīciōne eī dīxit, "Noctū et interdiū doleō quod Ulīxēs,
10 conjūnx amātus meus, ā terrā Trōjānā nōn rediit. Certē in longinquīs terrīs errāvistī. Vīdistīne eum?"

Ulīxēs Pēnelopae respondit, "Ōlim in Crētā virum quem comitēs Ulīxem appellābant vīdī. Vestem purpuream (*purple*) cum fībulā aureā gerēbat. In hāc fībulā erant figūrae canis et cervī parvī."

15 Pēnelopē lacrimāvit quod vestem et fībulam recognōvit. Deinde

Ulysses and the old nurse

dīxit, "Certē conjugem meum ipsum vīdistī. Illam vestem et illam fībulam Ulīxī ipsa dedī."

Ulīxēs respondit, "Sciō Ulīxem hōc annō ad patriam ventūrum esse."

Pēnelopē, magnō gaudiō mōta, jussit nūtrīcem pedēs mendicī lavāre. Nūtrīx fīda, ubi pedēs Ulīxis lavāre incēpit, lātam cicātrīcem (*scar*) recognōvit. 5

Magnopere excitāta, parvā vōce eī dīxit, "Rediistī, Ulīxēs."

Ulīxēs quidem celeriter respondit, "Nōlī clāmāre. Ego sum Ulīxēs. Nōlī appellāre mē nōmine meō."

Pēnelopē, quae haec verba nōn audīverat, dīxit, "Crās procī mē conjugem novum dēligere cōgent. Crās arcum in ātrium portārī jubēbō. Ille quī arcum Ulīxis tendere potuerit, mē in mātrimōnium dūcet." 10

arcus, -ūs, M., bow
dīmittō, -ere, -mīsī, -missum, dismiss, send away
fībula, -ae, F., brooch
ipse, ipsa, ipsum, myself, yourself, himself, herself, itself
jussū, M., *abl. sing.*, at the order
lavō, -āre, lāvī, lautum, bathe, wash
longaevus, -a, -um, aged, old
nūtrīx, -trīcis, F., nurse
praeter, *prep. with acc.*, except
tendō, -ere, tetendī, tentum, bend, stretch

DECLENSION AND USE OF *ipse*

The word **ipse** means *myself*, *yourself*, *himself*, *herself*, *itself*, *ourselves*, *yourselves*, or *themselves*. It is used for emphasis.

Dux ipse fūgit, *The leader himself fled.*

Ipse is declined like **ille** (p. 156), except that the neuter singular ends in **-um** in the nominative and accusative.

In the sentence above, **ipse** is masculine singular nominative, to agree with **dux.** The word **ipse** always agrees in gender, number, and case with the word to which it refers.

It is translated *myself, yourself, himself, herself, itself,* or *ourselves, yourselves, themselves,* according to the person, gender, and number of the word to which it refers.

Do not confuse the word **ipse** with the reflexive pronoun. Remember that the reflexive pronoun cannot be omitted without changing the thought of the sentence, whereas **ipse** merely gives additional emphasis.

MEANING OF THE FUTURE PERFECT

The *future perfect tense* represents an act to be completed before some specified or suggested time in the future.

I shall have finished the work in two weeks.

In English the future perfect is used less often than the other tenses. In Latin it is used somewhat more frequently than in English.

FORMATION OF THE FUTURE PERFECT ACTIVE

The future perfect active of a Latin verb has the tense sign **-eri-,** which is added to the perfect stem. The person endings are used as in the present tense. The future perfect is formed in the same way for all four conjugations.

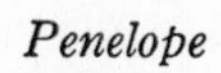

Penelope

SINGULAR

portā′verō, I shall have carried	**monu′erō,** I shall have warned
portā′veris, you will have carried	**monu′eris,** you will have warned
portā′verit, he, she, it will have carried	**monu′erit,** he, she, it will have warned

PLURAL

portāve′rimus, we shall have carried	**monue′rimus,** we shall have warned
portāve′ritis, you will have carried	**monue′ritis,** you will have warned
portā′verint, they will have carried	**monu′erint,** they will have warned

Notice that the **-i-** of the tense sign disappears before **-ō-** in the first person singular.

FUTURE PERFECT PASSIVE

The future perfect in the passive voice is formed by combining the perfect participle of the verb with the future indicative of **sum.** This is true of all four conjugations.

SINGULAR

portā'tus erō, I shall have been carried	**mo'nitus erō,** I shall have been warned
portā'tus eris, you will have been carried	**mo'nitus eris,** you will have been warned
portā'tus erit, he, she, it will have been carried	**mo'nitus erit,** he, she, it will have been warned

PLURAL

portā'tī erimus, we shall have been carried	**mo'nitī erimus,** we shall have been warned
portā'tī eritis, you will have been carried	**mo'nitī eritis,** you will have been warned
portā'tī erunt, they will have been carried	**mo'nitī erunt,** they will have been warned

PERFECT SYSTEM

You have now met all three tenses of the perfect system: the perfect, the past perfect, and the future perfect.

ACTIVE

Perfect = perfect stem + special person endings (**-ī, -istī,** etc.).
Past perfect = perfect stem + **-erā-** + regular person endings.
Future perfect = perfect stem + **-eri-** + regular person endings.

PASSIVE

Perfect = perfect passive participle with present tense of **sum.**
Past perfect = perfect passive participle with imperfect of **sum.**
Future perfect = perfect passive participle with future of **sum.**

1. Nēmō praeter longaevam nūtrīcem ipsam Ulīxem recognōvit. 2. Jussū ducis ipsīus domī mānsimus. 3. Item is dīxit sē jussū ducum ipsōrum omnēs dīmissūrum esse. 4. Nōlīte fībulam mātrī dare; date fībulam puellae ipsī. 5. Nōlī mēcum intrāre ātrium; manē in viā. 6. Este quiētī; canēs impetum in vōs nōn facient. 7. Tēlemachus scit patrem procōs occīsūrum esse. 8. Ubi procī arcum tendere temptāverint, Ulīxēs ipse arcum tendet. 9. Poteruntne procī arcum tendere?

Such nouns as **frāter** and **fēmina** are said to have *natural gender*. Latin nouns which do not have natural gender have grammatical gender: **gladius** (M.), **nāvis** (F.), **saxum** (N.).

HELP YOURSELF

Most nouns have only one gender; a few have two genders with different endings: **cervus, cerva.** Others have only one form but two genders, sometimes called *common gender:* **cīvis** (M. and F.). Still others have only one form and one gender but may also refer to the opposite sex: **leō** (M.), **avis** (F.).

In "Ulīxēs Recognōscitur" find examples of the two kinds of nouns with more than one gender.

LXXXVII. PENELOPE LIBERATA EST.

Postrīdiē eīdem procī ad magnum ātrium properāvērunt. Quisque (*each one*) quidem crēdidit Pēnelopam sē conjugem dēlēctūram esse. Ulīxēs, quī eandem vestem mendicī gerēbat, in ātriō aderat.

Tum procī dīxērunt, "Multōs annōs, Tēlemache, patrem tuum
5 expectāvistī; propter amōrem patris honōrem tibi rēctē dedimus, mātremque tuam in mātrimōnium contrā voluntātem dūcī nōn coēgimus. Sed jam prō certō scīmus Ulīxem numquam reditūrum esse."

Interim Pēnelopē arcum Ulīxis et sagittās, arma gravia, in magnum ātrium portāvit.

10 Tum procīs dīxit, "Audīte mē, procī nōbilēs. Nūntiāvistis ūnum ē numerō vestrō conjugem meum futūrum esse. Ecce, īdem arcus et eaedem sagittae quae Ulīxēs ōlim portābat! Ille quī hunc arcum tendere potuerit, mē in mātrimōnium rēctē dūcet."

Quamquam omnēs temptāvērunt, nēmō arcum tendere poterat.
15 Subitō mendicus dīxit, "Dā mihi arcum."

Sine difficultāte arcum tetendit; deinde magnā vōce clāmāvit, "Multa mīlia passuum nāvigāvī, contrā mīlle perīcula mē dēfendī. Jam ego Ulīxēs ipse adsum!"

Hīs verbīs audītīs, Tēlemachus arma cēpit et patrī auxilium dedit;
20 eōdem tempore servī fīdī et cīvēs, quī sēcrētō arcessītī erant, ātrium intrāvērunt ācriterque pugnāre incēpērunt. Omnibus procīs interfectīs, Pēnelopē fidēlis ad Ulīxem, conjugem amātum, properāvit.

īdem, eadem, idem, same
mīlle, *adj., indecl.,* a thousand; **mīlia, -ium,** N., *pl.,* thousands
passus, -ūs, M., pace; **mīlle passūs,** a mile
rēctē, *adv.,* rightly

LATIN ADVERBS AND ADJECTIVES

In English many adverbs are formed by adding *-ly* to adjectives: *slow, slowly; careful, carefully.* In Latin, also, most adverbs are formed from adjectives.

Many adverbs are formed from first- and second-declension adjectives by the addition of **-ē** to the base: **lātus,** *wide;* **lātē,** *widely.* What is the adverb from **cārus?** From **longus?**

Adverbs are also made from third-declension adjectives by the addition of **-ter** or **-iter** to the base (**-er** if base ends in **-nt**): **ācer, ācriter.**

From what adjectives do these adverbs come?

fortiter **graviter** **sapienter**

The neuter accusative of an adjective is sometimes used as an adverb.

facile, *easily* **multum,** *much*

The adverb corresponding to **magnus** is **magnopere,** to **bonus** is **bene.** Some adverbs do not have a corresponding adjective: **saepe,** *often,* **numquam,** *never,* and many others.

DECLENSION AND USE OF *īdem*

The declension of **īdem,** *same,* is as follows:

	SINGULAR		
	MASC.	FEM.	NEUT.
Nominative:	**ī'dem**	**e'adem**	**i'dem**
Genitive:	**ejus'dem**	**ejus'dem**	**ejus'dem**
Dative:	**eī'dem**	**eī'dem**	**eī'dem**
Accusative:	**eun'dem**	**ean'dem**	**i'dem**
Ablative:	**eō'dem**	**eā'dem**	**eō'dem**
	PLURAL		
Nominative:	**eī'dem, ī'dem**	**eae'dem**	**e'adem**
Genitive:	**eōrun'dem**	**eārun'dem**	**eōrun'dem**
Dative:	**eīs'dem, īs'dem**	**eīs'dem, īs'dem**	**eīs'dem, īs'dem**
Accusative:	**eōs'dem**	**eās'dem**	**e'adem**
Ablative:	**eīs'dem, īs'dem**	**eīs'dem, īs'dem**	**eīs'dem, īs'dem**

As you will observe, the forms of **īdem** are for the most part identical with those of **is** with the syllable **-dem** added. Before **d** a final **-m** is changed to **-n.**

Occasionally **īdem** is used as a pronoun meaning *the same person* (neuter, **idem,** *the same thing*). But it is commonly used as an adjective in agreement with a noun.

mīlle AND *mīlia*

The Latin word for *a thousand* is **mīlle,** an indeclinable adjective.

However, in referring to more than one thousand, Latin always uses a noun, **mīlia, mīlium,** which really means *thousands* and is therefore always followed by a genitive. **Mīlia** is declined like **īnsignia.**

Mīlle perīcula vīdī, *I have seen a thousand dangers.*

Duo mīlia hominum vīdī, *I saw two thousand men.*

ACCUSATIVE OF EXTENT OF SPACE

The accusative without a preposition is used to express extent of space.

Multa mīlia passuum nāvigāvī, *I have sailed many miles.*

Ad hortum suum, quī pauca mīlia passuum aberat, properāvit, *He hastened to his garden, which was a few miles away.*

1. In eō colle est oppidum; in eōdem colle est oppidum. 2. Frātrem ejus puerī videō; frātrem ejusdem puerī videō. 3. Eam legiōnem multa mīlia passuum mittēmus; eandem legiōnem mittēmus. 4. Amīcī eōrum hominum sumus; amīcī eōrundem hominum sumus. 5. Imperātōrēs ab eādem urbe discessērunt. 6. Eās epistulās eīdem servō rēctē dedī.

By translating the phrases make three sentences of each of the following.

1. Fābulam __ rēctē nārrāvī.
   to a small boy   *to other messengers*   *to the same messenger*
2. Multa mīlia mīlitum sunt __ .
   in the leader's army   *in the same army*   *in the same country*
3. Saepe __ ambulāvērunt.
   with the same friends   *with a few inhabitants*   *with the same soldier*
4. Illī virī sunt incolae __ .
   of the same city   *of the same country*   *of the same island*

HY

What English expression has the same form as **prō certō?** What tense is **potuerit?** What proves this?

LLT

The English word *mile* comes from the Latin **mille passuum,** which was often shortened to **mille.** Since the Roman pace was the distance covered by two steps—a step with each foot (about five feet)—the Roman mile was a little shorter than the English mile.

REVIEW OF UNIT XVIII LESSONS LXXXIV-LXXXVII

Nouns	*Verbs*	*Adjectives*	*Adverbs*
adventus, -ūs	accendō, -ere	certus, -a, -um	hūc
arcus, -ūs	*cōnsūmō, -ere	fidēlis, -e	item
àtrium, -ī	culpō, -āre	īdem, eadem, idem	rēctē
cāsus, -ūs	dīmittō, -ere	ipse, ipsa, ipsum	tam
fībula, -ae	*explōrō, -āre	longaevus, -a, -um	*Preposition*
jussū	intrō, -āre	mīlle	praeter
mīlia, -ium	lavō, -āre	vīgintī	
nūtrīx, -īcis	possum, posse		*Conjunction*
passus, -ūs	tendō, -ere	*Pronouns*	atque
procus, -ī	texō, -ere	ipse, ipsa, ipsum	
*suspīciō, -ōnis		nēmō	
vīnum, -ī			

I. Use a form of a word in the list above to complete each of the following sentences:

1. Ulīxēs dīcit sē in rēgiam īre __ . (*is able*)
2. Scīmus procōs in casam Eumaeī nōn __ . (*will enter*)
3. Nēmō sēnsit mendicum esse Ulīxem ipsum __ . (*could*)
4. Nūntiā Tēlemachō Ulīxem rēgiam __ . (*has entered*)
5. Nēmō, quidem, scit Ulīxem arcum in ātriō __ . (*will bend*)

II. In the list below, find the word or phrase needed to complete each of the sentences which follow.

eandem **eundem** **ipsīus** **mīlia passuum** **nōlīte** **poterunt**
este **ipsī** **ipsōs** **nōlī** **poterant**

1. __ fidēlēs, sociī. (*Be*) 2. __ timēre, virī, portum explōrāre. (*Don't*) 3. __ virum cotīdiē vidēmus. (*the same*) 4. Item Pēnelopē __ fībulam vīdit. (*the same*) 5. Quīnque __ nūtrīx longaeva ambulāvit. (*miles*) 6. Jussū Ulīxis __ Tēlemachus hūc vēnit. (*himself*) 7. Adventum Tēlemachī cēlāre __ . (*they will be able*) 8. Vigilēs __ captīvōs dīmittere rēctē cōnstituērunt. (*themselves*)

LATIN LIVES TODAY

Find in each sentence Latin derivatives equal to the number following it.

1. He was identified as the culprit. (2) 2. The case was tried before a judge. (2) 3. The mendicant consumed a large amount of nutritious food. (3) 4. It was not possible to dismiss the suspicion from his mind. (3) 5. His reputation for fidelity to duty attracted much attention. (4) 6. A few miles from the arch the explorers found a deserted village. (5)

UNIT

XIX

LXXXVIII. UTER FORTIOR ERAT?

Olim ūna legiō Rōmāna ā multīs Gallīs oppugnābātur. Cōpiae Gallōrum collēs altiōrēs circum castra Rōmāna occupāverant. Erant in exercitū Rōmānō duo centuriōnēs fortissimī, Pullō et Vorēnus nōmine; hī erant inimīcī. Uterque ā duce suō fēlīcissimus esse putābātur quod saepe in proeliīs perīculōsissimīs cum hostibus contenderat. Nēmō eōs occīdere potuerat.

"Uter fortior est?" aliī mīlitēs rogābant. "Estne Pullō potentior quam Vorēnus? Estne Vorēnus fidēlior quam Pullō?"

Itaque Pullō dīxit, "Cūr nunc dubius es, Vorēne? Jam virtūtem ostendere potes. Nōlī timēre! Hic diēs contrōversiam nostram fīniet."

Tum sōlus ex castrīs prōcessit impetumque in hostēs fēcit. Idem Vorēnus statim fēcit.

Pullō pīlum in hostēs conjēcit; ūnum ē Gallīs interfēcit. Cēterī Gallī in Pullōnem tēla sua conjēcērunt eumque circumvenīre temptāvērunt. Pullō gladium suum ēdūcere temptāvit, sed ejus balteus hastā trānsfīxus erat. Gladius post tergum mōtus erat. Hōc vīsō, hostēs impetum graviōrem in eum ācriter fēcērunt.

Tum Vorēnus ad auxilium inimīcī suī vēnit; celeriter currēbat; subitō cecidit (*fell*). Gallī, quī putāvērunt Pullōnem mortuum esse, eum relīquērunt, impetumque in Vorēnum fēcērunt.

Interim Pullō, quī nōn sōlum mortuus nōn erat, sed etiam nūllum vulnus accēperat, ad Vorēnum cucurrit, impetumque hostium frēgit. Ita duo inimīcī multōs Gallōs aut interfēcērunt aut vulnerāvērunt. Tum tūtī in castra rediērunt.

Uterque inimīcum servāvit. Uter fortior erat?

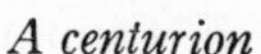

A centurion

balteus, -ī, M., belt, sword belt
centuriō, -ōnis, M., centurion
currō, -ere, cucurrī, cursum, run
ēdūcō, -dūcere, -dūxī, -ductum, lead out; draw
tēlum, -ī, N., weapon
trānsfīgō, -fīgere, -fīxī, -fīxum, pierce, transfix
uter, utra, utrum, which (of two)
uterque, utraque, utrumque, each (of two)
virtūs, -ūtis, F., valor, bravery

LATIN VERBS AND RELATED NOUNS AND ADJECTIVES

In Latin, as in English, many nouns and verbs have related forms and similar meanings: **culpō, -āre,** *to blame,* **culpa, -ae,** *blame;* **dōnō, -āre,** *to give,* **dōnum, -ī,** *gift;* **vulnerō, -āre,** *to wound,* **vulnus, -eris,** *wound.* Such a pair of related words is said to belong to the same *word family.*

You know what the verb **pugnō** means; what is the meaning of the noun **pugna?** You also know the noun **cēna**; what does the verb **cēnō** mean?

Verbs and adjectives are related in the same way: **timeō, -ēre,** *to fear,* **timidus, -a, -um,** *fearful;* **firmō, -āre,** *to make firm,* **firmus, -a, -um,** *firm.*

Give the meaning of each word in the following pairs of related words.

Verb	*Noun or Adjective*	*Verb*	*Noun or Adjective*
clāmō, -āre	**clāmor, -ōris**	**līberō, -āre**	**līber, -era, -erum**
cupiō, -ere	**cupidus, -a, -um**	**nōminō, -āre**	**nōmen, nōminis**
cūrō, -āre	**cūra, -ae**	**novō, -āre**	**novus, -a, -um**
fīniō, -īre	**fīnis, fīnis**	**rēgnō, -āre**	**rēgnum, -ī**
honōrō, -āre	**honor, -ōris**	**regō, -ere**	**rēgius, -a, -um**
jūdicō, -āre	**jūdex, jūdicis**	**serviō, -īre**	**servus, -ī**
labōrō, -āre	**labor, -ōris**	**spectō, -āre**	**spectātor, -ōris**
lacrimō, -āre	**lacrima, -ae**	**terreō, -ēre**	**terror, -ōris**
laudō, -āre	**laus, laudis**	**vestiō, -īre**	**vestis, vestis**

COMPARISON OF ADJECTIVES

Most English adjectives may be used in the *positive, comparative,* and *superlative.*

Positive: brave *Comparative*: braver *Superlative*: bravest

Latin adjectives also have positive, comparative, and superlative forms.

Positive:	**altus,** high	**fortis,** brave	**fēlīx,** happy
Comparative:	**altior,** higher	**fortior,** braver	**fēlīcior,** happier
Superlative:	**altissimus,** highest	**fortissimus,** bravest	**fēlīcissimus,** happiest

FORMATION OF THE COMPARATIVE AND THE SUPERLATIVE

The comparative of Latin adjectives regularly ends in **-ior** for the masculine and feminine and **-ius** for the neuter. These endings are added to the base. The base is found by dropping the masculine genitive ending of the positive form.

altus, genitive **altī,** base **alt-** *Comparative:* **altior, altius**
fortis, genitive **fortis,** base **fort-** *Comparative:* **fortior, fortius**
fēlīx, genitive **fēlīcis,** base **fēlīc-** *Comparative:* **fēlīcior, fēlīcius**

The superlative is formed regularly by adding **-issimus, -issima, -issimum** to the base.

altus, genitive **alti,** base **alt-** *Superlative:* **altissimus, -a, -um**
fortis, genitive **fortis,** base **fort-** *Superlative:* **fortissimus, -a, -um**
fēlīx, genitive **fēlīcis,** base **fēlīc-** *Superlative:* **fēlīcissimus, -a, -um**
potēns, genitive **potentis,** base **potent-** *Superlative:* **potentissimus, -a, -um**

DECLENSION OF COMPARATIVES AND SUPERLATIVES

Adjectives in the comparative are declined as third-declension adjectives. The ablative singular, however, ends in **-e,** and the genitive plural in **-um.**

	MASC. AND FEM.	NEUT.	MASC. AND FEM.	NEUT.
Nominative:	**lā'tior**	**lā'tius**	**lātiō'rēs**	**lātiō'ra**
Genitive:	**lātiō'ris**	**lātiō'ris**	**lātiō'rum**	**lātiō'rum**
Dative:	**lātiō'rī**	**lātiō'rī**	**lātiō'ribus**	**lātiō'ribus**
Accusative:	**lātiō'rem**	**lā'tius**	**lātiō'rēs**	**lātiō'ra**
Ablative:	**lātiō're**	**lātiō're**	**lātiō'ribus**	**lātiō'ribus**

The superlative of any adjective is declined like **bonus.**

TRANSLATION OF COMPARATIVES AND SUPERLATIVES

Sometimes a comparative is translated with *too* or *rather* instead of an English comparative, and a superlative with *very* instead of an English superlative.

flūmen lātius, *a rather wide river*
mōns altissimus, *a very high mountain*

1. Mārcus erat vir benignissimus. 2. Collēs Rōmae altissimī nōn sunt. 3. Illa arbor altissima est. 4. Mīdās erat rēx potentissimus. 5. Utrum cōnsilium tūtius erit? 6. Puer quī ē tēctō cucurrit est amīcus meus cārissimus. 7. Uter mīles validior erat? 8. Bracchium ejus sagittā trānsfīxum erat. 9. Virtūs mīlitis magna erat. 10. Balteus ducis erat validissimus. 11. Ēdūxitne Pullō gladium suum?

Translate the italicized words: 1. We know that *the leader* ran toward his men. 2. The same man can be either *very brave* or *very timid.* 3. A *very long* journey with good companions seems to be *very short.* 4. The days are *longer* in summer *than* in winter. 5. Who can be *more faithful* to a friend than was Pullo? 6. His belt *was pierced* by an arrow. 7. The *tallest* man was the *bravest.* 8. *Draw* your sword quickly, Vorenus.

HY

What is the difference in meaning between **uter** and **uterque?** Make a sentence containing each word.

LLT

The two words of each pair below have a common base, which is easy to see. You already know the meaning of both words in some pairs; in others you know one. In every case try to see the connection between the words of a pair and to give the meaning of both.

1. **acer** / **acrimonia**
2. **avis** / **aviarium**
3. **bonus** / **bonitas**
4. **centum** / **centurio**
5. **consul** / **consulatus**
6. **decem** / **decimus**
7. **fluo** / **flumen**
8. **nuntio** / **nuntius**
9. **odium** / **odiosus**
10. **quattuor** / **quartus**
11. **scribo (scriptum)** / **scriptura**
12. **solus** / **solitudo**
13. **specto** / **spectaculum**
14. **timeo** / **timidus**

At least one word of each pair has one or more English derivatives; sometimes both words have. Give yourself one point for each derivative you can think of without looking up any word. Fifteen is a good score, 20 very good, 30 excellent.

LXXXIX. TERROR EXERCITUM ROMANUM OCCUPAT.

Ariovistus, dux ācerrimus Germānōrum, in animō iter in Galliam facere et bonōs agrōs in illā regiōne occupāre habēbat. Cōnsilium Germānō ācrī facilius esse vidēbātur quod gentēs Galliae inter sē pugnābant.

5 Hōc cōnsiliō nūntiātō, Gallī territī auxilium ā Caesare, duce Rōmānō, quī sex legiōnēs in hanc regiōnem jam dūxerat, postulāvērunt.

Caesar, quī magnum perīculum sēnsit, exercitum suum dūxit ad oppidum, prope quod oppidum Ariovistus castra posuerat. Iter erat difficillimum, et mīlitēs erant dēfessī. In hōc oppidō erant multī 10 mercātōrēs, quī Ariovistum saepe vīderant. Hī mercātōrēs multa dē Germānīs fortissimīs nārrāvērunt.

Mox multī rūmōrēs nūntiātī dē ingentī magnitūdine corporum Germānōrum atque incrēdibilī virtūte atque magnā crūdēlitāte paucōs mīlitēs Rōmānōs maximē terruērunt. Brevī tempore similis 15 timor tōtum exercitum occupāvit et omnium mentēs animōsque maximē perturbāvit.

Etiam abditī in tabernāculīs mīlitēs magnum timōrem tegere nōn poterant.

Per tōta castra etiam testāmenta facta sunt. Hōrum vōcibus et 20 timōre mīlitēs veterānī et centuriōnēs perturbābantur. Multī quī sē timidōs aut humilēs exīstimārī nōn dēsīderābant, dīxērunt sē hostēs nōn timēre, sed angustiās itineris et magnitūdinem silvārum.

Dēnique Caesarī nūntiātum est mīlitēs propter timōrem magnum in proelium nōn prōcessūrōs esse.

abdō, -dere, -didī, -ditum, hide, put away
difficilis, -e, hard, difficult
dissimilis, -e, unlike
exīstimō, -āre, -āvī, -ātum, think, estimate
facilis, -e, easy
humilis, -e, low, humble
ingēns, *gen.* **ingentis,** huge
similis, -e, like, similar

A cavalryman in the Roman army

LATIN WORDS MADE WITH SUFFIXES

As you know, a *suffix* is an addition at the end of a word or at the end of the base. Thus, in *boldness*, the syllable *-ness* is a suffix, which forms a noun from the adjective *bold*.

Suffixes also make adjectives from nouns or other words. The adjective *golden* is made from the suffix *-en* and the noun *gold*.

Latin uses suffixes in the same way. Some suffixes used to form Latin nouns are **-ia, -tia, -tas, -tudo: angustia,** *narrowness* (from **angustus,** *narrow*); **crudelitas,** *cruelty* (from **crudelis,** *cruel*); **magnitudo,** *greatness* (from **magnus,** *great*).

What is the meaning of each of these Latin nouns?

brevitas **solitudo** **superbia**

Some Latin suffixes used to form adjectives are **-alis** or **-aris, -ilis, -anus, -inus, -bilis, -eus, -osus:**

naturalis, *natural,* from **natura**	**marinus,** *marine,* from **mare**
militaris, *military,* from **miles**	**credibilis,** *credible,* from **credo**
civilis, *civil,* from **civis**	**aureus,** *golden,* from **aurum**
urbanus, *urban,* from **urbs**	**curiosus,** *curious,* from **cura**

Many Latin suffixes have corresponding forms in English, as *-al* for **-alis** and *-ous* for **-osus.** The suffix **-aris** becomes *-ar* or *-ary* in many English words, and **-ilis** may be *-il* or *-ile* in English. In nouns, **-tas** often becomes *-ty* in English and **-tudo** becomes *-tude.*

Each word in the list below is connected with a Latin word you have already met.

1. Give the Latin word you know with which each is connected.
2. Give the meaning of each word, using a derivative whenever possible.

amabilis	**capitalis**	**fortitudo**	**lunaris**	**superbus**
amicitia	**consularis**	**gratia**	**mortalis**	**terribilis**
annualis	**credulitas**	**hostilis**	**odiosus**	**vigilia**
auxiliaris	**cupiditas**	**laudabilis**	**periculosus**	**vitalitas**
bellicosus	**curiositas**	**liberalis**	**Romanus**	**vocalis**
caninus	**equinus**	**libertas**	**servilis**	

Give an English synonym for as many of the derivative meanings as you can, as *warlike* or *quarrelsome* for *bellicose.*

COMPARISON OF ADJECTIVES IN *-er*

The superlative of adjectives ending in **-er** may be formed by adding **-rimus** to the nominative singular of the masculine. Their comparative is formed like that of other adjectives.

Positive:	**miser, -era, -erum**	**pulcher, -chra, -chrum**
Comparative:	**miserior, -ius**	**pulchrior, -chrius**
Superlative:	**miserrimus, -a, -um**	**pulcherrimus, -a, -um**

COMPARISON OF ADJECTIVES IN *-lis*

The superlative of five adjectives ending in **-lis** may be found by adding **-limus** to the base:

facilis, easy — **similis,** like — **humilis,** low
difficilis, difficult — **dissimilis,** unlike

Positive:	**facilis, -e**	**humilis, -e**
Comparative:	**facilior, -ius**	**humilior, -ius**
Superlative:	**facillimus, -a, -um**	**humillimus, -a, -um**

Most other adjectives ending in **-lis** form the superlative regularly with **-issimus.**

1. Haec via est brevissima, sed nōn est facillima. 2. Sapientissimum ducem dēlēgimus; sed nōn est fortissimus. 3. Urbēs tuae urbibus meīs sunt dissimilēs. 4. Illī ducēs fortēs sunt miserrimī quod ingentēs cōpiās nōn habent. 5. Sunt oppida pulchriōra in illā regiōne. 6. Mīlitēs atque ducēs quidem in silvā ingentī sē abdidērunt. 7. Nōnne centuriōnēs fortēs exīstimārī dēsīderāvērunt? 8. Mīles in locō humillimō positus erat.

Translate the italicized words: 1. These brothers are *very unlike,* but they are *very faithful* to our leader. 2. *The longest* routes are often *the easiest.* 3. The mountains of Europe are *very high* and *very beautiful.* 4. The victory will be *very difficult.* 5. The leaders thought the battles were *very easy.* 6. This hill is *lower* than the others.

HW Find out who Julius Caesar was and what he wrote.

LATIN LIVES TODAY For each blank supply an English word related to one of the following Latin words:

difficilis **dissimilis** **facilis** **humilis** **similis**

1. The boy was — when his dishonesty was revealed.
2. The — of the twins makes it — to tell them apart.
3. From the — with which he did the work, we knew it was easy for him.
4. Your tastes are so — that you will not enjoy the same things.

In such tents Caesar's soldiers were housed.

XC. DUX IRATISSIMUS

His rūmōribus audītīs, Caesar omnēs centuriōnēs convocāvit et eōs vehementer accūsāvit.

Īrātus dīxit: "Cūr vōs Germānōs ignāvōs timētis? Ariovistus ipse, dux pessimus, maximā cum cupiditāte amīcitiam populī Rōmānī petīvit; ego ipse cōnsul eram ubi, omnibus rēbus explōrātīs, Ariovistus amīcitiam grātiamque nostram āmittere nōn dēsīderāvit. Exercitūs nostrī exercitūs Germānōs saepe sustinuērunt; minimā difficultāte iterum exercitum Germānum superābimus.

"Nōs sumus mīlitēs meliōrēs quam Helvētiī, sed Helvētiī eōsdem Germānōs saepe superāvērunt nōn sōlum in fīnibus suīs, sed etiam in fīnibus ipsīs Germānōrum. Ariovistus multōs dolōs bellī scit, sed Rōmānī ejus dolōs timēre nōn dēbent.

"Mīlitēs Rōmānī quī dīcunt sē hostēs nōn timēre sed angustiās itineris et magnitūdinem silvārum sunt ignāvissimī. Haec sunt cūra ducis, nōn mīlitum. Multae gentēs Galliae frūmentum nōbīs dabunt; vōs ipsī brevī tempore dē perīculīs itineris jūdicābitis. Quārtā vigiliā castra movēbimus. Legiō decima nōn timet—ego cum decimā legiōne sōlā contrā Ariovistum ībō; ea legiō mihi erit praetōria cohors (*honor-guard*)."

Verba prīncipis autem decimae legiōnī grātissima erant. Ea legiō Caesarem jūdicium optimum dē sē fēcisse, sēque esse parātissimam gerere bellum cōnfirmāvit.

Hīs verbīs fortibus audītīs, omnium mentēs mūtātae sunt; maxima alacritās et cupiditās bellī omnem timōrem mīlitum expulērunt.

alacritās, -ātis, F., activity, readiness

sustineō, -tinēre, -tinuī, -tentum, support, endure, withstand

LATIN WORD FAMILIES

The following groups show how some Latin words are related. From the meaning of the first word in each group and from what you know about Latin prefixes and suffixes, try to deduce the meaning of each word.

duco	*sto*	*amo*	*cupio*	*teneo*
dux	**stabilis**	**amicus**	**cupidus**	**sustineo**
ductilis	**stabilitas**	**amicitia**	**cupido**	**attineo**
educo	**stabulum**	**amor**	**cupiditas**	**pertineo**
reduco	**stabulo**	**amabilis**		**retineo**
induco	**statio**	**inimicus**		**tenax**
deduco	**status**	**amator**		**tenacitas**
ductus	**statuo**			
ductor	**statua**			
perduco	**statura**			
aquaeductus	**statuarius**			

Make a word family for each of the following: **credo, porto, timeo.**

Select three of the word families on this page and give as many English derivatives as possible from each word in it.

ADJECTIVES COMPARED IRREGULARLY

There are a few adjectives which are compared irregularly. The most important are the following:

Positive	*Comparative*	*Superlative*
bonus, -a, -um, good	**melior, melius,** better	**optimus, -a, -um,** best
malus, -a, -um, bad	**pejor, pejus,** worse	**pessimus, -a, -um,** worst
magnus, -a, -um, large	**major, majus,** larger	**maximus, -a, -um,** largest
parvus, -a, -um, small	**minor, minus,** smaller	**minimus, -a, -um,** smallest
multus, -a, -um, much	—, **plūs,** more	**plūrimus, -a, -um,** most
———	**ulterior, ulterius,** farther	**ultimus, -a, -um,** farthest

In the singular, **plūs** is a neuter noun, with the genitive **plūris.** In the plural it is declined as an adjective with the forms **plūrēs, plūra,** etc.

1. Puer pessimus minimum saxum jēcit, sed virum optimum vulnerāvit. 2. Cīvēs meliōrēs lēgēs meliōrēs habēbunt. 3. Majōrēs cōpiās statim mittēmus, quod perīculum nunc majus est. 4. Casa tua est minor, sed casa mea est pulchrior. 5. Cōnsilium tuum est sapientissimum et optimum. 6. Rēgem accūsāvimus quod scelus ingēns fēcit. 7. Grātia centuriōnis erat maxima.

Translate the italicized words. 1. This city is *the best,* but it is not *the largest.* 2. This *very beautiful* temple is on a *very small* island. 3. This man is *worse* than his *father.* 4. I will give you a *larger reward* because your dangers have been *greater.* 5. His name was *more famous.*

LATIN LIVES TODAY

Sustineo alas (*I sustain the wings*) is a motto of the American Air Forces. Other branches of military service have Latin mottoes, too. What does each of these mottoes mean?

Arte et armis (202nd Coast Artillery, National Guard)
Curare (11th Med. Reg., Regular Army)
Descende ad terram (507th Parachute Infantry Reg.)
Facta non verba (124th Field Artillery, N. G.)
Fideliter servimus (15th Signal Battalion, RA Signal Corps)
Honoris custos (189th Field Arty., N. G.)
In bello paceque primus (122nd Inf., N. G.)
Monstrat viam (211th Coast Arty., N. G.)
Nihil timemus (121st Engineers, N. G.)
Non pro nobis sed pro aliis (105th Med. Reg., N. G.)
Non sibi sed omnibus (26th Quartermaster Reg., N. G.)
Nunc aut numquam (497th Field Arty., Reserve)
Primus aut nullus (First Field Arty., RA)
Pro Deo pro patria (145th Field Arty., N. G.)
Pro patria et gloria (107th Inf., N. G.)
Semper primus (First Inf., RA)
Vincere est vivere (101st Field Arty., N. G.)

A general addresses his troops.

Caesar lands in Britain.

XCI. CAESAR TAMESIM TRANSIT.

Postquam prīncipēs Galliae victī sunt, Caesar ad Britanniam cum cōpiīs majōribus etiam trānsīre cōnstituit. Itaque cum classe maximā ad illam īnsulam nāvigāvit.

Adventū Caesaris nūntiātō, Britannī territī in ūnum locum con-5 vēnērunt; pācem amīcitiamque inter sē fēcērunt. Anteā fuerant magnae contrōversiae inter omnēs gentēs īnsulae, sed jam nātiōnēs similēs commūnī perīculō jūnctae sunt.

Cassivellaunus dux dēlēctus est. Flūmen, quod Tamesis appellātur, fīnēs Cassivellaunī ā cīvitātibus maritimīs dīvidēbat. Is ēgregius dux 10 in animō habēbat prope flūmen in dēnsīs silvīs latēre impetūsque in mīlitēs Rōmānōs facere. Hoc flūmen in mare nōn longē fluit.

Hōc cōnsiliō cognitō, Caesar exercitum sine morā in fīnēs Cassivellaunī ad Tamesim celeriter dūxit. Id flūmen maximā cum difficultāte pedibus trānsīrī poterat.

15 Cōpiae hostium in rīpā īnstrūctae erant. Rīpa flūminis, autem, acūtīs sudibus (*stakes*) mūnīta erat. Hae sudēs, sub aquā positae, flūmine tegēbantur. Hīs rēbus per captīvōs cognitīs, Caesar tamen

mīlitēs suōs flūmen trānsīre jussit. Propter altitūdinem aquae, capita sōla mīlitum vidērī poterant. At hostēs hāc rē territī impetum Rōmānōrum sustinēre nōn poterant. Brevī tempore in silvās dēnsissimās sē abdidērunt.

anteā, *adv.*, before
at, *conj.*, but
commūnis, -e, common
īnstruō, -struere, -strūxī, -strūctum, build; provide; draw up

ADVERBS COMPARED REGULARLY

In adverbs derived from adjectives the comparative is regularly the same as the neuter accusative singular form of the comparative of the corresponding adjective. The superlative is made by adding **-ē** to the base of the superlative of the corresponding adjective.

Pos.	**lātē** (*from* **lātus**)	**ācriter** (*from* **ācer**)	**facile** (*from* **facilis**)
Comp.	**lātius**	**ācrius**	**facilius**
Super.	**lātissimē**	**ācerrimē**	**facillimē**

IRREGULAR ADVERBS

The following adverbs are irregular either in their formation or their comparison:

Positive:	**bene,** well	**male,** badly	**magnopere,** greatly
Comparative:	**melius,** better	**pejus,** worse	**magis,** more
Superlative:	**optimē,** best	**pessimē,** worst	**maximē,** very greatly

Positive:	**multum,** much	**parum,** little
Comparative:	**plūs,** more	**minus,** less
Superlative:	**plūrimum,** most	**minimē,** least

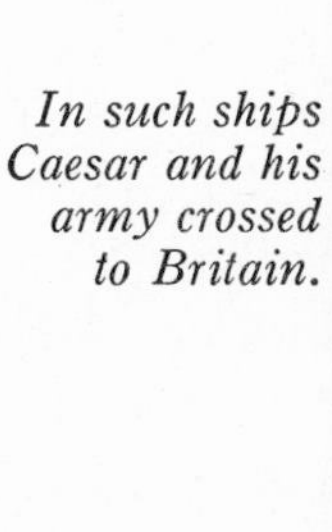

In such ships Caesar and his army crossed to Britain.

1. Minus facile castra oppugnāre poterimus quod flūmen est lātissimum. 2. Ducēs, īnstruite cōpiās vestrās in rīpā flūminis. 3. Cōpiae Britanniae nōn facile repellentur, sed legiōnēs fortissimē pugnābunt. 4. Captīvōs in illā regiōne facillimē inveniēmus. 5. Satis ācriter anteā pugnāvimus; satis lātē errāvimus. 6. Omnēs mīlitēs commūnī perīculō jūnctī sunt. 7. Scelere Germānī cognitō, hostēs Caesar oppugnāvit. 8. Paucī mīlitēs impetum sustinēre et cīvitātem servāre poterant. 9. Dux in proeliō ultimō pugnāverat.

Translate the italicized words: 1. The army came *rapidly* through the forest. 2. The legions *bravely* defended themselves and their camp. 3. The Gauls *formerly* wandered *more widely*. 4. The camp will be *better* defended by a *larger* army. 5. We fear the enemy *less*, but the common danger is *very great*. 6. Never before had we seen a *similar* danger. 7. Our forces were *badly* drawn up. 8. Since the man's crime *was known*, the leader accused him. 9. The soldiers withstood the attack *very bravely*.

HW Make questions of the first four sentences above, after you have translated them into Latin.

REVIEW OF UNIT XIX LESSONS LXXXVIII-XCI

Nouns

alacritās, -ātis
***altitūdō, -inis**
***amīcitia, -ae**
***angustiae, -ārum**
balteus, -ī
centuriō, -ōnis
***cīvitās, -ātis**
***crūdēlitās, -ātis**
***cupiditās, -ātis**
***cūra, -ae**
***grātia, -ae**
***magnitūdō, -inis**
***nātiō, -ōnis**
***rūmor, -ōris**
***superbia, -ae**
tēlum, -ī
***testāmentum, -ī**
***vigilia, -ae**
virtūs, -ūtis
***vulnus, vulneris**

Adjectives

commūnis, -e
***decimus, -a, -um**
difficilis, -e
dissimilis, -e
facilis, -e
humilis, -e
***incrēdibilis, -e**
ingēns, *gen.* ingentis
***odiōsus, -a, -um**
***quārtus, -a, -um**
similis, -e
ultimus, -a, -um
uterque, utraque, utrumque
***veterānus, -a, -um**

Verbs

abdō, -ere
***accūsō, -āre**
***circumveniō, -īre**
***cognōscō, -ere**
***creō, -āre**
currō, -ere
ēdūcō, -ere
exīstimō, -āre
***fīniō, -īre**
īnstruō, -ere
***jūdicō, -āre**
***perturbō, -āre**
sustineō, -ēre
trānsfīgō, -ere

Adverb

anteā
***lātē**

Pronoun

uter, utra, utrum

Conjunction

at

WORD MASTERY

I. Give an English noun from each Latin noun.

abundantia	**captivus**	**dignitas**	**omen**	**stabulum**
aedificium	**centurio**	**multitudo**	**religio**	**testimonium**

II. Give the Latin verb from which each English verb came.

defend	**narrate**	**observe**	**salute**
define	**navigate**	**remove**	**transcribe**

III. Give an English adjective corresponding to each Latin adjective.

caninus	**femininus**	**marinus**	**statuarius**
completus	**latens**	**navalis**	**temperatus**
expectans	**longus**	**ordinarius**	**veteranus**

IV. What does the prefix **in-** mean when added to an adjective? Give the meaning of each adjective.

incredibilis **infelix** **injustus** **invalidus**

V. Make compound verbs by adding each of these prefixes to another verb. Define each compound.

ab	**circum**	**contra**	**ex**	**re-**
ad	**com-**	**de**	**per**	**trans**

VI. From what noun and suffix was each adjective made?

civilis **militaris** **naturalis** **marinus**

VII. From what adjective and suffix was each of these nouns made?

amicitia **fortitudo** **libertas** **vitalitas**

VIII. From what adjective does each of these adverbs come? Give the meaning of the adverb.

acriter	**facile**	**graviter**	**longe**	**multum**
certe	**fortiter**	**libere**	**male**	**timide**

IX. Give the meaning of each member of this word family.

liber	**libertas**	**liberi**
liberalis	**liberator**	**libero**

X. Arrange these words in three word families.

admitto	**amicitia**	**amor**	**inimicus**	**remitto**
adventus	**amicus**	**circumvenio**	**invenio**	**revenio**
amabalis	**amo**	**committo**	**pervenio**	**venio**

A section of the Claudian Aqueduct, which once carried water to the homes, palaces, and baths of Rome

UNIT

XX

XCII. ARCHITECTI ET FABRI

Virī quī templa et tēcta cēteraque aedificia aedificant architectī appellantur. Multa aedificia antīqua quōrum pictūrās suprā in hōc librō vīdistī ā nōtīs architectīs Rōmānīs aedificātā sunt. Virīs illīs autem cūra formae urbium, aquaeductuum, viārum, arcuum 5 data est.

Virī quī ferrō aut lignō aut saxō aedificābant fabrī appellābantur. In bellō pontēs, castra, machinās bellī fabrī aedificābant; in pāce mūrōs, cloācās, fontēs, viās, pontēs, aquaeductūs, arcūs in Ītaliā et in prōvinciīs aedificābant.

10 Aquaeductus clārissimus Aqua Appia appellābātur, quod ab Appiō Claudiō aedificātus erat, et via clārissima causā eādem Via Appia appellābātur. Posteā Vitrūvius et Frontīnus erant architectī fabrīque ēgregiī nōn sōlum in pāce sed etiam in bellō.

Illī virī autem nōtissimī propter suōs librōs scrīptōs dē architec- 15 tūrā sunt. Hodiē etiam ex librīs illōrum architectī nostrī multa discunt.

The Romans had a branch of military service corresponding to our Engineering Corps. The captain was called *praefectus fabrum*. In walls, bridges, arches, temples, and amphitheaters (pp. 18, 59, 62, 63, 167, 178, and 206) are found architectural reminders of Roman occupation.

The modern architects who designed the Pennsylvania Railroad Station in New York followed the plans of the ancient architects who built the huge Baths of Caracalla, the walls of which still stand.

Other modern architects and engineers have admired and copied the architecture of the Romans. On pages 9, 16, 20, and 120 are pictured public buildings in our country which show the influence of ancient architecture. On page 10 is a photograph of a bridge in New York that looks like a Roman aqueduct, while the Jefferson Memorial on page 24 closely resembles a Roman temple.

Travelers who leave Rome by the Appian Way still pass through this ancient gateway, known as the Arch of Drusus. Once it supported a section of a Roman aqueduct.

XCIII. CORPUS JURIS CIVILIS

Jūstitia est cōnstāns et perpetua voluntās, jūs suum cuique (*to each*) tribuēns. Jūrisprūdentia est dīvīnārum atque hūmānārum rērum nōtitia, scientia justī atque injustī.

Initiō cīvitātis Rōmānae populus sine lēge certā, sine jūre certō 5 prīmum agere īnstituit omniaque manū ā rēgibus gubernābantur.

Posteā, autem, decem virī ā populō constitūtī sunt per quōs lēgēs in tabulīs scrīptae sunt. Itaque in cīvitāte lēx duodecim tabulārum et jūs cīvīle cōnstitūta sunt.

Jūs nātūrāle est jūs quod nātūra omnia animālia docuit. Et jūre 10 nātūrālī commūnia sunt omnium haec: āēr et aqua prōfluēns et mare et, per hoc, lītora maris. Nēmō igitur ad lītus maris appropinquāre prohibētur, quamquam ā vīllīs et monumentīs et aedificiīs abstinēre dēbet. Flūmina autem omnia et portūs sunt publica. Jūs piscandī (*of fishing*) igitur omnibus commūne est in portū flūminibusque. Sub 15 jūre gentium omnium est līberum jūs nōn sōlum per mare ipsum et per flūmen ipsum nāvigāre, sed etiam nāvem ad lītus maris aut ad rīpam flūminis appellere.

MIRABILE DICTU!

People who serve on juries in American courts are chosen by lot just as Roman jurors were selected two thousand years ago.

Unlike modern lawyers, however, Roman lawyers were not allowed to charge any fees, although they could accept gifts from their clients.

The famous Twelve Tables of Roman Laws written by the *decemvirs* were originally only ten. Two tables were added later, making twelve.

We say "To each his own"; the Romans said, **Suum cuique.**

Jus piscandi omnibus commune est.

Trial by jury goes back to Roman times.

USING LEGAL TERMS AND PHRASES FROM LATIN

The Romans had two words for *law:* **jus, juris** and **lex, legis. Jus** was a law based on a natural right; **lex** was a law proposed by a magistrate. The meanings of our related English words, *justice* and *legislation,* show that we make a similar distinction.

A **bona fide** salesman would never say, **"Caveat emptor!"** Since he acts in good faith, he does not need to warn the buyer to beware.

The *document* that sends a *criminal* to jail is called a **mittimus.** If a man is being wrongfully held in jail, a writ of **habeas corpus** may be secured to effect his release.

When Mr. Smith made his last will and *testament,* he *nominated* his bank as his *executor.* He *divided* his property **per capita** among his two sons and his granddaughter Mary. If the *estate* had been *divided* **per stirpes,** Mary would have received a smaller *legacy,* since the other *beneficiaries* were more closely *related* to the *testator* than she.

When a court or other body is adjourned **sine die,** no *definite* time is set for its next meeting.

As *collateral security,* Frank Jones *signed* a *promissory note dated January* 15, whereby he *promised* to pay the *principal* three years after *date,* with *six* **per cent.** *interest* **per annum.**

When a **subpoena** was served on Walter York, he knew that he was under *penalty* to appear before the Court.

The president of the *corporation* is **ex officio** chairman of the Board of *Directors.*

Every time you pay a *premium* on your *insurance* you are **de facto** making an *investment* in your *future security.*

The *defendant* was *confident* that he would not be *convicted* of the *crime* and that **ipso facto** he would be proved innocent.

Find and explain some other common legal expressions from Latin.

LATIN LIVES TODAY

What are the English nouns from **justitia, jurisprudentia, notitia, scientia?**

A *tribute* is bestowed on another as his due; what is the meaning of **tribuo?**

The house in which a *governor* lives is called a *gubernatorial* mansion. What does **guberno** mean?

What are the English adjectives from **civilis, communis, constans, divinus, humanus, injustus, justus, naturalis, perpetua?**

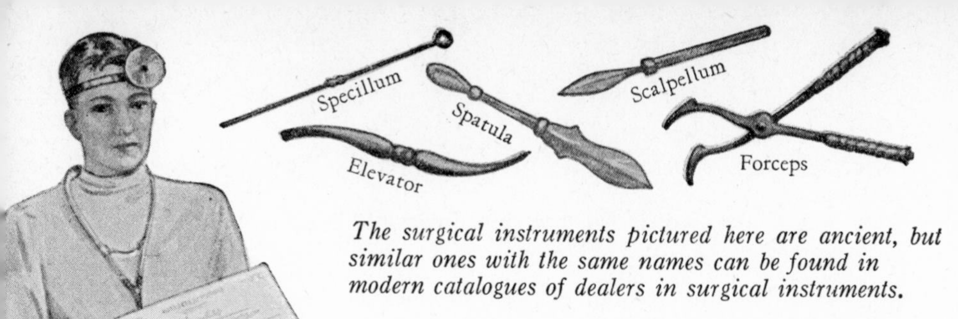

The surgical instruments pictured here are ancient, but similar ones with the same names can be found in modern catalogues of dealers in surgical instruments.

XCIV. MEDICAE ARTES

In patriā nostrā omnis medicus jūs jūrandum Hippocraticum dat. Antīquitus Hippocratēs, Graecus homō, clārissimus medicus erat.

Antīquissimus medicus fuit Aesculāpius. Is prīmō scientiam medicīnae didicit; posteā in numerō deōrum receptus est. Templa Aesculāpiī erant prīma valētūdināria. In hīs templīs aegrī dormiēbant et ā sacerdōtibus cūrābantur. Deus medicīnae etiam ā Rōmānīs honōrābātur. Hodiē ruīnae magnī templī Aesculāpiī vidērī in īnsulā Tiberis possunt. Rōmānī autem valētūdināria nōn sōlum domestica sed etiam mīlitāria habēbant, in quibus aegrī vulnerātīque sānābantur.

Multī Graecī medicī ad urbem Rōmam vēnērunt, ubi Rōmānōs dē medicīs artibus docuērunt et ipsī medicās artēs et chīrūrgiam tractābant. Galēnus etiam medicus persōnālis imperātōris Rōmānī erat. Fāma ejus erat maxima propter scientiam anatomiae et propter nōmina quae partibus corporis hūmānī dedit.

Quamquam Graecī clāriōrēs medicōs quam Rōmānī habēbant, tamen Rōmānī quoque medicōs clārōs habēbant. Inter eōs erat Celsus, quī fuit nōtissimus propter suōs librōs scrīptōs dē diaetā et exercitātiōne et chīrūrgiā et cēterīs rēbus.

THEN AND NOW

The Romans had **medici, medicae, vulnerarii** (or **chirurgi**), and **ocularii.** What would we call each of these today?

Medicamentum means "drug." Which picture shows the modern equivalent of a **medicamentarius?** Of a **medicus a dentibus?** Of a **nutrix?**

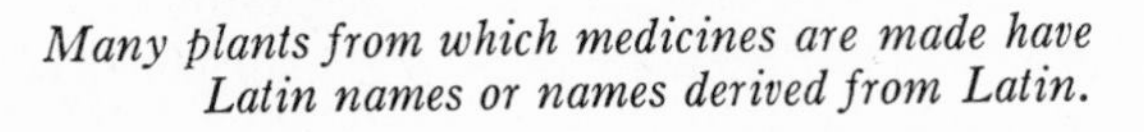
Many plants from which medicines are made have Latin names or names derived from Latin.

MIRABILE DICTU!

Digitalis is used as a heart stimulant. Can you see why it has a name meaning "thimble"?

Belladonna enlarges the pupil of the eye, and a drug from this plant has long been used to darken and beautify the eyes. The Italian name, *belladonna* (from Latin, **bella domina**), means "beautiful lady." What use do doctors now make of belladonna?

Sleeping drugs, often called "opiates," come from the juice of the **papaver.** What is our name for this plant?

Mentha piperita is found in the flavoring of candy and chewing gum, in toiletries, and in medicines. What is it?

Helleborus was believed by the ancients to cure insanity. Its powdered root is now used as an insecticide.

Aconitum gives us aconite, a sedative drug.

A doctor's prescription written in Latin can be filled by a pharmacist anywhere in the world.

THE ROMANS HAD A WORD FOR IT

Calvaria, *skull,* gave us the name *Calvary,* meaning "the place of the skull."

Musculus means "little mouse." The Romans thought a moving *muscle* looked like a mouse.

Patella, *kneecap,* is literally "a little pan."

Penicillum, *brush,* gave a name to the drug *penicillin,* made from a broom-shaped mold.

Find on the figure at the right the part of the body whose Latin name is related to each of the following English derivatives: *auricle, capital, cervical, clavicle, comet, digit, femoral, fibular, humeral, manual, nasal, oculist, oral, patellate, pedal, radius.*

The following parts are not pictured, but what English derivatives reveal their meaning? **appendix, arteria, cerebellum, cerebrum, corpusculum, cor (cordis), cuticula, nervus, palma, pulmo (pulmonis), vena, vertebra.**

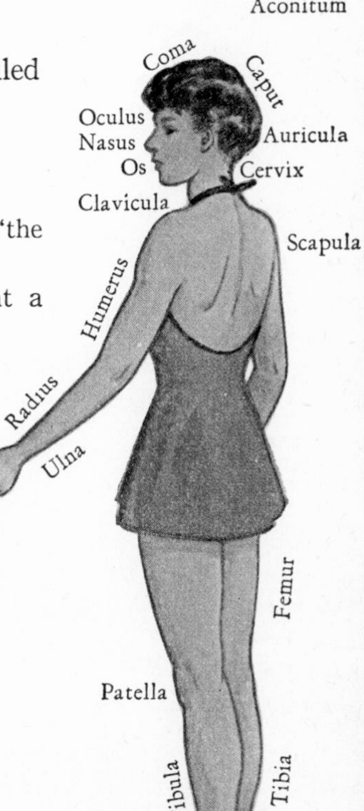

XCV. AGRICULTURA ROMANA

Antīquissimī Rōmānī habēbant agrōs parvōs quī ab agricolīs ipsīs et ā fīliīs eōrum colēbantur. Posteā autem multī Rōmānī maximōs fundōs habēbant quōs servī suī colēbant. Fundus optimus jūgerum CCXL esse putābātur.

Scrīptōrēs labōrēs agricolārum dēscrīpsērunt. Bovēs arātra, lignō dūrō facta, trahēbant. Prīmō vēre agricola impiger agrōs arābat; segetēs alternābat; serēbat frūmentum in agrō ubi anteā legūmina sēverat. Irrigātiōne solum āridum, dērīvātiōne solum palūdōsum juvābat.

Rōmānī frūmentum maximē serēbant. Segetēs falce caedēbantur; posteā trībulō frūmentum ā paleā sēparābātur. Hoc in āreā factum est.

Rōmānī autem bovēs, equōs, ovēs, caprōs colēbant. Animālibus optimīs dēlēctīs, agricolae pecora meliōra faciēbant. Apēs quoque saepe colēbantur, ā quibus mel acceptum est. Mel ā Vergiliō "caelestia dōna" appellābātur, quod sine magnō labōre acceptum est.

Vīta agricolārum minimē facilis erat, sed, ut Vergilius dīxit, "Labor omnia vīcit."

MIRABILE DICTU!

As a reward for military service, Roman soldiers were often given small sections of public lands. American soldiers likewise received part of their pay in land, after the American Revolution.

Vergil, Cato, and other Roman authors describe methods of cultivation that are both intelligent and scientific. Practices used by farmers two thousand years ago and still associated with successful farming are *rotation of crops, study of the soil, soil conservation, fertilizing, irrigation, drainage, pruning, threshing, culling of flocks, dipping of sheep, branding of cattle.*

At the left are a tribulum *and animals trampling out grain, with a modern thresher below. The space in the center—160 acres—equals CCXL* jugerum. *On the right are plows, old and new.*

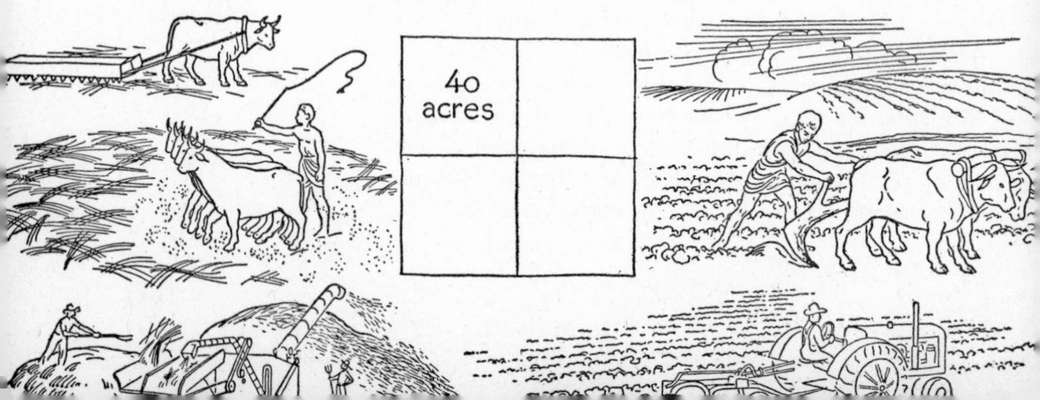

VOCABULARY FOR UNIT XX LESSONS XCII–XCV

arātrum, -ī, N., plow
caper, caprī, M., goat
chīrūrgia, -ae, F., surgery
chīrūrgus, -ī, M., surgeon
dērīvātiō, -ōnis, F., turning or drawing off (of water)
***diaeta, -ae,** F., diet
***ēlevātor, -ōris,** M., that which raises up; elevator
exercitātiō, -ōnis, F., exercise
faber, fabrī (*gen. pl.* **fabrum**), M., worker in wood, stone, or metal; engineer
falx, falcis, F., sickle, scythe
***forceps, -cipis** (*gen. pl.* **forcipium**), M. *and* F., tongs, pincers, forceps
fundus, -ī, M., bottom; farm
gubernō, -āre, -āvī, -ātum, pilot a ship; govern, direct
īnstituō, -ere, -uī, -ūtum, institute, establish, determine
***irrigātiō, -ōnis,** F., irrigation
jūgerum, -ī (*gen. pl.* **jūgerum**), N., juger (*two thirds of an acre*)
***jūrisprūdentia, -ae,** F., jurisprudence, the science of law
jūs, jūris, N., law; **jūs jūrandum, jūris jūrandī,** N., oath
legūmen, -inis, N., bean; any leguminous plant
medicāmentārius, -ī, M., druggist
medicāmentum, -ī, N., drug
***medicus, -a, -um,** of healing, medical; M. *and* F. *as noun*, physician, surgeon; **medicus ā dentibus,** dentist
mel, mellis, N., honey; sweetness
oculārius, -a, -um, of or relating to the eyes; M. *as noun*, oculist
ovis, ovis, F., sheep
palea, -ae, F., chaff
palūdōsus, -a, -um, marshy, boggy
pecus, pecoris, N., herd, cattle
praefectus, -ī, M., prefect, chief
sānō, -āre, -āvī, -ātum, heal, cure
***scalpellum, -ī,** N., scalpel; knife
***scientia, -ae,** F., knowledge, science
seges, -etis, F., crop
serō, -ere, sēvī, satum, sow, plant
solum, -ī, N., ground, earth
***spatula, -ae,** F., a broad piece; spatula
specillum, -ī, N., surgeon's probe
trībulum, -ī, N., threshing machine
ut, *adv.*, as
valētūdinārium, -ī, N., hospital
vēr, vēris, N., spring; **prīmō vēre,** in the beginning of spring
vulnerārius, -a, -um, of or relating to wounds; M. *as noun*, surgeon

LATIN LIVES TODAY

An *area* is now an amount of surface, but one meaning of the Latin word **area** is *a threshing floor*.

To the Romans, a person who was out of his mind was "out of the furrow" (**delirus,** from **de** + **lira**). What is the English word that describes this mental state?

To have *tribulations* literally means to be ground under and oppressed, as the Romans ground and pressed out their grain with a **tribulum.**

Work of an architect

A lawgiver

A doctor

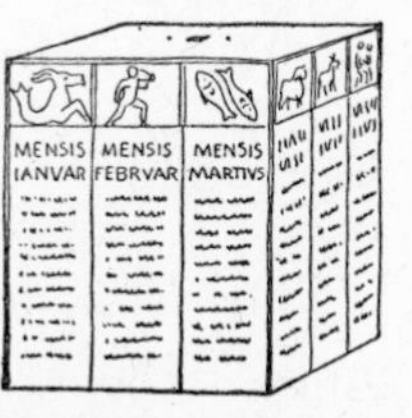

A calendar

Tria animālia in silvam iter faciēbant. Elephantus ante ursam ambulābat; ursa ante leōnem ambulābat; leō post ursam properābat.

Amīcī bonī per silvam et inter arborēs in locum apertum ambulāvērunt.

Sōl dē caelō per rāmōs fulgēbat (*was shining*). Animālia dēfessa sub arboribus sedēbant.

Posteā iterum ambulābant ursa cum leōne, elephantus sine comite. Ad flūmen pervēnērunt.

Piscēs (*fish*) in aquā vīsī ab ursā bonā capiēbantur. Interim elephantus sub aquam sē jēcit.

Tum elephantus trāns flūmen natāvit; cēnā parātā ab leōne ursāque, elephantus revēnit.

Post cēnam animālia circum arborēs currēbant. Leō suprā tergum elephantī saluit (*leaped*).

Nūbe vīsā, animālia ex silvā properāvērunt, timentia tempestātem.

Post hōrās grātās ad cavernam ubi ursa habitābat, animālia revēnērunt.

DE TRIBUS ANIMALIBUS

Read the story on page 352 and answer these questions.

1. Which prepositions in the story are followed by the accusative case?
2. Which are followed by the ablative?
3. Which prepositions may be followed by accusative or ablative? How can you tell which case is required?

Look at the pictures and answer these questions in Latin sentences, using prepositional phrases wherever you can.

1. Ante quod animal ursa in silvam ambulābat?
2. Post quod animal leō per silvam ambulābat?
3. Ubi animālia dēfessa sedēbant?
4. Ad quem locum animālia dēsīderantia aquam pervēnērunt?
5. Ā quō animālī piscēs in aquā vīsī capiēbantur?
6. Quid elephantus interim fēcit?
7. Ā quibus cēna parābātur?
8. Quid leō post cēnam fēcit?
9. Nūbe vīsā, quid animālia territa fēcērunt?

Make a Latin sentence using each of the following prepositional phrases.

circum vāllum	**dē perīculō**	**intrā mūrōs**	**prope flūmen**
contrā hostēs	**in hortum**	**per campōs**	**sine auxiliō**
cum difficultāte	**inter amīcōs**	**prō patriā**	**sub terram**

You can have fun working a Latin crossword puzzle. First copy the puzzle on a sheet of paper. This puzzle is made up of prepositional phrases: e.g., 1. *pro patria.* Watch your cases!

1. for country
2–9. before the lines of march
3–4. through ruins
5–6. within dry (places)
5–10. between kingdoms
7–8. after a journey
11. from a high (place)
12–13. in ships
14. from horses (on horseback)
15–16 into ships
17–18. across the forests
17–19. across the roof
19–20. with the mothers
21. under the stars
22–23. over the trees
24–27. against friends
25–26. without a horse

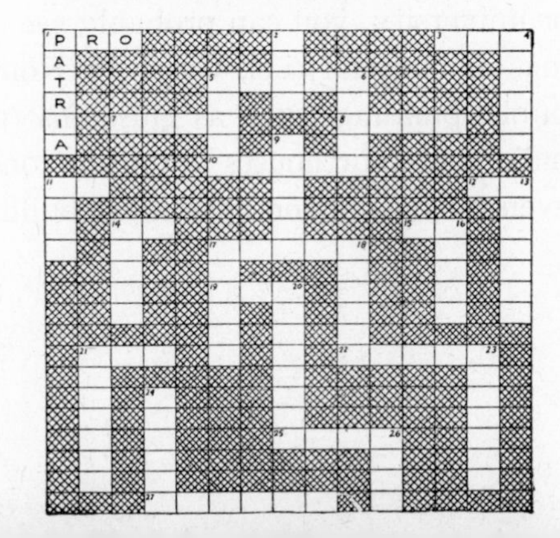

One of the famous buildings of ancie Rome was the Pantheon, a temp of all the gods.

ROME AND AMERICA

When Rome was at the height of its power, America had not yet been discovered. No Roman armies were ever sent out to conquer the territory now included within the boundaries of this country. Nevertheless, our daily lives in modern America are under the influence of the ageless civilization of Rome as surely as if our land had once been a part of the great Empire.

You have already seen that Latin lives today in the English language. One can scarcely speak or write a sentence without using words related to or taken directly from Latin. In fact, the number of our Latin derivatives is actually increasing. Among recent additions to the English language are *ignitron*, *ipsilateral*, *penicillin*, *prefabricate*, and *video*.

When you take a walk or a drive, you are almost certain to see buildings whose pillars, domes, and arches show that their designers were indebted to the architecture of Rome. If you live near a college or university, you can probably see on the campus one or more buildings of classical (i.e., Greek or Roman) design (p. 120). Moreover, public buildings such as museums (p. 16), state capitols (p. 17), city halls, and courthouses are often constructed in this style. You may even see houses and apartment buildings which reflect the influence of ancient architecture. In Washington, D.C., there are many such buildings—the Capitol (p. 9), the Supreme Court Building (p. 20), and the Jefferson Memorial (p. 24).

Architecture, however, is only one of the fields in which we find ourselves indebted to the Romans. In this book you have seen examples of Roman influence in the language of medicine and in its materials.

In law, too, you have observed that our use of Latin terms and our own legal procedures have been influenced by the language and laws of the Romans. Our great heritage of written law came to us from England, whose laws had for centuries been modeled after those of ancient Rome.

Modern science likewise owes a debt to Rome for many of its terms, since the Romans "had a word for it" when the English language had no suitable or convenient expression (pp. 67, 145, 146, 348-349). Some scientific practices have not changed much since Roman times, as you have seen in agriculture (pp. 350-351), as well as in medicine (pp. 348-349).

The books we read often reflect the influence of Latin language and literature in their titles, their allusions to Roman life, or their plots. Bulwer-Lytton's novel *The Last Days of Pompeii* has a Roman background, and Shakespeare's play *Julius Caesar* is based on Roman history. Thornton Wilder's *The Ides of March*, which gives a realistic picture of Rome in the time of Caesar, characterizes him and many of

The Low Library of olumbia University closely resembles the Pantheon

his contemporaries. Sometimes stories by Roman authors have been retold by modern writers; such tales make up Nathaniel Hawthorne's *A Wonder Book* and *Tanglewood Tales.* Ovid, an ancient writer who told in verse many myths of the Romans, provided Hawthorne with this story material. In this book you have read some of Ovid's stories (pp. 80, 115, 128, 132, 275).

In *Using Latin* there are also a number of stories taken from the Roman poet Vergil (pp. 124, 188, 223, 225, 231, 233, 236, 240, 243, 247, 250, 254, 257, 260), whose *Aeneid,* a long narrative in poetry, has been the source of many English poems and tales.

Julius Caesar—one of the greatest of the Romans—was famous not only for his military campaigns but also for the detailed accounts of them that he wrote. In these interesting commentaries on the experiences of Roman troops while fighting in Gaul, Germany, and Britain, he, as their commanding officer, provided accurate reports that were to become the basis for history. In much the same way, American officers in World War II—e.g., General George Marshall and General Dwight Eisenhower—sent back detailed reports from the front, some of which have appeared in book form. In each case the commander wrote history, though that was not his object.

In the realm of fine arts there are countless examples of classical influence. When we study music, we use many terms that come from Latin, e.g., *note, solo, duet, alto, major, minor, tempo, fugue, nocturne, furioso, maestoso.* Many Roman myths and legends are themes of operas, songs, and instrumental pieces. The operas *Orpheus and Eurydice, Paris and Helen,* and *Iphigenia in Aulis*—all by Christoph von

Gluck—and *Dido and Aeneas*, by Henry Purcell, are based on stories you have read in this book. Mozart's symphony in C Major, Opus 551, is known as the "Jupiter Symphony," while "The Pines of Rome" is a symphonic poem by Respighi.

An art gallery is an excellent place to observe classical influence. Here we see that the stories of ancient authors, including Ovid and Vergil, have inspired artists and sculptors. Anyone who knows the story behind a painting or a statue is able to understand and appreciate this work of art in a special way. Many of the paintings reproduced in this book are by famous artists, such as "Diana" (p. 64), by Correggio, and "The Cumaean Sibyl" (p. 118), by Michelangelo. The statue of "Paris and the Golden Apple" (p. 282) is by an ancient sculptor, while the head of Medusa (p. 138) is by the modern French artist Paul Dardon. Even in advertising art we find Roman influence. The picture of Icarus (p. 172) was used as a full-page advertisement in several magazines, and the drawing of Hercules (p. 98) is the symbol of a well-known powder company.

Thus, in our daily life, in work and play, we Americans are using and enjoying our heritage from ancient Rome to an extent unrealized until we study the language, literature, and life of the people who lived on the seven hills two thousand years ago.

LATIN WORDS AND PHRASES IN COMMON USE

Ad astra per aspera, to the stars through difficulties
Ad infinitum, to infinity; endlessly
Ad libitum (ad lib.), at pleasure
Alter ego, a second self
Anguis in herba, a snake in the grass
Ars est celare artem, it is (true) art to conceal art.
Ars longa, vita brevis, art (is) long, life (is) short.
Bis dat qui cito dat, he gives twice who gives quickly.
Carpe diem, seize the opportunity.
Causa sine qua non, an indispensable condition
Cave canem, beware of the dog!
Ceteris paribus, other things being equal
Cogito, ergo sum, I think, therefore I am.
Corpus delicti, the substantial facts that prove a crime (the body of a crime)
Cui bono, of what use is it? (To whom is it for a benefit?)
Cum grano salis, with a grain of salt
De novo, anew; afresh
Divide et impera, divide and rule.
Ecce homo, behold the man!
E pluribus unum, one out of many
Errare humanum est, to err is human.
Ex animo, from the heart; sincerely
Exempli gratia (e.g.), for example
Ex libris, from the books (of)
Fortes fortuna juvat, fortune favors the brave.
Hic jacet—, here lies—
Id est (i.e.), that is
In memoriam, in memory (of)
In toto, in the whole; entirely
Laborare est orare, to work is to pray.
Labor omnia vincit, labor conquers all things.
Lapsus linguae, a slip of the tongue
Lapsus memoriae, a slip of the memory
Loco citato (loc. cit.), in the place quoted
Magnum opus, a great work
Memoria in aeterna, in everlasting remembrance
Mens sana in corpore sano, a sound mind in a sound body
Mirabile dictu, wonderful to tell
Morituri te salutamus, we, about to die, salute you.
Multum in parvo, much in little
Natura abhorret a vacuo, nature abhors a vacuum.
Nota bene (N. B.), note well.
Pax vobiscum, peace (be) with you.
Pro bono publico, for the public good
Pro tempore, for the time being; temporarily
Qui docet, discet, he who teaches, learns.
Sic semper tyrannis, so (be it) ever to tyrants.
Sic transit gloria mundi, so passes away the glory of the world.
Status quo, the state in which (a thing is or was)
Summum bonum, the supreme good
Sursum corda, (lift) up your hearts.
Tempus fugit, time flies.
Veni, vidi, vici, I came, I saw, I conquered.
Via media, a middle way
Vice versa, the other way round; conversely
Vox populi, vox Dei, the voice of the people (is) the voice of God.

HORATIUS

Porsena, rēx Etrūscōrum

Sextus Tarquinius, fīlius Tarquiniī Superbī

Mamilius, rēx Tusculī, socius Porsenae

Scaena Prīma

Tarquinius Superbus, rēx Rōmānōrum, exul (*exile*)

Vigilēs, Etrūscī

Ducēs Mīlitum, Etrūscī

Scaena Secunda

Valerius, *Pulvillus* — cōnsulēs Rōmānī

Horātius Cocles, *Spurius Lartius*, *Titus Herminius* — senātōrēs Rōmānī

Vigil Prīmus, *Vigil Secundus* — Rōmānī

Cīvēs, Rōmānī

Mīlitēs, Etrūscī

SCAENA PRĪMA—IN CASTRĪS ETRŪSCŌRUM

Vesperī. Porsena ante tabernāculum suum stat; ā dextrā est Mamilius; ā sinistrā Tarquinius Superbus; ā tergō Sextus Tarquinius. Ante Porsenam ducēs mīlitum imperāta expectant. Longē ā dextrā stant vigilēs; hī Rōmam procul vident.

Porsena. Bene pugnāvistis hodiē, Ō ducēs, vōs et mīlitēs Etrūscī.

Ducēs. Grātiās tibi agimus, rēx maxime; prō patriā et prō tē fortiter pugnāvimus.

Porsena. Quō nōmine hic mōns appellātur, ubi jam castra posuimus?

Sextus. Jāniculum vocātur hic mōns.

T. Superbus. Jāniculum habēmus; facile erit Rōmam capere.

Ducēs. Bene nōs dūxit Mamilius, Ō rēx maxime.

Porsena. Hoc sciō; audīte. Dīc nōbīs, Mamilī, dē pugnā. Quō modō (*how*) Jāniculum cēpistī?

Mamilius. Ō rēx, Jāniculum tenēbat Pulvillus cōnsul cum centum mīlitibus; juvenis est et malus dux; imperāta ejus mala sunt, neque Rōmānī semper imperāta ejus faciunt. At diū resistēbant; neque facile erat illud parvum agmen dē monte pellere (*to drive*). Tandem centum mīlitēs circum montem mīsī; hī ā tergō Rōmānōs subitō oppugnāvērunt. Pulvillus territus tergum vertit (*turned*); cum quīnquāgintā (*fifty*) hominibus fūgit; cēterōs occīdimus.

Porsena. Bene fēcistī, Mamilī. Dīc nōbīs plūs.

Mamilius. Ille, tertius (*third*) in ōrdine (*rank*) ducum [ūnum ex ducibus mōnstrat], prīmus in summum montem pervēnit. Hostēs illum vulnerāverant et signiferum (*standard-bearer*) occīderant. Statim ille signum ē dextrā mortuī cēpit et in summō monte posuit.

Porsena. Bene fēcistī, Mamilī; bene fēcērunt tuī mīlitēs. Tū, dux vulnerāte, hūc venī. [Dux tertius lēniter appropinquat.] Laetus sum quod tam fortēs mīlitēs habeō. Accipe hoc praemium. [Ducī armillam (*bracelet*) dat. Tum dux in ōrdinem redit.] Crās Rōmam oppugnābimus.

Ducēs [laetīs clāmōribus]. Crās Rōmam capiēmus.

T. Superbus. Crās rēx iterum erō Rōmānōrum.

Sextus. Crās omnēs inimīcōs occīdam.

T. Superbus. Crās omnēs nōbilēs in vinculīs erunt.

Sextus. Dolor victīs! Nōs ex urbe expulērunt.

T. Superbus. Ignāvī hominēs rēgem habēre nōn dēsīderant; crās poenās dabunt (*they will pay the penalty*).

Ducēs [parvā vōce]. Fortēs, nōn ignāvī, sunt Rōmānī. Fortēs hostēs amāmus; ignāvōs nōn amāmus amīcōs.

Porsena. Quō tempore et quō modō Rōmam oppugnābimus?

Sextus. Statim hoc faciēmus; sī Rōmānī pontem (*bridge*) frangent, neque Tiberim trānsīre neque urbem intrāre poterimus.

Ducēs. Nōs quidem hodiē diū pugnāvimus; sine somnō mīlitēs nōn bene pugnābunt.

T. Superbus. Vigil! Vigil!

Vigil. Quid dēsīderās, Ō rēx?

T. Superbus. Quid nunc Rōmānī faciunt?

Vigil. Omnēs in urbem recessērunt. Vigilēs tamen ē moenibus spectant.

Porsena. Frēgēruntne pontem?

Vigil. Minimē, Ō rēx! Stat pōns.

Porsena. Eritne nox clāra aut obscūra?

Vigil. Obscūra; nūbēs in caelō sunt, neque lūna fulgēbit (*will be shining*). Etiam nunc vigilēs Rōmānōs vidēre nōn possumus; nōn jam pōns in cōnspectū est; hāc nocte caecī erunt vigilēs.

Porsena. Bene dīxistis, vigilēs. Hoc igitur cōnsilium audīte. Quārtā vigiliā, dum Rōmānī dormiunt, ad pontem silentiō appropinquābimus. Nōs neque vidēre neque audīre vigilēs poterunt. Nūllā morā pontem trānsībimus et per portam facile intrābimus, dum Rōmānī territī arma petunt. Resistere nōn poterunt.

Ducēs. Bonum cōnsilium cēpistī, Ō rēx. Vincēmus.

Porsena. Hoc cōnsilium, ducēs, mīlitibus nūntiāte. Deinde ad quārtam vigiliam dormīte.

Ducēs. Audīmus et imperāta faciēmus.

Porsena. Vigilēs, cum quārta vigilia erit, ē somnō nōs omnēs excitāte.

Vigilēs. Audīmus et imperāta faciēmus.

SCAENA SECUNDA—IN URBE ROMĀ

Ā sinistrā appārent (*appear*) moenia urbis; Tiberis praeter moenia fluit; rīpam ulteriōrem (*farther*) ad portam urbis jungit pōns. Vigilēs ē summīs moenibus spectant. In rīpā ulteriōre agmen Etrūscōrum ad pontem silentiō appropinquat, sed adhūc procul abest, cum sōl surgere (*to rise*) incipit. Prīmā lūce vigilēs hostēs vident.

Vigil I. Audīsne sonum?

Vigil II. Quam timidus es! Ventus aquam agitat.

Vigil I. Pedēs hominum audiō.

Vigil II. Nōlī hoc crēdere. Sōl mox surget; tum vidēre poterimus.

Vigil I. Hominēs videō.

Vigil II. Agmen est. Hostēs appropinquant.

Vigil I. Surgite (*arise*), Rōmānī. Hostēs adsunt.

Vigilēs. Surgite, Rōmānī. Hostēs adsunt.

Cīvēs armātī portam aperiunt et circumspectant. Valerius et Pulvillus in pontem currunt.

Valerius. Frangite pontem, cīvēs.

Pulvillus. Tempus nōn dabunt hostēs. Heu! Nōs prīmōs occīdent. Quid facere possumus? Ad quem locum fugere dēbēmus?

Valerius. Silē, ignāve! Cūr herī mīlitēs frangere pontem nōn jussistī? Tū imperātor erās. Hodiē ego imperāta dō. [Pulvillus in urbem redit. Multī cīvēs in portā appārent.] Audīte, cīvēs. Urbs dēfendī dēbet. Urbem dēfendēmus. Sī duo aut trēs breve tempus resistere poterunt, cēterī pontem frangent. Ita urbem servāre poterimus.

Horātius [inter cīvēs appāret]. Ego, Ō cōnsul, pontem dēfendam. Quis mēcum hoc prō patriā faciet?

Spurius [ex cīvibus prōcēdit]. Ego tuus socius erō, fortis Horātī.

Horātius. Tū bonus eris socius. Tēcum bene pugnābō. Tamen sī trēs erimus, tōtum hostium agmen facile repellēmus.

Titus [ex cīvibus prōcēdit]. Ecce, tertius erō. Prō Rōmā et Rōmānīs cum hīs comitibus pugnābō.

Horātius. Vōbīs agō grātiās. Vērī amīcī estis.

Cīvēs. Vōbīs grātiās agimus.

Etrūscī appropinquant.

Porsena. Currite, mīlitēs. Pontem occupāte.

Valerius. Properāte; currunt hostēs.

Trēs pontem trānseunt.

Horātius. Ego medius stābō; tū, Spurī, ā dextrā stā; Tite, tū ā sinistrā.

Etrūscī ad pontem perveniunt.

Porsena. Oppugnāte, mīlitēs. Illōs trēs occīdite et urbem intrāte.

Valerius. Secūrēs (*axes*) capite, cīvēs. Capite gladiōs. Frangite pontem.

Porsena. Mamilī, mēcum manē! Herī satis pugnābās. Sextus contrā suam urbem hominēs dūcet.

Valerius. Dā mihi secūrem, tū! Ita, ita, lignum (*the wood*) frangite.

Ipse pontem ferit (*strikes*) dum mīlitēs Etrūscī pontem oppugnant.

Spurius. Cavē (*beware*), Tite! Ā sinistrā oppugnābunt.

Titus. Parātus sum; ecce, undique veniunt.

Horātius. Dūra verbera (*blows*) date. Nōn multī eōdem tempore nōs oppugnāre possunt.

Pulvillus [in moenibus appāret]. Venīte, virī, ad moenia. [Multī cīvēs in moenia veniunt.] Sagittās mittite. Jacula jacite.

Sextus. Mēcum venīte, mīlitēs. Ego Horātium occīdam.

Cīvēs. Cujus vōcem audīmus?

Vigil I. Sextus Tarquinius hostēs dūcit.

Cīvēs. Apage (*begone*), perfide Sexte! Audēsne ad urbem revenīre?

Sextus. Mox alia clāmābitis, cum in vinculīs eritis.

Cīvēs. Occīde Sextum, Ō Horātī. Etiam sī hostēs nōs vīcerint, laetī erimus, quod perfidus Sextus mortuus erit.

Sextus Horātium oppugnat; Spurius et Titus contrā aliōs pugnant.

Pulvillus. Cavēte (*beware*), sagittāriī. Nōlīte nostrōs occīdere. Cavēte, jaculātōrēs (*javelin-throwers*). Suprā capita nostrōrum jacula jacite.

Vigil II. Uter vincet? Ecce, noster illum ferit!

Cīvēs. Iō triumphe (*Hurrah*)! Mortuus est Sextus.

Pulvillus. Minimē, surgit. Horātī, iterum ferī (*strike*).

Alter (*another*) Horātium oppugnat, dum Mamilius Sextum ē perīculō trahit.

Cīvēs. Quis Sextum juvat?

Pulvillus. Mamilius.

Cīvēs. Ecce, Sextum ē perīculō trahit.

Vigil I. Nunc redit; ipse Horātium oppugnābit.

Cīvēs. Heu! Nōn mortuus est Sextus.

Valerius. Auxilium date, cīvēs; ecce, paene frāctus est pōns.

Cīvēs. Spurius hostem occīdit; nunc alterum ferit.

Vigil II. Heu! Horātium vulnerāvit Mamilius.

Cīvēs. Heu! Spurī, auxilium dā.

Vigil I. Ecce, Mamilium repellunt.

Valerius [magnā vōce]. Redīte, Rōmānī. Paene frāctus est pōns. Jam jam (*right now*) redī, Horātī.

Cīvēs. Redīte, Rōmānī. Paene frāctus est pōns. Vōs servāte.

Horātius. Statim redīte, comitēs. Dum tempus manet, redīte.

Spurius. / *Titus.* Tū etiam nōbīscum redī. Sine tē nōn redībimus.

Cīvēs. Redīte, fortēs virī. Jam jam cadit (*is falling*) pōns.

Horātius. Redīte, comitēs. Cōnsilium habeō bonum; mē hostēs nōn occīdent.

Spurius.
Titus. } Imperāta tua faciēmus. Valē.

Ad portam redeunt.

Cīvēs. Nōlīte Horātium relinquere.
Spurius. Ipse imperāta dedit. Imperāta faciēmus.

Spurius et Titus nunc urbem intrant.

Cīvēs. Sērō (*too late*) redībis, Horātī. Cadit pōns.
Horātius [scūtum ad cīvēs jacit]. Capite, cīvēs, scūtum. Nōn laudābile est scūtum relinquere. [Gladium in hostēs jacit.] Hostēs, gladium capite. Tibi mē committō, Tiberis.

Dum pōns cadit, Horātius in flūmen sē jacit.

Pulvillus. Quid facit? Vulnerātus est; nōn potest natāre.
Cīvēs. Ita. Flūmen trānsit; ad portam natat.
Valerius. Jacite fūnēs (*ropes*)!

Cīvēs fūnem jaciunt.

Cīvēs. Fūnem capit. Trahite! Trahite!
Omnēs. Trahite! Trahite!

Cīvēs Horātium ex aquā in portam trahunt.

Valerius.
Pulvillus. } Senātus tibi grātiās agit.
Cīvēs. Populus Rōmānus tibi grātiās agit.
Omnēs. Rōmam servāvistī.

CIRCE

Ulīxēs, quī ad rēgnum suum iter facit

Eurylochus, comes et amīcus Ulīxis

Scaena Prīma

Aegyptius, *Philippus*, *Menexenus*, *Alexander*, *Crēsius* — nautae

Cēterī nautae

Scaena Secunda

Naupactōus, *Proxenus*, *Rhodius* — nautae

Circē, maga

Ancillae (maids) *quattuor*

Minister (butler)

Coquus (cook)

Servus alius

SCAENA PRĪMA—IN LĪTORE ĪNSULAE

In saxō stat Eurylochus; circum eum vīgintī nautae, aliī (*some*) in terrā sedent, aliī (*others*) stant; omnēs parvā vōce dīcunt.

Eurylochus. Nōlīte ducem nostrum culpāre.

Aegyptius. At quis nōs in īnsulam dēsertam dūxit?

Nautae. Respondē, Ō Euryloche! Nōnne Ulīxēs?

Eurylochus. Ita, magnus Ulīxēs vōs hūc dūxit; sed nōlīte illum culpāre.

Philippus. Cūr nōn dēbēmus illum culpāre?

Nautae. Respondē, Ō Euryloche. Cūr nōn dēbēmus illum culpāre?

Eurylochus. Quod dī immortālēs [caelum mōnstrat] nōs et illum in haec perīcula dūxērunt.

Menexenus. Sī dī Ulīxem nōn amant, nōn jam noster erit dux.

Nautae. Vērum dīcis; nōn jam noster erit dux.

Alexander. Ēsuriō (*I am hungry*); dā mihi cibum, Euryloche.

Omnēs. Ēsurīmus; dā nōbīs cibum, Euryloche.

Eurylochus. Nōnne magnus Ulīxēs in mediās silvās iit, quod cibum nōbīs petere cupiēbat?

Aegyptius. Sī bēstiās arcū occīdet, ipse eās edet (*he will eat*).

Omnēs. Ipse carnem (*flesh*) edet avium et bēstiārum.

Philippus. Nihil nōbīs dabit. Hoc prō certō habeō.

Omnēs. Nihil nōbīs dabit. Hoc prō certō habēmus.

Eurylochus. Ō stultī, fidēlis est noster dux; cibum vōbīs dabit.

Menexenus [quī circum sē spectat]. Hominem quī appropinquat videō.

Nautae. Estne hostis an (*or*) amīcus quī appropinquat?

Menexenus. Nesciō (*I don't know*); procul abest. Nōn possum bene vidēre.

Aliī nautae nunc stant.

Alexander. Ecce, dē summō colle dēscendit.
Nautae. Quis est? Quās vestēs, quae arma gerit?
Crēsius. Arcum sagittāsque portat; ad nōs venit.
Omnēs. Ulīxēs est.
Aegyptius. Quid umerīs portat?
Philippus. Animal portat.
Omnēs. Ō magnum Ulīxem! Ō optimum ducem!
Ulīxis Vōx. Cervum sagittā occīdī. Cibum ad vōs portō. Carnem (*meat*) edēmus omnēs.
Omnēs. Iō, Iō! (*hurrah*), Ō magnum Ulīxem! Ō optimum ducem!
Eurylochus. Ligna petite, nautae. Properāte!

Dum Ulīxēs appropinquat, nautae ligna per lītus petunt et in mediō pōnunt.

Menexenus. Rēmum (*oar*) frāctum invēnī, quī in lītore nōn procul jacēbat.
Alexander. Rāmōs portō, quī dē arbore cecidērunt (*fell*).
Crēsius. } Grave est id quod portāmus; gubernāculum (*rudder*)
Aegyptius. } portāmus nāvis nostrae, quod mare in lītus jēcit.

Ulīxēs appāret (*appears*) et cervum in terrā pōnit.

Eurylochus. Salvē (*hail*), Ulīxēs! Nautae, ignem accendite.

Nautae. Nōn possumus ignem accendere. Ō sapientissime omnium hominum [Ulīxī hoc dīcunt], hoc prō nōbīs fac, quod ēsurīmus et quam prīmum (*as soon as possible*) cēnāre cupimus.

Eurylochus [dum Ulīxēs ignem accendit]. Jam sapiēns et magnus est is quī pessimus ducum erat.

Ulīxēs in saxō sedet; nautae in summō igne cervum pōnunt. Tum circum Ulīxem et ignem sedent.

Ulīxēs. Per silvam errābam, cum hunc cervum vīdī—

Menexenus. Dulcis (*sweet*) est fūmus.

Ulīxēs. Mē post arborem cēlāvī—

Alexander [sonum labrīs (*lips*) facit]. Dulcem cibum jam gustō (*I taste*).

Ulīxēs. Ventus ad mē flābat (*blew*); nōn igitur mē olfacere (*smell*) cervus poterat.

Crēsius. Sed ego carnem olfaciō dulcissimam.

Ulīxēs. Sagittam arcumque parāvī.

Aegyptius. Nōs quidem cēnam parāmus.

Ulīxēs. Sagittā prīmā cervī caput trānsfīxī. Nōnne magna et pulchra sunt cornua, Ō Euryloche?

Philippus. Magna et pulchra erit cēna.

Menexenus. Jam certē tostus (*roasted*) est cervus. Ēsuriō. Statim edere cupiō.

Omnēs. Statim edere cupimus.

Ulīxēs. Edite, comitēs. Laetus sum quod nōn jam ēsuriētis.

Eurylochus. Edite, vōs quī suibus (*pigs*) estis similēs; nihil praeter cēnam cibumque in mentem vestram venit.

Nautae cervum dīvidunt et carnem vorant (*devour*). Interim Ulīxēs nārrat.

Ulīxēs. Postquam cervum occīdī, circum mē spectāre incēpī. Inter arborēs appārēbat tēctum. Fūmus inde (*from it*) ascendēbat.

Alexander. Sine dubiō cēnam parābant.

Nautae. Carō (*meat*) dulcis est! Libenter iterum carnem dulcem gustāmus.

Crēsius. Nōnne ad illud tēctum iistī, Ō dux?

Ulīxēs. Minimē. In mentem meam vēnit famēs (*hunger*) comitum meōrum. Ad vōs igitur quam prīmum cibum portāvī.

Aegyptius. Crās ad illud tēctum ībimus. Quid putātis, comitēs?

Nautae. Probāmus; ad eum locum ībimus.

Menexenus. Fortasse (*perhaps*) ibi multam carnem et bene tostam inveniēmus.

Eurylochus. Glandēs (*acorns*) in silvā inveniētis.

SCAENA SECUNDA—IN ĀTRIŌ CIRCAE

Nēmō in ātriō adest; sed per jānuam quae ā dextrā est nunc fēminās quae rīdent (*are laughing*), nunc suēs quī edunt audītis. Ā sinistrā intrant Ulīxēs et Eurylochus et trēs nautae, Naupactōus, Proxenus, Rhodius.

Naupactōus. Ubi sunt comitēs nostrī?

Proxenus. Eōs neque videō neque audiō.

Rhodius. At vōcēs audiō.

Eurylochus. Certē, fēminās quae rīdent audīs.

Naupactōus. Nōnne suēs audītis, comitēs, quī edunt?

Proxenus. Fēmina nunc cantat.

Ulīxēs. Circē, maga, pessima fēminārum, cantat quod nostrōs comitēs perdidit (*has destroyed*).

Rhodius. Nōnne nōs etiam perdet (*will destroy*)?

Ulīxēs. Priōrēs (*first*) eam oppugnābimus.

Naupactōus. At sī baculum (*wand*) illud agitābit, nōnne mortuī nōs omnēs erimus?

Ulīxēs. Sī omnia quae nunc jubēbō faciētis, eam vincēmus.

Eurylochus. Imperāta faciēmus, Ō dux noster, vir sapiēns. Quid jubēs?

Nautae. Imperāta tua faciēmus omnēs.

Ulīxēs. Apud (*in the house of*) hanc fēminam nōlīte edere (*eat*), nōlīte bibere (*drink*).

Omnēs. Nihil hīc edēmus, nihil bibēmus.

Ulīxēs. Etiam sī ego cibum et pōculum (*the bowl*) accipiam, nōlīte idem facere.

Rhodius. Cūr tū id faciēs quod nōs facere vetās (*you forbid*)?

Ulīxēs. Hunc quem teneō flōrem (*flower*) Mercurius mihi dedit. Dōnum mīrum est.

Proxenus. Quō modō tē dēfendere hic flōs potest?

Ulīxēs. Dum hunc olfaciō (*smell*), Circē mē laedere (*harm*) nōn poterit.

Eurylochus. Silēte omnēs. Quis jānuam aperit?

Ulīxēs. In memoriā tenēte id quod jussī, et imperāta mea facite!

Intrat Circē cum ancillīs quattuor.

Circē. Salvē, Ō Ulīxēs.

Ancilla I. Salvē, Ō Euryloche.

Ancilla II. Salvē, Ō Naupactōe.

Ancilla III. Salvē, Ō Proxene.

Ancilla IV. Salvē, Ō Rhodī.

Ulīxēs. Salvē, Ō rēgīna. Tē, quae meum nōmen scīs, quō modō (*how*) vocābō?

Eurylochus [ancillae I]. Quō modō (*how*) nōmen meum scīs?

Naupactōus [ancillae II]. Quō modō nōmen meum scīs?

Proxenus [ancillae III]. Quō modō nōmen meum scīs?

Rhodius [ancillae IV]. Quō modō nōmen meum scīs?

Circē. Salvēte (*greetings*), omnēs advenae. Nōmen meum nōlīte rogāre, sed vīnum meum bibite (*drink*) et carnēs meās edite (*eat*). [Signum dat.]

Intrat minister quī quīnque pōcula portat.

Minister. Adsum, O rēgīna.

Ancillae. Dā nōbīs pōcula.

Minister eīs quattuor pōcula dat. Circē signum dat. Intrat servus quī amphoram (*jar*) portat.

Servus. Adsum, Ō rēgīna.

Circē. Appropinquā, serve. [Dum baculum suprā amphoram agitat, venēnum (*poison*) in vīnum mittit.] Tibi, Ō Juppiter, vīnum cōnsecrō.

Ulīxēs [nautīs]. Cavēte (*beware of*) vīnum.

Servus vīnum in pōcula fundit (*pours*).

Servus [vōce magnā]. Aurea mīrō complēvī (*I have filled*) pōcula vīnō.

Circē. Mihi dā pōculum, Ō minister.

Minister [vōce magnā]. Hōc vīnō acceptō, Ulīxēs, sapientior eris.

Ulīxēs. Tum erō tam sapiēns quam vulpēs (*as wise as a fox*).

Circē. Hoc prōmittō. Accipe, Ō rēx. Rēgīna tibi vīnum dat.

Ancilla I. Accipe, Ō Euryloche: ancilla rēgīnae tibi vīnum dat.

Ancilla II. Accipe, Ō Naupactōe; ancilla rēgīnae tibi vīnum dat.
Ancilla III. Accipe, Ō Proxene; ancilla rēgīnae tibi vīnum dat.
Ancilla IV. Accipe, Ō Rhodī; ancilla rēgīnae tibi vīnum dat.

Virī ā fēminīs pōcula accipiunt. Rhodius sē post columnam cēlat.

Ulīxēs. Mē spectāte. [Interim Eurylochus et Naupactōus et Proxenus vīnum in terrā fundunt (*pour*), sed Rhodius bibit.] Vīnum bibō, grātus quod nōbīs advenīs tam benigna es, Ō rēgīna. [Flōrem olfacit, dum vīnum bibit (*drinks*).]

Omnēs Ulīxem diū spectant.

Ulīxēs. Cūr mē spectātis? Bonum est vīnum quod advenīs dās, Ō rēgīna; dī tibi praemium meritum (*deserved*) dabunt.
Circē [baculum agitat]. Vulpēs eris! Hoc jubeō.
Ulīxēs. Quid facis? Quid dīcis? [Rīdet.] Ah! Jam sciō; tam sapiēns sum quam vulpēs.
Ancilla I. Estne tibi vīnum grātum, Euryloche? Quid sentīs?
Eurylochus. Dulce est hoc vīnum.
Ancilla II. Et tū, Naupactōe, quid dīcis?
Naupactōus. Numquam anteā tam dulce vīnum bibī.
Ancilla III. Nōnne optimum est vīnum, Ō Proxene?
Proxenus. Deīs idōneum est—[sibi dīcit] sed nōn hominibus.
Ancilla IV. Tibine grātum est vīnum, Ō Rhodī?

Rhodius suis sonum facit et suī similis ex ātriō currit. Ulīxēs nihil videt.

Naupactōus. Vīdistīne suem quī ex ātriō currēbat?
Proxenus. Sed ubi est Rhodius? Maximē timeō.
Eurylochus. Nōlī timēre; Ulīxēs nōs servābit.
Ulīxēs. Dīc mihi, Ō rēgīna. Aliīne hīc adsunt apud (*with*) tē advenae?
Circē. Multās bēstiās apud mē habeō, sed hominēs nūllōs.
Ulīxēs. Ante hōs duōs diēs (*two days ago*) comitēs meī, nautae, ad tēctum tuum vēnērunt, quod ēsuriēbant.
Circē. Ita est. Illīs cibum dedī; hominēs mox discessērunt.
Ancillae [rīdent]. Suēs tamen apud nōs manent.
Nautae. Quid dīcitis? Nōn suēs erant comitēs nostrī, sed virī.

Circē signum dat. Intrat coquus quī cibum in paterā (*dish*) portat.

Coquus. Adsum, Ō rēgīna.

Circē. Quid portās?

Coquus [vōce magnā]. Ambrosiam (*ambrosia*) advenīs dulcem fēlīcibus portō.

Circē. Bibistis (*you have drunk*), Ō advenae; nunc edite (*eat*).

Ulīxēs [nautīs]. Cavēte cibum.

Circē [baculum suprā cibum agitat]. Tibi, Ō Juppiter, hunc cibum cōnsecrō. [Deinde Ulīxī dat.]

Omnēs cibum accipiunt.

Ulīxēs [subitō clāmat]. Ubi est Rhodius?

Dum omnēs circumspectant, nautae carnēs in terrā jaciunt.

Ancilla IV. Ex ātriō fūgit—[parvā vōce] sūs.

Rīdent ancillae.

Ulīxēs. Cibum edō et tibi, Ō rēgīna, grātiās agō.

Omnēs diū spectant.

Circē [baculum agitat]. Tandem vulpēs eris! Hoc ego, Circē, jubeō.

Ulīxēs [rīdēns]. Tē cognōscō, fēmina deīs hominibusque odiōsa, mala maga. Nihil facere potes. [Gladium capit.] Tē et tuās ancillās occīdam, quod multōs hominēs jam perdidistis.

Circē. Nōlī mē occīdere, Ō rēx! Nōn iterum hominēs laedam; hoc prōmittō.

Ulīxēs. Sī tē occīdam, hoc prō certō habēbō.

Eurylochus. Ubi sunt nostrī comitēs? Jubē eam, Ō Ulīxēs, hoc dīcere.

Circē. Sī tibi hoc dīcam, tūta erō?

Ulīxēs. Sī hoc faciēs, tūta eris.

Circē [baculum agitat]. Ō suēs, quī comitēs Ulīxis fuistis, este iterum hominēs.

Intrant cēterī nautae, quī comitēs salūtant.

Ulīxēs. Nōlī iterum hominem in bēstiae fōrmam mūtāre! Hoc jūrā (*swear*)!

Circē. Hoc jūrō.

Ancillae [lacrimant]. Hoc jūrāmus quod rēgīna jūrāvit.

Ulīxēs. Abīte (*begone*), miserae.

Fēminae discēdunt; nautae laetī sunt.

PUER AEGER

Octāvia, Titī māter
Medicus (*doctor*)
Titus, puer Rōmānus, duodecim annōs nātus (*twelve years old*)
Lūcius, *Pūblius* } Titī frātrēs, geminī, septem annōs nātī (*twins, seven years old*)

SCAENA—IN CUBICULŌ (*bedroom*) PUERŌRUM

A sinistrā stat lātus lectulus (*bed*); ibi dormiunt trēs puerī, Titus et Lūcius et Pūblius. Ā dextrā est fenestra, ā tergō jānua. Gallus (*rooster*) extrā (*outside*) cantat et puerōs ē somnō excitat.

Titus. Quota (*what*) hōra est?

Lūcius [ad fenestram currit]. Prīma hōra paene est. Sōl mox surget (*will rise*).

Titus. Ō mē miserum! Pēnsum (*lesson*) meum nōn fēcī. Quid magister dīcet?

Pūblius. Vērum dīcis. Quid faciet magister?

Titus. Jam ferulam (*rod*) sentiō. Ad lūdum (*school*) īre nōn audeō.

Lūcius. Laetus sum quod nōndum (*not yet*) ad lūdum īmus, ego et Pūblius.

Titus. Quālēs (*what kind of*) frātrēs estis! Quod vāpulābō (*I shall be beaten*) laetī estis.

Lūcius et Pūblius [saltant (*jump up and down*) et cantant]. Titus vāpulābit; Titus vāpulābit.

Titus [īrātus]. Vōs etiam vāpulābitis.

Frātrēs loculīs ferit (*strikes with his book-satchel*).

Lūcius et Pūblius [lacrimant]. Lacrimāmus, quod Titus vāpulābit. Lacrimāmus, quod Titus vāpulābit.

Titus. Quod vōs vāpulāvistis, lacrimātis. Iterum autem lacrimābitis, nisi (*unless*) bonum cōnsilium mihi inveniētis. Ego vāpulāre hodiē nōn dēsīderō.

Pūblius. Cōnsilium habeō.

Titus et Lūcius. Dīc nōbīs.

Pūblius. Manēte; cōgitō (*I am thinking*).

Titus. Celeriter, Pūblī. Ō mē miserum, vāpulābō.

Lūcius. Fortasse (*perhaps*) malum Pūblius habet cōnsilium; tum vāpulābis, Tite.

Titus. Nisi statim cōnsilium nārrābis, iterum idem accipiēs.

Loculōs sūmit (*he picks up*).

Pūblius. Cōgitāvī. Audīte cōnsilium. Vesperī apud Quīntum (*at Quintus' house*) cēnābās.

Titus. Illud jam scīmus.

Pūblius. Bene, ibi nimis ēdistī (*you ate too much*).

Titus. Quid dīcere temptās? Semper nimis edō (*I eat*); tū quoque et Lūcius.

Pūblius. Certē, at tū hodiē aeger es, quod nimis vesperī ēdistī.

Titus. At nōn aeger sum, frāter!

Lūcius. Ō stulte, nōnne intellegis (*understand*)? Hodiē aegrum simulābis (*play*).

Titus. Intellegō. Bene, Pūblī! Bonum cōnsilium invēnistī! Tū, Lūcī, ī ad mātrem; illī dē morbō (*sickness*) meō nārrā! [Exit Lūcius.] Pūblī, in aquam hunc pannum (*cloth*) pōne! Celeriter! Mātrem audiō; pannō meōs oculōs cēlā! Heu! heu! Quam miser sum!

Octāvia intrat cum Lūciō.

Octāvia. Hercle (*good heavens*)! Quam aeger es! Quid habēs, Tite?

Titus. Nunc calidus (*hot*) sum, nunc frīgidus.

Octāvia. Ō cāre Tite, medicum arcessam. Quis medicum venīre jubēbit?

Lūcius. Ego medicum arcessam, mea māter.

Pūblius. Et ego cum Lūciō ībō.

Octāvia. Īte, parvulī (*little boys*), et medicāmentum (*medicine*) portāre medicum jubēte.

Lūcius. Acerbum (*bitter*) medicāmentum portābit medicus.

Pūblius. Acerbum medicāmentum.

Exeunt geminī.

Titus. Aquam dēsīderō, māter cārissima!

Octāvia. Miser puer! Aquam frīgidam tibi dabō. Bibe (*drink*)!

Titus bibit.

Titus. Māter, nunc frīgidus sum. Ecce! Membra mea tremunt (*tremble*).

Octāvia. Tē tegam.
Titus. Māter, nimis calidus sum.
Octāvia. Heu! Quī morbus tē tenet? Quō tempore medicus veniet?
Titus. Quis jānuam pulsat (*is knocking at*)?

Medicus cum puerīs intrat.

Medicus. Salvēte (*greetings*)! Quis aeger est?
Octāvia. Salvē, medice! Fīlius meus aeger est.
Medicus. Salvē, puer! Aegerne es?

Titus annuit (*nods*).

Lūcius et Pūblius. Ita, medice. Maximē aeger est.
Medicus. Potesne tū edere (*eat*)?

Titus annuit.

Lūcius et Pūblius. Minimē. Nihil edere potest.
Medicus. Monstrā mihi linguam tuam. Quid herī ēdistī?
Titus. Nesciō (*I don't know*), medice.
Lūcius. Sciō equidem (*however*).
Pūblius. Et ego.
Lūcius. Apud Quīntum vesperī cēnābat.
Pūblius. Nimis ēdit—porcum (*pork*).
Lūcius. Et māla.
Pūblius. Et lība (*cakes*).
Lūcius. Et alia multa.
Octāvia. Minimē mīrum, sī hodiē aeger es.
Medicus. Minimē mīrum est. Medicāmentum tibi parābō.

Medicāmentum parat.

Lūcius. Quāle (*what kind of*) medicāmentum parās?
Pūblius. Estne medicāmentum acerbum?
Medicus. Acerbum est.
Lūcius et Pūblius. Acerbum est medicāmentum. Acerbum est medicāmentum.
Medicus. Dā mihi pōculum (*cup*), mātrōna! [Fundit (*he pours*).] Nunc bibe, puer!

Titus medicāmentum gustat (*tastes*).

Titus. Nōn dēsīderō bibere. Hoc pōculum numquam bibam.

Octāvia. Puer male, quō modō cūrārī poteris, nisi medicāmentum bibēs?

Lūcius et Pūblius. Titus bibere nōn dēsīderat. Titus bibere nōn dēsīderat.

Medicus. Necesse est bibere.

Lūcius et Pūblius. Acerbum est. Laetī sumus quod acerbum est medicāmentum.

Titus. Mox vāpulābitis.

Geminī audiunt et silent.

Octāvia. Statim bibe; sī id nōn faciēs, patrem vocābō.

Titus. Nōn dēsīderō bibere.

Exit Octāvia.

Patris Vōx. Tite, audīsne mē?

Titus. Ita, Ō pater.

Patris Vōx. Nōnne medicāmentum bibere dēsīderās?

Titus. Certē, Ō pater, bibam.

Dum bibit, Octāvia intrat.

Octāvia. Medicāmentum jam bibit Titus.

Medicus. Bene; deinde dormiēs. Mox validus iterum eris. Valē, mātrōna; valēte, puerī.

Omnēs. Valē, medice.

Exit Medicus.

Titus. Jam validior sum. Dēsīderō surgere, māter.

Octāvia. Nōn surgēs, Ō stulte. Tōtum diem in lectulō jacēbis. Et ego prope tē manēbō.

Titus. Nōn necesse est tibi, cārissima māter, prope mē manēre.

Octāvia. Meus es fīlius. Prope tē manēbō, dum aeger es.

Lūcius et Pūblius. Ō māter, dēsīderāmus in hortō lūdere.

Octāvia. Abīte (*go away*), geminī, et in hortō lūdite.

Lūcius et Pūblius. Titus in lectulō manēbit, tōtum diem in lectulō manēbit.

Exeunt Lūcius et Pūblius. Titus pugnum (*fist*) agitat.

LATIN SONGS

TRANSLATION—Mistress Mary

Mistress Mary,
Quite contrary,
How does your garden grow?
With silver bells
And cockle-shells
And hyacinths all in a row.

Adeste Fideles

O Come, All Ye Faithful[1]

1 O come, all ye faithful, joyfully triumphant;
To Bethlehem hasten now with glad accord.
Lo! in a manger lies the King of angels.
O come, let us adore Him, Christ the Lord.

2 Raise, raise, choirs of angels, songs of loudest triumph;
Through heaven's high arches be your praises poured.
Now to our God be glory in the highest;
O come, let us adore Him, Christ the Lord.

3 Amen, Lord, we bless Thee, born for our salvation;
O Jesus, forever be Thy name adored,
Word of the Father, late in flesh appearing.
O come, let us adore Him, Christ the Lord.

[1] The words of this hymn are based upon the Latin hymn *Adeste Fideles*, but they are not an exact translation.

Horner Jacculo

GAMMER GURTON, English
HENRICUS DRURY, Latin

Old Nursery Tune

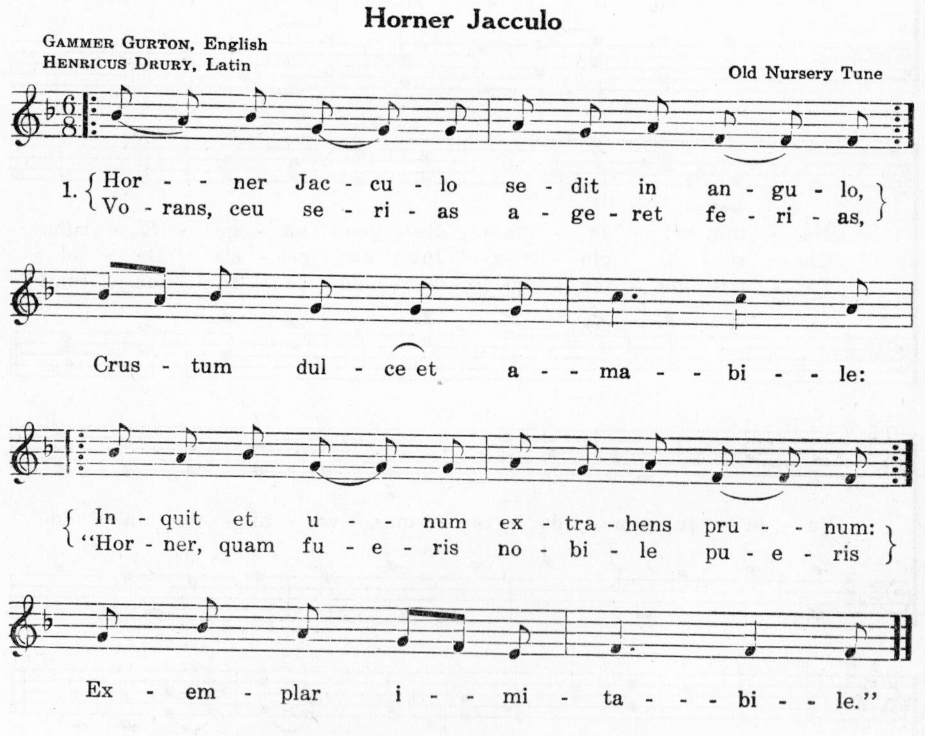

TRANSLATION—Little Jack Horner

Little Jack Horner
Sat in a corner,
Eating a Christmas pie.
He put in his thumb
And pulled out a plum,
And cried, "What a good boy am I!"

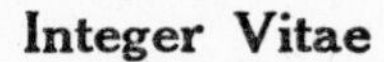

5 Pone me pigris ubi nulla campis
Arbor aestiva recreatur aura,
Quod latus mundi nebulae malusque
Juppiter urget;

6 Pone sub curru nimium propinqui
Solis, in terra domibus negata;
Dulce ridentem Lalagen amabo,
Dulce loquentem.

TRANSLATION

The man upright in life and free from guilt, needs not, O Fuscus, Moorish darts nor bow nor quiver loaded with envenomed arrows, whether his journey is to be over the boiling Syrtis or through the inhospitable Caucasus or in the places washed by the Hydaspes, famed in story. For while in the Sabine woods I was singing of my Lalage, and carefree was wandering beyond bounds, a wolf fled from me though I was unarmed. No such monster does the warlike Daunia nourish in its oak forest, nor does the land of Juba, that desert nurse of lions, produce the like. Place me where on the lifeless plains no tree is warmed to new life by the summer breeze, a region over which hang clouds and a gloomy sky; place me beneath the course of the sun as it draws too near the earth, in a land devoid of human dwellings; still will I love Lalage with her sweet smile and her sweet words.

SUMMARY OF GRAMMAR

NOUNS

FIRST- AND SECOND-DECLENSION NOUNS

1. ā-stems | **2.** o-stems

	1. ā-stems	2. o-stems				
	SINGULAR	SINGULAR				
Nom.	**rosa**	**amīcus**	**puer**	**ager**	**vir**	**templum**
Gen.	**rosae**	**amīcī**	**puerī**	**agrī**	**virī**	**templī**
Dat.	**rosae**	**amīcō**	**puerō**	**agrō**	**virō**	**templō**
Acc.	**rosam**	**amīcum**	**puerum**	**agrum**	**virum**	**templum**
Abl.	**rosā**	**amīcō**	**puerō**	**agrō**	**virō**	**templō**
	PLURAL	PLURAL				
Nom.	**rosae**	**amīcī**	**puerī**	**agrī**	**virī**	**templa**
Gen.	**rosārum**	**amīcōrum**	**puerōrum**	**agrōrum**	**virōrum**	**templōrum**
Dat.	**rosīs**	**amīcīs**	**puerīs**	**agrīs**	**virīs**	**templīs**
Acc.	**rosās**	**amīcōs**	**puerōs**	**agrōs**	**virōs**	**templa**
Abl.	**rosīs**	**amīcīs**	**puerīs**	**agrīs**	**virīs**	**templīs**

The vocative singular of **-us** nouns ends in **-e: amīce.**

3. THIRD DECLENSION

MASCULINE AND FEMININE CONSONANT STEMS

	SINGULAR			
Nom.	**lēx**	**mīles**	**frāter**	**homō**
Gen.	**lēgis**	**mīlitis**	**frātris**	**hominis**
Dat.	**lēgī**	**mīlitī**	**frātrī**	**hominī**
Acc.	**lēgem**	**mīlitem**	**frātrem**	**hominem**
Abl.	**lēge**	**mīlite**	**frātre**	**homine**
	PLURAL			
Nom.	**lēgēs**	**mīlitēs**	**frātrēs**	**hominēs**
Gen.	**lēgum**	**mīlitum**	**frātrum**	**hominum**
Dat.	**lēgibus**	**mīlitibus**	**frātribus**	**hominibus**
Acc.	**lēgēs**	**mīlitēs**	**frātrēs**	**hominēs**
Abl.	**lēgibus**	**mīlitibus**	**frātribus**	**hominibus**

Some masculine and feminine nouns of the third declension have the nominative ending **-s.** If the stem ends in **-c** or **-g,** the combination of the final **-c** or **-g** of the stem with **-s** gives **-x: dux,** nominative from the stem **duc-; lēx,** nominative from the stem **lēg-.** If the stem ends in **-d** or **-t,** the final consonant is dropped before **-s: laus,** nominative from the stem **laud-.**

In words of more than one syllable having **-e-** in the final syllable of the nominative, this regularly appears as **i** in the other cases: nominative **mīles,** genitive **mīlitis; prīnceps, prīncipis.**

Nouns with stems ending in **-tr** have the nominative ending in **-ter: frāter** from the stem **frātr-; māter** from the stem **mātr-.**

Nouns with stems ending in **-din** and **-gin** replace **-in** of the stem by **-ō** in the nominative: **virgō** from the stem **virgin-**; **multitūdō** from the stem **multitūdin-**. The nominative **homō** is also formed by replacing **-in** of the stem by **-ō**.

4. NEUTER CONSONANT STEMS

SINGULAR

Nom.	**flūmen**	**caput**	**corpus**	**iter**
Gen.	**flūminis**	**capitis**	**corporis**	**itineris**
Dat.	**flūminī**	**capitī**	**corporī**	**itinerī**
Acc.	**flūmen**	**caput**	**corpus**	**iter**
Abl.	**flūmine**	**capite**	**corpore**	**itinere**

PLURAL

Nom.	**flūmina**	**capita**	**corpora**	**itinera**
Gen.	**flūminum**	**capitum**	**corporum**	**itinerum**
Dat.	**flūminibus**	**capitibus**	**corporibus**	**itineribus**
Acc.	**flūmina**	**capita**	**corpora**	**itinera**
Abl.	**flūminibus**	**capitibus**	**corporibus**	**itineribus**

5. I-STEMS AND MIXED STEMS

SINGULAR

	MASCULINE AND FEMININE			NEUTER		
Nom.	**collis**	**nūbēs**	**nox**	**īnsigne**	**exemplar**	**animal**
Gen.	**collis**	**nūbis**	**noctis**	**īnsignis**	**exemplāris**	**animālis**
Dat.	**collī**	**nūbī**	**noctī**	**īnsignī**	**exemplārī**	**animālī**
Acc.	**collem**	**nūbem**	**noctem**	**īnsigne**	**exemplar**	**animal**
Abl.	**colle**	**nūbe**	**nocte**	**īnsignī**	**exemplārī**	**animālī**

PLURAL

Nom.	**collēs**	**nūbēs**	**noctēs**	**īnsignia**	**exemplāria**	**animālia**
Gen.	**collium**	**nūbium**	**noctium**	**īnsignium**	**exemplārium**	**animālium**
Dat.	**collibus**	**nūbibus**	**noctibus**	**īnsignibus**	**exemplāribus**	**animālibus**
Acc.	**collēs, -īs**	**nūbēs, -īs**	**noctēs, -īs**	**īnsignia**	**exemplāria**	**animālia**
Abl.	**collibus**	**nūbibus**	**noctibus**	**īnsignibus**	**exemplāribus**	**animālibus**

6. IRREGULAR NOUN

	SINGULAR	PLURAL
Nom.	**vīs**	**vīrēs**
Gen.	—	**vīrium**
Dat.	—	**vīribus**
Acc.	**vim**	**vīrēs, -īs**
Abl.	**vī**	**vīribus**

7. FOURTH DECLENSION, u-stems

	SING.	PLU.	SING.	PLU.
Nom.	**exercitus**	**exercitūs**	**cornū**	**cornua**
Gen.	**exercitūs**	**exercituum**	**cornūs**	**cornuum**
Dat.	**exercituī, -ū**	**exercitibus**	**cornū**	**cornibus**
Acc.	**exercitum**	**exercitūs**	**cornū**	**cornua**
Abl.	**exercitū**	**exercitibus**	**cornū**	**cornibus**

8. FIFTH DECLENSION, ē-stems

SING.	PLU.	SING.	PLU.
diēs	**diēs**	**rēs**	**rēs**
diēī	**diērum**	**reī**	**rērum**
diēī	**diēbus**	**reī**	**rēbus**
diem	**diēs**	**rem**	**rēs**
diē	**diēbus**	**rē**	**rēbus**

ADJECTIVES

9. FIRST AND SECOND DECLENSIONS

	SINGULAR			PLURAL		
	MASC.	FEM.	NEUT.	MASC.	FEM.	NEUT.
Nom.	bonus	bona	bonum	bonī	bonae	bona
Gen.	bonī	bonae	bonī	bonōrum	bonārum	bonōrum
Dat.	bonō	bonae	bonō	bonīs	bonīs	bonīs
Acc.	bonum	bonam	bonum	bonōs	bonās	bona
Abl.	bonō	bonā	bonō	bonīs	bonīs	bonīs
Nom.	miser	misera	miserum	miserī	miserae	misera
Gen.	miserī	miserae	miserī	miserōrum	miserārum	miserōrum
Dat.	miserō	miserae	miserō	miserīs	miserīs	miserīs
Acc.	miserum	miseram	miserum	miserōs	miserās	misera
Abl.	miserō	miserā	miserō	miserīs	miserīs	miserīs
Nom.	pulcher	pulchra	pulchrum	pulchrī	pulchrae	pulchra
Gen.	pulchrī	pulchrae	pulchrī	pulchrōrum	pulchrārum	pulchrōrum
Dat.	pulchrō	pulchrae	pulchrō	pulchrīs	pulchrīs	pulchrīs
Acc.	pulchrum	pulchram	pulchrum	pulchrōs	pulchrās	pulchra
Abl.	pulchrō	pulchrā	pulchrō	pulchrīs	pulchrīs	pulchrīs

10. THIRD DECLENSION

THREE TERMINATIONS—I-STEMS

	SINGULAR			PLURAL		
	MASC.	FEM.	NEUT.	MASC.	FEM.	NEUT.
Nom.	ācer	ācris	ācre	ācrēs	ācrēs	ācria
Gen.	ācris	ācris	ācris	ācrium	ācrium	ācrium
Dat.	ācrī	ācrī	ācrī	ācribus	ācribus	ācribus
Acc.	ācrem	ācrem	ācre	ācrēs, -īs	ācrēs, -īs	ācria
Abl.	ācrī	ācrī	ācrī	ācribus	ācribus	ācribus

11. TWO TERMINATIONS—I-STEMS

	SINGULAR	
	MASC. AND FEM.	NEUT.
Nom.	omnis	omne
Gen.	omnis	omnis
Dat.	omnī	omnī
Acc.	omnem	omne
Abl.	omnī	omnī
	PLURAL	
Nom.	omnēs	omnia
Gen.	omnium	omnium
Dat.	omnibus	omnibus
Acc.	omnēs, -īs	omnia
Abl.	omnibus	omnibus

12. ONE TERMINATION

	SINGULAR			
	MASC. AND FEM.	NEUT.	MASC. AND FEM.	NEUT.
Nom.	fēlīx	fēlīx	potēns	potēns
Gen.	fēlīcis	fēlīcis	potentis	potentis
Dat.	fēlīcī	fēlīcī	potentī	potentī
Acc.	fēlīcem	fēlīx	potentem	potēns
Abl.	fēlīcī	fēlīcī	potentī, -e	potentī, -e
	PLURAL			
Nom.	fēlīcēs	fēlīcia	potentēs	potentia
Gen.	fēlīcium	fēlīcium	potentium	potentium
Dat.	fēlīcibus	fēlīcibus	potentibus	potentibus
Acc.	fēlīcēs, -īs	fēlīcia	potentēs, -īs	potentia
Abl.	fēlīcibus	fēlīcibus	potentibus	potentibus

13. PRESENT PARTICIPLES

	SINGULAR		PLURAL	
	MASC. AND FEM.	NEUT.	MASC. AND FEM.	NEUT.
Nom.	**portāns**	**portāns**	**portantēs**	**portantia**
Gen.	**portantis**	**portantis**	**portantium**	**portantium**
Dat.	**portantī**	**portantī**	**portantibus**	**portantibus**
Acc.	**portantem**	**portāns**	**portantēs, -īs**	**portantia**
Abl.	**portante, -ī**	**portante, -ī**	**portantibus**	**portantibus**

14. IRREGULAR ADJECTIVES

alius	ūnus	alter
sōlus	tōtus	neuter
ūllus	nūllus	uter

SINGULAR

	MASC.	FEM.	NEUT.	MASC.	FEM.	NEUT.
Nom.	**sōlus**	**sōla**	**sōlum**	**alter**	**altera**	**alterum**
Gen.	**sōlīus**	**sōlīus**	**sōlīus**	**alterīus**	**alterīus**	**alterīus**
Dat.	**sōlī**	**sōlī**	**sōlī**	**alterī**	**alterī**	**alterī**
Acc.	**sōlum**	**sōlam**	**sōlum**	**alterum**	**alteram**	**alterum**
Abl.	**sōlō**	**sōlā**	**sōlō**	**alterō**	**alterā**	**alterō**

The plurals are like those of **bonus** and **miser.**

15. REGULAR COMPARISON OF ADJECTIVES

POSITIVE	COMPARATIVE	SUPERLATIVE
lātus	**lātior, lātius**	**lātissimus, -a, -um**
fortis	**fortior, fortius**	**fortissimus, -a, -um**
fēlīx	**fēlīcior, fēlīcius**	**fēlīcissimus, -a, -um**
miser	**miserior, miserius**	**miserrimus, -a, -um**
facilis	**facilior, facilius**	**facillimus, -a, -um**

16. IRREGULAR COMPARISON OF ADJECTIVES

POSITIVE	COMPARATIVE	SUPERLATIVE
bonus	**melior, melius**	**optimus, -a, -um**
malus	**pejor, pejus**	**pessimus, -a, -um**
magnus	**major, majus**	**maximus, -a, -um**
parvus	**minor, minus**	**minimus, -a, -um**
multus	**——, plūs**	**plūrimus, -a, -um**

17. DECLENSION OF COMPARATIVES

	SINGULAR		PLURAL	
	MASC. AND FEM.	NEUT.	MASC. AND FEM.	NEUT.
Nom.	**lātior**	**lātius**	**lātiōrēs**	**lātiōra**
Gen.	**lātiōris**	**lātiōris**	**lātiōrum**	**lātiōrum**
Dat.	**lātiōrī**	**lātiōrī**	**lātiōribus**	**lātiōribus**
Acc.	**lātiōrem**	**lātius**	**lātiōrēs, -īs**	**lātiōra**
Abl.	**lātiōre**	**lātiōre**	**lātiōribus**	**lātiōribus**

	SINGULAR		PLURAL	
	MASC. AND FEM.	NEUT.	MASC. AND FEM.	NEUT.
Nom.	——	plūs[1]	plūrēs	plūra
Gen.	——	plūris	plūrium	plūrium
Dat.	——	——	plūribus	plūribus
Acc.	——	plūs	plūrēs, -īs	plūra
Abl.	——	plūre	plūribus	plūribus

ADVERBS

18. REGULAR COMPARISON

POSITIVE	COMPARATIVE	SUPERLATIVE
lātē	**lātius**	**lātissimē**
fortiter	**fortius**	**fortissimē**
ācriter	**ācrius**	**ācerrimē**
facile	**facilius**	**facillimē**

19. IRREGULAR COMPARISON

POSITIVE	COMPARATIVE	SUPERLATIVE
bene	**melius**	**optimē**
male	**pejus**	**pessimē**
magnopere	**magis**	**maximē**
multum	**plūs**	**plūrimum**
parum	**minus**	**minimē**
prope	**propius**	**proximē**
saepe	**saepius**	**saepissimē**
diū	**diūtius**	**diūtissimē**

NUMERALS

20. LIST OF NUMBERS

ROMAN NUMERALS	CARDINAL	ORDINAL
I.	**ūnus, -a, -um**	**prīmus, -a, -um**
II.	**duo, duae, duo**	**secundus, alter**
III.	**trēs, tria**	**tertius**
IV.	**quattuor**	**quārtus**
V.	**quīnque**	**quīntus**
VI.	**sex**	**sextus**
VII.	**septem**	**septimus**
VIII.	**octō**	**octāvus**
IX.	**novem**	**nōnus**
X.	**decem**	**decimus**
XI.	**ūndecim**	**ūndecimus**
XII.	**duodecim**	**duodecimus**
XIII.	**tredecim**	**tertius decimus**
XIV.	**quattuordecim**	**quārtus decimus**
XV.	**quīndecim**	**quīntus decimus**
XVI.	**sēdecim**	**sextus decimus**
XVII.	**septendecim**	**septimus decimus**
XVIII.	**duodēvīgintī**	**duodēvīcēsimus**
XIX.	**ūndēvīgintī**	**ūndēvīcēsimus**
XX.	**vīgintī**	**vīcēsimus**
XXI.	**ūnus et vīgintī, vīgintī ūnus**	**vīcēsimus prīmus**
XXVIII.	**duodētrīgintā**	**duodētrīcēsimus**
XXIX.	**ūndētrīgintā**	**ūndētrīcēsimus**
XXX.	**trīgintā**	**trīcēsimus**
XL.	**quadrāgintā**	**quadrāgēsimus**

[1]Used in singular as noun only.

ROMAN NUMERALS	CARDINAL	ORDINAL
L.	quīnquāgintā	quīnquāgēsimus
LX.	sexāgintā	sexāgēsimus
LXX.	septuāgintā	septuāgēsimus
LXXX.	octōgintā	octōgēsimus
XC.	nōnāgintā	nōnāgēsimus
C.	centum	centēsimus
CI.	centum (et) ūnus	centēsimus (et) prīmus
CC.	ducentī, -ae, -a	ducentēsimus
CCC.	trecentī, -ae, -a	trecentēsimus
CCCC.	quadringentī	quadringentēsimus
D.	quīngentī	quīngentēsimus
DC.	sescentī	sescentēsimus
DCC.	septingentī	septingentēsimus
DCCC.	octingentī	octingentēsimus
DCCCC.	nōngentī	nōngentēsimus
M.	mīlle	mīllēsimus
MM.	duo mīlia	bis mīllēsimus

21. DECLENSION OF ***DUO***, ***TRĒS***, AND ***MĪLIA***

	MASC.	FEM.	NEUT.	MASC. AND FEM.	NEUT.	NEUT.
Nom.	duo	duae	duo	trēs	tria	mīlia
Gen.	duōrum	duārum	duōrum	trium	trium	mīlium
Dat.	duōbus	duābus	duōbus	tribus	tribus	mīlibus
Acc.	duōs, duo	duās	duo	trēs, trīs	tria	mīlia
Abl.	duōbus	duābus	duōbus	tribus	tribus	mīlibus

PRONOUNS

22. PERSONAL PRONOUNS

	FIRST PERSON		SECOND PERSON	
	SINGULAR	PLURAL	SINGULAR	PLURAL
Nom.	ego	nōs	tū	vōs
Gen.	meī	nostrum, nostrī	tuī	vestrum, vestrī
Dat.	mihi	nōbīs	tibi	vōbīs
Acc.	mē	nōs	tē	vōs
Abl.	mē	nōbīs	tē	vōbīs

There is no personal pronoun of the third person. Its place is taken either by a demonstrative pronoun (usually **is**, *he*, **ea**, *she*, **id**, *it*) or if the antecedent is the subject of the sentence or clause, by a reflexive pronoun.

23. REFLEXIVE PRONOUNS

	FIRST PERSON		SECOND PERSON		THIRD PERSON	
	SING.	PLU.	SING.	PLU.	SING.	PLU.
Gen.	meī	nostrī	tuī	vestrī	suī	suī
Dat.	mihi	nōbīs	tibi	vōbīs	sibi	sibi
Acc.	mē	nōs	tē	vōs	sē, sēsē	sē, sēsē
Abl.	mē	nōbīs	tē	vōbīs	sē, sēsē	sē, sēsē

24. POSSESSIVES

REFERRING TO SINGULAR ANTECEDENT

1st pers. **meus, -a, -um,** *my*
2d pers. **tuus, -a, -um,** *your* (of one person)
3d pers. {**suus, -a, -um,** *his, her, its* (reflexive)
{**ejus** (gen. sing. of **is**), *his, her, its* (not reflexive)

REFERRING TO PLURAL ANTECEDENT

1st pers. **noster, -tra, -trum,** *our*
2d pers. **vester, -tra, -trum,** *your* (of more than one person)
3d pers. {**suus, -a, -um,** *their* (reflexive)
{**eōrum, eārum, eōrum** (gen. pl. of **is**), *their* (not reflexive)

25. DEMONSTRATIVE PRONOUNS

	SINGULAR			PLURAL		
	MASC.	FEM.	NEUT.	MASC.	FEM.	NEUT.
Nom.	**hic**	**haec**	**hoc**	**hī**	**hae**	**haec**
Gen.	**hujus**	**hujus**	**hujus**	**hōrum**	**hārum**	**hōrum**
Dat.	**huic**	**huic**	**huic**	**hīs**	**hīs**	**hīs**
Acc.	**hunc**	**hanc**	**hoc**	**hōs**	**hās**	**haec**
Abl.	**hōc**	**hāc**	**hōc**	**hīs**	**hīs**	**hīs**
Nom.	**ille**	**illa**	**illud**	**illī**	**illae**	**illa**
Gen.	**illīus**	**illīus**	**illīus**	**illōrum**	**illārum**	**illōrum**
Dat.	**illī**	**illī**	**illī**	**illīs**	**illīs**	**illīs**
Acc.	**illum**	**illam**	**illud**	**illōs**	**illās**	**illa**
Abl.	**illō**	**illā**	**illō**	**illīs**	**illīs**	**illīs**
Nom.	**is**	**ea**	**id**	**eī, iī**	**eae**	**ea**
Gen.	**ejus**	**ejus**	**ejus**	**eōrum**	**eārum**	**eōrum**
Dat.	**eī**	**eī**	**eī**	**eīs, iīs**	**eīs, iīs**	**eīs, iīs**
Acc.	**eum**	**eam**	**id**	**eōs**	**eās**	**ea**
Abl.	**eō**	**eā**	**eō**	**eīs, iīs**	**eīs, iīs**	**eīs, iīs**

26. THE IDENTIFYING PRONOUN

	MASC.	FEM.	NEUT.
		SINGULAR	
Nom.	**īdem**	**eadem**	**idem**
Gen.	**ejusdem**	**ejusdem**	**ejusdem**
Dat.	**eīdem**	**eīdem**	**eīdem**
Acc.	**eundem**	**eandem**	**idem**
Abl.	**eōdem**	**eādem**	**eōdem**
		PLURAL	
Nom.	**eīdem, īdem**	**eaedem**	**eadem**
Gen.	**eōrundem**	**eārundem**	**eōrundem**
Dat.	**eīsdem, īsdem**	**eīsdem, īsdem**	**eīsdem, īsdem**
Acc.	**eōsdem**	**eāsdem**	**eadem**
Abl.	**eīsdem, īsdem**	**eīsdem, īsdem**	**eīsdem, īsdem**

27. THE INTENSIVE PRONOUN

	SINGULAR			PLURAL		
	MASC.	FEM.	NEUT.	MASC.	FEM.	NEUT.
Nom.	**ipse**	**ipsa**	**ipsum**	**ipsī**	**ipsae**	**ipsa**
Gen.	**ipsīus**	**ipsīus**	**ipsīus**	**ipsōrum**	**ipsārum**	**ipsōrum**
Dat.	**ipsī**	**ipsī**	**ipsī**	**ipsīs**	**ipsīs**	**ipsīs**
Acc.	**ipsum**	**ipsam**	**ipsum**	**ipsōs**	**ipsās**	**ipsa**
Abl.	**ipsō**	**ipsā**	**ipsō**	**ipsīs**	**ipsīs**	**ipsīs**

28. THE RELATIVE PRONOUN

	SINGULAR			PLURAL		
	MASC.	FEM.	NEUT.	MASC.	FEM.	NEUT.
Nom.	**quī**	**quae**	**quod**	**quī**	**quae**	**quae**
Gen.	**cujus**	**cujus**	**cujus**	**quōrum**	**quārum**	**quōrum**
Dat.	**cui**	**cui**	**cui**	**quibus**	**quibus**	**quibus**
Acc.	**quem**	**quam**	**quod**	**quōs**	**quās**	**quae**
Abl.	**quō**	**quā**	**quō**	**quibus**	**quibus**	**quibus**

29. THE INTERROGATIVE PRONOUN

	SINGULAR		PLURAL		
	MASC. AND FEM.	NEUT.	MASC.	FEM.	NEUT.
Nom.	**quis**	**quid**	**quī**	**quae**	**quae**
Gen.	**cujus**	**cujus**	**quōrum**	**quārum**	**quōrum**
Dat.	**cui**	**cui**	**quibus**	**quibus**	**quibus**
Acc.	**quem**	**quid**	**quōs**	**quās**	**quae**
Abl.	**quō**	**quō**	**quibus**	**quibus**	**quibus**

30. THE INTERROGATIVE ADJECTIVE

The interrogative adjective in the singular is the same as the relative pronoun (Section **28**), except that the nominative masculine may be either **quis** or **quī**. The plural of the interrogative adjective is the same as that of the interrogative pronoun (Section **29**).

31. INDEFINITE PRONOUNS

	SINGULAR		
	MASC.	FEM.	NEUT.
Nom.	**quīdam**	**quaedam**	**quiddam, quoddam**
Gen.	**cujusdam**	**cujusdam**	**cujusdam**
Dat.	**cuidam**	**cuidam**	**cuidam**
Acc.	**quendam**	**quandam**	**quiddam, quoddam**
Abl.	**quōdam**	**quādam**	**quōdam**

PLURAL

Nom.	**quīdam**	**quaedam**	**quaedam**
Gen.	**quōrundam**	**quārundam**	**quōrundam**
Dat.	**quibusdam**	**quibusdam**	**quibusdam**
Acc.	**quōsdam**	**quāsdam**	**quaedam**
Abl.	**quibusdam**	**quibusdam**	**quibusdam**

SINGULAR

Nom.	**aliquis, aliquī**	**aliqua**	**aliquid, aliquod**
Gen.	**alicujus**	**alicujus**	**alicujus**
Dat.	**alicui**	**alicui**	**alicui**
Acc.	**aliquem**	**aliquam**	**aliquid, aliquod**
Abl.	**aliquō**	**aliquā**	**aliquō**

PLURAL

Nom.	**aliquī**	**aliquae**	**aliqua**
Gen.	**aliquōrum**	**aliquārum**	**aliquōrum**
Dat.	**aliquibus**	**aliquibus**	**aliquibus**
Acc.	**aliquōs**	**aliquās**	**aliqua**
Abl.	**aliquibus**	**aliquibus**	**aliquibus**

VERBS

FIRST CONJUGATION

Principal parts: **portō, portāre, portāvī, portātum**

INDICATIVE

32. *ACTIVE*

PRESENT

SINGULAR	PLURAL
portō, *I carry*	**portāmus**, *we carry*
portās, *you carry*	**portātis**, *you carry*
portat, *he carries*	**portant**, *they carry*

IMPERFECT

portābam, *I was carrying, I carried*	**portābāmus**, *we were carrying*, etc.
portābās, *you were carrying*, etc.	**portābātis**, *you were carrying*, etc.
portābat, *he was carrying*, etc.	**portābant**, *they were carrying*, etc.

FUTURE

portābō, *I shall carry*	**portābimus**, *we shall carry*
portābis, *you will carry*	**portābitis**, *you will carry*
portābit, *he will carry*	**portābunt**, *they will carry*

PERFECT

portāvī, *I carried, I have carried*	**portāvimus**, *we carried*, etc.
portāvistī, *you carried*, etc.	**portāvistis**, *you carried*, etc.
portāvit, *he carried*, etc	**portāvērunt**, *they carried*, etc.

PAST PERFECT

SINGULAR	PLURAL
portāveram, *I had carried*	**portāverāmus,** *we had carried*
portāverās, *you had carried*	**portāverātis,** *you had carried*
portāverat, *he had carried*	**portāverant,** *they had carried*

FUTURE PERFECT

portāverō, *I shall have carried*	**portāverimus,** *we shall have carried*
portāveris, *you will have carried*	**portāveritis,** *you will have carried*
portāverit, *he will have carried*	**portāverint,** *they will have carried*

33. *PASSIVE*

PRESENT

portor, *I am carried*	**portāmur,** *we are carried*
portāris, -re, *you are carried*	**portāminī,** *you are carried*
portātur, *he is carried*	**portantur,** *they are carried*

IMPERFECT

portābar, *I was being carried, I was carried*	**portābāmur,** *we were being carried,* etc.
portābāris, -re, *you were being carried,* etc.	**portābāminī,** *you were being carried,* etc.
portābātur, *he was being carried,* etc.	**portābantur,** *they were being carried,* etc.

FUTURE

portābor, *I shall be carried*	**portābimur,** *we shall be carried*
portāberis, -re, *you will be carried*	**portābiminī,** *you will be carried*
portābitur, *he will be carried*	**portābuntur,** *they will be carried*

PERFECT

portātus sum, *I have been carried*	**portātī sumus,** *we have been carried*
portātus es, *you have been carried*	**portātī estis,** *you have been carried*
portātus est, *he has been carried*	**portātī sunt,** *they have been carried*

PAST PERFECT

portātus eram, *I had been carried*	**portātī erāmus,** *we had been carried*
portātus erās, *you had been carried*	**portātī erātis,** *you had been carried*
portātus erat, *he had been carried*	**portātī erant,** *they had been carried*

FUTURE PERFECT

portātus erō, *I shall have been carried*	**portātī erimus,** *we shall have been carried*
portātus eris, *you will have been carried*	**portātī eritis,** *you will have been carried*
portātus erit, *he will have been carried*	**portātī erunt,** *they will have been carried*

IMPERATIVE

PRESENT

Singular: **portā,** *carry* (said to one person)
Plural: **portāte,** *carry* (said to more than one)

INFINITIVES

	ACTIVE	PASSIVE
Pres.	**portāre,** *to carry*	**portārī,** *to be carried*
Perf.	**portāvisse,** *to have carried*	**portātus esse,** *to have been carried*
Fut.	**portātūrus esse,** *to be about to carry*	**portātum īrī,** *to be about to be carried*

PARTICIPLES

ACTIVE

Pres. **portāns,** *carrying*
Fut. **portātūrus,** *about to carry*

PASSIVE

Perf. **portātus,** *having been carried*

GERUND

Gen. **portandī,** *of carrying*
Dat. **portandō,** *to (for) carrying*
Acc. **portandum,** *carrying*
Abl. **portandō,** *from, by carrying*

SECOND, THIRD, AND FOURTH CONJUGATIONS

Principal parts: **moneō, monēre, monuī, monitum**
dūcō, dūcere, dūxī, ductum
capiō, capere, cēpī, captum
audiō, audīre, audīvī, audītum

INDICATIVE

34. *ACTIVE*

PRESENT

SINGULAR

moneō	**dūcō**	**capiō**	**audiō**
monēs	**dūcis**	**capis**	**audīs**
monet	**dūcit**	**capit**	**audit**

PLURAL

monēmus	**dūcimus**	**capimus**	**audīmus**
monētis	**dūcitis**	**capitis**	**audītis**
monent	**dūcunt**	**capiunt**	**audiunt**

IMPERFECT

SINGULAR

monēbam	**dūcēbam**	**capiēbam**	**audiēbam**
monēbās	**dūcēbās**	**capiēbās**	**audiēbās**
monēbat	**dūcēbat**	**capiēbat**	**audiēbat**

PLURAL

monēbāmus	**dūcēbāmus**	**capiēbāmus**	**audiēbāmus**
monēbātis	**dūcēbātis**	**capiēbātis**	**audiēbātis**
monēbant	**dūcēbant**	**capiēbant**	**audiēbant**

FUTURE

SINGULAR

monēbō	dūcam	capiam	audiam
monēbis	dūcēs	capiēs	audiēs
monēbit	dūcet	capiet	audiet

PLURAL

monēbimus	dūcēmus	capiēmus	audiēmus
monēbitis	dūcētis	capiētis	audiētis
monēbunt	dūcent	capient	audient

PERFECT

SINGULAR

monuī	dūxī	cēpī	audīvī
monuistī	dūxistī	cēpistī	audīvistī
monuit	dūxit	cēpit	audīvit

PLURAL

monuimus	dūximus	cēpimus	audīvimus
monuistis	dūxistis	cēpistis	audīvistis
monuērunt, -ēre	dūxērunt, -ēre	cēpērunt, -ēre	audīvērunt, -ēre

PAST PERFECT

SINGULAR

monueram	dūxeram	cēperam	audīveram
monuerās	dūxerās	cēperās	audīverās
monuerat	dūxerat	cēperat	audīverat

PLURAL

monuerāmus	dūxerāmus	cēperāmus	audīverāmus
monuerātis	dūxerātis	cēperātis	audīverātis
monuerant	dūxerant	cēperant	audīverant

FUTURE PERFECT

SINGULAR

monuerō	dūxerō	cēperō	audīverō
monueris	dūxeris	cēperis	audīveris
monuerit	dūxerit	cēperit	audīverit

PLURAL

monuerimus	dūxerimus	cēperimus	audīverimus
monueritis	dūxeritis	cēperitis	audīveritis
monuerint	dūxerint	cēperint	audīverint

35. *PASSIVE*

PRESENT

SINGULAR

moneor	dūcor	capior	audior
monēris, -re	dūceris, -re	caperis, -re	audīris, -re
monētur	dūcitur	capitur	audītur

PLURAL

monēmur	dūcimur	capimur	audīmur
monēminī	dūciminī	capiminī	audīminī
monentur	dūcuntur	capiuntur	audiuntur

IMPERFECT

SINGULAR

monēbar	dūcēbar	capiēbar	audiēbar
monēbāris, -re	dūcēbāris, -re	capiēbāris, -re	audiēbāris, -re
monēbātur	dūcēbātur	capiēbātur	audiēbātur

PLURAL

monēbāmur	dūcēbāmur	capiēbāmur	audiēbāmur
monēbāminī	dūcēbāminī	capiēbāminī	audiēbāminī
monēbantur	dūcēbantur	capiēbantur	audiēbantur

FUTURE

SINGULAR

monēbor	dūcar	capiar	audiar
monēberis, -re	dūcēris, -re	capiēris, -re	audiēris, -re
monēbitur	dūcētur	capiētur	audiētur

PLURAL

monēbimur	dūcēmur	capiēmur	audiēmur
monēbiminī	dūcēminī	capiēminī	audiēminī
monēbuntur	dūcentur	capientur	audientur

PERFECT

SINGULAR

monitus sum	ductus sum	captus sum	audītus sum
monitus es	ductus es	captus es	audītus es
monitus est	ductus est	captus est	audītus est

PLURAL

monitī sumus	ductī sumus	captī sumus	audītī sumus
monitī estis	ductī estis	captī estis	audītī estis
monitī sunt	ductī sunt	captī sunt	audītī sunt

PAST PERFECT

SINGULAR

monitus eram	ductus eram	captus eram	audītus eram
monitus erās	ductus erās	captus erās	audītus erās
monitus erat	ductus erat	captus erat	audītus erat

PLURAL

monitī erāmus	ductī erāmus	captī erāmus	audītī erāmus
monitī erātis	ductī erātis	captī erātis	audītī erātis
monitī erant	ductī erant	captī erant	audītī erant

FUTURE PERFECT

SINGULAR

monitus erō	ductus erō	captus erō	audītus erō
monitus eris	ductus eris	captus eris	audītus eris
monitus erit	ductus erit	captus erit	audītus erit

PLURAL

monitī erimus	ductī erimus	captī erimus	audītī erimus
monitī eritis	ductī eritis	captī eritis	audītī eritis
monitī erunt	ductī erunt	captī erunt	audītī erunt

IMPERATIVE

PRESENT

SINGULAR

monē	**dūc**[1]	**cape**	**audī**

PLURAL

monēte	**dūcite**	**capite**	**audīte**

INFINITIVES

ACTIVE

PRESENT

monēre	**dūcere**	**capere**	**audīre**

PERFECT

monuisse	**dūxisse**	**cēpisse**	**audīvisse**

FUTURE

monitūrus esse	**ductūrus esse**	**captūrus esse**	**audītūrus esse**

PASSIVE

PRESENT

monērī	**dūcī**	**capī**	**audīrī**

PERFECT

monitus esse	**ductus esse**	**captus esse**	**audītus esse**

FUTURE

monitum īrī	**ductum īrī**	**captum īrī**	**audītum īrī**

PARTICIPLES

ACTIVE

PRESENT

monēns	**dūcēns**	**capiēns**	**audiēns**

FUTURE

monitūrus	**ductūrus**	**captūrus**	**audītūrus**

PASSIVE

PERFECT

monitus	**ductus**	**captus**	**audītus**

36. *CONJUGATION OF SUM*

Principal parts: **sum, esse, fuī, futūrus**

INDICATIVE

PRESENT

SINGULAR	PLURAL
sum, *I am*	**sumus,** *we are*
es, *you are*	**estis,** *you are*
est, *he is*	**sunt,** *they are*

IMPERFECT

eram, *I was*	**erāmus,** *we were*
erās, *you were*	**erātis,** *you were*
erat, *he was*	**erant,** *they were*

FUTURE

erō, *I shall be*	**erimus,** *we shall be*
eris, *you will be*	**eritis,** *you will be*
erit, *he will be*	**erunt,** *they will be*

PERFECT

fuī, *I was, I have been*	**fuimus,** *we were, we have been*
fuistī, *you were, you have been*	**fuistis,** *you were, you have been*
fuit, *he was, he has been*	**fuērunt, -ēre,** *they were, they have been*

PAST PERFECT

fueram, *I had been*	**fuerāmus,** *we had been*
fuerās, *you had been*	**fuerātis,** *you had been*
fuerat, *he had been*	**fuerant,** *they had been*

FUTURE PERFECT

fuerō, *I shall have been*	**fuerimus,** *we shall have been*
fueris, *you will have been*	**fueritis,** *you will have been*
fuerit, *he will have been*	**fuerint,** *they will have been*

IMPERATIVE

PRESENT

Singular: **es,** *be* (said to one person)
Plural: **este,** *be* (said to more than one)

INFINITIVES

Pres. **esse,** *to be*
Perf. **fuisse,** *to have been*
Fut. **futūrus esse, fore,** *to be about to be*

PARTICIPLE

Fut. **futūrus,** *about to be*

37. *CONJUGATION OF* ***POSSUM***

Principal parts: **possum, posse, potuī**

INDICATIVE

PRESENT		PERFECT	
SINGULAR	PLURAL	SINGULAR	PLURAL
possum	**possumus**	**potuī**	**potuimus**
potes	**potestis**	**potuistī**	**potuistis**
potest	**possunt**	**potuit**	**potuērunt, -ēre**
IMPERFECT		PAST PERFECT	
poteram	**poterāmus**	**potueram**	**potuerāmus**
poterās	**poterātis**	**potuerās**	**potuerātis**
poterat	**poterant**	**potuerat**	**potuerant**
FUTURE		FUTURE PERFECT	
poterō	**poterimus**	**potuerō**	**potuerimus**
poteris	**poteritis**	**potueris**	**potueritis**
poterit	**poterunt**	**potuerit**	**potuerint**

INFINITIVES

Pres. **posse** *Perf.* **potuisse**

38. *CONJUGATION OF* ***EŌ***

Principal parts: **eō, īre, iī** *or* **īvī, itum**

INDICATIVE

PRESENT		IMPERFECT		FUTURE	
SINGULAR	PLURAL	SINGULAR	PLURAL	SINGULAR	PLURAL
eō	**īmus**	**ībam**	**ībāmus**	**ībō**	**ībimus**
īs	**ītis**	**ībās**	**ībātis**	**ībis**	**ībitis**
it	**eunt**	**ībat**	**ībant**	**ībit**	**ībunt**
PERFECT		PAST PERFECT		FUTURE PERFECT	
iī	**iimus**	**ieram**	**ierāmus**	**ierō**	**ierimus**
īstī, iistī	**īstis, iistis**	**ierās**	**ierātis**	**ieris**	**ieritis**
iit	**iērunt, -ēre**	**ierat**	**ierant**	**ierit**	**ierint**

Forms are sometimes found in the perfect system with the stem **īv-**, as **īvī, īveram**, etc.

IMPERATIVE

PRESENT

Singular: **ī** *Plural:* **īte**

INFINITIVES	PARTICIPLES
Pres. **īre**	*Pres.* **iēns**, *gen.* **euntis**
Perf. **īsse, iisse**	*Fut.* **itūrus**
Fut. **itūrus esse**	

REVIEW OF SYNTAX

39. AGREEMENT

(1) An adjective or a participle agrees with its noun in gender, number, and case.

(2) A relative pronoun agrees with its antecedent in gender and number, but its case depends on its use in its own clause.

(3) A noun in apposition is in the same case as the word it explains.

(4) A verb agrees with its subject in person and number.

CASES

40. NOMINATIVE

The nominative is the case of the subject or of the predicate noun.

41. GENITIVE

(1) The genitive is the case of the possessor. (*Genitive of Possession.*)

(2) The genitive, modified by an adjective, may be used to describe a person or thing. (*Genitive of Description.*)

(3) With words denoting a part, a dependent genitive may be used to denote the whole to which the part belongs. (*Genitive of the Whole* or *Partitive Genitive.*)

42. DATIVE

(1) The indirect object is in the dative case. (*Dative of Indirect Object.*)

(2) The dative is used in dependence on adjectives meaning *kind, friendly, pleasing, dear, useful, near, hostile,* and some others. (*Dative with Adjectives.*)

(3) Some Latin verbs have a special meaning which differs from their usual English translations. This meaning involves a dependent dative; e. g., **placēre,** *to be pleasing;* **resistere,** *to offer resistance;* **crēdere,** *give trust.* (*Dative with Special Verbs.*)

(4) Verbs compounded with **ante, ob, prae,** and **sub** frequently have a dependent noun or pronoun in the dative. This construction is sometimes found also with compounds of **ad, circum, cum (com-), in, inter, post, prō,** and **super.** (*Dative with Compounds.*)

43. ACCUSATIVE

(1) The direct object of a verb is in the accusative case. (*Accusative as Direct Object.*)

(2) A noun which tells how long an act or a situation continues is in the accusative. (*Accusative of Duration of Time.*)

(3) The accusative without a preposition is used to express extent of space. (*Accusative of Extent of Space.*)

(4) Certain prepositions have their objects in the accusative. (*Accusative with Prepositions.*)

44. ABLATIVE

(1) Verbs meaning to *separate, remove, deprive of, be absent,* and the like, take the ablative of separation, often with **ab, dē,** or **ex.** (*Ablative of Separation.*)

(2) With passive verbs, the noun or pronoun which denotes the person by whom the act is done is in the ablative with **ā** or **ab.** (*Ablative of Agent.*)

(3) The ablative with **in** denotes the place where something is or where some act occurs. (*Ablative of Place.*)

(4) The ablative with the preposition **cum** is used to denote the person with whom one is associated in doing an act. (*Ablative of Accompaniment.*)

(5) The time at which or within which an act takes place is regularly expressed by a noun or pronoun in the ablative case without a preposition. (*Ablative of Time.*)

(6) The ablative, frequently with the preposition **cum,** is used to express manner. (*Ablative of Manner.*)

(7) A word which denotes the means used to accomplish an act is in the ablative without a preposition. (*Ablative of Means.*)

(8) A noun or pronoun in the ablative, together with an adjective, a participle, or another noun in agreement, may be used to denote some circumstance or event loosely connected with the rest of the sentence. (*Ablative Absolute.*)

(9) The ablative without a preposition is used to indicate in what respect a statement is true. (*Ablative of Respect* or *Specification.*)

(10) The ablative modified by an adjective may be used to describe a person or thing. (*Ablative of Description.*)

(11) The ablative is used to express cause. (*Ablative of Cause.*)

45. VOCATIVE

The vocative denotes the person addressed.

MOODS

46. INDICATIVE

The indicative is used in a statement of fact and in a question which implies as its answer a statement of fact.

47. IMPERATIVE

The imperative is used to express commands.

48. INFINITIVE

(1) The infinitive is sometimes used to complete the meaning of another verb, by denoting an action of the subject of the verb. (*Complementary Infinitive.*)

(2) The infinitive with subject accusative is used with words of *saying, hearing, knowing, thinking, believing, seeing,* and the like. (*Indirect Discourse.*)

LATIN-ENGLISH VOCABULARY

In this vocabulary there are 711 words which may be considered basic forms (e.g., **amō**). Some additional entries (e.g., **amās**) are given as an aid to the beginner. The starred words (e.g., **abundantia**) have been taught through their likeness to English words.

A

ā, ab, *prep. with abl.*, by; from, away from
abdō, -dere, -didī, -ditum, hide, conceal, put away
***abdūcō, -dūcere, -dūxī, -ductum,** lead away, abduct
abstineō, -tinēre, -tinuī, -tentum, keep away from
absum, -esse, āfuī, āfutūrus, be away, be absent, be distant
***abundantia, -ae,** *f.*, abundance, plenty
accendō, -cendere, -cendī, -cēnsum, kindle, light, set on fire
accipiō, -cipere, -cēpī, -ceptum, accept, receive
***accommodātiō, -ōnis,** *f.*, adjustment
***accūsō, -āre, -āvī, -ātum,** accuse
ācer, ācris, ācre, sharp; fierce, eager
***ācrimōnia, -ae,** *f.*, sharpness
ācriter, *adv.*, vigorously, fiercely
acūtus, -a, -um, acute, sharp
ad, *prep. with acc.*, to, toward; until; near; at; for
***admittō, -mittere, -mīsī, -missum,** admit
***adōrnō, -āre, -āvī, -ātum,** adorn, decorate
***adōrō, -āre, -āvī, -ātum,** worship
adsum, -esse, -fuī, -futūrus, be present, be at hand, be here
advena, -ae, *m.*, stranger, foreigner
adventus, -ūs, *m.*, arrival; approach
***adversus, -a, -um,** unfavorable
aedificium, -ī, *n.*, a building
aedificō, -āre, -āvī, -ātum, build
aeger, -gra, -grum, ill, sick
āēr, āēris, *m.*, air
aestāte, in summer

ager

aeternus, -a, -um, everlasting, eternal
ager, agrī, *m.*, field, farm, land
agitō, -āre, -āvī, -ātum, drive, drive on, pursue; disturb, move; agitate, wave, shake
agmen, agminis, *n.*, column, line, line of march; army, band
agō, -ere, ēgī, āctum, drive, lead; act, do; spend, pass
agricola, -ae, *m.*, farmer
***agricultūra, -ae,** *f.*, agriculture

ala

āla, -ae, *f.*, wing
alacritās, -ātis, *f.*, alacrity, eagerness; activity
alba, *see* **albus**
***albeō, -ēre,** be white
albus, -a, -um, white
***aliēnus, -a, -um,** foreign; *m. as noun,* stranger
alius, -a, -ud, another, other; else
***alternō, -āre, -āvī, -ātum,** change, alternate
***altitūdō, -inis,** *f.*, height; depth
altus, -a, -um, high, tall; deep
***alumna, -ae,** *f.*, foster daughter
***alumnus, -ī,** *m.*, foster son, ward
***amābilis, -e,** worthy of love, amiable

amāmus, we love
amant, (they) love
amās, you love
amat, (he, she) loves
***amātor, -ōris**, *m.*, lover
ambulō, -āre, -āvī, -ātum, walk
***amīcitia, -ae**, *f.*, friendship
amīcus, -a, -um, friendly; *m. and f. as noun*, friend
amita, -ae, *f.*, aunt
āmittō, -mittere, -mīsī, -missum, lose, let go
amō, -āre, -āvī, -ātum, love
amoena, *see* **amoenus**
amoenus, -a, -um, pleasant
amor, -ōris, *m.*, love
***amplus, -a, -um**, ample
***anatomia, -ae**, *f.*, anatomy
***angelus, -ī**, *m.*, angel
angusta, *see* **angustus**
***angustiae, -ārum**, *f. pl.*, narrows
angustus, -a, -um, narrow
***animal, animālis**, *n.*, animal
animus, -ī, *m.*, mind, spirit; **in animō habēre**, intend
***annuālis, -e**, year old
annus, -ī, *m.*, year

animal

ante, *prep. with acc.*, before, in front of
anteā, *adv.*, formerly, before
antīqua, *see* **antīquus**
***antīquitās, -ātis**, *f.*, antiquity
antīquitus, *adv.*, long ago, in former times
antīquus, -a, -um, ancient, old
aperiō, -īre, -uī, apertum, open
aperta, *see* **apertus**
apertus, -a, -um, open
apis, apis, *f.*, bee

apis

appellō, -āre, -āvī, -ātum, call, name
appellō, -pellere, -pulī, -pulsum, drive, bring to; *with or without* **nāvem**, bring to land, come to land, land
appropinquō, -āre, -āvī, -ātum, approach, draw near
aqua, -ae, *f.*, water
***aquaeductus, -ūs**, *m.*, aqueduct
***aquila, -ae**, *f.*, eagle
***aquilīnus, -a, -um**, aquiline
āra, -ae, *f.*, altar
arānea, -ae, *f.*, spider
arbor, arboris, *f.*, tree
arca, -ae, *f.*, chest, box

aranea

arcessō, -ere, -īvī, -ītum, summon, call
architectūra, -ae, *f.*, architecture
***architectus, -ī**, *m.*, architect
arcus, -ūs, *m.*, bow, arch
***ārea, -ae**, *f.*, area; threshing floor; courtyard
***arēna, -ae**, *f.*, sand; arena
***āridus, -a, -um**, arid
arma, -ōrum, *n. pl.*, arms, weapons; tools
armātus, -a, -um, armed; *m. pl. as noun*, armed men, soldiers
arō, -āre, -āvī, -ātum, plow
ars, artis, *f.*, art; profession
arx, arcis, *f.*, citadel
***ascendō, -scendere, -scendī, -scēnsum**, ascend, climb, mount
at, *conj.*, but
atque, *conj.*, and, and also
ātrium, -ī, *n.*, atrium, *the principal room of a house*
***attendō, -tendere, -tendī, -tentum**, turn toward
attineō, -tinēre, -tinuī, -tentum, detain
audācia, -ae, *f.*, boldness, insolence
audeō, -ēre, dare
audiō, -īre, -īvī, -ītum, hear, listen to, listen

*audītōrium, -ī, *n.*, auditorium
audīvit, (he) heard
aureus, -a, -um, of gold, gold (*as adj.*), golden
aurum, -ī, *n.*, gold
aut, *conj.*, or; **aut . . aut,** either . . or
autem, *conj.* (*never stands first in a clause*), but, however, on the other hand; furthermore
***autumnus, -ī,** *m.*, autumn
***auxiliāris, -e,** auxiliary
auxilium, -ī, *n.*, help, aid
***aviārium, -ī,** *n.*, poultry yard, aviary

avis

avis, avis, *f.*, bird
avunculus, -ī, *m.*, uncle (*a mother's brother*)

B

balteus, -ī, *m.*, belt, sword belt
barbarus, -a, -um, barbarous; *m. as noun,* a barbarian; *pl.*, the barbarians
beātus, -a, -um, happy
***bellicōsus, -a, -um,** warlike, bellicose
bellum, -ī, *n.*, war
bene, *adv.*, well
benigna, *see* **benignus**
benignus, -a, -um, kind
bēstia, -ae, *f.*, beast, animal

bestia

bona, *see* **bonus**
***bonitās, -ātis,** *f.*, goodness
bonus, -a, -um, good
bōs, bovis, *m. and f.*, ox
bracchium, -ī, *n.*, forearm, arm
brevis, -e, short, brief
***brevitās, -ātis,** *f.*, brevity

boves

C

caecus, -a, -um, blind
caedō, -ere, cecīdī, caesum, cut
caelestis, -e, heavenly, belonging to heaven; of the sky
caelō, *see* **caelum**
caelum, -ī, *n.*, sky, heaven
calamitās, -ātis, *f.*, disaster, misfortune, calamity
campus, -ī, *m.*, plain, level plain, field, open country
***candēlābrum, -ī,** *n.*, candelabrum
***canīnus, -a, -um,** canine, of a dog
canis, canis, *m. and f.*, dog
cantō, -āre, -āvī, -ātum, sing; crow
***cantor, -ōris,** *m.*, singer, poet
capiō, -ere, cēpī, captum, take, seize, capture; receive
***capitālis, -e,** chief, important
***captīvus, -ī,** *m.*, captive, prisoner
caput, capitis, *n.*, head
cāra, *see* **cārus**
***cārē,** *adv.*, dearly
cārus, -a, -um, dear, precious
casa, -ae, *f.*, cottage, hut
castra, -ōrum, *n. pl.*, camp
cāsus, -ūs, *m.*, fall; accident, chance, disaster
***causa, -ae,** *f.*, cause, reason
***caverna, -ae,** *f.*, cavern, cave
celeriter, *adv.*, quickly, swiftly
cēlō, -āre, -āvī, -ātum, conceal, hide
cēna, -ae, *f.*, dinner, feast
***cēnō, -āre, -āvī, -ātum,** dine
***cēnsus, -ūs,** *m.*, registering of citizens and property by censors; census
centum, a hundred
centuriō, -ōnis, *m.*, centurion, *a subordinate officer in the Roman army*
cēra, -ae, *f.*, wax
certāmen, certāminis, *n.*, contest
certē, *adv.*, surely

certus, -a, -um, certain, definite; **prō certō,** for sure, for certain

cerva, -ae, *f.*, deer

cervus, -ī, *m.*, stag, deer

cēterī, -ae, -a, *pl.*, the other, the rest of, the others

cervus

cibus, -ī, *m.*, food

cicāda, -ae, *f.*, grasshopper, locust

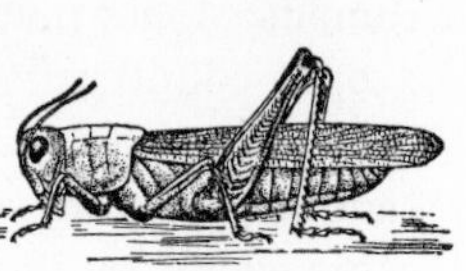

cicada

circum, *prep. with acc.*, around

***circumnāvigō, -āre, -āvī, -ātum,** circumnavigate, sail around

circumspectō, -āre, -āvī, -ātum, look around, look around at

***circumstō, -stāre, -stetī,** stand around, encircle

***circumveniō, -venīre, -vēnī, -ventum,** surround

***circus, -ī,** *m.*, circus

***cīvicus, -a, -um,** civic

***cīvīlis, -e,** civil, civic

cīvis, cīvis, *m. and f.*, citizen

***cīvitās, -ātis,** *f.*, the state, state

clāmō, -āre, -āvī, -ātum, shout, cry out, cry, scream

***clāmor, -ōris,** *m.*, shout, cry

***clangor, -ōris,** *m.*, noise

clāra, *see* **clārus**

clārus, -a, -um, bright, clear; famous

classis, classis, *f.*, fleet; division, class

claudō, -ere, clausī, clausum, shut, close; inclose

***clāvicula, -ae,** *f.*, little key; tendril; collarbone

cloāca, -ae, *f.*, sewer

***cognōscō, -nōscere, -nōvī, -nitum,** find out; know, recognize

cōgō, -ere, coēgī, coāctum, collect; compel

colit, tills, cultivates

***collēctiō, -ōnis,** *f.*, collection

***collēgium, -ī,** *n.*, college; union

collis, collis, *m.*, hill

collis

colō, -ere, coluī, cultum, cultivate, till

***color, -ōris,** *m.*, color

***columna, -ae,** *f.*, column, pillar

coma, -ae, *f.*, hair

comes, comitis, *m. and f.*, companion

***commemorō, -āre, -āvī, -ātum,** remember

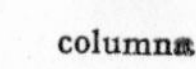

columna

***committō, -ere, -mīsī, missum,** commit, entrust

***commūnicō, -āre, -āvī, -ātum,** communicate

commūnis, -e, common, in common

***comparō, -āre, -āvī, -ātum,** compare

***cōnfirmō, -āre, -āvī, -ātum,** confirm, strengthen, establish

conjiciō, -jicere, -jēcī, -jectum, throw, hurl

***conjugālis, -e,** of marriage, conjugal

conjūnx, conjugis, *m. and f.*, husband, wife

***cōnscrīptiō, -ōnis,** *f.*, report

***consecrō, -āre, -āvī, -ātum,** consecrate, dedicate

***cōnsēnsus, -ūs,** *m.*, agreement

cōnsilium, -ī, *n.*, plan, counsel, design, advice

cōnsōbrīna, -ae, *f.*, cousin

cōnspectus, -ūs, *m.*, sight, view

***cōnstāns,** *gen.*, **-antis,** steady, firm, constant

cōnstituō, -stituere, -stituī, -stitūtum, erect, set up; determine, decide, decide on

cōnsul, cōnsulis, *m.*, consul, *a Roman magistrate*

***cōnsulāris, -e,** consular

***cōnsulātus, -ūs,** *m.*, office of consul

***cōnsūmō, -sūmere, -sūmpsī, -sūmptum,** consume, devour, destroy

***contendō, -tendere, -tendī, -tentum,** hasten; contend

contrā, *prep. with acc.*, against, contrary to

***contrādīcō, -dīcere, -dīxī, -dictum,** contradict

***contrādictōrius, -a, -um,** contradictory

***contrārius, -a, -um,** opposite

***contrōversia, -ae,** *f.*, controversy

conveniō, -venīre, -vēnī, -ventum, assemble, come together, meet, gather

convocō, -āre, -āvī, -ātum, call together

cōpia, -ae, *f.*, plenty, supply; *pl.*, forces, troops

cornū, -ūs, *n.*, horn; flank, wing (*of an army*)

corōna, -ae, *f.*, crown

***corporālis, -e,** of the body, corporal

corpus, corporis, *n.*, body

cotīdiē, *adv.*, every day, daily

crās, *adv.*, tomorrow

***crēdibilis, -e,** credible, believable

crēdō, -ere, crēdidī, crēditum, believe, trust

***crēdulitās, -ātis,** *f.*, credulity, ready belief

***creō, -āre, -āvī, -ātum,** elect, choose; make

crūdēlis, -e, cruel

***crūdēlitās, -ātis,** *f.*, cruelty

***culpa, -ae,** *f.*, blame

culpō, -āre, -āvī, -ātum, blame, censure, find fault with

cum, *prep. with abl.*, with

cum, *conj.*, when

***cupiditās, -ātis,** *f.*, desire

***cupīdō, -inis,** *f.*, desire

***cupidus, -a, -um,** desirous, fond

cupiō, -ere, -īvī, -ītum, wish, want

cūr, *adv.*, why

***cūra, -ae,** *f.*, care, anxiety

***cūrātor, -ōris,** *m.*, manager, curator

***cūriōsitās, -ātis,** *f.*, curiosity

cūriōsus, -a, -um, curious

cūrō, -āre, -āvī, -ātum, care for, take care of, look after, care; cure

currō, -ere, cucurrī, cursum, run

***cutīcula, -ae,** *f.*, skin

D

dē, *prep. with abl.*, down from, from; regarding, concerning, about

dea, -ae, *f.*, goddess

dēbeō, -ēre, -uī, -itum, owe; ought

dea

decem, ten

***decimus, -a, -um,** tenth

***decōrum, -ī,** *n.*, propriety

***dēdūcō, -dūcere, -dūxī, -ductum,** lead away, draw out

dēfendēbant, (they) defended

***dēfendō, -fendere, -fendī, -fēnsum,** defend

dēfessus, -a, -um, tired, tired out, weary, exhausted

***dēfīniō, -īre, -īvī, -ītum,** limit, define

deinde, *adv.*, next, then

dēleō, -ēre, -ēvī, -ētum, destroy, blot out

dēligō, -ligere, -lēgī, -lēctum, choose

***dēmōnstrō, -āre, -āvī, -ātum,** show, point out

dēnique, *adv.*, finally, at last
dēns, dentis, *m.*, tooth
***dēnsus, -a, -um,** dense, thick
***dēscendō, -scendere, -scendī, -scēnsum,** come down, descend

dens

dēscrībō, -ere, -scrīpsī, -scrīptum, describe
***dēscrīptiō, -ōnis,** *f.*, copy, description
dēserō, -serere, -seruī, -sertum, desert, abandon
dēsertus, -a, -um, deserted
dēsīderō, -āre, -āvī, -ātum, desire, want, long for; miss
dēsistō, -sistere, -stitī, -stitum, desist from, cease, stop
***dēspērō, -āre, -āvī, -ātum,** despair of, despair
deus, -ī, *m.*, a god; *nom. pl.* **dī,** gods
dextra, -ae, *f.*, right hand, right (*as opposed to left*); **ā dextrā,** on the right
dī, *see* **deus**
dīc, *imperative sing. of* dīcō
dīcit, (he, she) speaks, says
dīcō, -ere, dīxī, dictum, say, speak; appoint
***dictātor, -ōris,** *m.*, dictator
***dictum, -ī,** *n.*, remark, assertion
diēs, -ēī, *m. and f.*, day
difficilis, -e, difficult, hard
***difficultās, -ātis,** *f.*, difficulty

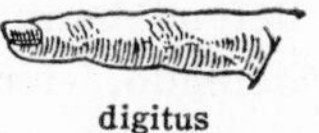
digitus

***digitus, -ī,** *m.*, finger
***dignitās, -ātis,** *f.*, worth, dignity
***dīligentia, -ae,** *f.*, diligence
dīmittō, -mittere, -mīsī, -missum, dismiss, send away, send out, let go; lose
discēdō, -cēdere, -cessī, -cessum, withdraw, depart, go away
discimus, we learn
***disciplīna, -ae,** *f.*, discipline
discō, -ere, didicī, learn
***discus, -ī,** *m.*, discus, disk
dissimilis, -e, unlike
diū, *adv.*, long, for a long time
***dīvidō, -ere, dīvīsī, dīvīsum,** divide, separate
***dīvīnus, -a, -um,** divine, of a deity
dīvitiae, -ārum, *f. pl.*, riches, wealth
dīxit, (he) said
dō, dare, dedī, datum, give, grant; afford
doceō, -ēre, -uī, doctum, teach, explain, instruct
doleō, -ēre, -uī, -itūrus, suffer; grieve, grieve for
dolor, -ōris, *m.*, sorrow, grief; pain
dolus, -ī, *m.*, trick, treachery, deceit; scheme
***domesticus, -a, -um,** domestic, belonging to the house
domī, at home
domicilium, -ī, *n.*, domicile, home
dominus, -ī, *m.*, master
***domus, -ūs (ī),** *f.*, house, home
***dōnō, -āre, -āvī, -ātum,** give
dōnum, -ī, *n.*, gift
dormiō, -īre, -īvī, -ītum, sleep
dracō, -ōnis, *m.*, serpent; dragon

draco

dubius, -a, -um, doubtful, dubious
dūcō, -ere, dūxī, ductum, lead; bring
***ductilis, -e,** that may be guided
***ductor, -ōris,** *m.*, commander
***ductus, -ūs,** *m.*, a leading; duct
dum, *conj.*, while, as long as
duo, duae, duo, two
***duodecim,** twelve
dūrus, -a, -um, hard, difficult; harsh
dux, ducis, *m.*, leader
dūxit, (he, she, it) led

E

ē, ex, *prep. with abl.*, from, from within, out of, of
ecce, behold! see!
***ēducātiō, -ōnis,** *f.*, education
***ēducātor, -ōris,** *m.*, tutor
ēdūcō, -ere, -dūxī, -ductum, draw out
ego, meī, I
ēgregius, -a, -um, excellent, distinguished, unusual
***elephantus, -ī,** *m.*, elephant
***ēloquentia, -ae,** *f.*, eloquence
eō, īre, iī (īvī), itum, go

elephantus

epistula, -ae, *f.*, letter
eques, equitis, *m.*, horseman; *pl.*, the cavalry
***equīnus, -a, -um,** of a horse
equus, -ī, *m.*, horse
erant, (they) were
erat, (he, she, it) was
eris, (you) will be
erit, (he, she, it) will be

equus

errō, -āre, -āvī, -ātum, wander; err
***error, -ōris,** *m.*, error, mistake
esse, *infinitive of* **sum,** to be
est, (he, she, it) is
este, *imperative pl. of* **sum,** be
et, *conj.*, and; **et . . . et,** both . . . and
etiam, *adv.*, even, also
***ēventus, -ūs,** *m.*, event
ex, *see* **ē**
***exaltō, -āre, -āvī, -ātum,** raise, exalt
excēdō, -cēdere, -cessī, -cessum, withdraw, depart, go out
excitō, -āre, -āvī, -ātum, stir up, rouse, arouse, excite, awake, alarm
exemplar, exemplāris, *n.*, example, copy, likeness
exeō, -īre, -iī, -itum, go forth, go out
exercitus, -ūs, *m.*, army
***exilium, -ī,** *n.*, exile
exīstimō, -āre, -āvī, -ātum, think, estimate
***exitus, -ūs,** *m.*, outcome, result, way out
***expectātiō, -ōnis,** *f.*, expectation
expectō, -āre, -āvī, -ātum, expect; await, wait for, wait
***expellō, -pellere, -pulī, -pulsum,** drive out
***explōrō, -āre, -āvī, -ātum,** explore
expugnō, -āre, -āvī, -ātum, capture, take by storm

F

fābula, -ae, *f.*, story, play
fac, *imperative sing. of* **faciō**
facile, *adv.*, easily
facilis, -e, easy
faciō, -ere, fēcī, factum, make; do
facit, (he, she, it) makes; does
factum, -ī, *n.*, deed, act
***facultās, -ātis,** *f.*, opportunity, chance; power of doing, ability
***falsus, -a, -um,** false, deceiving
***fāma, -ae,** *f.*, report; reputation
***familia, -ae,** *f.*, family
***fātum, -ī,** *n.*, fate
***fēlīnus, -a, -um,** of a cat, feline
***fēlis, -is,** *f.*, cat
fēlīx, *gen.* **fēlīcis,** happy, fortunate
fēmina, -ae, *f.*, woman
***fēminīnus, -a, -um,** feminine; like that of a woman
fenestra, -ae, *f.*, window
ferrum, -ī, *n.*, iron
ferus, -a, -um, fierce, wild

fībula, -ae, *f.*, brooch
fidēlis, -e, faithful
fīdus, -a, -um, faithful
***figūra, -ae,** *f.*, figure
fīlia, -ae, *f.*, daughter
fīlius, -ī, *m.*, son

fibula

***fīniō, -īre, -īvī, -ītum,** finish, limit
fīnis, fīnis, *m.*, end, boundary, limit; *pl.*, country, territory
***firmō, -āre, -āvī, -ātum,** make firm
***firmus, -a, -um,** firm
flamma, -ae, *f.*, fire, flame
flūmen, flūminis, *n.*, river
fluō, -ere, flūxī, flūxum, flow
foedus, -eris, *n.*, agreement, treaty
folium, -ī, *n.*, leaf

folia

fōns, fontis, *m.*, fountain
***fōrma, -ae,** *f.*, form; beauty
formīca, -ae, *f.*, ant
fortis, -e, brave; strong
fortiter, *adv.*, bravely
***fortitūdō, -inis,** *f.*, firmness, fortitude

formica

***fortūna, -ae,** *f.*, fortune
***fortūnātus, -a, -um,** fortunate
***fortūnō, -āre, -āvī, -ātum,** make happy, bless
***forum, -ī,** *n.*, forum, market place
***frāgmentum, -ī,** *n.*, fragment
frangō, -ere, frēgī, frāctum, break, break down
frāter, frātris, *m.*, brother
***frīgidus, -a, -um,** cold
frūmentum, -ī, *n.*, grain
fuga, -ae, *f.*, flight
fūgērunt, (they) fled
fugiō, -ere, fūgī, fugitūrus, flee
fūgit, (he, she, it) fled
***fugitīvus, -ī,** *m.*, fugitive
***fūmus, -ī,** *m.*, smoke, fume, vapor
funda, -ae, *f.*, sling
funditor, -ōris, *m.*, slinger

funda

***furia, -ae,** *f.*, fury; curse
furor, -ōris, *m.*, madness, frenzy

G

galea, -ae, *f.*, helmet
gaudium, -ī, *n.*, joy, happiness, delight, pleasure
gemma, -ae, *f.*, jewel, gem
gēns, gentis, *f.*, nation
genus, generis, *n.*, kind, sort
gerō, -ere, gessī, gestum, carry, **wear;** carry on, wage, do
***gladiātor, -ōris,** *m.*, gladiator
gladius, -ī, *m.*, sword
***glōria, -ae,** *f.*, fame, glory
grāmen, grāminis, *n.*, grass
grāta, *see* **grātus**
***grātia, -ae,** *f.*, favor, gratitude; **grātiās agere** (*takes dative*), thank
grātus, -a, -um, pleasing, welcome, grateful
gravis, -e, heavy; hard, severe, serious
graviter, *adv.*, severely; **heavily;** greatly, deeply

H

habēbant, (they) had
habēbat, (he, she, it) had
habent, (they) have
habeō, -ēre, -uī, -itum, have, **hold;** regard
habet, (he, she, it) has
habitō, -āre, -āvī, -ātum, live, live **in,** dwell
hasta, -ae, *f.*, spear
***herba, -ae,** *f.*, herb; grass
herī, *adv.*, yesterday
heu, alas!, oh me!

hic, haec, hoc, this; *pl.*, these; *as pronoun*, he, she, it; *pl.*, they
hīc, *adv.*, here
hieme, in winter
hodiē, *adv.*, today
homō, hominis, *m.*, man, human being
***honor, -ōris,** *m.*, honor, esteem
***honōrō, -āre, -āvī, -ātum,** honor
hōra, -ae, *f.*, hour
hortus, -ī, *m.*, garden
***hostīlis, -e,** hostile, of an enemy

hortus

hostis, hostis, *m.*, enemy (*a public enemy*); *pl.*, the enemy
hūc, *adv.*, to this place, here, hither
***hūmānitās, -ātis,** *f.*, humanity
***hūmānus, -a, -um,** human, relating to human beings
humilis, -e, low

I

ibi, *adv.*, there, in that place
īdem, eadem, idem, same, the same
idōneus, -a, -um, suitable, fit, favorable
igitur, *adv.*, therefore
ignāvus, -a, -um, idle; cowardly; *m. as noun*, coward
ignis, ignis, *m.*, fire
***ignōrantia, -ae,** *f.*, ignorance

ignis

ille, illa, illud, that; *pl.*, those; *as pronoun*, he, she, it; *pl.*, they
***imāginārius, -a, -um,** seeming, imaginary
***immortālis, -e,** immortal, deathless
***impedīmentum, -ī,** *n.*, impediment, hindrance
imperātor, -ōris, *m.*, general, commander, emperor
imperātum, -ī, *n.*, command, order; **imperāta facere,** obey commands
impetus, -ūs, *m.*, attack
impiger, -gra, -grum, energetic, industrious
in, *prep. with abl. or acc.; with abl.*, in, on, among; over; *with acc.*, into, to, on, against, at
incipiō, -cipere, -cēpī, -ceptum, begin
incola, -ae, *m. and f.*, inhabitant
***incrēdibilis, -e,** incredible
***indūcō, -dūcere, -dūxī, -ductum,** lead in, influence
***indulgentia, -ae,** *f.*, indulgence
īnfēlīx, *gen.*, **īnfēlīcis,** unlucky, unhappy
***īnfīnītus, -a, -um,** unlimited
***īnfirmitās, -ātis,** *f.*, weakness
***īnflātiō, -ōnis,** *f.*, inflation
īnflō, -āre, -āvī, -ātum, blow into, blow; play on
ingēns, *gen.* **-entis,** huge
inimīcus, -a, -um, unfriendly; *m. as noun*, enemy (*a personal enemy*)
initium, -ī, *n.*, beginning
***injūria, -ae,** *f.*, injury, wrong
injūstus, -a, -um, unfair, unjust
***īnsānus, -a, -um,** insane, crazy
īnsigne, īnsignis, *n.*, decoration, badge
***institūtiō, -ōnis,** *f.*, instruction
īnstruō, -struere, -strūxī, -strūctum, draw up; build; provide
īnsula, -ae, *f.*, island
***intelligentia, -ae,** *f.*, intelligence

insula

inter, *prep. with acc.*, between, among
interdiū, *adv.*, by day, during the day
interdum, *adv.*, sometimes
interficiō, -ficere, -fēcī, -fectum, kill, slay
interim, *adv.*, meanwhile, in the meantime
intrā, *prep. with acc.*, within
intrō, -āre, -āvī, -ātum, enter
***invalidus, -a, -um,** not strong

inveniō, -venīre, -vēnī, -ventum, find, find out, discover
invidiōsa, *see* **invidiōsus**
invidiōsus, -a, -um, jealous
invītō, -āre, -āvī, -ātum, invite
ipse, ipsa, ipsum, self, himself, herself, itself; *pl.*, themselves; the very
***īra, -ae,** *f.*, anger
īrāta, *see* **īrātus**
īrātus, -a, -um, angry
is, ea, id, that, this; *pl.*, those, these; *as pronoun*, he, she, it; *pl.*, they
ita, *adv.*, so, thus; yes; **ita est,** yes
itaque, *conj.*, and so, therefore
item, *adv.*, likewise
iter, itineris, *n.*, road; journey, march; route, course
iterum, *adv.*, again

J

jaceō, -ēre, -uī, lie, lie down
jaciō, -ere, jēcī, jactum, throw, hurl
jaculum, -ī, *n.*, javelin
jam, *adv.*, now, already; **nōn jam,** no longer
jānua, -ae, *f.*, door
jubeō, -ēre, jussī, jussum, order, command
jūdex, jūdicis, *m.*, judge, juror
jūdicium, -ī, *n.*, judgment, decision
***jūdicō, -āre, -āvī, -ātum,** judge
jungō, -ere, jūnxī, jūnctum, join, yoke, fasten together
jussū, at the order
***jūstus, -a, -um,** just, fair
jūstitia, -ae, *f.*, justice, uprightness, fairness
jūtus, *see* **juvō**
juvenis, juvenis, *m.*, young man, youth
juvō, -āre, jūvī, jūtum, help, assist

jaculum

L

***labor, -ōris,** *m.*, labor, task
labōrō, -āre, -āvī, -ātum, work, labor, toil
lacrima, -ae, *f.*, tear
lacrimō, -āre, -āvī, -ātum, weep, cry
***lacus, -ūs,** *m.*, lake
laeta, *see* **laetus**
laetus, -a, -um, happy, glad
***lāmentum, -ī,** *n.*, lament
lapis, lapidis, *m.*, a stone
***lātē,** *adv.*, widely
lateō, -ēre, -uī, lurk, hide, be concealed
lātus, -a, -um, wide, broad
***laudābilis, -e,** laudable, praiseworthy
laudāmus, we praise
laudant, (they) praise
laudat, (he) praises, does praise, approves of
laudō, -āre, -āvī, -ātum, praise
***laus, laudis,** *f.*, praise
lavō, -āre, lāvī, lautum, bathe, wash
***lēgālis, -e,** legal
legiō, -ōnis, *f.*, legion, *a Roman company of soldiers (4000 to 6000 men)*
legit, (he, she) reads
legō, -ere, lēgī, lēctum, read
lēniter, *adv.*, slowly
leō, -ōnis, *m.*, lion
***leōnīnus, -a, -um,** of a lion, leonine
lēx, lēgis, *f.*, law
libenter, *adv.*, willingly, with pleasure, gladly, freely
līber, lībera, līberum, free
liber, -brī, *m.*, book
lībera, *see* **līber**
***līberālis, -e,** of freedom, liberal
***līberātor, -ōris,** *m.*, liberator

leones

līberī, -ōrum, *m. pl.*, children
***līberō, -āre, -āvī, -ātum,** set free
***lībertās, -ātis,** *f.*, freedom, liberty
ligneus, -a, -um, wooden, of wood
lignum, -ī, *n.*, wood; *pl.*, firewood, wood
***līlium, -ī,** *n.*, lily
lingua, -ae, *f.*, tongue; language; speech
lītus, lītoris, *n.*, shore
***locālis, -e,** of a place
locus, -ī, *m.*, place; (*pl. usually n.*, **loca, -ōrum**)

lilia

longa, *see* **longus**
longaevus, -a, -um, aged, old
longē, *adv.*, far, at a distance
longinquus, -a, -um, distant
***longitūdō, -inis,** *f.*, length
longus, -a, -um, long
lucerna, -ae, *f.*, lamp
lūmen, -inis, *n.*, light

lucerna

lūna, -ae, *f.*, moon
***lūnāris, -e,** of the moon, lunar
lūx, lūcis, *f.*, light; **prīma lūx,** daybreak
***lympha, -ae,** *f.*, water, clear water
***lyra, -ae,** *f.*, lyre

M

***māchina, -ae,** *f.*, machine
maestus, -a, -um, sad, gloomy
maga, -ae, *f.*, enchantress
magicus, -a, -um, magical, magic
magis, *comparative of* **magnopere,** more, rather
magister, -trī, *m.*, master, teacher
***magistrātus, -ūs,** *m.*, official, magistrate
magna, *see* **magnus**
***magnanimus, -a, -um,** magnanimous
***magnificentia, -ae,** *f.*, magnificence
***magnitūdō, -inis,** *f.*, greatness, size, magnitude
magnopere, *adv.*, greatly, very much, very
magnus, -a, -um, large, great; loud
major, majus, *comparative of* **magnus,** larger, greater
male, *adv.*, badly
mālum, -ī, *n.*, apple
malus, -a, -um, bad

malum

māne, *adv.*, in the morning
maneō, -ēre, mānsī, mānsum, remain, wait, stay
manet, (he, she, it) remains, stays
manus, -ūs, *f.*, hand; band (*of armed men*)
mare, maris, *n.*, sea, ocean
***marīnus, -a, -um,** marine
maritima, *see* **maritimus**
maritimus, -a, -um, of the sea, maritime; **ōra maritima,** seacoast
māter, mātris, *f.*, mother
mātrimōnium, -ī, *n.*, marriage; **in mātrimōnium dūcere,** to marry
***mātrōna, -ae,** *f.*, matron
maximē, *superlative of* **magnopere,** especially; very greatly, very, very much
maximus, -a, -um, *superlative of* **magnus,** greatest
mē, *acc. or abl. of* **ego,** me
mea, *see* **meus**
***medicīna, -ae,** *f.*, medicine
medius, -a, -um, middle, middle of, in the middle; *n. sing. as noun,* the middle
melior, melius, *comparative of* **bonus,** better
melius, *comparative of* **bene,** better
***membrum, -ī,** *n.*, limb

***memoria, -ae,** *f.*, memory
mendicus, -ī, *m.*, beggar

mendicus

mēns, mentis, *f.*, mind; purpose
mēnsa, -ae, *f.*, table
mēnsis, mēnsis, *m.*, month
mercātor, -ōris, *m.*, trader, merchant
***meritum, -ī,** *n.*, merit
meus, -a, -um, my, mine
***migrō, -āre, -āvī, -ātum,** migrate, move
mihi, *dat. of* **ego,** to me, me (*as indirect object*)
mīles, mīlitis, *m.*, soldier
mīlia, *see* **mīlle**
***mīlitāris, -e,** military
***mīlitia, -ae,** *f.*, military service
mīlle (*pl.* **mīlia, -ium,** *n.*), thousand; **mīlle passūs** *or* **mīlle passuum,** a mile
minimē, *superlative of* **parum,** by no means, no; not at all
minimus, -a, -um, *superlative of* **parvus,** smallest, least
minor, minus, *comparative of* **parvus,** smaller, less
minus, *comparative of* **parum,** less
mīrus, -a, -um, strange, remarkable
miser, misera, miserum, unhappy, miserable, unfortunate
mittit, (he, she, it) sends, is sending
mittō, -ere, mīsī, missum, send; shoot
***moderātor, -ōris,** *m.*, director
***modus, -ī,** *m.*, manner, way
moenia, -ium, *n. pl.*, walls (*of a city*), fortifications
moneō, -ēre, -uī, -itum, warn, advise
***monitor, -ōris,** *m.*, monitor
mōns, montis, *m.*, mountain
mōnstrō, -āre, -āvī, -ātum, point out, show, display

mons

***mōnstrum, -ī,** *n.*, monster
***monumentum, -ī,** *n.*, monument
mora, -ae, *f.*, delay
mors, mortis, *f.*, death
***mortālis, -e,** subject to death, mortal
mortuus, -a, -um, dead; *m. sing. as noun,* a dead person
***moveō, -ēre, mōvī, mōtum,** move
mox, *adv.*, soon
multa, *see* **multus**
multae, *see* **multus**
***multitūdō, -inis,** *f.*, multitude, great number, crowd
***multum,** *adv.*, much, greatly
multus, -a, -um, much; *pl.*, many; *m. pl. as noun,* many (persons); *n. sing. as noun,* much; *n. pl. as noun,* many things
mūniō, -īre, -īvī, -ītum, fortify
mūrus, -ī, *m.*, wall

murus

***mūsa, -ae,** *f.*, muse; song, poem
mūtō, -āre, -āvī, -ātum, change, turn

N

nārrat, (he, she) tells
***nārrātor, -ōris,** *m.*, narrator
nārrō, -āre, -āvī, -ātum, tell, relate, tell a story
***nātiō, -ōnis,** *f.*, nation, tribe
natō, -āre, -āvī, -ātum, swim, float
***nātūra, -ae,** *f.*, nature
***nātūrālis, -e,** natural
nauta, -ae, *m.*, sailor
***nāvālis, -e,** naval
nāvigō, -āre, -āvī, -ātum, sail, navigate
nāvis, nāvis, *f.*, ship, boat
-ne, *attached to a word, to denote a question to be answered by "yes" or "no"*
necesse, *indeclinable adj.*, necessary; inevitable

necō, -āre, -āvī, -ātum, kill
nēmō, *dat.* **nēminī,** *acc.* **nēminem,** *no gen. or abl., m. and f.,* no one, nobody
neque, *conj.*, nor, and . . . not; **neque . . . neque,** neither . . . nor
nihil, *n., indeclinable,* nothing
nōbilis, -e, noble; well-known; *m. pl. as noun,* the nobles
nōbīs, *dat. and abl. of* **nōs,** we
noctū, *adv.*, at night
nōlī, *pl.* **nōlīte,** *imperative* be unwilling, do not
nōmen, nōminis, *n.*, name
***nōminālis, -e,** nominal
***nōminō, -āre, -āvī, -ātum,** name
nōn, *adv.*, not; **nōn sōlum . . . sed etiam,** not only . . . but also
nōnne, *used to introduce a question and to imply the answer "yes"*
nōs, *nom. and acc. pl. of* **ego,** we, us
noster, -tra, -trum, our, ours
nostra, *see* **noster**
nōta, *see* **nōtus**
***nōtitia, -ae,** *f.*, knowledge; notice, fame
nōtus, -a, -um, known, well-known, noted, familiar
nova, *see* **novus**
novem, nine

IX
novem

***novō, -āre, -āvī, -ātum,** renew
novus, -a, -um, new
nox, noctis, *f.*, night
nūbēs, nūbis, *f.*, cloud

nubes

nūllus, -a, -um, no, none
numerus, -ī, *m.*, number
numquam, *adv.*, never
nunc, *adv.*, now
nūntiō, -āre, -āvī, -ātum, announce, report
nūntius, -ī, *m.*, messenger; message, news
nūtrīx, nūtrīcis, *f.*, nurse
***nympha, -ae,** *f.*, nymph

O

Ō, O! oh!
obscūra, *see* **obscūrus**
obscūrus, -a, -um, dark, dim, obscure; invisible
***observō, -āre, -āvī, -ātum,** observe
occīdō, -cīdere, -cīdī, -cīsum, kill, slay
occupō, -āre, -āvī, -ātum, seize, occupy
octō, eight
oculus, -ī, *m.*, eye

oculus

***odiōsus, -a, -um,** odious, hateful
odium, -ī, *n.*, hatred
oecus, -ī, *m.*, large room for entertaining (*see p. 88*)
***officium, -ī,** *n.*, duty, service, office
ōlim, *adv.*, some day, sometimes; formerly, once upon a time
***ōmen, -inis,** *n.*, omen, sign, portent
omnis, -e, all, every, whole; *n. pl. as noun,* everything
***opīniō, -ōnis,** *f.*, opinion
oppidum, -ī, *n.*, town
***oppōnō, -pōnere, -posuī, -positum,** set against, oppose
oppugnō, -āre, -āvī, -ātum, attack
optimē, *superlative of* **bene,** best, in the best way
optimus, -a, -um, *superlative of* **bonus,** best
ora, -ae, *f.*, shore; **ōra maritima,** seacoast
***ōrāculum, -ī,** *n.*, oracle

*ōrātor, -ōris, *m.*, orator
*ōrdinārius, -a, -um, ordinary
*ōrnāmentum, -ī, *n.*, equipment, ornament
*ōrnātus, -a, -um, equipped, adorned
*ōrnō, -āre, -āvī, -ātum, equip
ōrō, -āre, -āvī, -ātum, beg for, ask for, pray to
ostendō, -tendere, -tendī, -tentum, show, display

P

paene, *adv.*, almost
palla, -ae, *f.*, long robe, mantle; curtain

palla

*palma, -ae, *f.*, palm, hand
parātus, -a, -um, prepared, ready
parō, -āre, -āvī, -ātum, get ready, prepare; obtain, get
*pars, partis, *f.*, part, direction; side
parum, *adv. and indeclinable noun*, too little, insufficiently, little
parva, *see* parvus
parvus, -a, -um, small, little
passus, -ūs, *m.*, pace; mīlle passūs *or* mīlle passuum, a mile

pastor

pāstor, -ōris, *m.*, shepherd
pater, patris, *m.*, father
*patientia, -ae, *f.*, patience
patria, -ae, *f.*, native country, country, one's country, native land
*patrimōnium, -ī, *n.*, patrimony
paucī, -ae, -a, *pl.*, few, a few
pāx, pācis, *f.*, peace
pecūnia, -ae, *f.*, money

pecunia

pejor, pejus, *comp. of* malus, worse
*pellō, -ere, pepulī, pulsum, beat; rout, drive
*pendulum, -ī, *n.*, pendulum
penna, -ae, *f.*, feather
per, *prep. with acc.*, through; all along
*perambulō, -āre, -āvī, -ātum, walk through, traverse
*perdūcō, -dūcere, -dūxī, -ductum, lead, bring, lead through
*perēmptōrius, -a, -um, peremptory
*perfectus, -a, -um, perfect
*perfidia, -ae, *f.*, treachery, perfidy
perfidus, -a, -um, treacherous; without faith
perīculōsa, *see* perīculōsus
perīculōsus, -a, -um, dangerous
perīculum, -ī, *n.*, danger, peril
peristȳlium, -iī, *n.*, an open court (*see p. 88*)
*perpetuus, -a, -um, continuous, perpetual
*persōnālis, -e, personal
*pertineō, -tinēre, -tinuī, -tentum, extend, reach
*perturbō, -āre, -āvī, -ātum, disturb, alarm
perveniō, -venīre, -vēnī, -ventum, arrive, come, arrive at, reach
pēs, pedis, *m.*, foot; pedibus, on foot

pes

pessimus, -a, -um, *superlative of* malus, worst
*pestilentia, -ae, *f.*, pestilence, plague
petō, -ere, petīvī, petītum, seek, look for; ask, ask for; attack
pictūra, -ae, *f.*, picture
piger, -gra, -grum, lazy
pīlum, -ī, *n.*, spear
pīrāta, -ae, *m.*, pirate
*plūma, -ae, *f.*, plume
plūrimus, -a, -um, *superlative of* multus
plūs, *gen.* plūris; *pl.*, plūrēs, plūra, *adj.*, more

pilum

poēta, -ae, *m.*, poet
pōnō, -ere, posuī, positum, place, put, station; **castra pōnere,** pitch camp
pōns, pontis, *m.*, bridge

pons

populus, -ī, *m.*, people
porta, -ae, *f.*, gate, door
portō, -āre, -āvī, -ātum, carry, bring
portus, portūs, *m.*, harbor

portus

possum, posse, potuī, be able, can
post, *prep. with acc.*, behind, after, back of; *adv.*, afterwards, later
posteā, *adv.*, afterwards, thereafter, later
postquam, *conj.*, after
postrīdiē, *adv.*, on the next day
postulō, -āre, -āvī, -ātum, demand
potēns, *gen.* **-entis,** powerful
potentia, -ae, *f.*, power
potestās, -ātis, *f.*, power, control
*__praejūdicium, -ī,__ *n.*, prejudice
praemium, -ī, *n.*, reward
praeter, *prep. with acc.*, past; except
pretiōsus, -a, -um, expensive, costly
pretium, -ī, *n.*, price
prīmō, *adv.*, at first, first
prīmum, *adv.*, first, at first; **quam prīmum,** as soon as possible
prīmus, -a, -um, first; **prīma lūx,** daybreak
prīnceps, prīncipis, *m.*, chief, prince, leader
*__prīncipālis, -e,__ first
*__prīvātus, -a, -um,__ private
prō, *prep. with abl.*, for, for the sake of, on behalf of; before, in front of
probō, -āre, -āvī, -ātum, approve, approve of
prōcēdō, -cēdere, -cessī, -cessum, proceed, advance, march
procul, *adv.*, at a distance, far
procus, -ī, *m.*, suitor, lover
proelium, -ī, *n.*, battle
prōfluō, -fluere, -flūxī, -flūxum, flow, flow forth
prohibeō, -hibēre, -hibuī, -hibitum, prohibit, forbid; prevent, hinder, keep away
prōmittō, -mittere, -mīsī, -missum, promise
prope, *prep. with acc.*, near
properō, -āre, -āvī, -ātum, hasten, hurry
propinqua, *see* **propinquus**
propinquus, -a, -um, near, neighboring, nearby
propter, *prep. with acc.*, on account of
prōvincia, -ae, *f.*, province
prōvocō, -āre, -āvī, -ātum, challenge; summon
*__prūdentia, -ae,__ *f.*, prudence
pūblicus, -a, -um, public
puella, -ae, *f.*, girl
puer, puerī, *m.*, boy, youth
*__pugna, -ae,__ *f.*, fight, combat, battle
pugnō, -āre, -āvī, -ātum, fight
*__pugnus, -ī,__ *m.*, fist
pulcher, -chra, -chrum, beautiful
pulchra, *see* **pulcher**
putō, -āre, -āvī, -ātum, think

Q

quam, *adv.*, how, as, than; **quam prīmum,** as soon as possible; *with superlatives*, as . . . as possible
quamquam, *conj.*, although
*__quārtus, -a, -um,__ fourth

IV
quattuor

quattuor, four
-que, *conj. attached to a word*, and

quī, quae, quod, *interrog. adj.*, which, what
quī, quae, quod, *rel. pron.*, who, which, that
quid, *interrog. pron.*, what
quidem, *adv.* (*never stands first in a clause*), indeed, certainly
quiēta, *see* **quiētus**
quiētus, -a, -um, quiet
quinque
quīnque, five
quis, quid, *interrog. pron.*, who, what
quod, *conj.*, because
quoque, *conj.* (*never stands first in a clause*), also

R

***radius, -ī,** *m.*, rod, staff; spoke (*of a wheel*); ray
rāmus, -ī, *m.*, branch, bough
ramus
rāna, -ae, *f.*, frog
***rapidus, -a, -um,** rapid
re- (*prefix*), back, again
recēdō, -cēdere, -cessī, -cessum, go back, retreat, withdraw
***receptāculum, -ī,** *n.*, receptacle
***recessus, -ūs,** *m.*, retreat
recipiō, -cipere, -cēpī, -ceptum, receive; take back
***recitātiō, -ōnis,** *f.*, reading aloud
recognōscō, -cognōscere, -cognōvī, -cognitum, recognize
rēctē, *adv.*, rightly
recūsō, -āre, -āvī, -ātum, refuse
redeō, -īre, -iī, -itum, go back, return
***redūcō, -dūcere, -dūxī, -ductum,** lead back, bring back
***refugiō, -fugere, -fūgī, -fugitūrus,** flee
***rēgālis, -e,** regal
rēgia, -ae, *f.*, palace
rēgīna, -ae, *f.*, queen
regiō, -ōnis, *f.*, region, district
***rēgius, -a, -um,** kingly, regal
***rēgnō, -āre, -āvī, -ātum,** rule
rēgnum, -ī, *n.*, kingdom; royal power
***regō, -ere, rēxī, rēctum,** direct; rule
***religiō, -ōnis,** *f.*, moral obligation
relinquō, -linquere, -līquī, -lictum, leave, leave behind, abandon
***remittō, -mittere, -mīsī, -missum,** send back
***removeō, -movēre, -mōvī, -mōtum,** remove, withdraw
repellō, -pellere, reppulī, repulsum, drive back, repel, repulse
***reportō, -āre, -āvī, -ātum,** carry back; report
rēs, reī, *f.*, thing; affair, fact, circumstance, matter
***resistō, -ere, -stitī,** resist
respiciō, -spicere, -spexī, -spectum, look back, look back at
respondeō, -spondēre, -spondī, -spōnsum, answer, reply
***retineō, -tinēre, -tinuī, -tentum,** retain
***reveniō, -īre, -vēnī, -ventum,** come back
rēx, rēgis, *m.*, king
rīpa, -ae, *f.*, bank (*of a stream*)
rogō, -āre, -āvī, -ātum, ask
***rosa, -ae,** *f.*, rose
rosa
rōstrum, -ī, *n.*, beak
***ruīna, -ae,** *f.* (*often in the plural*), ruin
***rūmor, -ōris,** *m.*, rumor
rostrum

S

sacer, -cra, -crum, sacred, holy
sacerdōs, -dōtis, *m. and f.*, priest, priestess
***sacrificium, -ī,** *n.*, sacrifice
***sacrificō, -āre, -āvī, -ātum,** sacrifice

*sacrum, -ī, n., sacred rite, religious custom or observance
saepe, adv., often
sagitta, -ae, f., arrow
sagitta
sagittārius, -ī, m., archer
salūs, salūtis, f., safety; salūtem dīcit, gives greetings, greets
*salūtō, -āre, -āvī, -ātum, greet
sanguis, -inis, m., blood
*sānus, -a, -um, sane, healthy
sapiēns, gen. -entis, wise
*sapienter, adv., wisely
sapientia, -ae, f., wisdom
satis, adv., sufficiently, enough
saxum, -ī, n., stone, a stone, rock
*scaena, -ae, f., scene
scelus, sceleris, n., crime; scelus facere, commit a crime
schola, -ae, f., school
sciō, scīre, scīvī, scītum, know, know how
scrībit, (he, she) writes
scrībō, -ere, scrīpsī, scrīptum, write
*scrīptor, -ōris, m., writer
*scrīptum, ī, n., written composition
*scrīptūra, -ae, f., writing
*sculptūra, -ae, f., sculpture
scūtum, -ī, n., shield
sēcrētō, adv., secretly
*sēcrētus, -a, -um, secret
scutum
secundus, -a, -um, second; favorable
*sēcūritās, -ātis, f., freedom from anxiety
sed, conj., but
sedeō, -ēre, sēdī, sessum, sit, be seated; settle, settle down
semper, adv., always
*senātor, -ōris, m., senator
*senātus, -ūs, m., senate
sentiō, -īre, sēnsī, sēnsum, feel, notice, think, know, believe, realize
sēparō, -āre, -āvī, -ātum, separate

septem, seven
*sepulchrum, -ī, n., sepulcher
serpēns, -entis, f., serpent, snake
serpens
serva, -ae, f., female slave, maidservant
*servīlis, -e, slavish, servile
*serviō, -īre, -īvī, -ītum, serve
servō, -āre, -āvī, -ātum, save, preserve, keep
servus, -ī, m., slave, servant
*sevēritās, -ātis, f., sternness, severity; seriousness
*sevērus, -a, -um, stern, severe
sex, six
sī, conj., if
sīc, adv., thus, so
significō, -āre, -āvī, -ātum, mean
*signō, -āre, -āvī, -ātum, mark; seal
*signum, -ī, n., sign, mark, standard, signal; seal
silentium, -ī, n., silence; silentiō, in silence, silently
sileō, -ēre, -uī, be silent
silva, -ae, f., forest
similis, -e, like, similar
sine, prep. with abl., without
sinistra, -ae, f., left hand, left; ā sinistrā, on the left
*sistō, -ere, stitī, statum, plant, set
socius, -ī, m., ally, comrade, companion
sōl, sōlis, m., sun
*sōlitūdō, -inis, f., solitude
sol
sōlus, -a, -um, alone, only; single; nōn sōlum . . . sed etiam, not only . . . but also
somnium, -ī, n., dream
somnus, -ī, m., sleep
sonus, -ī, m., sound, noise

soror, -ōris, *f.*, sister
***spectāculum, -ī,** *n.*, spectacle, sight, show, exhibition
***spectātor, -ōris,** *m.*, spectator
spectō, -āre, -āvī, -ātum, watch, look at, look
spēlunca, -ae, *f.*, cave, den
spīna, -ae, *f.*, thorn
***stabilis, -e,** firm, stable
***stabilitās, -ātis,** *f.*, stability
***stabulō, -āre,** put in a stable
***stabulum, -ī,** *n.*, stable, stall
***stadium, -ī,** *n.*, stadium
***stāmen, -inis,** *n.*, thread
statim, *adv.*, at once, immediately
***statiō, -ōnis,** *f.*, station
***statua, -ae,** *f.*, statue
***statuārius, -a, -um,** statuary
***statuō, -ere, -uī, -ūtum,** set up
***statūra, -ae,** *f.*, height, stature
***status, -ūs,** *m.*, station, position
stella, -ae, *f.*, star
***stimulus, -ī,** *m.*, goad, spur

stella

stō, stāre, stetī, stātūrus, stand
***strātum, -ī,** *n.*, covering, layer
stultus, -a, -um, foolish, stupid
***stupidus, -a, -um,** stupid
sub, *prep. with acc. or abl.*, under, below
subitō, *adv.*, suddenly
suī (*gen.*), *reflexive pron.*, of himself, herself, itself, themselves
sum, esse, fuī, futūrus, be
summus, -a, -um, highest, greatest, utmost; highest part of, top of
sunt, (they) are
superba, *see* **superbus**
***superbia, -ae,** *f.*, pride, haughtiness
superbus, -a, -um, proud, haughty
superō, -āre, -āvī, -ātum, defeat, overcome, conquer; surpass
suprā, *adv., and prep. with acc.; as adv.*, above, before; *as prep.*, above, over
sūs, suis, *m. and f.*, pig, hog, swine

sus

***suspīciō, -ōnis,** *f.*, suspicion
sustineō, -tinēre, -tinuī, -tentum, uphold, withstand, support, endure
suus, -a, -um, his, her, its, their; *in reflexive meaning,* his own, her own, its own, their own

T

tabernāculum, -ī, *n.*, tent

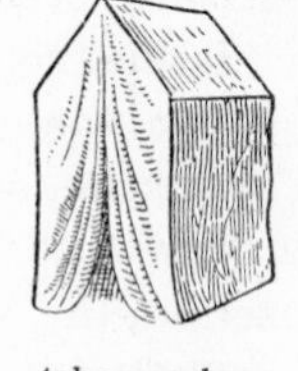

tabernaculum

tablīnum, -ī, *n.*, room next to the atrium (*see p. 89*)
***tabula, -ae,** *f.*, table
taeda, -ae, *f.*, torch
tam, *adv.*, so
tamen, *adv.*, still, nevertheless, however
tandem, *adv.*, at length, finally, at last
taurus, -ī, *m.*, bull

taurus

tē, *acc. or abl.* of **tū,** you (*sing.*)
tēctum, -ī, *n.*, house; roof
tegō, -ere, tēxī, tēctum, cover, protect
tēlum, -ī, *n.*, weapon
***temperantia, -ae,** *f.*, temperance
***temperō, -āre, -āvī, -ātum,** restrain oneself, be temperate
***tempestās, -ātis,** *f.*, storm, tempest; weather
templum, -ī, *n.*, temple
***temporālis, -e,** temporary
***temporārius, -a, -um,** temporary

temptō, -āre, -āvī, -ātum, try
tempus, temporis, *n.*, time
***tenācitās, -ātis,** *f.*, holding fast, tenacity
***tenāx, -ācis,** holding fast, tenacious
tendō, -ere, tetendī, tentum, bend
teneō, -ēre, -uī, hold, hold to; keep, keep back
tergum, -ī, *n.*, back, rear; **ā tergō,** at the rear, from the rear
terra, -ae, *f.*, land, country; the earth
terreō, -ēre, -uī, -itum, frighten, terrify
***terribilis, -e,** terrible
territa, *see* **territus**
territus, -a, -um, frightened
***terror, -ōris,** *m.*, terror, fright, fear
***testāmentum, -ī,** *n.*, testament, will
***testimōnium, -ī,** *n.*, testimony
texō, -ere, -uī, textum, weave
tibi, to you, you (*as indirect object*)
timent, (they) fear
timeō, -ēre, -uī, fear, be afraid of
timet, (he, she, it) fears, is afraid of
***timidus, -a, -um,** timid, cowardly
timor, -ōris, *m.*, fear
***toga, -ae,** *f.*, toga, *a garment worn by Roman men*

toga

***tormentum, -ī,** *n.*, torment; instrument of torture
tōtus, -a, -um, whole, all
tractō, -āre, -āvī, -ātum, treat, handle, manage
trahō, -ere, trāxī, tractum, drag, draw, pull
trāns, *prep. with acc.*, across
***trānscrībō, -scrībere, -scrīpsī, -scrīptum,** transcribe
trānseō, -īre, -iī, -itum, cross
trānsfīgō, -fīgere, -fīxī, -fīxum, pierce
***trānsportō, -āre, -āvī, -ātum,** transport
trēs, tria, three
tribuō, -ere, -uī, -ūtum, bestow, assign, give

tuba

tū, you (*sing.*)
tua, *see* **tuus**
tuba, -ae, *f.*, trumpet
tum, *adv.*, then, at that time
***tumultus, -ūs,** *m.*, tumult
tumulus, -ī, *m.*, mound, tomb
tūtus, -a, -um, safe, unharmed
tuus, -a, -um, your, yours (*of one person*)

U

ubi, *adv. and conj.*, where; when
ultimus, -a, -um, last
umerus, -ī, *m.*, upper arm, shoulder
unda, -ae, *f.*, wave
undique, *adv.*, on all sides, from all sides
ūnus, -a, -um, one
***urbānus, -a, -um,** of the city

urna

urbs, urbis, *f.*, city
urna, -ae, *f.*, jar, pitcher
ursa, -ae, *f.*, bear
***ūsus, -ūs,** *m.*, use
ut, *conj.*, as
uter, utra, utrum, which (*of two*)
uterque, utraque, utrumque, each (*of two*), both
uxor, -ōris, *f.*, wife

ursa

V

vadum, -ī, *n.*, shallow place, ford, shoal
valē, *imperative sing. of* **valeō,** farewell, good-by

valeō, -ēre, -uī, -itūrus, be well, be strong
validus, -a, -um, strong, well
vāllum, -ī, *n.*, rampart, wall
vāstō, -āre, -āvī, -ātum, lay waste, destroy, devastate
vehementer, *adv.*, violently, strongly, earnestly, very much, very
*__vehiculum, -ī,__ *n.*, vehicle
vellus, velleris, *n.*, fleece

vehiculum

veniō, -īre, vēnī, ventum, come
venit, (he, she, it) comes
vēnit, (he, she, it) came
ventus, -ī, *m.*, wind
verbum, -ī, *n.*, word
vērus, -a, -um, true
vesperī, in the evening
vester, -tra, -trum, your, yours (*of more than one person*)
vēstīgium, -ī, *n.*, footstep, track
*__vestiō, -īre, -īvī, -ītum,__ clothe
vestis, vestis, *f.*, clothing, garment
*__veterānus, -a, -um,__ veteran, old
via, -ae, *f.*, street, road, way
*__victor, -ōris,__ *m.*, conqueror, victor

via

*__victōria, -ae,__ *f.*, victory
vidēmus, we see
vident, (they) see
videō, -ēre, vīdī, vīsum, see
videor, -ērī, vīsus sum, seem
videt, (he, she, it) sees
vīdit, (he, she, it) saw
vigil, vigilis, *m.*, sentinel, watchman, guard
*__vigilantia, -ae,__ *f.*, wakefulness, vigilance
*__vigilia, -ae,__ *f.*, watch, *one fourth of the night*
vigilō, -āre, -āvī, -ātum, keep watch, watch, keep awake
vīgintī, twenty
*__vīlla, -ae,__ *f.*, farmhouse, country house
vincō, -ere, vīcī, victum, defeat, conquer, overcome
vinculum, -ī, *n.*, chain, bond

vinculum

vīnum, -ī, *n.*, wine
*__vīpera, -ae,__ *f.*, viper, snake
vir, virī, *m.*, man
virgō, -inis, *f.*, maiden, girl
virtūs, virtūtis, *f.*, manliness, bravery, courage, valor
vīta, -ae, *f.*, life
*__vītālis, -e,__ vital
*__vītālitās, -ātis,__ vitality
vīvō, vīvere, vīxī, vīctum, live, exist
*__vīvus, -a, -um,__ alive, living
*__vōcālis, -e,__ vocal
vocō, -āre, -āvī, -ātum, call, summon
volō, -āre, -āvī, -ātūrus, fly
voluntās, -ātis, *f.*, wish, desire; will
vōs, *nom. or acc., pl. of* **tū,** you (*pl.*)
vōx, vōcis, *f.*, voice, word; **magna vōx,** a loud voice; **parva vōx,** a low voice
vulnerō, -āre, -āvī, -ātum, wound
*__vulnus, vulneris,__ *n.*, a wound

ENGLISH-LATIN VOCABULARY

A

abandon, dēserō, -serere, -seruī, -sertum
(**able**), **be able,** possum, posse, potuī
about, dē, *prep. with abl.*
above, suprā, *prep. with acc.*
(**absent**), **be absent,** absum, -esse, āfuī, āfutūrus
(**account**), **on account of,** propter, *prep. with acc.*
accuse, accūsō, -āre, -āvī, -ātum
across, trāns, *prep. with acc.*
adorn, adōrnō, -āre, -āvī, -ātum
advance, prōcēdō, -cēdere, -cessī, -cessum
advise, moneō, -ēre, -uī, -itum
after, post, *prep. with acc.*
afterwards, posteā, *adv.*
again, iterum, *adv.*
against, contrā, *prep. with acc.*
agitate, agitō, -āre, -āvī, -ātum
aid (*noun*), auxilium, -ī, *n.*
aid (*verb*), juvō, -āre, jūvī, jūtum
all, tōtus, -a, -um; omnis, -e
ally, socius, -ī, *m.*
alone, sōlus, -a, -um
already, jam, *adv.*
also, quoque, *conj.*
altar, āra, -ae, *f.*
am, I am, sum
among, inter, *prep. with acc.*
and, et, *conj.*
and so, itaque, *conj.*
animal, bēstia, -ae, *f.;* animal, animālis, *n.*
announce, nūntiō, -āre, -āvī, -ātum
another, alius, -a, -ud
answer, respondeō, -spondēre, -spondī, -spōnsum
archer, sagittārius, -ī, *m.*
are, (they) are, there are, sunt
armed, armātus, -a, -um; **armed man,** armātus, -ī, *m.*
arms, arma, -ōrum, *n. pl.*
army, exercitus, -ūs, *m.*
arrive, perveniō, -venīre, -vēnī, -ventum
arrow, sagitta, -ae, *f.*
as, quam, *adv.*
as long as, dum, *conj.*
ask, rogō, -āre, -āvī, -ātum
at, ad, *prep. with acc.*
at once, statim, *adv.*
attack (*noun*), impetus, -ūs, *m.*
attack (*verb*), oppugnō, -āre, -āvī, -ātum
aunt, amita, -ae, *f.*
(**away**), **be away,** absum, -esse, āfuī, āfutūrus
away from, ā, ab, *prep. with abl.*

B

back of, post, *prep. with acc.*
bad, malus, mala, malum
badge, īnsigne, īnsignis, *n.*
badly, male, *adv.*
bank, rīpa, -ae, *f.*
barbarian, barbarus, -ī, *m.*
battle, proelium, -ī, *n.*
be, sum, esse, fuī, futūrus
be able, can, possum, posse, potuī
be absent, absum, -esse, āfuī, āfutūrus
be here, adsum, -esse, -fuī, -futūrus
be near, adsum, -esse, -fuī, -futūrus
be present, adsum, -esse, -fuī, -futūrus
bear, ursa, -ae, *f.*
beautiful, pulcher, pulchra, pulchrum
because, quod, *conj.*
bee, apis, apis, *f.*

before (*adv.*), anteā; (*prep.*), ante (*acc.*); prō (*abl.*)
beggar, mendicus, -ī, *m.*
begin, incipiō, -cipere, -cēpī, -ceptum
believe, crēdō, -ere, crēdidī, crēditum
belt, balteus, -ī, *m.*
bend, tendō, -ere, tetendī, tentum
best, optimus, -a, -um
better (*adj.*), melior, melius
better (*adv.*), melius
between, inter, *prep. with acc.*
big, magnus, magna, magnum
bird, avis, avis, *f.*
blind, caecus, -a, -um
body, corpus, corporis, *n.*
boldness, audācia, -ae, *f.*
book, liber, -brī, *m.*
boy, puer, puerī, *m.*
branch, rāmus, -ī, *m.*
brave, fortis, -e
bravely, fortiter, *adv.*
break, frangō, -ere, frēgī, frāctum
bright, clārus, -a, -um
bring, portō, -āre, -āvī, -ātum
brother, frāter, frātris, *m.*
build, aedificō, -āre, -āvī, -ātum
building, aedificium, -ī, *n.*
bull, taurus, -ī, *m.*
but, sed, *conj.*
by, ā, ab, *prep. with abl.*

C

call, vocō, -āre, -āvī, -ātum; appellō, -āre, -āvī, -ātum
call together, convocō, -āre, -āvī, -ātum
camp, castra, -ōrum, *n. pl.*
can, be able, possum, posse, potuī
captive, captīvus, -ī, *m.*
care for, cūrō, -āre, -āvī, -ātum
carry, portō, -āre, -āvī, -ātum
cavalry, equitēs, -um, *m. pl.*
cave, caverna, -ae, *f.*
cavern, caverna, -ae, *f.*
certainly, certē, *adv.*
chain, vinculum, -ī, *n.*
change, mūtō, -āre, -āvī, -ātum
chief, prīnceps, prīncipis, *m.*
children, līberī, -ōrum, *m. pl.*
choose, dēligō, -ligere, -lēgī, -lēctum
citadel, arx, arcis, *f.*
citizen, cīvis, cīvis, *m. and f.*
city, urbs, urbis, *f.*
cloud, nūbēs, nūbis, *f.*
color, color, -ōris, *m.*
come, veniō, -īre, vēnī, ventum
common, commūnis, -e
companion, comes, comitis, *m.*
conceal, cēlō, -āre, -āvī, -ātum
conflict, certāmen, certāminis, *n.*
conquer, vincō, -ere, vīcī, victum
consul, cōnsul, -ulis, *m.*
contend, contendō, -tendere, -tendī, -tentum
contest, certāmen, certāminis, *n.*
cottage, casa, -ae, *f.*
country, terra, -ae, *f.*; **native country,** patria, -ae, *f.*
cousin (*girl, woman*), cōnsōbrīna, -ae, *f.*
cowardly, ignāvus, -a, -um
crime, scelus, sceleris, *n.*
crown, corōna, -ae, *f.*

D

danger, perīculum, -ī, *n.*
dangerous, perīculōsus, perīculōsa, perīculōsum
dare, audeō, -ēre
dark, obscūrus, obscūra, obscūrum
daughter, fīlia, -ae, *f.*
day, diēs, -ēī, *m. or f.*
(**day**), **by day,** interdiū, *adv.*
(**day**), **during the day,** interdiū, *adv.*
(**day**), **next day,** postrīdiē, *adv.*
daybreak, prīma lūx; **at daybreak,** prīmā lūce
dead, mortuus, -a, -um

death, mors, mortis, *f.*
decide, cōnstituō, -stituere, -stituī, -stitūtum
decoration, īnsigne, īnsignis, *n.*
defeat, superō, -āre, -āvī, -ātum; vincō, -ere, vīcī, victum
defend, dēfendō, -fendere, -fendī, -fēnsum
demand, postulō, -āre, -āvī, -ātum
den, spēlunca, -ae, *f.*
desert, dēserō, -serere, -seruī, -sertum
desire, dēsīderō, -āre, -āvī, -ātum
destroy, dēleō, -ēre, -ēvī, -ētum; vāstō, -āre, -āvī, -ātum
devastate, vāstō, -āre, -āvī, -ātum
difficult, difficilis, -e
dim, obscūrus, -a, -um
dinner, cēna, -ae, *f.*
discover, inveniō, -venīre, -vēnī, -ventum
distant, longinquus, -a, -um
don't, nōlī, nōlīte, *imperative*
door, jānua, -ae, *f.*
drag, trahō, -ere, trāxī, tractum
dragon, dracō, -ōnis, *m.*
draw (out), ēdūcō, -ere, -dūxī, -ductum
draw up, īnstruō, -struere, -strūxī, -strūctum
dream, somnium, -ī, *n.*
drive, agō, -ere, ēgī, āctum
drive back, repellō, -pellere, reppulī, repulsum
drive out, expellō, -pellere, -pulī, -pulsum
dry, āridus, -a, -um
during the day, interdiū, *adv.*

E

earth, terra, -ae, *f.*
easy, facilis, -e
eight, octō, *indeclinable numeral*
either . . . or, aut . . . aut, *conj.*
emperor, imperātor, -ōris, *m.*
elephant, elephantus, -ī, *m.*
enemy, inimīcus, -ī, *m.* (*a personal enemy*); hostis, hostis, *m.* (*a public enemy*)
enter, intrō, -āre, -āvī, -ātum
escape, fugiō, -ere, fūgī, fugitūrus
(evening), **in the evening,** vesperī
every, omnis, -e
evil, malus, mala, malum
example, exemplar, exemplāris, *n.*
expect, expectō, -āre, -āvī, -ātum
explore, explōrō, -āre, -āvī, -ātum
eye, oculus, -ī, *m.*

F

faithful, fīdus, -a, -um; fidēlis, -e
famous, clārus, -a, -um; nōtus, -a, -um; ēgregius, -a, -um
farmer, agricola, -ae, *m.*
farmhouse, vīlla, -ae, *f.*
fast, celeriter, *adv.*
father, pater, patris, *m.*
fear, timeō, -ēre, -uī
feather, penna, -ae, *f.*
few, a few, paucī, -ae, -a, *pl.*
field, ager, agrī, *m.*
fierce, ferus, -a, -um; ācer, ācris, ācre
fight (*verb*), pugnō, -āre, -āvī, -ātum
finally, dēnique, *adv.*; tandem, *adv.*
find, inveniō, -venīre, -vēnī, -ventum
fire, flamma, -ae, *f.*; ignis, ignis, *m.*
first, prīmus, -a, -um; **at first,** prīmō, *adv.*
five, quīnque, *indeclinable numeral*
fled from (they), fūgērunt
flee, fugiō, -ere, fūgī, fugitūrus
fleece, vellus, velleris, *n.*
fleet, classis, classis, *f.*
fly, volō, -āre, -āvī, -ātūrus
food, cibus, -ī, *m.*
for, prō, *prep. with abl.*
forces, cōpiae, -ārum, *f. pl.*

form, fōrma, -ae, *f.*
formerly, ōlim, *adv.*, anteā, *adv.*
fortify, mūniō, -īre, -īvī, -ītum
forum, forum, -ī, *n.*
four, quattuor, *indeclinable numeral*
free, līber, lībera, līberum
friend, amīcus, -ī, *m.*
frightened, territus, -a, -um
from, ē, ex; dē; ā, ab, *preps. with abl.*
(**front**), **in front of,** ante, *prep. with acc.*

G

garden, hortus, -ī, *m.*
garment, vestis, -is, *f.*
gate, porta, -ae, *f.*
gem, gemma, -ae, *f.*
general, imperātor, -ōris, *m.*
gift, dōnum, -ī, *n.*
girl, puella, -ae, *f.*
give, dō, dare, dedī, datum; **I give,** dō; **he gives,** dat
glad, laetus, -a, -um
go, eō, īre, iī, itum; **go across,** trānseō, -īre, -iī, -itum; **go back,** redeō, -īre, -iī, -itum; **go out, go forth,** exeō, -īre, -iī, -itum
god, a god, deus, -ī, *m.* (*nom. pl.* dī)
goddess, dea, -ae, *f.*
golden, aureus, -a, -um
good, bonus, bona, bonum; **very good,** optimus, -a, -um
grass, grāmen, grāminis, *n.*
grasshopper, cicāda, -ae, *f.*
gratitude, grātia, -ae, *f.*
great, magnus, -a, -um; **greater,** major, majus; **very great,** maximus, -a, -um
grieve, grieve for, doleō, -ēre, -uī, -itūrus
ground, terra, -ae, *f.*
guard (*noun*), vigil, vigilis, *m.*
guard (*verb*), dēfendō, -fendere, -fendī, -fēnsum; vigilō, -āre, -āvī, -ātum

H

hair, coma, -ae, *f.*
happy, laetus, -a, -um; fēlīx, *gen.* fēlīcis
hasten, properō, -āre, -āvī, -ātum
have, habeō, -ēre, -uī, -itum; **I have,** habeō; **has, does have,** habet
head, caput, capitis, *n.*
hear, audiō, -īre, -īvī, -ītum
heavily, graviter, *adv.*
helmet, galea, -ae, *f.*
help (*noun*), auxilium, -ī, *n.*
help (*verb*), juvō, -āre, jūvī, jūtum
her (*possessive*), *when reflexive,* suus, -a, -um; *when not reflexive,* ejus
here, hīc, *adv.*
(**here**) **be here,** adsum, -esse, -fuī, -futūrus
hide, cēlō, -āre, -āvī, -ātum
high, altus, alta, altum
hill, collis, collis, *m.*
himself, herself, itself, *when reflexive, gen.* suī; *when not reflexive,* ipse
his, her, its, *when reflexive,* suus, -a, -um; *when not reflexive,* ejus
home, domicilium, -ī, *n.*; **at home,** domī
horse, equus, -ī, *m.*
horseman, eques, equitis, *m.*
hour, hōra, -ae, *f.*
house, casa, -ae, *f.*; tēctum, -ī, *n.*
how, quam, *adv.*
hurl, jaciō, -ere, jēcī, jactum
hurry, properō, -āre, -āvī, -ātum
husband, conjūnx, conjugis, *m.*

I

I, ego
immediately, statim, *adv.*
in, in, *prep. with abl.*
in front of, ante, *prep. with acc.*
industrious, impiger, -gra, -grum

inhabitant, incola, -ae, *m. and f.*
insigne, īnsigne, īnsignis, *n.*
intend, in animō habēre
into, in, *prep. with acc.*
invite, invītō, -āre, -āvī, -ātum
is, there is, est
island, īnsula, -ae, *f.*

J

jewel, gemma, -ae, *f.*
journey, iter, itineris, *n.*
judge, jūdex, jūdicis, *m.*

K

keep watch, vigilō, -āre, -āvī, -ātum
kill, interficiō, -ficere, -fēcī, -fectum; necō, -āre, -āvī, -ātum
kind, benignus, benigna, benignum
kindle, accendō, -cendere, -cendī, -cēnsum
king, rēx, rēgis, *m.*
kingdom, rēgnum, -ī, *n.*
know, sciō, scīre, scīvī, scītum
known, well-known, nōtus, nōta, nōtum

L

lamp, lucerna, -ae, *f.*
land, terra, -ae, *f.*; **native land,** patria, -ae, *f.*
large, magnus, magna, magnum; **larger,** major, majus; **largest,** maximus, -a, -um
last, ultimus, -a, -um
lead, dūcō, -ere, dūxī, ductum
leader, dux, ducis, *m.*
leave, relinquō, -linquere, -līquī, -lictum
led, dūxit
(left), on the left, ā sinistrā
legion, legiō, -ōnis, *f.*
less, minus, *adv.*
letter, epistula, -ae, *f.*
level plain, campus, -ī, *m.*
lie, lie down, jaceō, -ēre, -uī
light, lūmen, -inis, *n.*
like, amō, -āre, -āvī, -ātum; **we like,** amāmus; **they like,** amant
limit, fīnis, fīnis, *m.*
line of march, agmen, agminis, *n.*
lion, leō, -ōnis, *m.*
listen, audiō, -īre, -īvī, -ītum
little, parvus, parva, parvum
live, vīvus, -a, -um, *adj.*
live, habitō, -āre, -āvī, -ātum; vīvō, -ere, vīxī, vīctum
long (*adj.*), longus, longa, longum
long, for a long time (*adv.*), diū
look around, circumspectō, -āre, -āvī, -ātum
look at, spectō, -āre, -āvī, -ātum
lose, āmitto, -mittere, -mīsī, -missum
loud, magnus, -a, -um
love, amō, -āre, -āvī, -ātum; **I love,** amō; **you love,** amās; **he, she loves,** amat
low, humilis, -e

M

magic, magicus, -a, -um
make, faciō, -ere, fēcī, factum
man, vir, virī, *m.*; homō, hominis, *m.*
many (*as noun*), multī, -ōrum, *m. pl.*
many (*adj.*), multī, multae, multa
march, prōcēdō, -cēdere, -cessī, -cessum
matter, rēs, reī, *f.*
me, *dat.*, mihi; *acc. and abl.*, mē
meanwhile, interim, *adv.*
medicine, medicīna, -ae, *f.*
merchant, mercātor, -ōris, *m.*
message, nūntius, -ī, *m.*
messenger, nūntius, -ī, *m.*
mile, mīlle passūs
mine, *see* **my**
money, pecūnia, -ae, *f.*
monster, mōnstrum, -ī, *n.*
moon, lūna, -ae, *f.*

(**morning**), **in the morning,** māne, *adv.*
mother, māter, mātris, *f.*
mountain, mōns, montis, *m.*
move, moveō, -ēre, mōvī, mōtum
much, multus, -a, -um, *adj.*; multum *adv.*
my, mine, meus, mea, meum

N

name, nōmen, nōminis, *n.*
narrow, angustus, -a, -um
nation, gēns, gentis, *f.*
native country, patria, -ae, *f.*
near, prope, *prep. with acc.*
near, propinquus, propinqua, propinquum, *with dat.*
(**near**), **be near,** adsum, -esse, -fuī, -futūrus
nearby, propinquus, -a, -um
never, numquam, *adv.*
new, novus, -a, -um
news, nūntius, -ī, *m.*
next day, postrīdiē, *adv.*
night, nox, noctis, *f.*; **at night,** noctū
nine, novem, *indeclinable numeral*
no (*adj.*), nūllus, -a, -um
no longer, nōn jam, *adv.*
noble, nōbilis, -e
nobody, nēmō, *m. and f.*
noise, sonus, -ī, *m.*
not, nōn, *adv.*, **and not,** neque, *conj.*
now, nunc, *adv.;* jam, *adv.*
nymph, nympha, -ae, *f.*

O

odious, odiōsus, -a, -um
often, saepe, *adv.*
old, antīquus, -a, -um
omen, ōmen, -inis, *n.*
on, in, *prep. with abl.*
on account of, propter, *prep. with acc.*
on all sides, undique, *adv.*
one, ūnus, -a, -um
only, sōlus, -a, -um
open, apertus, aperta, apertum
or, aut, *conj.*
order (*noun*), imperātum, -ī, *n.*; **by the order,** jussū
order (*verb*), jubeō, -ēre, jussī, jussum
other (*adj.*), cēterī, -ae, -a, *pl.*; alius, -a, -ud
others, the others (*pron.*), cēterī, -ōrum, *m. pl.*
ought, dēbeō, -ēre, -uī, -itum
our, noster, nostra, nostrum
out of, ē, ex, *prep. with abl.*
over, suprā, *prep. with acc.*
overcome, superō, -āre, -āvī, -ātum
ox, bōs, bovis, *m.*

P

peace, pāx, pācis, *f.*
people, populus, -ī, *m.*
picture, pictūra, -ae, *f.*
pierce, trānsfīgō, -fīgere, -fīxī, -fīxum
pirate, pīrāta, -ae, *m.*
pitch camp, castra pōnere
place (*noun*), locus, -ī, *m.* (*pl.* loca, *n.*)
place (*verb*), pōnō, pōnere, posuī, positum
plain, campus, -ī, *m.*
plan, cōnsilium, -ī, *n.*
pleasant, amoenus, -a, -um
plow, arō, -āre, -āvī, -ātum
poet, poēta, -ae, *m.*
point out, mōnstrō, -āre, -āvī, -ātum
praise, laudō, -āre, -āvī, -ātum; **he, she praises,** laudat; **we praise,** laudāmus; **they praise,** laudant
prepare, parō, -āre, -āvī, -ātum
present (*noun*), dōnum, -ī, *n.*
(**present**), **be present** (*verb*), adsum, -esse, -fuī, -futūrus
priest, priestess, sacerdōs, -ōtis, *m. and f.*

promise, prōmittō, -mittere, -mīsī, -missum
proud, superbus, -a, -um
province, prōvincia, -ae, *f.*

Q

quickly, celeriter, *adv.*

R

rapidly, celeriter, *adv.*
ray, radius, -ī, *m.*
read, legō, -ere, lēgī, lēctum; **he reads,** legit
ready, parātus, -a, -um
receive, accipiō, -cipere, -cēpī, -ceptum
recognize, recognōscō, -cognōscere, -cognōvī, -cognitum
refuse, recūsō, -āre, -āvī, -ātum
region, regiō, -ōnis, *f.*
remain, maneō, -ēre, mānsī, mānsum; **he remains,** manet
remarkable, ēgregius, -a,-um
repel, repellō, -ere, reppulī, repulsum
reply, respondeō, -spondēre, -spondī, -spōnsum
(rest of), the rest of, cēterī, -ae, -a, *pl.*
return, redeō, -īre, -iī, -itum
reward, praemium, -ī, *n.*
river, flūmen, flūminis, *n.*
road, iter, itineris, *n.*; via, -ae, *f.*
rock, saxum, -ī, *n.*
roof, tēctum, ī, *n.*
route, iter, itineris, *n.*
ruin, ruīna, -ae, *f.*
rule, regō, -ere, rēxī, rēctum
run, currō, -ere, cucurrī, cursum
run away, fugiō, -ere, fūgī, fugitūrus

S

sacrifice, sacrificō, -āre, -āvī, -ātum
safe, tūtus, -a, -um
sail, nāvigō, -āre, -āvī, -ātum
sailor, nauta, -ae, *m.*
salute, salūtō, -āre, -āvī, -ātum
same, īdem, eadem, idem
save, servō, -āre, -āvī, -ātum
say, dīcō, -ere, dīxī, dictum
scream, clāmō, -āre, -āvī, -ātum
sea, mare, maris, *n.*
seacoast, ōra maritima, *f.*
seashore, ōra maritima, *f.*
secretly, sēcrētō, *adv.*
see, spectō, -āre, -āvī, -ātum; videō, -ēre, vīdī, vīsum; **I see,** videō; **he sees,** videt; **we see,** vidēmus; **they see,** vident
seek, petō, -ere, petīvī, petītum
seem, videor, -ērī, vīsus sum
seize, occupō, -āre, -āvī, -ātum; capiō, -ere, cēpī, captum
(self), himself, herself, itself, ipse, ipsa, ipsum; **reflex.,** suī, sibi, sē
send, mittō, -ere, mīsī, missum
separate, sēparō, -āre, -āvī, -ātum
seriously, graviter, *adv.*
settle, sedeō, -ēre, sēdī, sessum
severely, graviter
seven, septem, *indeclinable numeral*
shepherd, pāstor, -ōris, *m.*
shield, scūtum, -ī, *n.*
ship, nāvis, nāvis, *f.*
shore, ōra, -ae, *f.*; lītus, lītoris, *n.*
short, brevis, -e
show, mōnstrō, -āre, -āvī, -ātum
sick, aeger, -gra, -grum
signal, signum, -ī, *n.*
(silence), in silence, silentiō
similar, similis, -e
sing, cantō, -āre, -āvī, -ātum
sister, soror, -ōris, *f.*
sit, sedeō, -ēre, sēdī, sessum
six, sex, *indeclinable numeral*
sky, caelum, -ī, *n.*
slave, servus, -ī, *m.*
slay, interficiō, -ficere, -fēcī, -fectum; necō, -āre, -āvī, -ātum

sleep, dormiō, -īre, -īvī, -ītum
sling, funda, -ae, *f.*
slinger, funditor, -ōris, *m.*
slowly, lēniter, *adv.*
small, parvus, parva, parvum
so, ita, *adv.*
soldier, mīles, mīlitis, *m.*
so long, tam diū, *adv.*
sometimes, interdum, *adv.*
son, fīlius, -ī, *m.*
Spain, Hispānia, -ae, *f.*
spear, hasta, -ae, *f.*
spider, arānea, -ae, *f.*
stag, cervus, -ī, *m.*
stand, stō, stāre, stetī, statūrus
star, stella, -ae, *f.*
statue, statua, -ae, *f.*
stay, maneō, -ēre, mānsī, mānsum
stone, saxum, -ī, *n.*
(**storm**), **take by storm,** oppugnō, -āre, -āvī, -ātum
story, fābula, -ae, *f.*
strange, novus, -a, -um; mīrus, -a, -um
stranger, advena, -ae, *m.*; aliēnus, -ī, *m.*
street, via, -ae, *f.*
strong, validus, -a, -um
stupid, stultus, -a, -um
suddenly, subitō, *adv.*
sufficiently, satis, *adv.*
suitable, idōneus, -a, -um
suitor, procus, -ī, *m.*
(**summer**), **in summer,** aestāte
summon, arcessō, -ere, -īvī, -ītum
surely, certē, *adv.*
swiftly, celeriter, *adv.*
swim, natō, -āre, -āvī, -ātum
sword, gladius, -ī, *m.*

T

table, mēnsa, -ae, *f.*
take, occupō, -āre, -āvī, -ātum
take by storm, oppugnō, -āre, -āvī, -ātum
take up, capiō, -ere, cēpī, captum
tall, altus, -a, -um
teacher, magister, -trī, *m.*
tell, nārrō, -āre, -āvī, -ātum
temple, templum, -ī, *n.*
ten, decem, *indeclinable numeral*
tent, tabernāculum, -ī, *n.*
terrified, territus, -a, -um
terror, terror, -ōris, *m.*
than, quam, *adv.*
that (*pl.* **those**), ille, illa, illud; is, ea, id
their, *when reflexive,* suus, -a, -um; *when not reflexive,* eōrum, eārum
themselves (*reflexive*), *gen.* suī
then, tum, *adv.*
there, ibi, *adv.;* (**there**) **is,** est
these, hī, hae, haec; eī, eae, ea
thing, rēs, reī, *f.*
think, putō, -āre, -āvī, -ātum
this (*pl.* **these**), hic, haec, hoc; is, ea, id
those, illī, illae, illa; eī, eae, ea
three, trēs, tria
through, per, *prep. with acc.*
throw, jaciō, -ere, jēcī, jactum; conjiciō, -jicere, -jēcī, -jectum
thus, sīc, *adv.*
time, tempus, temporis, *n.*
timid, timidus, -a, -um
tired, tired out, dēfessus, -a, -um
to, ad, in, *preps. with acc.*
today, hodiē, *adv.*
too, quoque, *conj.*
tooth, dēns, dentis, *m.*
torch, taeda, -ae, *f.*
toward, ad, *prep. with acc.*
town, oppidum, -ī, *n.*
trader, mercātor, -ōris, *m.*
treacherous, perfidus, -a, -um
treaty, foedus, foederis, *n.*
tree, arbor, arboris, *f.*
troops, cōpiae, -ārum, *f. pl.*

true, vērus, -a, -um
trumpet, tuba, -ae, *f.*
try, temptō, -āre, -āvī, -ātum
two, duo, duae, duo

U

uncle, avunculus, -ī, *m.*
under, sub, *prep. with acc. or abl.*
unhappy, miser, -a, -um
unjust, injūstus, -a, -um
unlike, dissimilis, -e
us, *dat. and abl.*, nōbīs; *acc.*, nōs

V

very great, maximus, -a, -um
very much, maximē, *adv.*
very small, minimus, -a, -um
victor, victor, -ōris, *m.*
victory, victōria, -ae, *f.*

W

wage (war), gerō, -ere, gessī, gestum
walk, ambulō, -āre, -āvī, -ātum
wall, mūrus, -ī, *m.;* vāllum, -ī, *n.*
wander, errō, -āre, -āvī, -ātum
want, dēsīderō, -āre, -āvī, -ātum; cupiō, -ere, -īvī, -ītum
war, bellum, -ī, *n.*
warn, moneō, -ēre, -uī, -itum
watch (*verb*), spectō, -āre, -āvī, -ātum; vigilō, -āre, -āvī, -ātum
watchman, vigil, vigilis, *m.*
water, aqua, -ae, *f.*
wax, cēra, -ae, *f.*
we, nōs
weapons, arma, -ōrum, *n. pl.*
wear, gerō, -ere, gessī, gestum
weary, dēfessus, -a, -um
weep, lacrimō, -āre, -āvī, -ātum
well, bene, *adv.*
well-known, nōtus, -a, -um
what (*interrog. pron.*), quid
while, dum, *conj.*
white, albus, alba, album
who (*interrog. pron.*), quis, quid; (*rel. pron.*), quī, quae, quod
whole, tōtus, -a, -um
why, cūr, *adv.*
wicked, malus, mala, malum
wide, lātus, -a, -um
widely, lātē, *adv.*
wife, uxor, -ōris, *f.*; conjūnx, -jugis, *f.*
will, voluntās, -ātis, *f.*
wind, ventus, -ī, *m.*
window, fenestra, -ae, *f.*
wing, āla, -ae, *f.*
(winter), in winter, hieme
witch, maga, -ae, *f.*
with, cum, *prep. with abl.*
within, intrā, *prep. with abl.*
without, sine, *prep. with abl.*
withstand, sustineō, -tinēre, -tinuī, -tentum
woman, fēmina, -ae, *f.*
woods, silvae, -ārum, *f. pl.*
word, verbum, -ī, *n.*
work, labōrō, -āre, -āvī, -ātum
worse, pejor, pejus
wound, vulnerō, -āre, -āvī, -ātum
write, scrībō, -ere, scrīpsī, scrīptum; **he writes,** scrībit

Y

year, annus, -ī, *m.*
yesterday, herī, *adv.*
yoke (together), jungō, -ere, jūnxī, jūnctum
you (*sing.*), *nom.*, tū; *dat.*, tibi; *acc.*, tē
you (*pl.*), vōs
young man, juvenis, juvenis, *m.*
your, *of one person,* tuus, tua, tuum; *of more than one person,* vester, -tra, -trum
youth, juvenis, juvenis, *m.*

SUMMARY OF LATIN PRONUNCIATION

SOUNDS OF VOWELS

LONG	SHORT
ā = *a* in *father*	**a** = first *a* in *aha*
ē = *e* in *they*	**e** = *e* in *net*
ī = *i* in *machine*	**i** = *i* in *this*
ō = *o* in *hole*	**o** = *o* in *domain*
ū = *u* in *rude*	**u** = *u* in *full*

SOUNDS OF DIPHTHONGS

ae = *i* in *like*
au = *ou* in *round*
oe = *oi* in *boil*
ei = *ei* in *vein*
eu = short *e* + *oo*
ui almost = *ui* in *ruin*

CONSONANTS

The consonants are, in general like English. But note that:

c is always like *k*	**p** is always as in *spin*	**t** is always as in *stop*
g is always as in *go*	**qu** = *qu* in *quick*	**x** is always like *ks*
j = *y* as in *yes*	**s** is always as in *say*	**bs** = *ps;* **bt** = *pt;* **v** = *w*

ch = *c* in *can;* **ph** = *p* in *put;* **th** = *t* in *ten*

SYLLABLES

A syllable must always have a vowel or a diphthong.

1. A consonant between two vowels is taken with the vowel which follows it: **pō-nō, ha-be-ō.**

2. Two consonants between two vowels are divided, one going with the vowel which precedes and one with the vowel which follows: **par-va, ter-ra.**

> EXCEPTIONS. (1) If the first of the two consonants is a stop consonant[1] and the second is **l** or **r**, both are taken with the vowel following: **pa-trī.** (2) In the division of a compound verb into syllables, the prepositional element is separated from the simple verb: **ad-est.**

3. When there are more than two consonants between two vowels, all but the first go with the following vowel: **ob-scū-ra.**

ACCENT

1. All words of two syllables are accented on the first syllable: **a′mō, lau′dant.**

2. In a word of more than two syllables the accent falls on the penult (the syllable before the last) if the penult is long; that is, if it has a long vowel (**mo-nē′mus**) or a diphthong (**a-moe′na**) or if it ends in a consonant (**in-ter′dum, pu-el′la**).

> EXCEPTION. If the first of two consonants is a stop consonant[1] (or **f, ph, th, ch**) and the second is **l** or **r**, they do not make the penult long.

3. If the penult is not long, the accent falls on the antepenult (the second syllable from the last): **pe-cū′ni-a, a-gri′co-la, e-pis′tu-la.**

---

[1]The stop consonants are **b, p, d, t, g, c, k, q.** The combinations ch, ph, th are treated as stop consonants.

PROPER NAMES

Achillēs, *nom.*; **Achillis,** *gen.*; **Achillem,** *acc.*; *m.*, Achilles (ə kil′ēz), *Greek hero in the Trojan War*

Aeacus, -ī, *m.*, Aeacus (ē′ə kəs), *legendary Greek king, grandfather of Achilles*

Aegyptius, -ī, *m.*, Aegyptius (i jip′shəs), *a man's name*

Aenēās, *nom.*; **Aenēae,** *gen. or dat.*; **Aenēam,** *acc.*; **Aenēā,** *abl.*; *m.*, Aeneas, (ē nē′əs), *Trojan leader, hero of Vergil's* Aeneid

Aesculāpius, -ī, *m.*, Aesculapius (es′kū lā′pi əs), *god of medicine*

Aethiopia, -ae, *f.*, Ethiopia (ē′thi ō′pi ə), *country in Africa* (map, p. 60)

Aetna, -ae, *f.*, Etna (et′nə), *volcano in Sicily* (map, p. 60)

Āfrica, -ae, *f.*, Africa (af′ri kə) (map, p. 60)

Agamemnōn, -onis, *m.*, Agamemnon (ag′ə mem′non), *Greek leader in the Trojan War*

Albānus, -a, -um, Alban (ôl′bən); **Lacus Albānus,** *Alban Lake* (map, p. 60)

Alexander, -drī, *m.*, Alexander (al′ig zan′dər), *a man's name*

Allēctō, *nom.*, *f.*, Allecto (ə lek′tō), *one of the three Furies*

Amāta, -ae, *f.*, Amata (ə mä′tə), *queen of Latium*

Anchīsēs, *nom.*, *m.*, Anchises (an kī′sēz), *father of Aeneas*

Androclēs, *nom.*; **Androclem,** *acc.*; **Androcle,** *abl.*; *m.*, Androcles (an′drō klēz), *Roman slave*

Andromeda, -ae, *f.*, Andromeda (an drom′ə də), *Ethiopian princess*

Anna, -ae, *f.*, Anna, *name of a girl or woman*

Apollō, Apollinis, *m.*, Apollo (ə pol′ō), *god of the sun*

Appius Claudius, Appiī Claudiī, *m.*, Appius Claudius (ap′i əs klô′di əs), *patriotic Roman citizen famed for his public works*

Aqua Appia, Aquae Appiae, *f.*, the Appian Aqueduct

Arachnē, *nom.*, *f.*, Arachne (ə rak′ni), *a girl skilled in weaving*

Arcadia, -ae, *f.*, Arcadia (är kā′di ə), *a country in Greece* (map, p. 60)

Ariadna, -ae, *f.*, Ariadne (ar′i ad′ni), *Cretan princess*

Ariovistus, -ī, *m.*, Ariovistus (ā′ri ō vis′təs), *king of a German tribe*

Ascanius, -ī, *m.*, Ascanius (as kā′ni əs), *son of Aeneas*

Athēna, -ae, *f.*, Athena (ə thē′nə), *goddess of wisdom*

Athēnae, -ārum, *f. pl.*, Athens (ath′ənz), *a city* (map, p. 60)

Aulidem, *acc.*, *f.*, Aulis (ô′lis), *a town* (map, p. 60)

Aurōra, -ae, *f.*, Aurora (ô rô′rə), *goddess of the dawn*

Babylōnius, -a, -um, Babylonian (bab′i lō′ni ən), *of Babylonia* (map, p. 60)

Britannia, -ae, *f.*, Britain (brit′ən), (map, p. 60)

Britannus, -ī, *m.*, a Briton (brit′ən), *an inhabitant of Britain*

Caesar, Caesaris, *m.*, Caesar (sē′zər), *Roman general and author*
Calchās, *nom.*; **Calcham,** *acc.*; *m.*, Calchas (kal′kəs), *Greek prophet*
Callistō, *nom., f.*, Callisto (kə lis′tō), *Arcadian princess, changed to a bear*
Camillus, -ī, *m.*, Camillus (kə mil′əs), *Roman general*
Campus Mārtius, *nom., m.*, Campus Martius (kam′pəs mär′shəs), *field of Mars*
Capitōlium, -ī, *n.*, the Capitol (kap′i təl), *a temple of Jupiter; also* the Capitoline (kap′i tə līn, *one of the seven hills of Rome*
Capua, -ae, *f.*, Capua (kap′ū ə), *a city* (map, p. 60)
Caracalla, -ae, *m.*, Caracalla (kar′ə kal′ə), *Roman emperor*
Carthāgō, -inis, *f.*, Carthage (kär′thij), *a city* (map, p. 60)
Cassiopēa, -ae, *f.*, Cassiopeia (kas′i ō pē′ə), *queen of Ethiopia*
Cassivellaunus, -ī, *m.*, Cassivellaunus (kas′i və lô′nəs), *British chief*
Celsus, -ī, *m.*, Celsus (sel′səs), *Roman physician*
Cerberus, -ī, *m.*, Cerberus (sėr′bər əs), *three-headed watchdog of the lower world*
Cerēs, Cereris, *f.*, Ceres (sēr′ēz), *goddess of agriculture*
Charōn, *nom., m.*, Charon (kãr′on), *ferryman in the lower world*
Circa (*or* **Circē**), **-ae,** *f.*, Circe (sėr′si), *enchantress*
Cloelia, -ae, *f.*, Cloelia (klēl′yə), *brave Roman girl*
Clytemnestra, -ae, *f.*, Clytemnestra (klī′təm nes′trə), *wife of Agamemnon*
Colchidem, *acc.*; **Colchide,** *abl.*; *f.*, Colchis (kol′kis), *a country* (map, p. 60)
Colossēum, -ī, *n.*, the Colosseum (kol′ə sē′əm), *Roman amphitheater*
Cōnsidius, -ī, *m.*, Considius (kon sid′i əs), *officer in Caesar's army*
Cornēlia, -ae, *f.*, Cornelia (kôr nēl′yə), *name of a girl or woman*
Cornēlius, -ī, *m.*, Cornelius (kôr nēl′yəs), *name of a boy or man*
Corsica, -ae, *f.*, Corsica (kôr′si kə), *an island* (map, p. 60)
Crēsius, -ī, *m.*, Cresius (krē′shəs), *one of Ulysses' sailors*
Crēta, -ae, *f.*, Crete (krēt), *an island* (map, p. 60)
Cūmae, -ārum, *f. pl.*, Cumae (kū′mē), *a city* (map, p. 60)
Cupīdō, Cupīdinis, *m.*, Cupid (kū′pid), *god of love*

Daedalus, -ī, *m.*, Daedalus (ded′ə ləs), *character of Greek legend*
Daniēl, *nom.*; **Daniēlī,** *dat.*; **Daniēlem,** *acc.*; *m.*, Daniel (dan′yəl), *Hebrew prophet*
Daphnē, *nom.*; **Daphnēn,** *acc.*; *f.*, Daphne (daf′ni), *woodland nymph*
Dēlos, *nom., f.*, Delos (dē′los), *an island* (map, p. 60)
Deucaliōn, -ōnis, *m.*, Deucalion (dū kā′li ən), *character of Greek legend*
Diāna, -ae, *f.*, Diana (dī an′ə), *goddess of hunting*
Dīdō, *nom., f.*, Dido (dī′dō), *queen of Carthage*
Dioclētiānus, -ī, *m.*, Diocletian (dī′ə klē′shən), *Roman emperor*
Discordia, -ae, *f.*, Discordia (dis kôr′di ə), *goddess of discord*
Dīviciācus, -ī, *m.*, Diviciacus (di′vish i ā′kəs), *Haeduan chief*
Dumnorīx, *nom.*; **Dumnorīgem,** *acc.*; *m.*, Dumnorix (dum′nôr iks), *brother of Diviciacus*

Epimētheus, -ī, *m.*, Epimetheus (ep′i mē′thüs), *husband of Pandora*
Etrūria, -ae, *f.*, Etruria (i trür′i ə), *a country in Italy* (map, p. 60)
Etrūscī, -ōrum, *m. pl.*, Etruscans (i trus′kənz), *people of Etruria*
Eumaeus, -ī, *m.*, Eumaeus (ū mē′əs), *swineherd of Ulysses*
Eurōpa, -ae, *f.*, Europe (ūr′əp), (map, p. 60)
Euryalus, -ī, *m.*, Euryalus (ū rī′ə ləs), *young Trojan warrior*
Eurydicē, *nom.*; **Eurydicēs,** *gen.*; **Eurydicēn,** *acc.*; *f.*, Eurydice (ū rid′i sē), *wife of Orpheus*
Eurylochus, -ī, *m.*, Eurylochus (ū ril′ə kəs), *companion of Ulysses*
Evander, -drī, *m.*, Evander (ē van′dėr), *founder of an early Italian city*

Fortūna, -ae, Fortuna (fôr tū′nə), *Roman goddess*
Frontīnus, -ī, *m.*, Frontinus (fron tī′nəs), *Roman architect*
Fulvia, -ae, *f.*, Fulvia (ful′vi ə), *name of a girl or woman*
Furiae, -ārum, *f. pl.*, Furies (fūr′iz), *three goddesses of vengeance*

Galba, -ae, *m.*, Galba (gal′bə), *name of a man or boy*
Galēnus, -ī, *m.*, Galen (gā′lən), *Greek physician*
Gallia, -ae, *f.*, Gaul (gôl), (map, p. 60)
Gallicus, -a, -um, Gallic (gal′ik)
Gallus, -ī, *m.*, a Gaul (gôl), *an inhabitant of Gaul*
Germānus, -a, -um, German (jėr′mən); *m. pl. as noun,* the Germans
Gideōn, *nom., m.*, Gideon (gid′i ən), *hero of Israel*
Graecia, -ae, *f.*, Greece (grēs), (map, p. 60)
Graecus, -a, -um, Greek (grēk); *m. as noun,* a Greek

Harpyia, -ae, *f.*, Harpy (här′pi), *mythical creature, half bird and half woman*
Hector, -oris, *m.*, Hector (hek′tər), *Trojan prince slain, by Achilles*
Helena, -ae, *f.*, Helen (hel′ən), *queen of Sparta, abducted by Paris, called the most beautiful woman in the world*
Helenus, -ī, *m.*, Helenus (hel′ən əs), *Trojan prince and soothsayer*
Helvētiī, -ōrum, *m. pl.*, the Helvetians (hel vē′shəns), *Gallic tribe*
Herculāneum, -ī, *n.*, Herculaneum (hėr′kū lā′ni əm), *a city* (map, p. 60)
Herculēs, *nom.*; **Herculem,** *acc.*; *m.*, Hercules (hėr′kū lēz), *hero of Greek mythology*
Hippocratēs, -is, *m.*, Hippocrates (hi pok′rə tēz), *Greek physician*
Hippocrāticus, -a, -um, Hippocratic (hip′ō krat′ik)
Hispānia, -ae, *f.*, Spain (spān), (map, p. 60)
Hispānus, -ī, *m.*, a Spaniard (span′yərd)
Homērus, -ī, *m.*, Homer (hō′mər), *blind Greek poet, author of two long poems, the* Odyssey *and the* Iliad
Horātius, -ī, *m.*; **Horātī,** *voc.*; Horatius (hō rā′shəs); **Horātius Cocles,** Horatius Cocles (kō′klēz), *Roman hero*

Īcarus, -ī, *m.*, Icarus (ik′ə rəs), *son of Daedalus*
Īda, -ae, *f.*, Ida (ī′də), *mountain near Troy* (map, p. 60)
Īphigenīa, -ae, *f.*, Iphigenia (if′i ji nī′ə), *daughter of Agamemnon*
Isrāēlīta, -ae, *m.*, an Israelite (iz′ri əl īt), *a descendant of Israel; a Hebrew*
Ītalia, -ae, *f.*, Italy (it′ə li), (map, p. 60)
Ithaca, -ae, *f.*, Ithaca (ith′ə kə), *an island* (map, p. 60)

Jāniculum, -ī, *m.*, the Janiculum (jə nik′ū ləm), *one of the seven hills of Rome*
Jānus, -ī, *m.*, Janus (jā′nəs), *god of doors and beginnings*
Jāsōn, -ōnis, *m.*, Jason (jā′sən), *Greek hero*
Jovis, *gen. of* **Juppiter; Jovem,** *acc.* of **Juppiter; Jove,** *abl.* of **Juppiter**
Jūlia, -ae, *f.*, Julia (jül′yə), *name of a girl or woman*
Jūlius, -ī, *m.*, Julius (jül′yəs), *name of a man or boy*
Jūnō, -ōnis, *f.*, Juno (jü′nō), *queen of the gods*
Juppiter, Jovis, *m.*, Jupiter (jü′pi tər), *king of the gods*
Jūstīniānus, -ī, *m.*, Justinian (jus tin′i ən), *Roman emperor responsible for the Roman legal code,* **Corpus Jūris**
Jūturna, -ae, *f.*, Juturna (jü tėr′nə), *nymph, sister of Turnus*

Labiēnus, -ī, *m.*, Labienus (lā′bi ē′nəs), *officer in Caesar's army*
Labyrinthus, -ī, *m.*, Labyrinth (lab′i rinth), *maze of passages in Crete*
Lāocoōn, -ontis, *m.*, Laocoön (lā ok′ō on), *Trojan priest*
Lār, Laris, *m., usually pl.,* **Larēs, -um,** lares (lãr′ēz), *Roman family gods*
Latīnus, -a, -um, Latin (lat′in); *m. pl. as noun,* Latins, *people of Latium*
Latīnus, -ī, *m.*, Latinus (lə tī′nəs), *king of Latium*
Latium, -ī, *n.*, Latium (lā′shi əm), *a country* (map, p. 60)
Lātōna, -ae, *f.*, Latona (lə tō′nə), *mother of Apollo and Diana*
Lāvīnia, -ae, *f.*, Lavinia (lə vin′i ə), *Latin princess, bride of Aeneas*
Līberālia, -ium, *n. pl.*, Liberalia (lib′ər al′i ə), *annual Roman festival held on March 17*
Lūcia, -ae, *f.*, Lucia (lü′shə), *name of a girl or woman*
Lūcius, -ī, *m.*, Lucius (lü′shəs), *name of a man or boy*
Lūcrētia, -ae, *f.*, Lucretia (lü krē′shə), *name of a girl or woman*

Mamilius, -ī, *m.*; **Mamilī,** *voc.*; Mamilius (mə mil′i əs), *king of Tusculum*
Mānlius, -ī, *m.*, Manlius (man′li əs), *Roman who saved the Capitol*
Mārcus, -ī, *m.*, Marcus (mär′kəs), *name of a man or boy*
Marius, -ī, *m.*, Marius (mãr′i əs), *Roman consul*
Mārs, Mārtis, *m.*, Mars (märz), *god of war*
Mārtius, -a, -um, *pertaining to Mars;* **Campus Mārtius,** Campus Martius (kam′pəs mär′shəs), *field of Mars, used for military drill*
Mēdēa, -ae, *f.*, Medea (mi dē′ə), *princess of Colchis, an enchantress*

Mediterrāneus, -a, -um, Mediterranean (med′i tə rā′ni ən); **Mare Mediterrāneum,** the Mediterranean Sea (map, p. 60)
Medūsa, -ae, *f.*, Medusa (mi dū′sə), *a Gorgon, a creature with snakes for hair*
Melita, -ae, *f.*, Malta (môl′tə), *an island* (map, p. 60)
Menelāus, -ī, *m.*, Menelaus (men′ə lā′əs), *king of Sparta*
Menexenus, -ī, *m.*, Menexenus (men ek′sə nəs), *one of Ulysses' sailors*
Mercurius, -ī, *m.*, Mercury (mėr′kū ri), *messenger of the gods*
Messāna, -ae, *f.*, Messina (me sē′nə), *a city* (map, p. 60)
Mīdās, *nom., m.*, Midas (mī′dəs), *king who was granted the golden touch*
Midianīta, -ae, *m.*, a Midianite (mid′i ə nīt); *pl.*, the Midianites
Minerva, -ae, *f.*, Minerva (mi nėr′və), *goddess of wisdom*
Mīnōtaurus, -ī, *m.*, Minotaur (min′ə tôr), *mythical monster with the head of a bull and the body of a man*
Mīsēnum, -ī, *n.*, Misenum (mī sē′ nəm), *ancient town* (map, p. 60)

Naupactōus, -ī, *m.*, Naupactous (nô′ pak tō′əs), *companion of Ulysses*
Neptūnus, -ī, *m.*, Neptune (nep′tūn), *god of the sea*
Nīsus, -ī, *m.*, Nisus (nī′səs), *a young Trojan warrior*

Octāvia, -ae, *f.*, Octavia (ok tā′vi ə), *name of a girl or woman*
Orcus, -ī, *m.*, Orcus (ôr′kəs), *lower world*
Orestēs, *nom.*; **Orestem,** *acc.*; *m.*, Orestes (ō res′tēz), *son of Agamemnon*
Orpheus, -ī, *m.*, Orpheus (ôr′fūs or ôr′fi əs), *mythical character*
Ōstia, -ae, *f.*, and **Ōstia, -ōrum,** *n. pl.*, Ostia (os′ti ə), *port of Rome* (map, p. 60)

Pallās, *nom., m.*, Pallas (pal′əs), *son of Evander*
Pandōra, -ae, *f.*, Pandora (pan dō′rə), *mythical character*
Paris, *nom.*; **Paridis,** *gen.*; **Paridī,** *dat.*; **Paridem,** *acc.*; **Paride,** *abl.*; *m.*, Paris (par′is), *Trojan prince*
Penātēs, -ium, *m. pl.*, penates (pe nā′tēz), *household gods of the ancient Romans*
Pēnelopa (or **Pēnelopē**), **-ae,** *f.*, Penelope (pi nel′ə pi), *wife of Ulysses*
Perseus, -ī, *m.*, Perseus (pėr′süs or pėr′si əs), *legendary Greek hero*
Phaëthōn, *nom., m.*, Phaëthon (fā′i thon), *son of Apollo*
Philippus, -ī, *m.*, Philip, *a man's name*
Phoenīcia, -ae, *f.*, Phoenicia (fi nish′ə), *a country* (map, p. 60)
Pīcus, -ī, *m.*, Picus (pī′kəs), *legendary king, changed to a woodpecker*
Plīnius, -ī, *m.*, Pliny (plin′i), *the Elder, Roman writer and military leader; the Younger, nephew of Pliny the Elder, also a writer*
Plūtō, -ōnis, *m.*, Pluto (plü′tō), *king of the lower world*
Polydectēs, *nom.*; **Polydectem,** *acc.*; *m.*, Polydectes (pol′i dek′tēz), *a legendary king*

Polydōrus, -ī, *m.*, Polydorus (pol′i dō′rəs), *Trojan prince*
Pompeiī, -ōrum, *m. pl.*, Pompeii (pom pā′ē), *a city* (map, p. 60)
Porsena, -ae, *m.*, Porsena (pôr′sən ə), *king of the Etruscans*
Priamus, -ī, *m.*, Priam (prī′am), *king of Troy*
Prōserpina, -ae, *f.*, Proserpina (prō sėr′pi nə), *daughter of Ceres*
Proxenus, -ī, *m.*, Proxenus (prok′sən əs), *companion of Ulysses*
Pūblius, -ī, *m.*, Publius (pūb′li əs), *name of a boy or man*
Pullō, -ōnis, *m.*, Pullo (pu̇l′ō), *centurion in Caesar's army*
Pulvillus, -ī, *m.*, Pulvillus (pu̇l vil′əs), *Roman consul*
Pylade, *abl.*, *m.*, Pylades (pī′lə dēz), *friend of Orestes*
Pyrrha, -ae, *f.*, Pyrrha (pir′ə), *character of Greek legend*
Pyrrhus, -ī, *m.*, Pyrrhus (pir′əs), *king of a country in Greece*

Quīntus, -ī, *m.*, Quintus (kwin′təs), *name of a man or boy*

Rhēnus, -ī, *m.*, the Rhine (rīn), *river which divided Gaul from Germany* (map, p. 60)
Rhodanus, -ī, *m.*, the Rhone (rōn), *river in Gaul* (map, p. 60)
Rhodius, -ī, *m.*, Rhodius (rō′di əs), *companion of Ulysses*
Rōma, -ae, *f.*, Rome (rōm), (map, p. 60); *also* Roma (rō′mə), *a goddess*
Rōmānus, -a, -um, Roman (rō′mən), *m. as noun*, a Roman
Rutulus, -a, -um, Rutulian (rə tül′yən)
Rutulus, -ī, *m.*, a Rutulian (rə tül′yən); *pl.*, Rutulians (rə tül′yənz), *people of a nation of central Italy* (map, p. 60)

Sardinia, -ae, *f.*, Sardinia (sär din′i ə), (map, p. 60)
Secunda, -ae, *f.*, Secunda (sə kün′də), *name of a girl or woman*
Seleucus, -ī, *m.*, Seleucus (sə lü′kəs), *legendary pirate*
Sertōrius, -ī, *m.*, Sertorius (sėr tôr′i əs), *general under Marius*
Sextus, -ī, *m.*, Sextus (seks′təs); **Sextus Tarquinius, -ī,** *m.*, Tarquin (tär′kwin)
Sibylla, -ae, *f.*, Sibyl (sib′il), *prophetess*
Sibyllīnus, -a, -um, Sibylline (sib′i līn), *pertaining to a Sibyl*
Sicilia, -ae, *f.*, Sicily (sis′i li), (map, p. 60)
Silvia, -ae, *f.*, Silvia (sil′vi ə), *daughter of Tyrrhus*
Sinōn, *nom.*, *m.*, Sinon (sī′nən), *Greek spy in Trojan War*
Sparta, -ae, *f.*, Sparta (spär′tə), *a city* (map, p. 60)
Spurius, -ī, *m.*, **Spurī,** *voc.*; Spurius (spür′i əs), *a Roman name*; **Spurius Lartius** (lär′shəs), *Roman senator*
Stygem, *acc.*, *f.*, Styx (stiks), *river in the lower world*
Sulla, -ae, *m.*, Sulla (sul′ə), *Roman dictator*

Tamesis, *nom.*; **Tamesim,** *acc.*; *m.*, Thames (temz), *river in Britain* (map, p. 60)
Tarentīnī, -ōrum, *m. pl.*, Tarentines (tə ren′tēnz)

Tarentum, -ī, *n.*, Tarentum (tə ren′təm), *a town* (map, p. 60)

Tarquinius, -ī, *m.*, Tarquin (tär′kwin), *king of Rome*; **Tarquinius Superbus** (sü pėr′bəs), Tarquin the Proud, *last king of Rome*

Taurōrum, *gen., m. pl.*, Taurians (tô′ri ənz), *inhabitants of a peninsula in the Black Sea* (map, p. 60)

Tēlemachus, -ī, *m.*, Telemachus (ti lem′ə kəs), *son of Ulysses*

Thēseus, -ī, *m.*, Theseus (thē′süs or thē′si əs), *slayer of the Minotaur*

Thetis, *nom., f.*, Thetis (thē′tis), *mother of Achilles*

Thrācia, -ae, *f.*, Thrace (thrās), *region north of Greece*

Tiberis, *nom.* or *gen.*; **Tiberim,** *acc.*; *m.*, the Tiber (tī′bər), *river on which Rome is situated* (map, p. 60)

Titus, -ī, *m.*, Titus (tī′təs), *name of a man or boy*; **Titus Herminius,** Titus Herminius (hėr min′i əs), *Roman senator*

Trōja, -ae, *f.*, Troy (troi), *city in Asia Minor* (map, p. 60)

Trōjānus, -a, -um, Trojan (trō′jən), *m. as noun*, a Trojan

Tullia, -ae, *f.*, Tullia (tül′yə), *name of a girl or woman*

Turnus, -ī, *m.*, Turnus (tėr′nəs), *king of the Rutulians*

Tusculum, -ī, *n.*, Tusculum (tus′kū ləm), *town in Latium*

Tyrrhus, -ī, *m.*, Tyrrhus (tir′əs), *shepherd of King Latinus*

Ulīxēs, *nom.*; **Ulīxis,** *gen.*; **Ulīxī,** *dat.*; **Ulīxem,** *acc.*; **Ulīxe,** *abl.*; *m.*, Ulysses (ū lis′ēz), *king of Ithaca, hero of Homer's* Odyssey

Valerius, -ī, *m.*, Valerius (və lēr′i əs), *Roman consul*

Veiī, -ōrum, *m. pl.*, Veii (vē′yī), *Etruscan city near Rome* (map, p. 60)

Venus, *nom.*; **Venerī,** *dat.*; **Venerem,** *acc.*; **Venere,** *abl.*; *f.*, Venus (vē′nəs), *goddess of love*

Vergilius, -ī, *m.*, Vergil (vėr′jil), *Roman poet, author of the* Aeneid

Vesuvius, -ī, *m.*, Vesuvius (vi sü′vi əs), *volcano in Italy* (map, p. 60)

Via Appia, Viae Appiae, *f.*, Appian Way (ap′i ən wā), *famous Roman road* (map, p. 60)

Vitrūvius, -ī, *m.*, Vitruvius (vi trü′vi əs), *Roman architect*

Vorēnus, -ī, *m.*, Vorenus (vô rē′nəs), *centurion in Caesar's army*

Vulcānus, -ī, *m.*, Vulcan (vul′kən), *god of fire*

VOCABULARY FOR CLASSROOM USE

The following vocabulary of Latin expressions and grammatical terms will be helpful when Latin is used in the classroom.

Good morning, Salvē (*pl.* Salvēte).
Rise (*imperative*), Surge (*pl.* Surgite).
Open the window, Fenestram aperī.
Give me the chalk, Crētam mihi dā.
Recite, Recitā (*pl.* Recitāte).
Close the door, Jānuam claude.
Please, Sīs (*pl.* Sultis)
Thank you, Grātiās tibi (*pl.* vōbīs) agō.
Be seated, Cōnsīde (*pl.* Cōnsīdite).
Write on the blackboard, Scrībe (*pl.* Scrībite) in tabulā.
Lay aside your book, Pōne librum (*pl.* Pōnite librōs).
Take paper and pencil, Sūme chartam et stilum (*pl.* Sūmite chartam et stilōs).
Place your papers on the table, Chartās in mēnsā pōnite.
Give me your paper, Mihi chartam tuam dā (*pl.* chartās vestrās date).
Good-by, Valē (*pl.* Valēte).

noun, nōmen
adjective, adjectīvum
pronoun, prōnōmen
verb, verbum
  transitive, trānsitīvum
  intransitive, intrānsitīvum
adverb, adverbium
preposition, praepositiō
conjunction, conjūnctiō
interjection, interjectiō
case, cāsus
  nominative, nōminātīvus
  genitive, genitīvus
  dative, datīvus
  accusative, accūsātīvus
  ablative, ablātīvus
  vocative, vocātīvus
gender, genus
  masculine, masculīnum
  feminine, fēminīnum
  neuter, neutrum
person, persōna
  first, prīma
  second, secunda
  third, tertia
number, numerus
  singular, singulāris
  plural, plūrālis
tense, tempus
  present, praesēns
  imperfect, imperfectum
  future, futūrum
  perfect, perfectum
  past perfect, praeteritum perfectum
  future perfect, futūrum perfectum
voice, vōx
  active, actīva
  passive, passīva
mood, modus
  indicative, indicātīvus
  imperative, imperātīvus
  infinitive, īnfīnītīvus
conjugation, conjugātiō
declension, dēclīnātiō
blackboard, tabula
paper, charta
chalk, crēta
pencil, stilus
question, interrogātiō
answer, respōnsum

ILLUSTRATIONS

Extent of the Roman Empire

PAGE

Map of the Roman Empire..... 60
Britain, Hadrian's Wall..... 18, 178
Mosaic..... 47
Villa..... 48-49
Silver plates..... 143
Roman helmets..... 180
Public baths..... 228
Sicily, Roman bridge..... 59
Austria, Roman arch..... 62

PAGE

Portugal, Temple of Diana..... 62
Russia, Storage pit for fish..... 63
Africa, Roman arches..... 63
Bas-relief..... 126
Spain, Roman aqueduct..... 70
Scabbard..... 161
Roman school..... 196
France, Amphitheater at Arles..... 167
Roman bridge..... 206

Maps

America and Europe..... 12
Roman Empire..... 60
Rome..... inside front cover
Italy..... inside back cover

Exploring the Past

Seacoast view of Herculaneum. 15
Hadrian's Wall in England. 18, 178
The Colosseum..... 21, 219
From a coin..... 351
The Roman Forum..... 22, 93, 214
Arch in Pompeii..... 40
Houses in Pompeii..... 41
Excavating Herculaneum..... 42
Mosaic found in England..... 47
Apartment house at Ostia..... 90
Courtyard at Herculaneum..... 105
Silver plates found in England..... 143
Baths at Bath, England..... 229
Shrine from Pompeii..... 267
Statue of a lar from Pompeii..... 267
Site of Troy today..... 306

Landmarks in and Near Rome

Pictorial map of
Rome..... inside front cover
Claudian Aqueduct..... 10, 344
Colosseum..... 21, 219
The Roman Forum..... 22, 93, 214
House in Herculaneum..... 34
Vesuvius seen through an arch
in Pompeii..... 40
Houses in Pompeii..... 41
House of Cornelius Rufus. 88-89
Apartment house at Ostia..... 90
Courtyard in Herculaneum..... 105
Bay of Naples..... 141
Vesuvius..... 164
Mulvian Bridge over the Tiber..... 183
Mills at Ostia..... 193
Arch on the Appian Way..... 345
Pantheon..... 354
Pictorial map of
Italy..... inside back cover

Ancient Architecture in Modern Structures

PAGE

National Capitol, Washington, D. C. 9
High Bridge, New York 10
Museum of Science and Industry, Chicago 16
Capitol of Arkansas, Little Rock 17
U. S. Supreme Court Building .. 20
Jefferson Memorial 24
Dome of Massachusetts Institute of Technology 120
Library of Columbia University, New York 355

The Roman House and Its Furnishings

Mosaic of a rabbit 13
Wall painting of a villa 33
House in Herculaneum 34
Gold and silver dishes 37
Houses in Pompeii 41
Wall painting 43
Mosaic of doves 44
Mosaic of donkey-cart and driver 46
Mosaic found in England 47
Roman villa in Britain 48 49
Door of a Roman house 56
Wall paintings in a Pompeian villa 74
Chest for valuables 85
House of Cornelius Rufus ... 88-89
Section of an ancient house ... 88-89
Model of an apartment house .. 90
Apartment building in Ostia 90
Plan of a Roman house 90
Mosaic dining-room floor 103
Courtyard in Herculaneum 105
Fresco of Cupids picnicking 109
Decorative urn 115
Silver plates found in England .. 143
Plate—victory of Pyrrhus 148
Corner of a Pompeian kitchen .. 152
Heating stove 152
Bathtub 153
Table 153
Lamp 154
Glassware 154
Goblets 154
Egg dish 154
Wall painting of a Roman house 176
Fresco of Cupids working in a shop 193
Fresco of Iphigenia 308
Pompeian wall painting of Iphigenia 310

Roman Dress and Adornment

Toga 121
Stola and palla 121
Necklace 122
Ring 122
Shoes 122
Bracelet 123
Hairdress 123
Boy's tunic 291
Boy's toga and bulla 295
Bulla 295

Schools

Books and writing materials 71
Roman schools in Spain 196
Wax tablets 290
Abacus 290
Ancient letter 290
Roman schoolboy 291
Young man reading a book 291
Papyrus growing 291

Religion

PAGE

Temple of Diana in Portugal... 62
Diana....................64, 95
Temple of Neptune at Paestum 83
Ceres.......................92
Temples in the Roman Forum 93, 214
Roman altar................ 96
Cumaean Sibyl..............118
Aeneas and the Sibyl in Hades..125
Apollo and Daphne...........129
Minerva and Arachne.........144
Lavinia and the evil omen......225
Jupiter................257, 266
Juno...................257, 266
Spring festival...............265
Mars........................266
Minerva.....................266
Pompeian shrine..............267
Lar.........................267

Law and Government

The Roman Forum......22, 93, 214
Appius Claudius in the Senate..158
Ancient and modern law.......346
Justinian, the lawgiver.......351

Amusements

Colosseum...............21, 219
Theater in Spain.............. 31
Banquet.....................108
Cupids picnicking............109
A Roman theater.............136
Actors' masks...............137
Amphitheater at Arles.........167
Chariot race.................168
Charioteers 168
Child with pet goose..........185
Roman triumph...........186-187
Women at a public bath........228
Roman public baths at Bath, England..................228

Military Life

Hadrian's Wall in Britain...18, 178
Triumphal procession in Forum. 93
Plate commemorating victory of Pyrrhus..................148
Scabbard....................161
Roman helmets..........180, 223
Etruscan shield..............181
Roman triumph..........186-187
Military equipment...........197
Roman trumpeter.............200
Outside a Roman camp.......201
Roman military insignia...210, 211
Insignia of U. S. Armed Forces...........211, 212, 339
Ancient warships.........232, 341
Treaty, from a Roman coin....250
Roman centurion.............330
Roman Cavalryman...........334
Roman tents.................337
Caesar addressing his troops....339
Caesar's troops landing on coast of Britain...............340

Language and Books

Books and writing materials.... 71
Monk copying Latin manuscript 112
Initial letter of First Psalm.....112
Vergil reading the *Aeneid*......239
Ancient letter...............290
Man reading a book..........291
Papyrus growing.............291
De Tribus Animalibus........352

Agriculture

	PAGE
Plow and oxen	75
Farmer and plow	76
Ceres, goddess of agriculture	92
Farm products	101
Olive grove	195
Oxen and cart	195
Ancient threshing floor	350
Ancient and modern threshing	350
Ancient plow in use	350
Modern tractor-drawn plow	350
Calendar used by Roman farmers	351

Industry and Business

	PAGE
The Roman Forum	22, 93, 214
Roman merchant ships	28, 97, 268
Storage pit for fish in Russia	63
Ancient ships	28, 84
Chest for valuables	85
Loaf of bread from a bakery	109
Roman coins	117
Shops	165, 194
Cupids in a dye shop	193
Mills at Ostia	193
Blacksmith shop	194
Abacus, used for calculation	290

Literature and Myths

	PAGE
Latona and the farmers	53
Diana	64, 95
The Great Bear	67
Perseus and Andromeda	81
Ceres	92
Roman emperor in the garb of Hercules	98
Cumaean Sibyl	118
Aeneas and the Sibyl in Hades	125
Aeneas, Anchises, and Ascanius	126
Apollo and Daphne	129
Deucalion and Pyrrha	132-133
Medusa	138
Minerva and Arachne	144
The ant and the grasshopper	155
Human offerings to the Minotaur	169
The Minotaur	171
Icarus	172, 173
Sylvia's wounded stag	188
Daniel in the lions' den	204
Homer with a child	208
Lavinia and the evil omen	225
Aeneas and comrades in Africa	236
Dido watching Aeneas' departure	237
Vergil reading the *Aeneid*	239
Trojans bringing gifts to Latinus	240
Evander showing Aeneas the site of Rome	243
Vergil and two of the Muses	247
Jupiter and Juno	257
Death of Turnus	260
The golden fleece	269
Orpheus and Cerberus	275
Pandora	278
Paris and the golden apple	282
Helen fleeing with Paris	285
Achilles in disguise	289
Helen at Troy	292
Helen being taken to Troy	293
The wooden horse	297
Achilles	301
Iphigenia	304, 308
Sacrifice of Iphigenia	310
Rescue of Iphigenia	311
Iphigenia and Orestes	314
Telemachus and Penelope	317
Ulysses	319
Ulysses recognized by his aged nurse	323
Penelope	324
Aesculapius	351

Ancient Legend, Myth, and History in the Fine Arts

PAGE

Latona and the farmers, Adam Elsheimer . . . 53
Estaque, a scene on the Mediterranean, Paul Cezanne . . . 61
Diana, Antonio Correggio . . . 64
Perseus and Andromeda, Piero di Cosimo . . . 81
Ceres, after François Millet . . . 92
Diana and her maidens, Hans Makart . . . 95
Cumaean Sibyl, Michelangelo . . . 118
Aeneas and the Sibyl in Hades, Jan Brueghel . . . 125
Apollo and Daphne, Antonio Pollaiuolo . . . 129
Head of Medusa, Paul Dardon . . . 138
Plate—victory of Pyrrhus . . . 148
Appius Claudius in the Senate, Cesare Maccari . . . 158
Human offerings to the Minotaur, Ernest-Augustin Gendron . . . 169
Icarus on door panels in Wright Memorial . . . 173
Roman triumph, Antoine-Charles-Horace Vernet . 186-187
Specialty shop—a bas-relief . . . 194
Blacksmith shop—a bas-relief . . . 194
Daniel in the lions' den, Breton Rivière . . . 204
Homer, after François Gérard . . . 208
Dido watching Aeneas' departure 237
Vergil reading the *Aeneid* . . . 239

PAGE

Evander showing Aeneas the site of Rome, Giorgione da Castelfranco . . . 243
Vergil and the Muses in mosaic . . 247
Roman festival, Lawrence Alma-Tadema . . . 265
Jupiter . . . 266
Juno . . . 266
Mars . . . 266
Minerva . . . 266
A lar . . . 267
Orpheus and Cerberus, Thomas Crawford . . . 275
Pandora, Dante Gabriel Rossetti . . . 278
Paris and the golden apple . . . 282
Helen fleeing with Paris, Rudolf von Deutsch . . . 285
Achilles in disguise, Pompeo Girolamo Batoni . . . 289
Helen of Troy, Frederic Leighton 292
Helen being taken to Troy—a Greek vase painting . . . 293
Iphigenia, Anselm Feuerbach . . . 304
Rescue of Iphigenia, Giovacchino Agricola . . . 311
Telemachus and Penelope—a Greek vase painting . . . 317
Ulysses . . . 319
Penelope . . . 324
Caesar addressing his troops—a bas-relief . . . 339

Science

Arachnida . . . 145
Formicidae . . . 146
Picidae . . . 220
The medical profession . . . 348
Surgical instruments . . . 348
Medicinal plants . . . 349
Anatomical figure . . . 349
Aesculapius . . . 351

INDEX OF GRAMMAR

ā, ab, preposition with ablative, 59, 125, 352
  prefix, 273, 276
ABLATIVE CASE
  absolute, 234
  of accompaniment, 231
  of agent, 142, 232
  of manner, 232
  of means, 130, 232
  of time at which, 313
ACCENT, 428 (*see also* 95, 101, 104, 113)
ACCUSATIVE CASE
  of direct object, 24
  with prepositions, 125
  in indirect discourse, 286
  of duration of time, 312
  of extent of space, 328
ACTIVE VOICE, defined, 140
ad, preposition with accusative, 125, 353
  prefix, 273, 276
ADJECTIVES, defined, 11
  agreement, 16, 19, 30, 45, 51, 96, 113, 116, 287
  comparison of, 331, 336, 338
  declension of
    first and second, 99-100, 113
    third, 269, 273
  demonstrative, 145, 156, 174
  interrogative, 165
  numeral, 279
  position of, 13
  possessive, 113, 189
  predicate, 14
  two modifying one noun, 19
  used as nouns, 116
  with dative, 47
ADVERBS, 119, 327, 341
ANSWERS TO QUESTIONS, 77
ante, preposition with accusative, 125, 352
ANTECEDENT, defined, 76
APPOSITION, defined, 54
ARTICLE, lack of in Latin, 13

BASE
  of a noun, 54
  of an adjective, 332

CARDINAL NUMERALS, 279
CASE, defined, 24
  uses, 24, 29, 44, 51, 54
CASE ENDINGS OF NOUNS
  first declension, 24, 29, 44, 51, 54
  second declension, 106
  third declension, 198
  fourth declension, 298
  fifth declension, 312
cēterī, plural, 170
circum, preposition with accusative 164, 352
  prefix, 273, 276
CLAUSE, defined, 58
  dependent, 58
  independent, 58
COMPARATIVE ADJECTIVES
  declension of, 332
  formation of, 332, 336
  translation, 332
COMPARISON
  of adjectives, 331, 336, 338
  of adverbs, 341
COMPOUND VERBS, defined, 160
CONJUGATION, defined, 32
  first, 35, 69, 79, 86, 141, 170, 182, 226, 306, 324
  second, 133, 139, 141, 170, 182, 226, 306, 324
  third, 238, 241, 251, 255, 258, 306, 324
  fourth, 248, 251-252, 255-256, 259, 306-307, 324-325
CONJUNCTIONS, defined, 58

CONSONANTS, 428 (*see also* 9, 12, 15, 34, 53, 98, 209)
contrā, preposition with accusative, 159
prefix, 273, 276
cum, preposition with ablative, 51, 125, 231, 352
ablative of pronouns with, 284, 303
conjunction, 71

DATIVE CASE, 44, 47, 48, 57, 396
dē, preposition with ablative, 53, 125, 352
prefix, 273, 276
DECLENSION, defined, 54
of adjectives
first and second declension, 99, 113
third declension, 269-270, 273
of comparative and superlative adjectives, 332
of nouns
how determined, 54, 94, 197, 298, 312
first declension, 54
second, 93, 99, 102, 106
third, 197, 202, 207, 209, 211
fourth, 298
fifth, 312
of participles, 218, 277, 318
DEMONSTRATIVES, 145, 156, 174
agreement, 156
DIPHTHONGS, 428 (*see also* 18, 57, 145, 161, 164)
DIRECT OBJECT, 16, 19
dō, present, 45
imperfect, 104
future, 71
imperative, 65
"do" in negative sentences and in questions, 17
duo, declension of, 279

ē, *ex*, preposition with ablative, 51, 125, 352
distinguished from *ā*, *ab*, 59
prefix, 273, 276
ego, declension of, 302
ENCLITICS: *-cum*, 284, 303; *-ne*, 76
eō, conjugation of, 293, 321
compounds of, 294, 321
EXPLETIVE "there," 51

FUTURE PERFECT TENSE, 324-325
FUTURE TENSE, 68, 133, 182, 258

GENDER
in first declension, 96
in second declension, 96, 99, 102, 106
in third declension, 211
in fourth declension, 298
in fifth declension, 312
GENITIVE CASE, 29, 48

hic, declension of, 145
distinguished from *ille*, 156
distinguished from *is*, 174
pronoun, 175
homō and *vir* distinguished, 202

īdem, declension of, 327
pronoun, 327
ille, declension of, 156
distinguished from *hic*, 156
distinguished from *is*, 174
pronoun, 175
IMPERATIVE MOOD, defined, 65
first conjugation, 65
second conjugation, 134
third conjugation, 238, 242
fourth conjugation, 248
eō and *sum*, 321
negative commands, 321
IMPERFECT TENSE, 85, 133, 170, 255
in, preposition with ablative, 51, 125-126, 352
prefix, 273, 276
preposition with accusative, 126, 352
INDICATIVE MOOD, defined, 65
INDIRECT DISCOURSE, 286, 310
INDIRECT OBJECT, defined, 44
dative of, 44
phrase with "to" as equivalent, 44, 126
position of, 48

INFINITIVES, defined, 35
active
present, 35, 80, 134, 238, 248, 261
future, 318
perfect, 309
passive
present, 261, 309
perfect, 309
in indirect discourse, 286, 310
inter, preposition with accusative, 164, 352
INTERROGATIVE ADJECTIVE, 165
INTERROGATIVE PRONOUN, 76, 162, 284
INTRANSITIVE VERBS, defined, 38
ipse, declension of, 323, 324
is, declension of, 174

jam and *nunc* distinguished, 119

meus, use of, 113
mīlle and *mīlia*, 328
MOOD
imperative, 65, 134, 238, 242, 248, 321
indicative, 65
infinitive, 35, 286

-ne, sign of a question, 76, 94
NEGATIVE COMMANDS, 231
"no," how expressed in Latin, 77
NOMINATIVE CASE, 13, 19, 24, 227
nōnne, sign of a question, 94
nōs, declension of, 302
NOUNS, defined, 10
classes of, 198, 202, 207, 209, 211
nūllus, declension of, 98
NUMBER
of nouns, 19
of verbs, 32
NUMERALS, 120, 279
nunc and *jam* distinguished, 119

OBJECT
direct, 16, 24
indirect, 44, 126
ORDER OF WORDS, 13, 16, 48, 119, 218

PARTICIPLES, defined, 218
agreement, 218, 277
position of, 218
present, 276, 277
perfect, 218
future active, 318
used in infinitives, 318
PASSIVE VOICE, defined, 140
first conjugation, 141, 170, 182, 226, 307, 324
second conjugation, 141, 170, 182, 226, 307, 324
third conjugation, 238, 241, 251, 256, 258, 307, 324
fourth conjugation, 248, 251, 256, 259, 307, 324
PAST PERFECT TENSE, 306
per, preposition with accusative, 125, 352
prefix, 273, 276
PERFECT SYSTEM OF VERBS, 325
PERFECT TENSE
active, 78, 139, 251
passive, 226, 251
contrasted with imperfect, 85
PERSON ENDINGS OF VERBS, 35, 79, 142
PERSON OF VERBS, 32
PERSONAL PRONOUNS, 76, 302
PHRASE, defined, 19
POSSESSIVE ADJECTIVES AND PRONOUNS, 113, 189, 190
POSSESSIVE CASE, 24, 29
possum, conjugation of, 321, 397
post, preposition with accusative, 125, 352
PREDICATE, defined, 13
adjective, 14, 287
noun, 13, 19, 287
with passive, 227
PREFIXES, prepositions as, 273, 276
verbs compounded with, 273, 276
PREPOSITIONS, as prefixes, 273, 276
with ablative, 51, 59, 231, 353
with accusative, 125, 126, 353

PRESENT SYSTEM OF VERBS, 86
PRESENT TENSE
first conjugation, 35, 141
second conjugation, 133, 141
third conjugation, 238, 241
fourth conjugation, 248
PRINCIPAL PARTS OF VERBS, 220, 221, 224, 252
PRONOUNS, defined, 76
demonstrative, 156
interrogative, 76, 162
omitted in Latin as subject, 23
personal, 76, 302
reflexive, 186, 286, 303
relative, 283, 284; with *-cum*, 284
PRONUNCIATION, 9, 12, 15, 18, 23, 28, 34, 37, 43, 57, 428, 429-435

QUESTIONS, 76, 77, 94
quī, declension of, 283
quī, quis, declension of, 165
quis, declension of, 162
QUOTATIONS: direct, 286; indirect, 286

re-, prefix, 273, 276
REFLEXIVE PRONOUNS, 186, 286, 303
RELATIVE PRONOUNS, 283, 284

SENTENCES, defined, 10
sine, preposition with ablative, 146, 352
sōlus, declension of, 104 (footnote)
SOUNDS, summary of, 428
STEMS OF VERBS, 221
sub, preposition with ablative and accusative, 156, 352
SUBJECT, defined, 10
in indirect discourse, 286
omission of, 23
SUBSTANTIVE USE OF ADJECTIVES, 116
SUFFIXES, 335
sum, conjugation of, 32, 71, 80, 86, 321
compounds of, 160
SUPERLATIVE, 332, 336, 341
suus, use of, 189
SYLLABICATION, 428 (*see also* 43, 46, 98, 101, 104, 113, 159)

TENSE, defined, 68
present, 35, 133, 141, 238, 241, 248
imperfect, 85, 133, 170, 255
future, 69, 133, 182, 258
perfect, 78, 85, 139, 226, 251
past perfect, 306
future perfect, 324
signs of tenses
imperfect, 86
future, 68, 259
past perfect, 306
future perfect, 324
"there," as an expletive, 51
"to," in English phrases
place to which, 126
equivalent to indirect object, 44, 126
trāns, preposition with accusative, 125, 352
prefix, 273, 276
tōtus, declension of, 185
TRANSLATION, defined, 14
trēs, declension of, 279
tū, declension of, 302

VERBS, defined, 10
agreement, 32
person and number of, 32
position of, 16
principal parts of, 220
stems of, 221
transitive and intransitive, 38
see also CONJUGATION, MOOD, TENSE, VOICE
vir and *homō* distinguished, in meaning, 202
VOCATIVE CASE, 66, 106
VOICE, 140
vōs, declension of, 302
VOWELS, 428 (*see also* 9, 12, 15, 23)

WORD ORDER, 13, 16, 48, 119, 218

"yes," how expressed in Latin, 77
"you," Latin equivalents, 33

ACKNOWLEDGMENTS

For permission to reproduce pictures on the following pages, grateful acknowledgment is made to: A Century of Progress, Chicago, 90 (top); The Alaoui Museum, Le Bardo, Tunis, 126, 247; Archives du Touring-Club de France, 206; Arkansas Resources and Development Commission, 17; Art Reference Bureau, New York, 81, 125, 308, 311; Austrian National Tourist Office, New York, 62 (top); A. & C. Black, Ltd., London, England, 200, 201; R. H. Blomgren, Lincoln, Nebraska, 21, 40, 141, 344, 345; British Museum, 143, 180 (from *A Guide to the Antiquities of Roman Britain*); Chicago Natural History Museum, 153 (bottom); The Chicago Tribune, 16; Decou from Ewing Galloway, 195 (bottom); Denoyer-Geppert Company (copyright by Denoyer-Geppert Co., Chicago), 301; ENIT, Italian Tourist Information Office, Chicago, 291 (bottom); Ewing Galloway, 355; Georgia T. First, Rock Island, Ill., 219; Fitzwilliam Museum, Cambridge, England, 53; Fogg Museum of Art, Harvard University, 278, 310; French Embassy, Press and Information Division, New York, 63 (bottom); Goodyear Tire & Rubber Company, Inc., 172; Gramstorff Bros., Inc., Malden, Mass., 95, 118, 285, 314; Gurlitt History Pictures, 340; Oliver Wendell Holmes Memorial Library, Phillips Academy, Andover, Mass., 188; Anna Dale Kek, Indianapolis, Ind., 214; Thomas Peters Lake, 9, 20; Rudolph Lesch Fine Arts, New York, 304; Maiuri, *Passegiate Campane*, published by Ulrico Hoepli, Milan, Italy, 43; Massachusetts Institute of Technology, 120; Donald McLeish, London, England, 18, 178; Museum of Fine Arts, Boston, 275; Ernest Nash, 420 Riverside Drive, New York, 10; Philadelphia Commercial Museum, 28; Margaret and Alexander Potter, School of Architecture, University of Liverpool, England, and Penguin Books, Ltd., 48-49 (from *The Building of London*); Reuter-photo, P.A.-Reuter Photos, Ltd., London, England, 47; Royal Ontario Museum of Archaeology, Toronto, Canada, 122 (bottom); J. Salmon, Ltd., for the picture from a water-color drawing by A. R. Quinton, copyright by J. Salmon, Ltd., Sevenoaks, England, 229; Signal Corps, U. S. Army, 24; Society for Visual Education, Chicago, 193 (top); Sovfoto, New York, 63 (top); the Superintendent of Antiquities for Southern Etruria, Rome, Italy, 148; Albert H. Travis, 31; Underwood-Stratton, 306; United Artists, 31, 334; Photographic Archives of the Vatican, Vatican City, 103.

Pictures on the following pages are reproduced by courtesy of: The Colonial Art Company, Oklahoma City, Oklahoma, 204, 265; The Metropolitan Museum of Art, 61, 115, 186-187, 267 (top); A. J. Nystrom & Co., Chicago, Cybulski pictures, 33, 41, 44, 56, 84, 88-89 (bottom), 96, 97, 112, 117, 161, 176, 197, 232, 268, 337, and 341, the Lehman Colored History Picture, 88 (top), and the Hoffmann-Schmidt pictures, 37, 168 (top).

The pictures on pages 136, 165, 196 are taken from Latin Picture Cards by Grainger, by permission of G. Bell and Sons, London, England.

Colored pictures on the following pages are after photographs used by courteous permission of the institutions or individuals named: The Bettmann Archive, 169; R. H. Blomgren, 164; Evans from Three Lions, 57; Frick Art Reference Library, 208; Gramstorff Bros., Inc., 64, 289, 292; Oliver Wendell Holmes Memorial Library, Phillips Academy, Andover, Mass., 225, 236, 240, 257, 260; and The Metropolitan Museum of Art, 13. The special kindness of Miss Carol M. Vinson, Director of Publications of the National Gallery, London, in connection with the picture on 129, is gratefully acknowledged.

The pictures on 101, 132-133 were painted especially for this book by A. F. and M. S. Hurford; the pictures on 108, 228, 269, 297, 363, 366, by Herbert Rudeen. The cover design and the small decorations were drawn by Seymour Fleishman. The maps on pages 12 and 60 and the end sheets are by Raymond Craig.

The plays "Horatius," "Circe," and "Puer Aeger" (all adapted from *Decem Fabulae*) are used with the kind permission of E. Ryle.

4 5 6 7 8 9 10 11 12 13 14 15 16 17 18 19 20 21 22 23 24 25 63 62 61 60 59 58 57 56